Mahjong

Mahjong

A Chinese Game and the Making of
Modern American Culture

ANNELISE HEINZ

OXFORD
UNIVERSITY PRESS

OXFORD
UNIVERSITY PRESS

Oxford University Press is a department of the University of Oxford. It furthers
the University's objective of excellence in research, scholarship, and education
by publishing worldwide. Oxford is a registered trade mark of Oxford University
Press in the UK and certain other countries.

Published in the United States of America by Oxford University Press
198 Madison Avenue, New York, NY 10016, United States of America.

Portions of chapter 4 appear in Annelise Heinz, "Performing Mahjong in the 1920s:
White Women, Chinese Americans, and the Fear of Cultural Seduction," *Frontiers:
A Journal of Women Studies* 37, no. 1 (2016): 32–65. © The Frontiers Editorial Collective.
Portions of chapters 9 and 10 appear in Annelise Heinz, "'Maid's Day Off': Leisured Domesticity
in the Mid-Twentieth-Century United States," *American Historical Review* 125,
no. 4 (October 2019): 1316–1331. Published by Oxford University Press.

Library of Congress Cataloging-in-Publication Data
Names: Heinz, Annelise, author.
Title: Mahjong : a Chinese game and the making of
modern American culture / Annelise Heinz.
Other titles: Mah jong
Description: New York : Oxford University Press, [2021] |
Includes bibliographical references and index.
Identifiers: LCCN 2020041162 (print) | LCCN 2020041163 (ebook) |
ISBN 9780190081799 (hardback) | ISBN 9780190081812 (epub) |
ISBN 9780190081829
Subjects: LCSH: Mah jong—Social aspects—United States. |
United States—Civilization—Chinese influences.
Classification: LCC GV1299.M3 H45 2021 (print) | LCC GV1299.M3 (ebook) |
DDC 795.34—dc23
LC record available at https://lccn.loc.gov/2020041162
LC ebook record available at https://lccn.loc.gov/2020041163

DOI: 10.1093/oso/9780190081799.001.0001

1 3 5 7 9 8 6 4 2

Printed by Sheridan Books, Inc., United States of America

for Katie and for Jane

Contents

Preface   ix

Introduction: What's in a Game?   1

1. The Mahjong Phenomenon   14

2. Cosmopolitan Roots in Shanghai   41

3. Making a Transpacific Game   55

4. Moderns and Mandarins   75

5. White Women and a Chinese Game   95

6. Inside and Outside Chinese America   122

7. Asian Exclusion and Enforced Leisure   144

8. The Americanization of Mahjong   162

9. Suburban Migrations and Summer Bungalows   187

10. The Paradoxes of Postwar Domesticity   203

Epilogue: Reading the Tiles   221

Acknowledgments   229

Notes   235

Selected Bibliography   317

Index   325

Preface

MAHJONG IS PLAYED with tiles instead of cards, but like a deck of cards these tiles have suits. Now and in the past, Chinese tiles are "chunky": over an inch long, about an inch wide, and at least half an inch deep, they are thick enough to stand on their ends. American tiles are thinner and stand upright with the help of a rack. Players line their "hands," or set of selected tiles, up in front of them much as card players fan their hand of cards to see their options away from the prying eyes of others.

Like playing cards, the backs of the tiles are identical to ensure that players cannot identify which tiles others have. On the face of the tiles are markings that differentiate three suits: Circles, Bamboo, and Characters. (The character tiles include Chinese numbers and, most often, the character for ten thousand, or *wan*.) These designs originate from stylized depictions of money. For example, Chinese coins with holes in the middle were the circles, and long strings of these coins evolved into sticks of bamboo.[1] In American parlance, these are known most commonly as Dots, Bams, and Craks. There are four sets of tiles 1 to 9 in each suit, totaling 36 in each. As in much of mahjong, there are intricacies in the designs: the "1 bam" tile, for example, depicts a bird rather than a single rod of bamboo.

In addition, there are two groups of nonsuited tiles: "honor tiles" and "flowers." Honors include the four cardinal directions ("Winds") and three colors (white, green, and red) known in the West as "dragons." Since there are four of each of these sets, there are a total of 28 honor tiles. "Flowers" can have a variety of scenic images. Their name draws from one of the most common designs, with flowers that represent the seasons in traditional Chinese art. In more elaborate carvings, the tiles can be lined up in a row and recreate a scene from an iconic Chinese opera or paint a picturesque landscape. Most commonly, these markings are engraved or recessed into the face of the tiles, so experienced Chinese players take pride in knowing which tiles they draw simply by feeling the grooves with their thumbs.

Flowers have been the most controversial tiles and have varied in number at times. The standard form, however, is with eight flower tiles that all look different from each other. After 1960, the National Mah Jongg League changed the tiles by adding a specific set of Joker tiles as well, to differentiate from the previous practice of using flowers as wild cards. Taiwanese mahjong sets have introduced a "100 uses" tile similar to American jokers, while other regional styles play with different numbers of tiles. With the exception of Japanese and Vietnamese sets, most styles of play without jokers use sets with 144 tiles. With jokers, the tiles in American sets total 152.

All over the world, there are different ways of playing mahjong, some of which have branched quite far from the original form.[2] However, there are some core historic commonalities. Though there are many variations, these are the standard elements of play.

To begin, four players begin by mixing, or "washing," the tiles face down in the center of a square table. The clatter of the tiles against each other and the table can be quite noisy, and mahjong players often cover the tabletop with a cloth or felt to soften the racket. The players then work together to quickly build a (rough) square from the tiles. Each side of the wall is a double-decker stack of two facedown tiles. The combined steps of mixing and building the wall work together as a highly effective shuffling strategy.

The roll of dice determines where in the wall to begin drawing tiles. Each player takes four tiles in turn, as the players complete the initial draw. Experienced players zip along as the central square wall quickly fragments into each player's hand of 13 tiles. In the American style, players then exchange tiles in an additional shuffling process known as "the Charleston." Expert American players say that the game is won or lost in the Charleston, when players determine which hands they are best set up to win. In both Chinese and American standard forms, the goal is to complete a hand with a final additional tile, resulting in a winning combination of 14 tiles.

We'll learn more about how American mahjong came to be distinct from Chinese play, but, in brief, the Chinese version is fairly similar to the card game gin rummy: most winning hands involve four sets of three tiles and a pair, and until the birth of the National Mah Jongg League in the late 1930s, most Americans played that way, too. After the League came into existence, they established a more limited number of acceptable hands with more variations in combinations, which change on an annual basis. For both, rules govern how tiles can be drawn from the wall or snatched from the discard pile, and how winning hands are scored. Penalties for discarding tiles that another player uses to complete a winning hand encourage defensive play: one of the hallmarks of skilled mahjong players, whichever style they play, is an ability to track which tiles have been played, which remain, and which hands other players are likely vying to complete.[3]

Mahjong is primarily a game of skill. Luck is always present; debates over the use of flowers or jokers have centered on whether to introduce more luck, and if that reduces the game's challenge. Learning the basics of the traditional game does not take long—like gin rummy, it can be learned in the span of an afternoon. Mastering the scoring and strategy, however, can take a lifetime. The American game has a slightly steeper initial learning curve, in part because the strategy revolves around a smaller number of acceptable hands. Adherents of the different styles tend to be fiercely loyal to their own and will defend the merits of its intellectual demands or, depending on their experience, the friendly socializing it fosters. The game of bridge is a frequent point of comparison, and many American mahjong players play bridge as well. Unlike bridge, which demands constant concentration to simply play the game (in part because it is a partnered game and one player's performance affects a partner), mahjong involves individual players and can be played along a spectrum of competitiveness. All forms of mahjong can be played in highly competitive, fast-paced, and demanding games. Alternatively, most forms can also be played more socially, and regular groups form according to preference. In almost any scenario, however, chatting *during* play, or delaying the next player's turn through slowness or inattention, is not suffered lightly.

Each element of the game—the way the tiles look and feel, the rhythms of play, and the intellectual and social satisfaction it provides—has intersected with specific historical contexts to create social meanings. It is that history that this book reveals.

Mahjong

Introduction

THE TILES CLATTER across the table. Eight hands push and sweep them back and forth, mixing them into an erratic mass before flipping over any exposed faces to show only blank backs. The tiles are smooth and cool to the touch, small enough to be held easily with thumb against forefinger. As fingers quickly pluck tiles from the center of the table, voices punctuate the air. Nimble movements bring the tiles close to the edge of the square table and four walls made of two layers of stacked tiles quickly take shape. A pair of hands holds two dice and rolls them in the center of the table. The mahjong game is about to begin.

Envision these players in an 1890 Shanghai courtesan house. The four men do not look up as a young woman in embroidered silk pulls aside the cloth door covering to enter the room, bringing wine with her. The men's queues hang down the backs of their long robes as they focus on calculating their points; the winner will cover half their party's bill for the evening's drink and company. A tasseled lantern hangs from the ceiling. Two other "sing-song girls," also known as "flowers," stand supportively behind their patrons' wooden chairs, looking over their shoulders at the bone-and-bamboo tiles, watching for wine glasses to refill and ready to whisper advice if asked.[1]

In an American household in 1921 Beijing, the table is in a living room of a traditional *hutong* house. Bright cushions on a black sofa sit near a Chinese desk and chair of dark wood. Two couples play mahjong together in elegant dress, the women in pressed waists and men in suits despite the heat. Wearing a long white robe, a Chinese servant, knowledgeable in English and the preferences of these foreigners, refreshes their tea and cocktails. If he plays mahjong he does not tell them, while they delight in their knowledge of this Chinese game sweeping the foreign social scene in Beijing and Shanghai.[2]

The new fad travels to the United States, where a photographer poses four young white women, fashionably wearing bobbed hair and flowing sleeveless gowns, in ornately carved Chinese chairs. The women's eyes stay focused on the tiles before them. Their photographed game will accompany the text in a 1923 instruction manual helping introduce newcomers to the game that is exploding in popularity across the nation. French readers will eventually view their likenesses as well, in a translated edition that will compete with a cascade of other instruction manuals and media chatter about the game.[3]

On market day at a Chinese American general store in Los Angeles during the early years of the Depression, a group of older men in button-down shirts play at a table in the back. Their years of labor do not slow the quickness of their hands in the game they have played for almost a decade. A long wooden chest of drawers holding dried herbs stands near the front door; on other shelves are newly arrived mail, outgoing remittances from the local clientele, and the mahjong set when it is not in use. A child in a pink pinafore watches them; later that month she will play mahjong with her grandmother during the Chinese New Year holiday.[4]

Two decades later, players' hands mix the tiles again, now made of plastic. On a grassy lawn, four women sit around a metal card table with a quilted fabric cover. A stone's throw away, a path leads to bungalow vacation homes, all occupied by Jewish families. A coin purse rests near one of the player's sandaled feet and a cigarette case is by her hand. Their children swim and dig for worms—most important, they are out of sight. This game will be followed by another and another this afternoon and the next. It is summer in the Catskill Mountains of upstate New York.[5]

* * *

Mahjong is a game of the senses. The tiles hold beauty—earthy tones of bone and bamboo or yellowed butterscotch of aged plastic. They are heavy in the hand, with rounded edges rubbing against each other like river pebbles. Thumbs bump against grooves in the tiles from impossibly intricate carvings or brightly colored embossed images. Nothing else mimics the clatter of mahjong tiles running over each other on a hard table surface; even a felt top does not entirely soften the din. Regardless of when and where the game is played, these experiences remain. They are part of what makes mahjong unique and are no small part of its boundary-crossing appeal. Mahjong is both a cultural form and a material object that is made, bought, and bequeathed. Within the spaces between the tiles and the moments between games, distinct social cultures flourished. Despite the universal elements of how the game is played—and the common feel of it—mahjong reflected, and helped express, a range of meanings, especially: emerging American modernity, Chinese American heritage, and Jewish American women's culture. In the holds of steamships, mahjong traveled from China to the United States and became a quintessentially American game—not in spite of but because of its diverse manifestations. Its history of adaptation, amalgamation, and self-making offers unexpected insight into race, gender, class, and leisure in modern American culture.

This book follows the history of one game to think about how, in their daily lives, individuals create and experience cultural change. Playing a game from a culture across the globe helped Americans create group identities and address issues of inclusion and exclusion. Mahjong, like other forms of leisure, played a significant role in the cultural transformations of the twentieth century. There is no single answer to why the game was so resonant across different contexts, but the fact that it was, and that it inspired rich

FIGURE I.I Bone and bamboo composed most mahjong sets during the 1920s fad. Many came in wooden boxes with pullout drawers and a sliding front cover. More desirable sets were made in China, as advertised on the front cover of this box. Author's Collection.

game-playing cultures, connects to some of the most important themes in modern American history. Its story is a window onto three pivotal areas of change in the twentieth-century United States: What did it mean to become "modern" in the early twentieth century? How did American ethnicities take shape in the years leading up to and after World War II? How did middle-class women experience and shape their changing roles in society, before the social revolutions of the late twentieth century? How are these things related?

Mahjong's history also prompts closer considerations of the meaning of leisure. Although players understood mahjong first and foremost as a fun and challenging game, the specific social patterns they created on a broad scale had ramifications beyond any individual's conscious intent. Mahjong not only reflected larger social changes but also allowed diverse groups to shape behaviors and ideas that had consequences of their own. During the 1920s mahjong fad, for example, white women in elaborate Chinese costumes experimented with exotic personae and newly accessible forms of sexuality, Chinese American mahjong instructors capitalized on the fad as an economic and cultural opportunity, and critics of the game recoiled from the social mobility of both white women and Chinese Americans. Each group's interactions with mahjong were an important part of enacting—or coming to terms with—a modern national culture that included new gender norms and increasing racial diversity.

Perhaps more than other popular games, mahjong had a complex cultural journey. Its history connects American expatriates in Shanghai, Jazz Age white Americans, urban Chinese Americans in the 1930s, Japanese Americans in wartime camps, Jewish American suburban mothers, and Air Force officers' wives in the postwar era. Over time, the material game changed—bone and bamboo mimicked ivory; later the new plastics preserved the heft and feel of the tiles without relying on natural materials. So, too, its significance shaped American understandings of Asia, the boundaries of gender and race, and ideas about leisure.

Though rarely considered as part of American popular culture, mahjong has in fact been a part of the nation's recreation for nearly a century. Its American story began in 1922, when newspapers on the West Coast started buzzing about the "new-old" Chinese game. Unlike its marketing image as an "ancient game," it had only recently become popular in a few urban centers in China, after its development as one of many male gambling games in the mid-to late-1800s. A growing elite class of Chinese intermediaries facilitated mahjong's introduction to Shanghai's burgeoning American population in the late 1910s. Promoters and travelers spread the game to the United States.

Soon the most elite Americans from President and First Lady Harding to Hollywood starlets were playing it. Just two years after its introduction, Americans made mahjong sets Shanghai's sixth largest export to the United States—Congress even added a tax law specifically targeting mahjong sets in 1924. As the American market developed a voracious appetite for the game, Chinese and Western merchants launched large-scale mahjong factories in Shanghai that standardized production with artisanal workmanship. Mahjong helped inaugurate an era of fads—crosswords, miniature golf, flag-pole sitting, and dance marathons all gained a rapt audience in the 1920s. Although forgotten today, the craze defined the era for decades afterward.

Mahjong exploded into American consciousness at the height of immi-gration restrictions, nativism, and the mainstream national revival of the Ku Klux Klan. The irony of its popularity illuminates the complexities of con-sumerism, race, and the wary embrace of selective aspects of Chinese culture. In the 1920s, Americans imagined themselves learning a game of Confucius, a pastime of royalty and the misty "Celestial" ancients. Advertisers and players alike gleefully celebrated the "great, exciting, hundreds of years old, national Chinese game, now the craze of America."[6] Yet mahjong also represented the vulnerabilities of Western civilization: even the stalwart game of bridge might fall before the sneaky pleasures of a "Yellow Peril" pastime. The racial (and often racist) tenor of the 1920s fad was unmistakable.

In an era of pervasive xenophobia, why did this Chinese game achieve such widespread resonance? Its popularity was not just a result of individual ap-peal and enjoyment. The game itself allows for adaptability that meant a wide range of people could use the game both for entertainment, and for cultural purposes. In part, mahjong helped Americans navigate the tensions of moder-nity: the simultaneous nostalgic yearnings and excited embrace of progress that marked the decade. Advertisers promised that it would provide players with an experience of ancient Eastern mystery, modern cosmopolitanism, and Jazz Age glamour. Society pages featured mahjong matrons dressed in Chinese costume, from club women in Los Angeles to the Vanderbilts in Manhattan. Even small mahjong parties allowed for experimentation in cos-tume and exotic food. Embodying premodern authenticity and modern inno-vation, the mix of tiles, rules, and meanings created a site of play for the era's contradictions. It also fit into larger consumer patterns of the era: even as ac-tual contact with Chinese individuals became less likely for most Americans, most also became more likely to consume something Chinese—or that claimed to be Chinese—from silk pajamas and chinoiserie lamps to chop suey. At the same time, Chinese Americans leveraged mahjong's popularity for economic opportunities in a discriminatory economy as new players hired Chinese teachers to help them master the rules. The idea that the game embodied some essence of Chinese culture could serve multiple purposes.

The idea of China has been powerful for its symbolism. In addition to the famously derided "coolie" caricature, China has also represented a highly civilized past. More broadly, however, it exemplifies a potent abstract concept of foreignness, one that is disconnected from China itself for modern Americans. Therefore, references to China can serve as a proxy for other social boundaries of inclusion and exclusion within the United States. Unlike card games that have become assimilated as American over time, because the mahjong sets themselves bore material signs and engravings of their Chinese origins, the game retained its link to China and its ability to evoke a misty Orient. This liminal positioning, always linked both to China and the United States, made the game particularly malleable and enduring in building American identities.

In China, the American-led global fad raised the game's profile and it became known as a "national treasure;" its meaning changed for Chinese Americans, too. For most Chinese Americans, the game evolved from its urban nightlife roots to become more domestic as white Americans engaged with the game for, ironically, its exotic appeal. In the interwar era, Chinese Americans found the game useful for navigating tensions associated with Americanization, including pressure to foster inclusion, survive exclusion, and nurture intra-cultural cohesion. Mahjong could be a point of commonality across generations because it was both Chinese and American—a Chinese game whose cultural meaning was transformed by American consumption.

The history of how mahjong "became American" is also a story of particular communities "becoming American" in the twentieth century. Mahjong is woven into the uneven history of how the nation came to identify itself as a multiracial democracy and how different groups experienced the possibilities, limitations, and potential costs of integration. By "playing mandarin," white Americans momentarily stepped out of their established identities through this Chinese game and its trappings, acculturating to a changing nation.[7] Chinese Americans used this transpacific consumer good to help them navigate questions of otherness and belonging. In America (and in other countries), other Asian groups adopted the game: Japanese Americans first played the game in the fad years and picked it up again as one form of much-needed recreation while confined in so-called internment camps. And more marginal "white" Americans contributed to the complexity, as Jewish families made mahjong their own. The cultures mahjong players created highlight ethnicity as constantly produced and unstable, rather than natural or unchanging.[8]

By the 1930s, mahjong continued to evolve in a national context that led to styles of play and forms of the game that became uniquely American. Formed in 1937 during an era of virulent anti-Semitism, the National Mah Jongg League never emphasized its strongly Jewish leadership, but its connection to Jewish women enabled the League's game to grow and become a key part of modern Jewish American culture even as its game became known as "National" and eventually "American" mahjong. The League emphasized mahjong as a philanthropic activity, during World War II promoting both its link to Allied Chinese culture and, more important, enabling patriotic fundraising. Meanwhile, other specifically American variants have continued, though in smaller numbers than the Chinese versions and the League's game. Since World War II, the Officers' Wives Club in the Air Force has spread their version—known as "Wright-Pat rules" after the Wright-Patterson Air Force Base—to bases around the world, establishing ties in transient military life.

Jewish American women had been playing mahjong since the 1920s fad, but the Cold War era nurtured a flourishing gendered mahjong culture linked to the National Mah Jongg League. After World War II, the push toward increasingly suburban housing and widely shared entrance into full-time domesticity created a need for ways to overcome young mothers' frequently experienced isolation. Middle-class Jewish women also had the unique resource of culturally specific patterns of vacation communities to build upon. They were able to use the rhythms forged in bungalow colonies to claim time and space for themselves, not just for productive work (as in philanthropic or community groups), and not just during daytime or with husbands, but—crucially—in ways that reimagined domesticity itself. By creating a community marker, they also shaped what it meant to be a middle-class Jewish woman in Cold War America.

A diverse cast of characters people this history—from the stereotyped Chinese gambler and Jewish matron to influential individuals, including the oil representative-cum-mahjong entrepreneur Joseph Babcock, the Chinese American sociologist Pardee Lowe, and a forgotten founder of what would become "American mahjong," Dorothy Meyerson. They not only harnessed the game to preexisting cultural meaning, but also created meaning unique to this game. Thus, people are not the only actors in this story. Sometimes mahjong will serve as a lens, and sometimes as an agent. Taking this approach allows for distinguishing between the view of the interpreter, or what mahjong allows us to see, and the meaning of the cultural form for the people who interacted with it, or the work mahjong does in the world. At times, such as in the wartime incarceration of Japanese Americans, or in the development of plastics industries, mahjong offers a window into larger political and economic stories. In other contexts, people attached ideas to the physical game, particularly ideas of foreignness and difference, and those ideas gave mahjong a shaping force. The game rules also carried certain rhythms and ways for people to interact, including across multiple generations.

Perhaps another game could have served these social functions. However, mahjong had a unique combination of qualities. In addition to its sensory appeal, including the beauty and feel of the tiles, it took skill and concentration, not just luck; it was played in an intimate setting with regular groups of four or five people; and—importantly—it had a certain rhythm that facilitated communication and conversation. The tiles must be shuffled and stacked after each round of play, every fifteen to twenty minutes, creating pauses that last longer than it takes to shuffle a deck of cards. The distinctive qualities of mahjong are also key to understanding how this Chinese game became a vital part of women's culture in the postwar era. Outside Asian American communities, it had already become a women's game, not a game played by married couples. In those moments of pause, women created social bonds. At mahjong, one player explained, women would "let their hair down" in ways they did not during other games.[9]

Mahjong's trajectory charts the fraught relationship of leisure in American culture, particularly along lines of class, ethnicity, and gender. Underlying the ability to play mahjong is time without intentional productive purpose. After decades of effort from labor unions, the growth of a middle class, and a mass consumer economy, leisure and recreation became a defining aspect of modern American life in the twentieth century, held out as a marker of progress.[10] Most clearly, leisure has been associated with class privilege. In the early days of the mahjong fad, advertisers featured scenes with maids and mahjong, since both were signs of aspirational wealth. Yet leisure is a knottier issue than it first appears.

Following the trail of mahjong reveals sometimes surprising and often overlooked realms of leisure: of psychological survival, of community building, of cultural creation. Chinese immigrant laundry workers in the early twentieth century were a far cry from the "leisured classes," yet exhaustion did not prevent them from incorporating mahjong into weekly rituals and nighttime games. The social aspects of leisure, felt most keenly in new, uprooted environments, like postwar suburban subdivisions, and Air Force bases all over the world, provided opportunities to build relationships. For

Jewish Americans, women's games of mahjong helped mark a shared territory in a middle-class context that risked assimilation into Christian America and created new cultural norms. Leisure activities have been just as foundational to ethnic formation as labor, education, and politics.

Yet leisure that is not chosen—the enforced leisure of imprisonment, of anxious boredom, of endless uncertain waiting—is a terrible burden. The tensions between inclusion and exclusion defined the Asian American experience during the era of immigration restriction. In the 1920s and 1930s, male migrants detained at the Angel Island Immigration Station used recreation to carve out social spaces in a dehumanizing context. In a very different environment, Japanese Americans played mahjong as a release from the pressures of disruption and anxiety in camps during World War II, while some tried to prevent recreation from turning into destructive gambling.

The image of idleness has often been unsettling for Americans. For Chinese Christians and Christian missionaries, mahjong carried a specter of the insidious dangers of a softened and respectable gambling game. In reality, mahjong has long straddled the spectrum of gambling—to be both a game where large sums of money are won, lost, and fought over, as well as a family-friendly game played with pennies. By the time mahjong entered popular culture, Protestant moralists and local governments had increasingly targeted gambling in particular as a threat to an orderly, meritocratic, industrial society based on the growing strength of middle-class mores around personal saving, work, and restraint over an embrace of luck.

Examined outside these moral frameworks, gambling can also be understood as part of a mindset that embraces luck in an uncertain world. For the working poor, trying one's hand at dice, cards, or mahjong promised greater reward than a dead-end job ever would.[11] Of course, the same factors that spark a desire for building community, mental stimulation, and relief of uncertainty can trigger addiction. Chinese immigrants were strongly associated with gambling and frequently targeted by police—in part because of long traditions of widespread gambling among migrant men, and in part because of simplistic stereotypes of moral lassitude. As a Chinese game, mahjong seemed to dance on the edge of danger.

In the face of such judgments, proponents of the game have struggled to legitimize their use of leisure by stressing perceptions of skill and money involved. Throughout the game's history in the United States, players and commentators have debated the appropriate combination of luck and skill present in the game. Experts in the game of bridge often unfavorably compared mahjong to the intelligence and rational logic needed for bridge and urged mahjong players to avoid incorporating more luck into the format of the game. Democratic pressures worked against their warnings, and over time multiple forms of mahjong have included more luck—though not without controversy. In the 1920s, the democratization of the game across social classes risked hurting its reputation (according to its elite "chaperones") as rubes and poorly made sets entered the milieu.[12] Founded by wealthy women, the National Mah Jongg League became the architect of American mahjong and its eventual strong association with the middle class. For decades, the League has emphasized its role as a philanthropic organization. Recently, a Modern Orthodox player felt her group's donation to the synagogue "lent more class" to what could otherwise be seen as a wasteful or inappropriate pastime—as did the participation of the rabbi's wife.[13] The philanthropic element of mahjong overlaps with a tradition of women's entertainment being put to obviously useful purposes in fundraising teas and galas.

Many of the criticisms launched against mahjong have been particularly barbed in gendered terms. As the game became increasingly associated with women, mahjong players in the United States have often been viewed through the lens of motherhood and mahjong's influence on distracted or self-centered mothering. In the 1920s, mahjong-playing mothers were castigated for the juvenile delinquency of their wayward children. In the 1960s, an association between mahjong and vacuous, all-consuming mothers became part of the "Jewish mother" stereotype. Alternatively, it could be seen as frivolous, for layabout women who had "nothing better to do."[14] More appropriate for women, long tradition held, was the belief that a woman's work is never done. In contrast, an equivalently gendered game like poker has not suffered the same loss of prestige as a game for men who have nothing better to do.

This history also revises interpretations of the roles women have played in each stage of transnational consumerism. Women have been predominantly viewed as iconic consumers: from Gilded Age matrons acquiring objects from the Near and Far East as participants in American empire, to housewives as consumer advocates and consumer-citizens in postwar America.[15] Historians of women have also challenged assumptions about the limited range of women's lives largely by identifying involvement outside the home.[16] This history reimagines women's labor in twentieth-century consumer culture both within and outside their homes. From Shanghai social clubs to Chinatown apartments to Philadelphia townhouses, domestic space served as an arena not only for cultural transmission but also for cultural creation through mahjong as both a game and a springboard for community engagement.

Mahjong-playing women combined consumption, production, and marketing when they worked as instructors and gamesmiths and were vital members of family manufacturing and distribution industries. As hostesses of mahjong parties in Shanghai and in the United States, women helped create spaces for cultural exchange, social interaction, and political maneuvering; as mahjong instructors, they built their own and their family businesses. From 1920s Manhattan to 1930s San Francisco to 1950s Wichita, women also used their homes as venues for female leisure in new ways. White women experimented with social boundaries via "exotic" Chinese costuming in the 1920s, Chinese American women established new access to respectable leisure, and Jewish women demarcated women-only zones of home-based recreation after World War II. These moves were part of cultural negotiations over women's place in the home. The history of mahjong highlights leisure as a meaningful site of both change and contestation, which could also bring domestic spaces into the ostensibly public world of politics and business.

* * *

Uncovering this history relies on a diversity of sources as complex as its makers, players, and promoters. There is no archive for mahjong. Throughout its history, game producers, players, critics, and storytellers have left a range of evidence: photographs from 1920s factories in Shanghai; plays, paintings, and songs of Jazz Age Americans in thrall to the game; sociological notes from 1930s California Chinatowns; and newspapers and diaries from Japanese American incarceration camps during World War II. A dusty room off a boardgame factory floor in Massachusetts held the remnants of business files from the Mah Jongg Sales Company of America, the company that launched the global mahjong fad, while the Schlesinger Library's women's history archive housed the records of an early instructor of the game. These sources demonstrate the broad range of expression that mahjong inspired, as well as the different registers of society that it connects.

Mahjong was widespread in the rituals and contours of interwar Chinese American society and midcentury Jewish life, but in both cases the activities of these individuals' daily lives were rarely kept in written records. The richest sources for these stories proved to be oral histories. Transcribed interviews with Chinese men and women who had been detained at Angel Island Immigration Center in the 1920s and 1930s, as well as elderly Chinese Los Angelenos in the 1970s, revealed essential textures of community and individual lives. I also conducted dozens of interviews, one of which captured the rare perspective of a small-scale manufacturer of mahjong. Most of the interviews were with Jewish American mahjong players and their children, resulting in more than fifty conversations in varying geographic locations and from a range of class strata. The size of the sample set was important in making arguments about specific patterns to allow for variations in circumstance, memory, and reliability. In addition, I sought out accounts from women who did not play mahjong or who actively disliked it in order to mitigate the biases that emerge from those eager to discuss a given topic. Together, they revealed remarkably consistent patterns around mahjong. From Atlanta to Philadelphia to Los Angeles, groups across the country played the same game, at parallel places and times, while noshing on similar snacks. These commonalities created a widely shared culture that reached its height in the postwar years of upward mobility, experienced in particularly pronounced ways by Jewish Americans.

This study unfolds in two parts, from its Chinese origins to the transpacific consumer fad to American Chinatowns and suburbs. The first half is focused on mahjong's history as related to consumerism, with a close examination of its economic and cultural origins. Paying attention to transpacific entrepreneurs, white women who dressed in Chinese costume to play the game, and Chinese Americans who asserted their ostensibly authentic ties to China reveals how mass consumerism in a global frame helped Americans define what it meant to be "modern" in newly self-conscious ways. Chapter 1 begins in the midst of the 1920s fad, as the mahjong industry connected novel forms of doing business with established markets for "Oriental" goods and patterns of home entertainment and sociability. Chapters 2 and 3 focus on the development and production of the game in the cosmopolitan world of Shanghai at the turn of the century. They reveal the social milieu of Americans living in China where the game took root and the Chinese factory workers who produced it while the exploding international market accelerated its reach. In Chapters 4 and 5 the story recrosses the Pacific to examine the cultural dynamics of the massive mahjong vogue in the early 1920s, when American consumers capitalized on the game to navigate new gender dynamics and racial ideologies.

The second half of the book explores how mahjong interwove with the experiences of inclusion and exclusion in the evolving definition of what it means to be American. While Chapter 6 traces mahjong in the development of Chinatowns between the world wars and the game as a point of identity-building inclusion, Chapter 7 looks at mahjong as survival strategy in the exclusion of Chinese migrants at Angel Island Detention Center and Japanese Americans in wartime incarceration camps. Chapter 8 focuses on the creation of specifically American forms of the game, which lay the groundwork for the mahjong culture created by Jewish American women in postwar communities. Chapters 9 and 10 chart the development of Jewish American ethnicity through leisure, gender roles, and residential geography. An epilogue follows the recent history of the game, which parallels the nation's continued diversification in the late twentieth century, to showcase today's growing mahjong revival.

Mahjong's American trajectory is a history of a mass-produced game that crossed and re-crossed the Pacific, creating economic waves at the height of its popularity, and creating a potent cultural symbol in its wake. It tells the story of the tensions between assimilation and cultural continuity that encouraged the creation of identifiably ethnic communities. It also reveals the ways in which women leveraged a game to gain access to respectable leisure—and the backlash that often followed.

Because the sets themselves carried specific visual markers as Chinese, the game could retain a certain element of foreignness, even as it became Americanized in style and form. Its associations with China were an essential part of the game's appeal, either as a new and exotic good, or as a connection to cultural heritage. The game's adaptability created barriers as well as bridges as players pushed the evolution of distinctive mahjong variants. Mahjong was—in essential ways—both outside and inside American culture. The link to China and the attendant American associations with difference provided an avenue for formation of simultaneous American identities, both related to and entirely independent of its Chinese origins. Mahjong players, promoters, entrepreneurs, and critics tell a broad story of American modernity. The apparent contradictions of the game—as both American and foreign, modern and supposedly ancient, domestic and disruptive of domesticity—reveal the tensions that lie at the heart of modern American culture.

I

The Mahjong Phenomenon

MEN AND WOMEN hurried from autos and streetcars toward the bright lights of the Granada Theatre in San Francisco. It was September 23, 1922, and the "spectacular stage production 'Mah-Jongg Blues'" was about to start. Inside, young white women in Chinese costumes sold raffle tickets. The lucky winner would take home a Mah-Jongg Sales Company mahjong set, with tiles of engraved bone and bamboo made by workers in Shanghai. The crowd had been reading articles for the last several months about the "queer Chinese game" that was sweeping the West Coast. Expectations were high, stoked by the Mah-Jongg Sales Company's advertising campaign, which included publicizing the lyrics to "The Mah-Jongg Blues" a few weeks before the show. These highlighted elements of the game in their translated "Chinese" imagery: "When I build that Chinese wall, / Dragons, winds and bamboos all, / Something seems to thrill me—WOW!" Some attendees had likely been in the privileged audience at an elaborate mahjong-inspired summer pageant at the Fairmont Hotel on Nob Hill. Those unfamiliar with this brand-new game need not worry; instructors were in the balcony, charging one dollar to teach the game, all proceeds going to charity. Ushers handed eager moviegoers programs explaining the evening's entertainment, which would conclude with a silent film melodrama. Before the screen curtain went up, the stage was filled by a "Chinese fantasie." "The Mah-Jongg Blues" debuted with choreographed musical numbers "suggested by the new Chinese game."[1]

This San Francisco movie palace was at the vanguard of a fad that would quickly become all the rage: the Chinese game mahjong. Later that year, the Columbia Theatre in Seattle staged its own Mah-Jongg Blues production. Mahjong devotees did not have to rely on live performances; soon they could listen at home to the Atlantic Dance Orchestra's recording of the upbeat

"Blues."[2] In the early 1920s, it was nearly impossible to live anywhere in the United States without encountering at least some chatter about the game, from Spanish-language media in Texas and small-town newspapers in the Northwest, to films screened across the country and everything from fashionable shoes to ragtime tunes named after the game.[3] How had mahjong become an overnight sensation?

However delightful it was to play, mahjong was still an utterly unfamiliar game to most Americans when marketers first introduced it, and there was no guarantee they would be receptive. Yet key changes in popular culture and the economy—most importantly, the growth of mass consumerism and a market for goods from the "exotic East"—primed the pump for a mahjong craze in the 1920s. Unlike card games, mahjong required a unique type of game set in order to play; those sets and their weighty carved tiles provided much of the game's appeal—but they did not sell themselves. Entrepreneurs made use of the latest techniques in advertising, store display, and new forms of media like film to create and corner a mahjong market, which involved building relationships with retailers as well as moving to squash competition through patents and litigation. The mahjong industry connected novel forms of production, distribution, and marketing with established markets for "Oriental" goods and patterns of home entertainment.

"Attract attention, create a desire and supply merchandise that will sell"

The single most significant early promoter of mahjong was Joseph Park Babcock's Mah-Jongg Sales Company of America. In the 1910s, Joseph Park Babcock was a Standard Oil representative from Indiana. Eventually stationed in Suzhou, just outside Shanghai, he learned enough language to communicate with the locals—an unusual skill for a foreigner.[4] As his wife Norma explained, "we were in close contact with interesting Chinese people, we had few amusements in our small community of Americans and Europeans. My husband became an expert player and close student of the Chinese game."[5] After picking up the game from acquaintances, Babcock claimed to have changed it in part through combining styles he learned from "constant association with natives."[6] He began working on a set of tiles with English letters and numerals, as well as written rules to help his friends, who had struggled to learn the game. His 1920 printed English-language rules, which simplified elements such as the counting of points, helped spread the game among the

Anglo-American community in Shanghai.[7] Within a decade, he had built a mahjong empire in the United States.

Mainland Americans first began hearing about mahjong when the Babcocks introduced it in the summer of 1920 to wealthy Angelenos vacationing on Catalina Island, off Southern California.[8] They hoped this would serve as a useful test case for the game's potential popularity. They were right. After California high society pounced on the game, the Babcocks returned to Shanghai to pursue their ambitious entrepreneurial plans.[9] Together with his friend Anton Lethin and Lethin's superior at the International Correspondence School Albert Hager, who had the financial backing for the "Mah-Jongg Company of China," Joseph Babcock worked to spread his version of the game among Westerners in Shanghai and hoped to create an export market.[10] Babcock and Hager joined with lumber merchant William A. Hammond to set up the new "Mah-Jongg Sales Company of America" headquarters near the Port of San Francisco Ferry Building, where Hammond began receiving sets early in 1922. They, along with their vice president and general manager J. M. Tees, launched an aggressive national marketing campaign.[11] In the summer of 1922, they papered the country with advertisements for "high-class specialty men wanted as sales agents. Must be organizers able to train men and to handle a big proposition." Poised for rapid expansion, they hoped to hire in at least ten cities from New York and Boston to Indianapolis, Louisville, New Orleans, and El Paso.[12]

When the Pacific Mail steamship *Hoosier State* docked in San Francisco in May 1922, the local press was ready to meet her high-society passengers who brought with them an exciting new Chinese import: mahjong sets. The game had only been in the country "a few months," though transpacific communication had already revealed that mahjong was sweeping American expatriate circles in China.[13] Passengers included members of New York and Atlanta society whose skills as "experts in the game" were tested during the two mahjong tournaments held during the ocean crossing.[14] The fad had dominated steamship social halls during the three-week voyage.[15] The enterprising ship's barber sold seventy sets to passengers to take home, while stateside shops specifically marketed mahjong sets as "steamer gifts."[16] Passengers brought with them more than twenty-four additional mahjong sets "to introduce it to their friends in this country," as the game was already quickly gaining popularity on the West Coast. Just two days later, a department store advertised in the *Los Angeles Times* for "Mah-Jongg, that fascinating new-old game that is sweeping the country by storm!"[17]

Babcock and his business partners knew that the trend-setting New York market was critical for reaching the rest of the nation, and by the fall of 1922 they had failed to make significant inroads in the Northeast. Although readers of the *New York Times* had recently learned of "China's fascinating super game" in a September article about the game's popularity among returned visitors to Shanghai, there was no ensuing media frenzy.[18] The Mah-Jongg Company needed to create buzz around their branded product and to spark a sense of competition among those who were at the cutting edge of new trends. So Babcock gave his high-end sets to Hollywood film stars with a national reach like Douglas Fairbanks, who posed for photos playing the game with a set of tiles housed in an elaborately carved wooden cabinet.[19]

In November 1922, Mah-Jongg Company Vice President J. M. Tees arrived at the grand Hotel Pennsylvania in midtown Manhattan, which had been acclaimed as "the greatest hotel centre in the world."[20] He brought with him news of "the most fascinating game in the world" and its rapid spread across the Pacific Rim social scene, from Shanghai to San Francisco. Without mentioning his business interests as a promoter of the game, Tees positioned

FIGURE 1.1 Joseph Babcock and Douglas Fairbanks posed for a photo shoot with an example of an early high-end Mah-Jongg Sales Company set, showing Fairbanks consulting Babcock's "Red Book of Rules." The case that held the tiles, not shown here, was a detailed wooden box, with picturesque carved scenes. Courtesy of Christopher Berg.

himself as a traveling expert player who had bested players in the West but could simply not find "worthy opponents" in New York. " 'If there's anybody in your Hotel who knows Mah-Jongg, for Heaven's sake, send them to me,' he pleaded" on the front page of the hotel's in-house newspaper.[21] Bellboys silently delivered the paper each morning to the rooms of the movers and shakers who stayed there.

Tees cleverly pitched a match with the opera star Giovanni Martinelli and his wife, Adele Previtali, as "his only game in New York." The clip of his Hotel Pennsylvania challenge was sent to Mah-Jongg Company of China partner Albert Hager with a note: "Bert: — This is what your friend Morris did. He said that isn't anything yet!" Sure enough, a few days later the New York *Sun* published a photograph of the famous couple playing with a Mah-Jongg Sales Company set featured front and center while Previtali pored over a copy of Babcock's copyrighted book of rules.[22] The article credited a recent opera tour of Asia for Martinelli's knowledge of the "ancient game of China," but the trademarked product placement was clear. A month later, "there came to Washington from New York engraved invitations for a mah-jongg party" hosted for the Washington military elite by Lou Henry Hoover, wife of Secretary of Commerce Herbert Hoover.[23]

Settling into the circulatory routes of leisured wealth, mahjong coursed through Newport, Rhode Island; the Berkshires in Massachusetts; and Palm Beach, Florida.[24] Norma Babcock proudly claimed mahjong as the first good not only to spread from the United States to the rest of the world, but from the West Coast to boot. Its "widespread popularity and international social fame," she asserted, "conclusively proves that the Pacific Coast now holds the point of vantage over the Atlantic, and explodes the idea that all worth-while things must be introduced in an eastern metropolis to prove successful."[25] As their business strategy showed, however, the Mah-Jongg Sales Company understood that the East Coast still held outsized cultural influence. By the end of 1922, mahjong was officially a "craze." Throughout the next two years, African American clubwomen in Newark, married couples in Chicago, teenagers in Boston, white socialites in Seattle, and housewives in Atlanta helped spread the game in their communities, while the initial coastal markets continued to increase their consumption.[26] As Tees explained in 1923, "We feel that we have accomplished what we have set out to do. Attract attention, create a desire and supply merchandise that will sell."[27]

For the Mah-Jongg Sales Company of America, the game's explosive success was a mixed blessing. The company sought early on to retain control over and dominate the mahjong market. Hager registered a trademark and

Babcock filed a patent for the game to be known under the name of Mah-Jongg, with the hyphen and double g marking the "genuine" article, but the patent was slow in coming.[28] Hager filed for additional patents on behalf of the Mah-Jongg Company of China for the ornate wooden "cabinets for holding games" and the pieces used to keep score.[29] Meanwhile, other manufacturers in Shanghai and the United States proliferated and sold mahjong under a wealth of brand names, from "Pah-Lukk" and "Pung Chow" to "The Ancient Game of the Mandarins." In a particularly egregious attempt to horn in on the Mah-Jongg brand, a company producing a cheap cardboard set in Chicago highlighted its "Muh-Jung" title while explaining it was actually "pronounced Mew Yoonk," and therefore, they insinuated, clearly innocent from copyright infringement.[30]

Babcock's company advertised its sets for sale in "authorized stores and hotels," even as it quickly lost an uphill battle to control what and who could market mahjong—or, as they preferred to think of it, Mah-Jongg-like games.[31] In 1922, the Mah-Jongg Sales Company tried to enforce brand loyalty by suing the high-profile San Francisco home furnishings store Gump's, which specialized in Asian luxury goods, "for sales of apparatus and rules for playing the Chinese domino game, in violation, it is alleged, of patent rights and copyrights."[32] It also sued the San Francisco importers H. S. Crocker Company and Philip Naftaly.[33] Babcock demanded their imposter inventory be destroyed and argued that such companies skimmed unearned profits while "for years he diligently studied the game."[34] Naftaly, for his part, continued building his reputation as a mahjong rulebook author, but published his second book under the title of "Ma Cheuck."[35] Two years later, Babcock unsuccessfully tried to halt manufacturers in Amsterdam and Frankfurt as the game spread across Europe.[36] Despite the Mah-Jongg Sales Company's best efforts, after the game's initial introduction it was never again the only major distributor.

Even as Babcock filed a patent for his "Improvement in Games," the game was spreading along various other routes.[37] Not company sales agents, but rather society matron Carolyn Snowden Andrews Fahnestock introduced the game to politicos and military leadership in Washington, DC, in November 1922.[38] While the widow of financier Gibson Fahnestock reportedly "picked up her set in Europe," others brought sets from San Francisco. Lelia Montague Barnett carried the game back from Asia after accompanying her husband, Commandant of the Marine Corps General George Barnett, on an official trip to Japan. Representative Harry Hawes of St. Louis further spread the game when he gifted mahjong sets to more than a dozen Washington households, thus ensuring he could find players and, presumably, talk politics over the game.[39] Illustrating the ineffectiveness of the Mah-Jongg Sales Company's claims to patented exclusivity, an article about mahjong in "Capital Society" described the wide variety of sets emerging on the DC scene, "made by many manufacturers in China, since there are no patents on the game."[40]

Parker Brothers, the well-known toy-maker based in Massachusetts, eventually brought their heft to the Mah-Jongg Sales Company's efforts. George Parker had turned down an early partnership offer with Babcock, wary of his own recent lackluster game sales and weak results from an early trial of Mah-Jongg he conducted in a few Manhattan department stores.[41] By the spring of 1923, with mahjong mania in full swing, Parker approached the Mah-Jongg Sales Company and purchased Babcock's "trademarks, good will, and copyrights."[42] The two businessmen shared a motivation to corner the market. Two decades earlier, Parker's competitors had successfully diluted his proprietary "Ping-Pong" to a generic "table tennis," and Parker did not want this to happen again.[43] Under Parker Brothers, the Mah-Jongg Company adopted the motto "If it isn't marked Mah-Jongg it isn't genuine!" but even that was soon copied.[44] It seemed as though everyone was playing mahjong, and they did not need official Mah-Jongg approval to do so. The same elements that combined to generate enormous profits for the Mah-Jongg Sales Company of America—the game's Chinese origins, its wide appeal, and new national distribution and mass marketing techniques—helped prevent the company's control over the product.

"Something different this time"

Mahjong benefited from the established vogue of Asian-inspired goods. As a Los Angeles Times reporter asserted, "Half the fascination about the game is the quaint 'Chinesyy' al-about it [sic]."[45] Stores like Vantine's in New York, a famed emporium whose catalog displayed a wide range of goods to fill "an Oriental room or sun porch or special corner in one's home," dedicated an entire department to mahjong.[46] Smaller importers also integrated mahjong into a larger collection of Asian goods that were part of the American market for japonisme, chinoiserie, and an Orientalist mixture of Near- and Far-Eastern aesthetics.[47] Advertisers played up a sense of the foreign as anachronistic and strange that created an exotic appeal for all things Eastern.[48]

American Orientalism lumped together items and ideas about the Islamic World, South Asia, and East Asia to emphasize their difference from the West. Orientalist thought and representation made their way into everyday material and visual culture, including ideas of "the Orient" as feminine, luxurious, and backward.[49] Romanticized and simplified imaginings painted these cultures as presumably ancient societies that existed outside Western modernity.[50] These concepts were commodified by advertisers and producers of a wide range of cultural and material goods, promising their customers access to a cosmopolitanism for their homes through Orientalist consumerism.[51] With the expansion of *chinoiserie*—both Chinese imports and Western-made goods inspired by a Chinese aesthetic—and lavish paintings of the Arab world came "cosey corners" where Americans draped fabric in their own living rooms to create a harem aesthetic.[52] Armchair travelers hosted gatherings with global and exotic themes, from mahjong parties to Japanese tea socials to project their fashionable knowledge of the world.[53]

Orientalist consumerism reached a high point around the turn of the twentieth century, but it was built on long-term European and American fascination with tea and Chinese luxury goods including spices, porcelain, silk, and furniture. Until the nineteenth century, the Chinese empire carried a global reputation of cultured civilization, but as prejudice rose against the migrants from Southern China who entered the United States as part of a global diaspora, Chinese products came to be associated with cheapness and inferiority.[54] Chinese immigrant Andrew Kan remembered that, when he started his own import business in 1880s Portland, Oregon, he intentionally misnamed it a "Japanese Bazaar." "At that time, everybody cares buy Japanese goods—Chinese goods not amount to much," he explained.[55] The dynamic flipped again when anti-Japanese sentiment spread in the 1910s, especially in California. By that time, Chinese goods were fully integrated in a pastiche of Asian products. Andrew Kan started a successful new business in Seattle— this time named the China Trading Company—where he soon sold mahjong along with silk kimonos, mandarin coats, incense, lunch cloths, and Chinese baskets.[56]

Mahjong combined with a mishmash of Orientalist references and consumer aesthetics that were widely distributed throughout American popular culture, from movie theaters to clothing. In 1922, the same year that launched the mahjong craze, mass Orientalist consumerism exploded with the British archaeological discovery of King Tutankhamen's tomb. The extraordinary treasure trove of precious metals and art inspired a range of fashions and cosmetics, and furthered the popularity of films such as *The Sheik*.[57] Art movements such as modernism and Art Deco incorporated Asian designs and artistic styles, which filtered through architecture, advertising, and domestic objects into a mainstream Western aesthetic.[58]

FIGURE 1.2 On the cover of *Auction Bridge and Mah-Jongg Magazine*, a white woman in faux-Chinese dress paints designs on a larger-than-life mahjong set. Behind her glows a golden Chinese dragon screen, at once alluring and ominous. Exemplifying the massive American cultural output inspired by mahjong, the illustration highlights how the Chinese game and its accoutrement helped form a 1920s "Oriental" aesthetic. Library of Congress.

The visual culture of Orientalism made its way into American popular culture by the late nineteenth century.[59] The enormously successful 1893 Chicago World's Fair introduced its visitors to a highly consumable, simplistic, and often denigrated vision of foreign colonized and aboriginal peoples. The Fair explicitly linked the nation's success to a vision of racial hierarchy, physically separating Anglo-American civilizational progress displayed in the grand halls of the "White City" from the living dioramas of highly exoticized cultures organized along the Midway Plaisance.[60]

The Fair was also the setting for mahjong's overlooked initial debut in the United States. British Sinologist William H. Wilkinson, who reported collecting the "dominoes" from Ningbo in 1892, gave the set for inclusion in a games exhibit to anthropologist Stewart Culin.[61] Although many of the Chicago World's Fair's 27 million attendees must have glimpsed the mahjong set, it would have been meaningless without instruction and with the added barrier of unfamiliar tiles without numerals. These foreigner-friendly features enabled the global fad two decades later. While the Fair did not play a significant role for mahjong specifically, it helped spread Orientalist consumerism from highbrow culture to decorative objects available to the masses.

When the United States' military presence in the Pacific expanded into China, American consumer trends followed. After European, American, and Japanese forces suppressed the anti-imperialist Boxer Rebellion in 1900, they ransacked Beijing's Forbidden Palace. British soldiers returned with Pekingese dogs of the Chinese court, fostering a boom in this breed among British and then Americans.[62] Americans began to see themselves as a force for Western civilization as they simultaneously built a Pacific military and economic presence, perceiving themselves as promoting modern capitalist and democratic uplift.[63] In the process, they embraced consumer goods that evoked the trappings of empire.

One of the most celebrated purveyors of Asian goods exemplifies how American Orientalist consumerism evolved. In the early twentieth century, Grace Nicholson built a national reputation for her elaborate "Treasure House of Oriental Art" in Pasadena, near Los Angeles. She advertised mahjong prizes and novelties "Fashioned from Colorful Old Chinese Embroideries," using one material from the China trade to build on another.[64] Nicholson had first created her business by marketing Native American baskets, but as American tastes changed, she catered to the market for an Asian aesthetic.[65]

Although much of mahjong's consumer appeal was steeped in the allure of the exotic, its foreignness could prove controversial as well—particularly in its relationship to the game of bridge. In the world of home-based recreation, mahjong most directly paralleled that popular and esteemed pastime. Both games served the purpose of marking status, as bridge was associated with the social clubs, homes, and philanthropic events of the wealthy. Like mahjong, learning how to play bridge well took a significant investment of time in instruction, practice, and play.

In contrast to mahjong, bridge had a long and venerable history associated with British culture in American popular consciousness. Bridge-Whist, a
combination of late-nineteenth century card games, became popular among
Americans who enjoyed the intellectual challenge and its dynamic strategy
between partners and opponents. Its epicenter was New York and it was
spread by social elites. Couples and single-sex groups eagerly picked up the
four-person partner game, playing after dinner and with friends. It was played
with familiar cards and, notably, came to the United States via Europe.[66]
Mahjong, in contrast, entered the United States via the Pacific, from direct
contact with China. The tiles retained their visible Chinese origins with
carvings of Chinese characters and symbols.

Seen through the lens of bridge, mahjong was a successor, a usurper, or an
interloper. Virtually every early newspaper article and commentator weighed
in on whether mahjong would supplant bridge.[67] In echoes of the immigration
debate, some warned in racialized language that the "yellow peril" of mahjong
would overtake the European game.[68] The satirical (and pro-imperialist) *Judge*
magazine featured a huddled group of bridge players fending off an onrushing
horde of assailants who were armed with mahjong game pieces, mandarin
robes, and a smoke-billowing Chinese dragon.[69] The word play in its title,
"Horatius at the bridge," linked a legendary defense of ancient Rome with the
embattled card game that was ostensibly rooted in "Western Civilization."
From social scientists to song lyrics, mahjong's qualities were always seen in
comparison to bridge.[70] Eventually both games coexisted, but during the initial years of the mahjong fad, players and promoters frequently defended the
game by engaging in the terms of debate set by bridge's proponents.

Mahjong's differences from bridge, though critiqued in racial terms, also
provided a welcome change for some. Both bridge and mahjong needed four
players, but in a key distinction from the partnered pairs of bridge, mahjong
play was individualized. It offered a reprieve from high-pressure games
in which partners depended on each other to make the best play.[71] Others
claimed mahjong was, variously, more challenging, easier to learn, and more
strategic than bridge.[72] The tiles were also especially satisfying. One society
woman described the sensory appeal and fresh change of pace as "We were
getting a little tired of cards, cards, cards, all the time. I just love playing with
the little tiles. They are so pretty for one thing, that it is a pleasure to handle
them."[73] The cost of high-end tiles and insider knowledge of foreign phrases
appealed to status-seekers, too, as the game could be "more exclusive than
bridge."[74]

Horatius at the bridge.

FIGURE 1.3 This rendition of an epic battle between bridge defenders and a threatening mahjong army filled the first page of the satirical magazine *Judge*, in a 1924 issue focused on mahjong-related humor. Its visual depiction reinforced the association of bridge with Anglo-American culture and mahjong with Chinese and Chinese-influenced interlopers. HathiTrust Digital Library.

Those who embraced mahjong compared it favorably to bridge for its merits as a game, as a status marker, and as emblematic of America's modern future. "Bridge, then, is about where it was, and mah jong is about where it is," a *New York Times* feature asserted. While bridge represented the Old World, "America turned to the other side of the world and mah jong it was."[75] In this version, the United States paved the way, its leadership marked in part by trumping competition in modern entertainments. A cartoon Uncle Sam with his hands full of sports trophies taunted a befuddled and portly empty-handed

Brit, asking, "Can you play 'mah jongg'?"[76] For nationalist mahjong promoters, the United States had not only usurped Britain's leadership in geopolitical terms, but was also outplaying them in the recreational arena.

Rudyard Kipling's 1889 poetic assertion of an indelible cultural and racial divide, "East is East and West is West, and never the twain shall meet," often featured in poetry, advertisements, and articles.[77] Marketers emphasized stereotypes of Chinese as inexorably foreign to heighten the allure of mahjong as a way to experience the otherwise inaccessible world of Chinese culture. In so doing, they reinforced the idea that China stood as the most extreme pole of the "Other."[78] "There is a mysticism about the Oriental and his mode of life that challenges the imagination," wrote mahjong promoter L. L. Harr. "The dress of the Chinese, their strange customs, their difficult language, and their apparently impenetrable masklike faces appeal to the fancy and throw a veil of mystery around even the commonplace."[79] Inevitably in these accounts, mahjong became the meeting point between East and West, disproving the idea of an uncrossable divide. However, such depictions relied upon the surprising American embrace of a markedly foreign game, and thus simultaneously portrayed mahjong as a cultural bridge while reinforcing the idea of essential difference.

Writing about the mahjong craze, a Phoenix journalist explained, "'East is East and West is West' but there is nothing West likes better than to dress up and pretend itself Eastern for a space."[80] Mahjong fit with a larger pattern of consuming markers of "the East" with "Incense, beaten brass, lacquer and porcelain for our living rooms, and jade, [em]broidered silks and Ivory hair pins in which to array ourselves, anything for the exotic breath of the East. But it[']s something different this time."[81] By creating recognizable foreign symbols, the game and its aesthetic unified a branch of Orientalist consumerism around mahjong.

Beyond the game sets, a whole range of goods specifically marked the game's imagery, as well as game-play objects like tile racks and tables, were patented, produced, and sold.[82] Mahjong tiles, often carved with beautifully intricate images, were part of the appeal of the game and designers quickly took inspiration for fashions and fabrics.[83] "Whether the vogue of Mah Jong, the Chinese game, is responsible for Chinese designs and colorings in textiles, or the other way about, the fact remains that the two are progressing together," a commentator observed. "In fact, the textile designers have borrowed many of the designs that appear upon the playing pieces of the Mah Jong sets."[84] In 1924, retailers advertised a silk stocking named "Mah Jongg," embroidered with flowers mimicking the game's tile designs.[85] "Made to retail at a popular price" but "suggestive of the richness of high-priced Chinese kimonos" worn by elite women, the stockings provided affordable mahjong-related finery.[86] Mahjong sandals merely riffed off the popularity of the game and its Orientalist consumer resonance: an article reporting on the "Mah Jongg Shoes" that had begun appearing in Massachusetts stores explained, "the shoes are not Chinese except in name. However, the name sells a lot of shoes these days, and other goods, too."[87] Some even named high-status animals after the game: the *New York Times* featured a prize Pekingese, a Chow Chow, a winning racehorse, and a champion steer all named Mah Jongg.[88] The breadth of items marked by mahjong reveals the rapidly expanding world of goods for sale to a mass market obsessed with the exotic.

Alongside renditions of mahjong tiles—whether carefully stitched onto cloths to protect tables and soften the din made from shuffling the tiles, or painted on chairs, or printed on mahjong party invitations and score cards—were reductionist images of Chinese people. These included girls with umbrellas, lanterns, and the exaggerated queues of Chinese boys and men swirling through the air.[89] A "Mah Jongg Kid" doll sold by the Averill Company in New York had no obvious reference to mahjong, but it had a soft and squeezable body, a buttoned jacket, and a long queue.[90] It was a "Mah Jongg Kid" by virtue of its commodified, anachronistic, and ultimately accessible vision of Chinese culture. Mahjong both rode the wave of Orientalist consumerism and furthered its reach.

Luxury, Leisure, and the Masses

Mahjong found special purchase in the 1920s self-conscious obsession with mass consumerism. Business leaders and politicians viewed consumerism, even more than production, as a positive and necessary economic engine for the modern American economy.[91] Due especially to changes in financial credit systems and spending patterns, Americans were able to buy consumer goods—from durables such as home appliances, automobiles, and radios to ready-made fashion and cosmetics—on an entirely new scale in the 1920s.[92] The growing field of male advertisers increasingly imagined the prototypical shopper as a middle-class white matron, dubbed "Mrs. Consumer" by home economist Christine Frederick, and they targeted their efforts with women's anxieties and desires as purchasers for their families in mind.[93] The mirror image of the homemaker-consumer was the personification of the rising generation's youth culture: the flapper. Advertisers sought to capture the growing numbers of young women entering the wage-earning economy and their discretionary purchasing power. Such women working in the growing service industries faced both possibilities and pressures in presenting a stylish appearance. At the same time, Hollywood starlets promoted a sexualized image of white beauty shaped by newly respectable makeup and body hair removal.[94]

Mass consumerism was bound up with widespread leisure as more—though certainly not all—Americans could purchase ready-made necessities while enjoying more time for recreation. Sports culture bloomed in this environment too; tennis, baseball, football and golf all surged in popularity, while promoting a bodily aesthetic of slim fitness. Mahjong was closely tied to the leisure classes given the time investment necessary to learn the game as well as to play it. Hands, which bear the evidence of manicures, also feature prominently in mahjong.[95] Fingers take center stage during shuffling and picking tiles during a game. In 1925, the influential photographer Edward Steichen featured the disembodied hands of Ilka Chase, daughter of *Vogue* editor Edna Woolman Chase, "as she plays with mah-jongg tiles: rope of pearls wrapped around one wrist; on the other arm an emerald and diamond bracelet (the emerald conceals a timepiece), and a diamond bracelet; an emerald-cut diamond ring; all from Cartier."[96] The manicured hands, clearly unfamiliar with physical labor or dishwashing, were merely vehicles for displaying jeweled wealth and moving tiles. Mahjong also connected players with other products and enabled them to present themselves as leisured and knowledgeable consumers. A *Los Angeles Times* columnist surmised that "the ladies may take up mah jongg or golf as a pastime," but "they merely serve as a starring vehicle for that new frock or golf suit."[97] In this rendition, the "ladies" who took up recreation were mostly motivated as fashion-oriented consumers and the opportunities each new activity offered to buy things.

Mahjong quickly became seen as a game of the wealthy as it took hold across the country. However, as the development of mass consumerism meant that many manufactured products were available to a wide range of shoppers, its class spread was more diverse than its image. Most mahjong distributors carried multiple versions of sets at a range of prices, from under $10 to over $300, making sets accessible to a spectrum of buyers. The ubiquitous bone-and-bamboo sets often retailed at $20–$40, roughly equivalent to the cost of a dress from an urban department store—substantially more than a set of dominoes, but less than a decent radio set.[98] While Americans with lower incomes could sacrifice to buy an inferior-quality game, mahjong particularly attracted America's super-elite in its initial heyday and upwardly striving players in their wake.[99]

Middle-class players brought mahjong into their homes and social circles, influenced by newspapers and advertisers. By the 1910s, middle-class men's and women's social clubs were increasingly important in community life and frequently hosted card parties and charity fundraisers.[100] Mahjong became a social necessity, as parodied in a comic strip entitled "That Guiltiest Feeling," wherein an invitation to join a friend's game at home reduces a grown man to tears by "the disgrace" of not knowing how to play mahjong.[101] Wealthier hostesses could stage elaborate garden performances of plays such as *Mah-Jongg: The Play of One Hundred Intelligences* and grant starring roles to favored friends.[102] Most household entertainments, however, revolved instead around hosting game-playing social gatherings. By the turn of the century, evening bridge games had become de rigueur for middle-class Americans. "Play while the ice cream freezes," urged an advertisement for the Auto Vacuum ice cream maker. The readers of *Good Housekeeping* could rely on this appliance instead of servants or handmade refreshments to provide "frozen dainties with hardly any trouble" for their bridge or mahjong-playing guests.[103]

African American social clubs in Northern and Midwestern cities adopted the game as well. In February 1924, the club columnist for the African American newspaper the *Chicago Defender* covered "the first Mah Jong club" in Newark, while August saw the birth of "The Mah Jong Social club, one of Washington's newest elite clubs."[104] The *Chicago Defender's* national edition carried news of mahjong clubs and events happening throughout urban Black communities, from Kansas, Missouri, and Washington State, to Washington, DC, New Jersey, and Michigan.[105] Marketers did not miss the opportunity to peddle mahjong accoutrement to a growing Black following, such as a "mah jong ring" with engraved Chinese characters, supposedly "worn by fashionable society." For only $1.98, the ring promised the wearer "Unseen powers, riches, health, happiness, good luck in love."[106]

The game's social standing as a marker of elite respectability likely made it particularly appealing to certain segments of the Black upper class. The African American press featured mahjong almost exclusively in the context of Black women's clubs. Both white and Black society women in the interwar period were active members of social clubs, which promoted social causes, planned charity events, and sponsored lecture series for their members' edification. In the context of Jim Crow segregation and white supremacy, Black women's clubs had additional meaning as groups that would serve the needs of the Black community as well as manage and mold the potentially damaging image of working-class African Americans. For "race women," mahjong clubs would have also served as an opportunity to perform the politics of respectability.[107] When African American women desired to learn the game, however, they were unlikely to have access to or, perhaps, desire for private instruction from the white women who were the majority of mahjong instructors. African American women of means in New Jersey hired "N. Yam, native Chinese," to whom they credited their "wonderful strides in mastering the difficult Chinese game of Mah Jong."[108] Such a notice contrasted with white society reports, which rarely mentioned in-home Chinese instructors, and never by name.

Within white society, as mahjong became the pastime of "the smart set," women also used the game to engage their compatriots in philanthropic activities.[109] Bridge fundraisers had been commonplace: participants might pay for tickets and donate any winnings to the cause. By 1922, mahjong had joined bridge as a game to generate funds and contributed an additional "exotic" element with Chinese costumes and mahjong-inspired performances. The media also began to cover such high-profile events. In August 1922, for example, The World's Art Salon presented the first "fashion pageant and Mah Jongg tea," complete with "the leading modistes of the city" dancing and singing to Chinese songs, while others "in full Oriental costume" taught mahjong at an elaborately decorated Fairmont Hotel in downtown San Francisco.[110] News of the tea soon spread across the nation. Readers in Omaha, Nebraska, learned of mahjong's local debut when the *World-Herald* reported on a San Francisco visitor's dinnertime games en route to New York.[111] Not to be outdone, the following year Virginia Fair Vanderbilt chaired a "Ma-Jung Fete" in Manhattan as a fundraiser for the Catholic, Protestant, and Jewish Big Sisters Organizations.[112] The Fete at the Plaza Hotel featured a ballet starring the principal male dancer of the Ziegfeld Follies, while costumed members of the rich and famous "went slowly through some intricate movements" amid the creations of Broadway set designer Ned Wayburn, representing the game as "gaudy, almost fantastic Orientals."[113] Mahjong galas and fundraising events soon spread across the nation. While few were as high profile as the Fairmont tea and Plaza fete, many wealthy clubwomen staged mahjong benefits.[114] In the winter of 1922, a group of "young matrons" initiated the first mahjong teas in Seattle, "at which a silver offering will be taken, the proceeds to be used for various charities."[115] Middle-class housewives also hosted mahjong parties as fundraisers for their local sections' California Home Economics Association dues.[116]

FIGURE 1.4 The elaborate "Mah Jong Fete" of 1923 starred, among other members of high society, the twenty-three-year-old Muriel Vanderbilt as a lotus blossom representing the "flower" tiles of a mahjong set. Supper tables at the event in Manhattan's Plaza Hotel sold for $100 for charity, while newspapers discussed the rivalries over rare ivory sets owned by the wealthiest attendees. Courtesy of the Department of Special Collections, Stanford University Libraries.

As the popularity and availability of mahjong spread, department stores competed for customers by marketing themselves as modern emporiums of consumer delights.[117] Using the new marketing technique of "confessional" text, a melodramatic Macy's ad featured the woeful tale of a "lady [who] meditates ending it all!" Her fabulously wealthy life was already complete, having "divorced three husbands, including a Duke; shot African lions in

Somaliland," and completed her motherly duties by marrying off her son to an heiress. "What more does life hold for me?," she cried. In the department store's self-promotional fantasy, "The lady came to Macy's, where she found—just as you will find, when you come, a perfectly captivating Ma-Chiang set—in a department devoted exclusively to the Chinese game." Shoppers would, the ad assured, find imported sets at a range of prices as well as "Chinese dolls for the hostess whose decorations breathe the 'Ma-Chiang' atmosphere." In the advertisers' consumerist reverie, both the game and the store promised an elite and pleasurably exotic experience accessible to the middle-class masses who could, in turn, imagine themselves as "everybody who is anybody."[118]

Just as Macy's promised, department stores sold shoppers a full Oriental experience through new types of elaborate showrooms as well as window displays dedicated to mahjong and its associated products. In Los Angeles, white salesgirls with Chinese-style hairdos and embroidered dresses greeted Bullock's shoppers with an entire section promoting mahjong. The display cases featured sets from diverse manufacturers, as well as yet more Chinese dolls and mahjong-themed decorations. The products on sale nestled under Chinese lanterns, tapestries, and gongs. With echoes of earlier Orientalist "cosey corners," such displays engaged customers and encouraged them to create their own immersive "mahjong dens" at home.[119] Farther north, the Rhodes Brothers store in Tacoma, Washington, created a sensation when its mahjong window display "was veritably a miniature China, representing a fantastic land of dragons, figured screens, gold and purple silks," reported the *Tacoma Ledger*. Crowds gathered to watch "three dainty little maids" (young white women dressed in Chinese robes) play the game among the hanging lanterns and Oriental rugs, such that "the atmosphere of the whole northwest corner off 11th and Broadway seemed permeated with the spirit of ancient China and the mystery of Mah-Jongg."[120] Stores frequently showcased players in windows and hired instructors to teach shoppers the alluring new game.[121]

Because many of the mass-marketing techniques promoting mahjong were new, industry literature educated their audience about how best to draw consumers. The 1923 Mah-Jongg Sales Company catalog dedicated four pages to featuring ornate store displays like the Ville de Paris in Los Angeles, with whole "Mah-Jongg departments." Parker Brothers later coached potential drug-store purveyors of mahjong on successful mahjong exhibits and "staged demonstration by local Chinese experts" with a column in *National Drug News*. Aware of their audience outside department stores, Parker Brothers encouraged these smaller retailers that "a more modest display, backed by a newspaper announcement, will result in many profitable sales."[122]

FIGURE 1.5 The "Mah Jongg Section" of Bullock's department store in Los Angeles included a variety of mahjong sets in a range of boxes. The level of ornate detailing indicated the overall quality and cost of the set. Alongside mahjong sets made in China for the Mah-Jongg Sales Company and the American-made Piroxloid Corporation's "Ancient Game of the Mandarins," displays included a range of Orientalist consumer goods sold by young white women in Chinese-inspired dress. Bullock's Department Store Collection of Photographs. The Huntington Library, San Marino, California.

The industry magazine *The Moving Picture World* informed its readers of movie houses working with department stores for dual promotion, as when "a masked masquerader played against three Chinese girls in a department store window to advertise the game" alongside the 1922 film *The Masquerader*. The magazine included an informative photograph of the life-size window display, wherein a masked gentleman and three white women in mandarin robes passed tiles amid *chinoiserie* figurines and displayed mahjong sets.[123] Although mahjong did not play an important role in the film, the display capitalized on its chic associations to bring shoppers into the store and into the theater. When, following the example of San Francisco's Granada Theatre, the Columbia Theater in Seattle staged "an exceptionally artistic number 'The Mah Jongg Blues' " as a short pre-film stage production, *Moving Picture World* detailed how the theater manager's "stage setting was effective with Chinese art panels, and bowers of greens and blossoms."[124] In a move borrowed from department stores, a mahjong set "in a glass case in a lobby" complemented the dancing girls and singing mandarins.

Creative theater owners harnessed the game's popularity to simultaneously link themselves with the latest trend and raise attendance. By 1924, movie houses faced stiff competition from other entertainments. Theater owners bemoaned the twin threats of mahjong and radio drawing away customers' time and attention, and they strove to compete.[125] Thus, to show *Miami*, the Fox-Oakland Theatre in California recreated a beach and hotel veranda, complete with palms in the lobby and a stage set with "fashionably attired ladies arguing over Mah Jong or absorbed in bridge."[126] Their efforts were rewarded with "exceptionally big business." A movie house in Nashville raised enough funds to show the 1924 film *Flowing Gold* by linking local merchants' interests with "many hooks" in the film—an early variation on product placement in reverse. For example, a local jeweler urged potential customers to first see the film stars play mahjong in the movie, "and then order a set" from the store.[127] Middle-class patrons were inundated with images of mahjong. Although marketers sought to retain an association with the wealthy elite to build a sense of desirability and exclusivity, they depended upon broadening the customer base for the game.

In reality, players also came to mahjong because it was enjoyable. It offered entertainment that could be played casually or with great concentration and competitiveness. Players could sit for a few rounds or for many hours, building skills of strategy and scoring, hearing the sounds of the tiles, and feeling their smooth, cool shapes between their fingers. Amid Prohibition, the *Los Angeles Times* agreed that mahjong's affordable entertainment value "is an item well worthy of consideration in this day of persistent landlords, [and] high priced hootch."[128] The *Washington Post* published a little ditty about one man's mahjong conversion. After his wife "tells me in her way emphatic Mah Jong's so aristocratic," he balks at the price of the $30 set "for some Chinese game." But, thanks to his wife, the appeal of the game pulled him in: "in spite of all my jawing I forgot the cost and sat in and played, and that is that!"[129]

As mahjong became integrated into the pastimes available to "regular folk," at least some guardians of social hierarchy worried that the game risked losing its status. In a lengthy *New York Times* article, columnist Helen Bullitt Lowry wrote about both inappropriate methods of consumption and consumption by those deemed inappropriate.[130] Arguing that the "actual democratizing" of the game was driven by commercial interests, Lowry viewed the proliferation of cheap sets and slap-dash instruction as posing a "great danger" to the quality of mahjong. Despite the fact that the game's popularity was inherently linked to business interests, for Lowry the commercialization of mahjong bore the stain of crass ignorance. She bemoaned the move away from imagined Chinese players of yore at "ebony tables with 'tiles' of ivory and pearl, the while their thoughts turn toward Confucius, the heaven blest." In contrast, uncultured Americans "play it on the edge of the kitchen cupboard table with 'pieces' of something or other that looks like bone and smells like celluloid, it is described as 'that Chink game' and the stakes, at a tenth of a cent a point, are likely to be kept to a mere shadow of the two hundred and fifty thousand dollar pot they may reach upon the tables of the Mandarins." Equally critical of self-promotional socialites and common consumers, Lowry hoped that proper game-playing folks could make mahjong align with the "scientific" skill and decorous play of bridge. The game's popularity had long escaped the "chaperonage" Lowry desired.

"Smart Women"

Just as the *Washington Post* poet credited his wife with introducing him to the game as both status marker and entertainment, women drove mahjong's rapid spread into homes across the nation. Women often bore the bulk of mixed-sex social responsibilities, whether they worked outside the home or not: hosting visitors, maintaining relationships, keeping an eye on children's entertainments, and fostering their own female networks. A California mahjong "expert" and instructor explained, "Many of the women buy sets as soon as they have learned the game and take them home and teach the whole family."[131] In so doing, women were the primary shoppers for their families, but they were also creators of social trends.

Articles and advertisements told women how they could be, in an oft-repeated phrase, "smart hostesses."[132] To be "smart" one had to be in the know—and demonstrate that knowledge by serving things like "Mah Jong Cakes" surrounded by Chinese-themed decorations.[133] In the 1920s, this ubiquitous rhetoric conveyed that women's "smartness" had less to do with intelligence and more to do with an urbane, upwardly mobile, and charmingly frivolous self-presentation.[134] Mahjong fit into this limited mold as a chic leisure activity of socialites, while some middle-class matrons helped create a market for mahjong by connecting family and friends with the new pastime. It communicated a form of armchair worldliness and of consumable cosmopolitanism—and ignorance of the game risked social censure.[135] Others pursued mahjong instruction as a rare path toward independent income or, for white women, an opportunity within the growing retail industry of department stores.

In contrast to bridge, mahjong provided an opportunity for hostesses to dress up their homes and demonstrate their collection of fashionable Chinese decor. In the social realm, a leisure activity like mahjong ironically involved a great deal of effort and housework. For the wealthy women whose mahjong luncheons graced column after column in society news across the country, a typical elaborate "affair took place in the Chinese room and the guests numbering eighteen were seated around a long table, which held as centerpieces huge baskets filled with spring flowers and dainty Chinese place cards and favors."[136] Such a production would likely have involved the labor of household servants, like the maid pictured at a formal mahjong party in a Jell-O advertisement.[137] Images of uniformed servants transferred a sense of elite entertainment to those of more modest means, as well. Newspapers and home or fashion magazines educated their middle-class readers about what "society" was doing and how they could do it, too. The *Los Angeles Times* recipes column offered advice for a more manageable mahjong luncheon for four, featuring California avocados stuffed with olive oil and ginger.[138] "If it is your turn to be hostess, surprise and delight your guests by decorating your table with a pagoda cake and making Mah Jongg sandwiches," advised *Ladies Home Journal*.[139] These suggestions were within reach for homemakers with little or no paid domestic help and could still add some Orientalist flair to their tables.

A homemaker named Florence Currier offers an intimate glimpse into how individuals created the mahjong fad and how they incorporated this new activity into their social lives. After her husband gave her a mahjong set as a birthday gift in September 1923, Florence dove into the game with her family and friends in Belmont, Massachusetts.[140] While financially comfortable, they were a far cry from the Vanderbilts and Astors. Their family vacations were to nearby New Hampshire, and Florence and their daughter Peggy did the domestic labor, with occasional paid help from "Mrs. Fitzgerald." Both Florence and her husband Frank would have heard much about the game, as newspapers had been heralding its spread for the previous year and nearby shops promoted it. Living near Boston, Frank Currier could have easily purchased a set from a department store like R. H. White or Jordan Marsh, which advertised the "fascinating game."[141]

In her diary, Florence recorded her diligent study of the game a week after its arrival. Her notes reveal the patterns of domestic labor and leisure that shaped how mahjong's popularity spread. After she "made 6 glasses grape conserve, went to School St. Stores, wrote to Mary + looked over bills," Florence "read in a Mah jongg book."[142] It is quite possible her book was Joseph Babcock's "Red Book," which accompanied all the Mah-Jongg Company sets. Over the following year, mahjong made frequent appearances in her diary. It temporarily supplanted cards as the Curriers' main social activity. In their own and in friends' homes, Florence and Frank played mahjong as an evening activity with other married couples. One Friday night, after a day of cleaning the house and making desserts, Florence hosted their friends for mahjong "until 11.15 again!"[143] Female friends occasionally dropped by for afternoon games, but Florence's days were usually busy with housekeeping, social clubs, and church activities. After "A lovely day" of Peggy's help with cleaning and a late afternoon of shopping, she did the mending and "played mah jongg."[144] Soon the teenaged Peggy began playing as well, and Florence and Peggy could play together. In June 1924, *"Peggy had hair bobbed,"* her mother exclaimed, and the next day she debuted her stylish new hairdo with friends who "came to play mahjongg."[145] In 1924, mahjong was part of daily rhythms of labor and leisure as a fashionable trend for the young as well as their parents.

Had they known her, the Curriers might have thanked Marion Angeline Howlett, a nearby mahjong entrepreneur and traveling lecturer, for her role in catapulting their new pastime to national acclaim. Howlett was at the forefront of a growing number of women who headed to Asia alone or with other women to work their way to tourism and adventure.[146] From an established middle-class New England family in Cambridge, Massachusetts, Howlett, after a single college course at Radcliffe, traveled with her sister to California in her early twenties with ten dollars in her pocket and kept heading west across the Pacific.[147] She arrived in China with travel experience and money she had earned in Los Angeles, Honolulu, and Manila. Howlett later recounted her initial experience with the game as an itinerate journalist in 1921, traveling in Nankou near Beijing: "The Ching Er Hotel officials joined us to teach us Mah Jong. All of us huddled around the table learning Mah Jong *from* Chinese *in* Chinese with the help of Chinese pidgin-English and much pantomime."[148] She capitalized on her experiences in China to enter the American business world, launch a successful career as mahjong instructor, land on the society pages of the *New York Times*, and build a speaking tour.

Howlett was in many ways the ideal candidate for successfully using mahjong to build a self-supporting career. In the right place at the right time, she encountered mahjong just before the American craze exploded. Once it did, she marketed her skills as a mahjong instructor aided by her silk robes and the bone-and-bamboo mahjong set she bought in the Chinese section of Shanghai in 1921.[149] Her connection to "authentic" mahjong was important for Howlett to market her credibility, but the version she famously taught in the United States she must have learned from expatriates, as it was imbued with exactly the same rhetoric and styles of play associated with Western promoters. However, foreign instructors made for a less marketable story than the Nankou encounter.[150]

While recounting her adventures in exotic locales, Howlett offered her students opportunistic zeal in a socially acceptable package—Chinese authenticity along with white respectability. Her skills teaching etiquette in Hawaii and the Philippines likely made her even more adept at navigating her high-society mahjong customers. Giving mahjong instruction in Berkshire area hotels frequented by wealthy Northeasterners on vacation, Howlett helped solidify the game's association with the leisured wealthy. She also taught mahjong in the winter in Palm Beach, Florida, the "playground for millionaires."[151] With her she brought an embroidered mandarin coat from her travels, which the *Boston Globe* explained, "furnished a bit of realism that was reminiscent of the land of Confucius, touching up afresh the somewhat bored imagination of the leisure class with its medley of brilliant colors."[152]

A series of photos taken in Palm Beach in 1924 launched Howlett into the national spotlight as the instructor of "Mah Jong on the beach."[153] Motivated by their own need for marketable images, photographers eagerly posed Howlett playing mahjong in the sand and even floating on a rubber raft.[154] Despite her later protestations that her mahjong instruction never actually occurred on the sand, the pictures flew across publications and "water mah jongg" effectively became "one of the season's novelties."[155]

At the center of the mahjong fad, Howlett helped advertise the game's association with the wealthy while also bringing it into middle-class homes through instruction in department stores and touring events. Immediately after Christmas of 1923, when Santa Claus had distributed thousands more mahjong sets, the *Attleboro Sun* in southeastern Massachusetts hosted an enormous free mahjong lesson taught by Howlett.[156] The three hundred tickets were all claimed in advance, with representatives from a Rhode Island department store and the local chamber of commerce eagerly joining in. Howlett also garnered a number of ongoing business opportunities through private lessons in the area.

Public instructors like Howlett hoped to gain references for in-home instruction, which was far more lucrative than promoting sets in department stores. Customers at R. H. White in Boston would pay her 75 cents for an

FIGURE 1.6 Instructor Marion Angeline Howlett posed for a Palm Beach photo shoot with props that communicated her status as an authority on the game. She acquired the mahjong set from Shanghai and mandarin coat from Beijing while living in China. A Mah Jongg doll gifted to Howlett by its designer sits propped against the mahjong case. Schlesinger Library, Radcliffe Institute, Harvard University.

hour's instruction from Howlett in the store, a fee that would be waived for buyers of new sets.[157] But she pulled in "$10 an hour–that is $30 or $40 an evening" for private lessons while wintering among the wealthy in Palm Beach.[158] Howlett was able to use mahjong to help fuel her lecturing career, which lasted longer than the mahjong craze. After a trip to remote Alaskan villages in 1928, she embarked on a full-time speaking circuit, describing her adventures, promoting "International Good Will," and eventually focusing on the evils of communist Russia after her trip to the Soviet Union in 1931.[159] Like many other lecturers, she circulated especially among women's clubs, which sponsored speakers with international perspectives for the edification and cosmopolitan sensibilities of their middle- and upper-class female audiences.[160]

For both married and single women, mahjong provided an opportunity to earn their own income. The game's popularity quickly generated opportunities for instructors.[161] Along with department stores, women taught in cafés, at galas, or in private homes. While the Mah-Jongg Sales Company had peppered the country with ads for "specialty men" as sales agents, newspapers featured classified ads for "female help" in Manhattan as "Mah Jong Teachers and Experts."[162] Still early in the mahjong craze, in

September 1922 the *San Francisco Call* reported, "A new form of activity for women along business lines is teaching the Chinese game, Mah Jongg."[163] Soon after, California newspapers began carrying reports of an enterprising Mrs. Brown, who taught mahjong in stores and homes throughout Northern and Central California.[164] Traveling instructors like Brown and Howlett were important in bringing knowledge of how to play the game to places like Merced and Santa Rosa in California and Attleboro in Massachusetts, where the buzz of the game had sparked interest but aspiring new players desperately needed instruction. Women who did not need added revenue could still stand to raise their social profile by serving as instructors at philanthropic mahjong galas.[165] Some instructors could advertise their link to the "authentic" game, as Howlett did with her Chinese set and stories.[166] Yet the majority were white women who had no link to China but who, because of their race and gender, were able to gain access to other women's homes and gatherings without suspicion.

The success these instructors experienced rested on the explosive popularity of the game. Babcock and the many marketers who followed him successfully promoted an image of the game that linked it to social elites, enabling it to ride the shirttails of media attention to activities of the rich and famous. However, mahjong's appeal—both as a game and as a form of class aspiration—spread across lines of class, race, and region, and its varied forms made the game available to the masses.

In popular understandings of economic history, men operated as catalytic entrepreneurs while women participated as consumers, discrete from the operations of business. There is some truth in these generalizations. However, the making of the mahjong market blurred these distinctions, as individuals were often both purchasers and distributors. Amid a male-dominated business world, numerous individual women played an essential but easily overlooked role in creating the mahjong phenomenon as informal importers, entrepreneurial instructors, or businesswomen involved behind the scenes in their husbands' family businesses. On a societal level, elite and middle-class women were crucial in spreading the game as hostesses at home and social planners of large public events. Their role—and the cultural contradictions embedded in Orientalist consumerism—had been present since the early days of the game's popularity with Americans in China.

2

Cosmopolitan Roots in Shanghai

"VISITORS TO SHANGHAI who ride past any of the clubs," satirist Elsie McCormick wrote in Shanghai's *China Press* in 1921, often heard a strange clicking. But the sound, she continued with racially and class-inflected humor, was not "the daily dishwashing stunt of Ah Ling in the pantry and the subsequent chipping of perishable porcelain." Rather, they were hearing "the galloping ivories of China," which were "rounding out their usual sixteen-hour day in the foreign community." Thus, the American McCormick informed her readers of the burgeoning expatriate love affair with mahjong. In a widely circulated quip, McCormick even facetiously posed the unthinkable: a future in which the esteemed game of bridge was unknown. "The day may not be far off when an innocent little daughter will sidle up to mother with a dusty card in her hand and ask what it was all about. 'That's what people used to write the score on in a game called bridge,' mother will explain. . . . 'Better hide that card, or everybody will think we're old-fashioned. Now run along and find amah. Mama wants to play mah-jongg.'"[1]

Shortly after World War I, Americans in Shanghai began writing home to their families about a new game sweeping their social circles, the only Chinese pastime that took hold and threatened bridge's sacrosanct status among Westerners in semi-colonial foreign enclaves. Situated near mahjong's points of origin in the Lower Yangzi Delta, Shanghai brought together the people, social worlds, and businesses that propelled mahjong into an international phenomenon. Mahjong's cultural and geographic roots set the stage for entrepreneurs to transport this Chinese game to the United States.

Mahjong had been spreading throughout China's urban centers for four decades before the rest of the world began playing it. Although Americans would later imagine it as an ancient game juxtaposed against their own modern identity, for Chinese cultural commentators, mahjong already symbolized the possibilities and perils of modern society. A new elite class of Chinese intermediaries eventually helped introduce mahjong to American businessmen and travelers, for whom it served similar purposes of community, entertainment, and posturing as it did for Chinese players. Mahjong soon found pride of place in expatriate homes and social clubs.[2] While male social circles were the most visible, the growing numbers of both American women and Western-educated Chinese women helped create new patterns and places of interaction. The seeds of the gender shift from predominately male to female players originated in the expat world. Mahjong's path through American social circles highlights the dynamics of leisure, domestic labor, and social competition that underwrote the patterns of foreign life in semi-colonial China.

Origins

Mahjong's story begins during the final decades of the Qing (1644–1912), the last era of dynastic rule in China. The exact origins of mahjong in China are murky, but it likely evolved as a gambling game in the mid-to-late 1800s—not the age of Confucius, as American marketers advertised. Its creators combined paper and tile games, collectively called *pai*; its suits likely originated from paper cards that referenced units of money.[3] By the early 1910s, the game was well known across social classes in Shanghai, in the confines of the Forbidden City in Beijing, among gamblers in Hong Kong, and in the Southwest urban center of Chengdu. The roots of the game lay in the broader Lower Yangzi Delta, an area that had a long history of game development. As one of the wealthiest parts of the Ming and Qing empires, the Delta was a diverse and bustling region, connected via trade routes and print culture to the imperial capital of Beijing to the north. Before Shanghai emerged as China's major port after the First Opium War, nearby cities like Suzhou and Hangzhou (known in English at the time as Soochow and Hangchow) functioned as centers of wealth and urban cultural production.[4]

By the turn of the twentieth century, Lower Yangzi Delta elites played a recognizable form of mahjong as one among many primarily male gambling games. Clear predecessors of the game survive from the early 1870s as a handful of Western scholars and government employees carefully recorded a "species of Dominoes" from Fuzhou and Ningbo in the Lower Yangzi.[5] The essentials of mahjong's set, rules, and name likely stabilized by the 1890s around Ningbo and Shanghai, though the game continued to evolve over time.[6] Its name, 麻雀, pronounced as *moziang* in Shanghainese, meant "sparrow." Mahjong's developers took designs from paper cards, including some elements of the earlier game of madiao with its four-person configuration, and combined the cards with the domino-like form of tile games. Other substantive changes in play differentiated mahjong as well, particularly the structure of individual play in which each player operated only for himself rather than three operating against the fourth "leader," as in madiao. The individual style of play would become a defining feature of mahjong, as would its particular mix of luck and strategy.

It did not take long for mahjong to proliferate in Lower Yangzi urban centers, spread northward to Beijing, and then outward to major trading cities like Chengdu far in the interior and Canton on the southern coast. In 1885, the Shanghai newspaper *Shenbao* reported a "brand-new" gambling game of *moziang* in Jiaxing, a region just north of Shanghai on the Grand Canal, en route to Beijing. Over the next few decades, mahjong spread to Beijing and its nearby areas, pronounced in the North as *májiàng* and eventually written as 麻將.[7] By the early 1920s, a newspaper editor in Hebei, the province surrounding Beijing and the nearby treaty-port of Tianjin, reported that "In recent years, a new token has entered the district from other areas. The common name for the game is majiang." It was associated with city life; as the article explained, "Majiang is not often seen in surrounding villages, but it is already gradually becoming popular in the city. Before long, it will spread to the entire district."[8] The game had already taken hold of Shanghai.

Shanghai's unique culture transformed and broadcast mahjong into the rest of China and internationally. By the time of mahjong's debut, Shanghai had become a semi-colonial treaty-port city; its structure was rooted in the history of trade and imperialism that had wrought massive changes in China over the previous century. Trade and consumer goods had long driven Western involvement in the Pacific, but the nineteenth century marked a new era. For many years, China held the upper hand, as vigorous European markets clamored for Chinese goods.[9] By the 1840s, European desires to control trade and reduce competition to maximize profits matched increasing European military strength.[10] Meanwhile, a struggling Chinese government faced population pressures and multivalent imperial challenges while it also worked to prevent the illegal importation of opium from British India.[11] A series of military defeats resulted in treaties primarily with France, Britain, Russia, the United States, and Japan. Early twentieth-century Chinese nationalists later knew these pacts collectively as the "Unequal Treaties" because of their one-sided obligations, the first of which forcibly opened Shanghai and four other Chinese ports as treaty-ports to foreign trade and zones of international settlement.[12]

Located midway between the British colony of Hong Kong to the south and the historic political center of Beijing to the north, Shanghai was China's most important international trading center. People and goods flowed in and out of Shanghai's port and overland routes. It was a city often described in hyperbole, with alluring nightlife, crowded streets, and extremes of wealth and poverty.[13] Unlike colonies such as Hong Kong, which the British directly controlled, the Chinese government held limited sovereignty with "foreign concessions." The relatively small foreign population primarily operated in separate residential and commercial districts, particularly the International Settlement and the French Concession. The International Settlement was formed from the merger of the British and American enclaves, though it housed a mixed population from a range of nations and was governed by the locally elected, British-dominated, and very powerful Shanghai Municipal Council.[14] By 1920, Japanese residents outnumbered all other foreign populations in Shanghai combined.[15] Although they lacked equal administrative representation in the foreign-run enclaves, Chinese residents vastly outnumbered any other group in every district. Among the Chinese, newcomers from multiple regions in turn outnumbered those originally from Shanghai.[16]

Shanghai's multiple jurisdictions made it a haven for radicals and the underworld. Authorities intermittently enforced anti-gambling statutes, and as mobile gambling enterprises were closed down, they could profitably reopen in a more welcoming jurisdiction.[17] Mahjong was played primarily as a gambling game along a spectrum of stakes and was thoroughly enmeshed in social spaces like courtesan halls and teahouses. There women who trained in the arts of flirtation, sexual pleasure, and entertainment encouraged customers to spend money at mahjong.[18] Courtesans were integrated into Shanghai's social fabric, influencing fashion and even issuing special tokens accepted as local currency. Mahjong meshed well with the masculine culture that courtesans helped facilitate: customers invited friends to evenings in hotel rooms and banquets with food, drink, and mahjong or cards at courtesan halls to demonstrate their wealth and to curry favor with the madams who controlled access to the women known as "flowers."[19] As one client advised his friend in the 1892 serialized novel *The Sing-song Girls of Shanghai*, "if you favored them with a dinner party and a game of mah-jongg, how they'd fuss over you!"[20] Courtesan houses did not take cuts like gambling houses, but benefited from players losing money to courtesans, paying to access their company, and spending on food and drink. The novel of late-Qing courtesan culture depicted multiple scenes of mahjong parties with various and diverse players, from male and female servants in the "Hall of Beauties," to clients and courtesans at opium-infused "sing-song house parties."[21] Mahjong served as an arena for competition, banter, and conflicting motivations: male clients tried to keep their mahjong losses to a minimum while feeling pressure "to appease the courtesans" by playing. Playing with higher stakes helped establish reputations essential to doing business in Shanghai.[22]

Mahjong existed in an ambiguous position to Qing edicts against gambling.[23] It could be played without monetary stakes and was therefore not always considered illegal. Although maximizing points was a major part of the game's strategy, it could also be played in a simpler version that just made specific combinations of tiles, or it could be played for very low stakes. As a *Sing-song* courtesan patron advised his friend with illustrative circular logic, "mah-jongg parties don't count as gambling. Well, as long as you don't gamble."[24] Holidays, however, continued to be a legally acceptable time for gambling during the Qing era and the subsequent Republic, and especially during these times mahjong could be found in diverse spaces. Shortly after the 1911–1912 Republican Revolution, the (all-male) Shanghai printers' guild

FIGURE 2.1 Courtesans and their clients play mahjong in Shanghai, likely on a river "flower boat" at the turn of the twentieth century, when both mahjong and courtesan culture had become increasingly pervasive in the city. As shown here, Chinese players stood the tiles on end, in contrast to the racks American players later adopted. From R. Barz, *Sketches of Present-Day Shanghai.*

celebrated Mid-Autumn Festival with rounds of mahjong to cap an evening of respectable celebration, including a vegetarian feast overseen by chanting Buddhist monks.[25]

Key elements of the game's appeal were present in its early history and would help the game adapt to widespread play in China and abroad. The tiles' carved beauty set them apart from other domino games. Unlike many other gambling games, mahjong provided a mix of luck and strategy. Because it could be played along a spectrum of stakes and necessary pauses were taken between rounds for shuffling the tiles, it was well suited to sociability across a range of classes. Mahjong did not stay in courtesan houses, but instead moved up to the realm of elite respectability—including, most controversially, bourgeois women's homes.[26] "Respectable" women began to play the game as well. As it continued to spread, the rhythms of a mahjong game—the pacing of breaks between rounds of play, and the dynamics of individuals facing off against each other—meant that mahjong games could be used as settings for friendship, to build relationships, or to demonstrate power moves of posturing and strategy.

The game took Beijing by storm in the last years of the Qing court, among both men and women. During the early 1900s, the Empress Dowager Cixi embraced the game and would "constantly have her ladies-in-wait[ing] play it with her."[27] As a symbol of pleasure-centered idleness, mahjong also fit in with the Dowager court's reputation for corrupt indulgence. Chinese historian Xu Ke reported that court officials, eunuchs, and servants "were all obsessed with the game" shortly before the Revolution. "When the game was at its most popular," historian Xu Zhiyan wrote in 1917, "it reached everybody from palace residents and noble families to itinerant merchants in their sedan chairs. Nobody failed to take pleasure in it." Evoking the sounds that would become a hallmark of the game, Xu described: "Journeying through the narrow alleys of the city, you always heard the clinking of tiles. After celebrations, when there was a little free time, people always played it. In the twisting lanes of the hutong and in the courtyards, people wallowed day and night in the game."[28]

The game crossed political lines too, as reformist journalists pondered its social potential, even while decrying mahjong's conservative royal fan.[29] In the midst of debates over modernization, a few advocates in Shanghai for Western-style changes suggested using the game as a tool for ideological mass education. One innovator carved the English alphabet into mahjong tiles to make a spelling game and "imbue it with more civilized concepts."[30] In 1904, another reformer who hoped "to draw upon common knowledge of the game in order to alleviate the ignorance of the people" imagined changing the names of the tiles to instruct players on global styles of government and modern geopolitics. Notably, tiles symbolizing "republicanism" were worth twice as much as those for constitutionalism, while Qing "autocracy" netted zero points. Flower tiles underwent a makeover, too. No longer adorned with Confucian-inspired depictions of the traditional Four Noble Plants, they depicted powerful new technologies such as steamships, railroads, and hot-air balloons. Each technology, as well as other tiles representing commercial and military prowess, had to be matched with the appropriate continent or ocean in order to explore or establish dominance.[31]

In this highly politicized era, reformers could see mahjong as an indicator or even instigator of social degeneration. These philosophical and political debates particularly raged in Shanghai. In part because of the strong associations with teahouses and courtesan halls, commentators still linked mahjong with pleasure-seeking men and lower-status women. Mahjong smacked of indulgence and leisure, and skill in play became a marker of "ill-spent youth."[32] Even worse, reformers feared the effects on the new republican nation of distracted mothers corrupted by the game that had moved into respectable homes by the early twentieth century.[33] Labor organizers in the mid-1920s complained about mahjong's spread of indolence, as "on holidays these workers go downtown to amuse themselves or stay home to play mahjong. Only a few enlightened workers engage in proper pastimes."[34] In 1925, an anti-union official used mahjong to actively encourage worker apathy by bribing Shanghai workers with modern treasures of phonographs and mahjong sets to reduce union membership.[35]

Other critics associated mahjong with an overall disordered society, from the corruption of the Qing court to modern perils. After the Republican Revolution of 1912, intellectuals blamed mahjong, among other elements of Chinese culture, for the fall of the dynasty. Some linked the game's origins to gambling Taiping leaders of the destabilizing mid-nineteenth century Taiping Rebellion that devastated the region just south of Shanghai.[36] In 1914, a Shanghai satirist linked mahjong with disruptive forces, as a "Great King of Majiang" joined other fictional "heroic bandits" to end the crumbling Qing dynasty. The story explained, "the Qing had lost all control and the empire was in disorder," requiring the mixed blessings of the Kings of Sex, Money, Railroads, Prostitution, and Opium to end the Qing and unify the empire. Each imagined warlord embodied the pitfalls of modernity and social ills that also reeked of foreign influence. The Great King of Majiang, as a Chinese innovation imbued with cosmopolitanism and decadence, provided the crowning blow by unifying the populace where others could not. Game playing became ironic battle, as "people from all classes, at every hour of the day, including men, women, the elderly, and children, engaged in the fight in big and small ways." Progressive intellectuals lauded the end of the corrupt Qing, but used mahjong's popularity to question the possibility of a modern future.[37] Mahjong's cultural meaning extended far beyond the game as it reflected and sometimes furthered changes in each social context, from Shanghai courtesan houses to reformist proposals. In turn, the social segregation of Shanghai as a semi-colonial city shaped how foreigners approached the game.

Shanghai and the Mahjong Explosion

When Elsie McCormick reported in 1921 about the "swelling popularity" of mahjong, she satirized the craze by imagining "enthusiasts" who proposed "little portable tables that can be carried around the neck for practice in ricshas; others are suggesting electric torches with each set, so that the game can be played at the movies."[38] Mahjong swept the expat social scene, first in Shanghai and soon in Beijing. Most foreigners coming to China landed first in Shanghai, and it was the final destination for the increasing numbers of American sojourners.[39] Even if businessmen were transferred elsewhere, they stayed there a few weeks to acclimate while being shepherded through the International Settlement's well-developed framework of social networks and services. Disembarking in Shanghai, the American Janet Wulsin first encountered a new game she called "Maja" in 1921 when she and her husband landed to explore China on behalf of the National Geographic Society.[40] Wulsin was immediately introduced to the "Chinese gambling game" in the home of a Mrs. Nichols. The Wulsins soon left for Beijing, where mahjong entered their social circles by Christmas. It is notable that a person like Janet Wulsin, the daughter of a wealthy East Coast railroad family who cared about social exclusivity, embraced this Chinese game. Many foreigners in China were invested in reinforcing a hierarchical and colonial-style isolation from Chinese culture, so the spread of mahjong was an unusual point of crossover.

Mahjong shaped the worlds of the three major types of Westerners who lived in Shanghai's International Settlement in the 1920s. They included the long-established and predominantly British "Shanghailanders," the rapidly growing ranks of European and American newcomers, including businessmen and educators, and the predominantly American missionaries.[41] Old-guard wealthy British settlers dominated the Municipal Council that governed the International Settlement and scorned the new arrivals as strivers, but both groups played mahjong. In contrast, the missionaries actively discouraged their flocks from playing the gambling game. As one American woman observed, in the status-conscious society of "the caucasians in Shanghai . . . the missionaries and the business men do not love each other at all out here."[42] Growing numbers of American merchants shaped the burgeoning American scene in Shanghai, particularly as missionaries focused more on interior China.[43] Among and outside these groupings a wide variety of businessmen, adventurers, hedonists, and radicals also lived in the city. Lines of class, national origin, and race shaped the lives of Shanghai's residents, but the main social differentiation was between Chinese and Westerners, enforced most enthusiastically by the established Shanghailanders.[44]

The key players in the cultural transfer of mahjong were the growing numbers of Chinese intermediaries and non-missionary Americans as mahjong continued to gain popularity among Chinese players in Shanghai and Beijing. By the 1920s and 1930s, many of the new political and business Chinese elites had been educated abroad or by American missionaries, spoke English, and served a vital role in Shanghai.[45] Forging extensive personal networks, this diverse group of officials, middlemen, compradors, industrialists, merchants, racketeers, and partisans knit Shanghai together and bridged the divide between foreigners and Chinese, though only rarely in social settings.[46] Although Chinese residents made up the majority of the population, speaking Chinese was largely unnecessary for foreigners, whose only regular interpersonal interaction with Chinese people were servants who often had basic or pidgin English skills.[47] Chinese elites and those educated in the West began introducing mahjong to foreigners by having numerals carved on the Chinese-numbered tiles, an innovation for which mahjong exporter Joseph Babcock would later take credit.[48] Even monolingual Westerners or Chinese businessmen who kept to Chinese circles might be invited to a dinner party held by intermediaries.[49]

Shanghai's International Settlement provided the key environment to adopt the game and transform it into an international phenomenon. Americans in particular quickly integrated mahjong as a major social activity in their social clubs and domestic circles. Perhaps these non-missionary Americans picked up the game more quickly because many were relative newcomers and less invested in the predominantly British Shanghailanders' established ways of emphasizing their separation from China.[50] For Americans like Janet Wulsin, mahjong may have provided a way to consume Chinese culture while maintaining class exclusivity and demonstrating knowledge of a fashionable pastime. Babcock's spheres of influence may also have disproportionately affected Americans, as he worked to spread his rules for the game through the expatriate community. Soon, however, mahjong was played throughout the foreign community and it alone would come to challenge the supremacy of bridge.

Shanghai's foreign community was ideally structured for the spread of mahjong. It was built on access to leisure underwritten by the labor of Chinese servants and revolved around male social clubs and home-based social networks facilitated by expatriate women.[51] Among the elites, the International Settlement also fostered diverse business connections that entrepreneurial individuals could work to their advantage.[52] Babcock and his business partners may have leveraged such connections in establishing their mahjong production and export business.

Not unlike the Chinese native-place associations, the male social clubs provided a modicum of familiar community far from home and facilitated essential networks.[53] In these clubs, men fraternized, drank, played card games, and gambled on horse races. For their national communities, clubs indicated local prestige and geopolitical strength.[54] Within the clubs, particularly the American ones, the game quickly spread, facilitated by key promoters like Babcock. Conveniently, Babcock's business partner, Anton Lethin, was a resident of the American Columbia Country Club when they began to see commercial possibilities for the game in 1919.[55] Along with their partner Albert Hager, they actively encouraged the game in social clubs through their company.[56] In addition, game expert Robert Foster credited "two brothers named White [who] took a fancy to the game of Mah Jong and introduced it to English-speaking clubs" by 1921.[57] Although evidence indicates that Babcock, Hager, and Lethin took the leading early role, doubtless many individuals contributed to its spread in the influential social clubs.[58]

Mahjong may have made an early foreign club appearance in the Union Club, an unusual organization founded in 1919 originally called the "ABC Club" for its express purpose of bringing together elite Americans, Britons, and Chinese.[59] Soon after, Babcock began circulating his first printed rules for the game. By 1925, American advertisements trumpeted the "copyrighted Babcock's rules" as "the recognized standardized rules adopted by all the leading Clubs of Shanghai, (the American Shanghai Union and Country Clubs)" as the clubs carried transpacific prestige for consumers abroad.[60]

Most established social clubs for elite Shanghailanders, especially the famous Shanghai Club for British residents, prided themselves on extreme exclusivity: only wealthy men, and certainly no Chinese, need apply.[61]

However, the significant demographic changes in Shanghai and growing Chinese nationalist resistance in the 1910s and 1920s challenged the British Shanghailanders' dominance of the International Settlement's social scene. Although it remained relatively small, the American population more than doubled from 1914 to nearly 3,000 in 1921, while Japanese residents also increased and "White Russian" tsarist refugees provided a new European underclass.[62] An American school, businessmen's club, country club, and church sprang up on Shanghai's landscape, just as the United States strengthened its position as a major trading and diplomatic partner for China.

At its grand opening in 1925, the American Club building's million-dollar architecture communicated civilized elegance, including an exotic Chinese mahjong retreat. Their new club building helped Anglo-Americans define their unique brand of elite internationalism. In fact, its grandeur and expense overshadowed even the preeminent Shanghai Club, and Americans reveled in their community's statement of power and permanence.[63] The American Club denied Chinese members until 1929 (after the more open German Club and Cercle Sportif Français, but well before the British). The club's elegant rooms, from the dining room to the billiard parlor, conveyed a unified 1920s American aesthetic, with the one exception being the Chinese-inspired "Mah Jong Room."[64] Inside, the dark mahogany-carved furniture, lanterns, and painted eaves echoed a Chinese aesthetic and created a space where members could partake in a game deemed "Chinese" without loss of status.[65]

Although American women were peripheral to the club environment, they nurtured mahjong cultures at home. Their involvement was essential to the spread of the game internationally.[66] Clubs were the most splashy and visible social spaces for foreigners in Shanghai, but mahjong also fit neatly into domestic life in semi-colonial China. Social dinners and long lunches provided time to learn and play the game, as did paid domestic labor. Along with the rising tide of commercial interests came wives of businessmen whose "feminine invasion," as US Commercial Attaché to China Julean Arnold called it, transformed the American Shanghai social scene.[67] Their presence and roles moved social and business networks from club to home. In January 1922, Janet Wulsin told her parents about playing "Ma Chang, a fascinating Chinese game," with Gordon Wilson and his wife. She noted that he was the "No. 2 at Andersen Meyer," one of the largest companies in China.[68] Foreigners socialized to facilitate and cement high-power relationships, and in letters they communicated mahjong's elite associations to their own wealthy families.

Women also used personal networks and mahjong parties to build rare relationships across the Chinese-foreign divide with other influential

The Mah Jong Room

Library

The American Club, Shanghai

The Card Room

The American Eagle in the Lobby

FIGURE 2.2 As the showpiece of the American community in Shanghai, the American Club building was meant to be stately and imposing. Among its varied places for recreation, the room dedicated to mahjong play stood out for its traditional Chinese aesthetic, complete with ornate painted ceiling. The Far Eastern Review. University of California, Los Angeles.

women. As educated Chinese women increasingly joined public events, particularly in the company of elite and American-educated Chinese men, they facilitated the small but growing interaction with foreign communities.[69] Rhoda Cunningham was a progressive counterpart to her conservative Shanghailander husband, US Consul-General Edwin Cunningham. She initiated some of the first integrated social gatherings when she "invited a few of the wives of distinguished Chinese to her famous curry tiffin parties, and asked them to stay on for mah-jongg."[70] Among the attendees was Wellesley graduate Mayling Soong, soon known internationally as Madame Chiang Kai-shek.[71] Rhoda Cunningham's outsized social influence offered some protection from the social censorship of other Westerners who socialized with Chinese and her efforts inaugurated "a new era in the social life in Shanghai," American journalist Edna Lee Booker later remembered.[72] Booker, who had learned the game from the rules circulated by Joseph Babcock and Albert

Hager, played mahjong with wealthy Chinese women who hosted gatherings in their Shanghai apartments (and who, in a show of hospitality, allowed Booker to win).[73]

Enterprising single women as well as matrons led the American Shanghai "feminine invasion," and they incorporated mahjong into their communities as well.[74] Thyra Pedersen traveled to China as a young woman and supported herself by teaching Chinese students at the missionary Union Girls' School in Hangzhou outside Shanghai in 1923–1924. Although her primary community in China was the Midwestern Baptist missionaries who rejected mahjong, and the modernizing Chinese government of Hangzhou proscribed mahjong along with other gambling games, such restrictions did not stop Pedersen and her small group of foreign teacher friends. Pedersen explained in a letter home, "The city of Hangchow forbids Mah Jong except for three days of the Chinese New Year," a time traditionally associated with luck and gaming. "However we play but no one would suspect that we were Mah Jong players and therefore no one investigates. Besides we do not play for money and that is the great evil of the Chinese who play."[75] Pedersen, a self-described secular person, may have encountered the game during her surreptitious "devilish" forays into Shanghai's nightlife. Or, she may have played at other integrated gatherings like the bridge party hosted by Chinese students returned from studying abroad, held during the Chinese New Year.[76]

Women broadcast knowledge of their new pastime across the Pacific via correspondence. Maintaining ties with families and friends at home, they sent hundreds of letters by steamer across the Pacific describing the daily life of Americans in China. Wulsin, who had earlier come across the game she called "maja" in Shanghai, embraced it by the winter of 1921, playing "every night" in December with her husband and compatriots in Beijing. Writing home, she endorsed " 'majen,' a Chinese game that you would love."[77] Two years after Wulsin arrived in China, her stateside family became swept up in the craze as well. By 1923, Wulsin could complain of her expat friend being "too busy with Mah Jongg and bridge to allow a free afternoon for these glorious sunny days" without needing to remind her readers of an unfamiliar Chinese game.[78] After hearing that "father is quite a Mah Jongg player," Wulsin wrote hopefully: "We will have to have some family games someday."[79]

By the time the global mahjong fad roared to life in the 1920s, the game had already traversed multiple social spaces within Chinese and foreign society, from courtesan halls to bourgeois homes. The new access respectable women had to the game would shape its trajectory in the United States, and for both Chinese and American women, playing it continued to draw scrutiny from cultural commentators. Early patterns—mahjong's association with urban sexuality, cosmopolitan allure, and its flexible gaming potential—set templates for the game's transformative American career.

3

Making a Transpacific Game

A MAHJONG CRAFTSMAN at the Mei Ren Company factory in Shanghai bent over his work. The fifteen-year-old hailed most recently from Ningbo, having negotiated an agreement with his new employer to offset the vulnerabilities of piecework wages. He worked in a new kind of mahjong factory that combined elements of Chinese workshops, such as artisanal techniques and task specialization, with Western expectations for standardized design and streamlined output. He specialized in one task, building a reputation as a "bamboo-engraver," as he etched the parallel lines of the bamboo images on the bone faces. After carving the designs, another worker added the vibrant pigment that would make the grooves stand out, rubbing the green, red, and blue paint into the furrows, while still another wiped off the excess. Depending upon their skill and experience, as well as the production pressures they faced, his fellow engravers' images might range from rough gouges to delicate line paintings. Buyers with deeper pockets could request an individualized set of engravings.

Before reaching this decorative step, the tiles were first constructed by transforming bamboo pieces and bovine shinbones into rectangular domino-like tiles. Other craftsmen, ranging in age from late childhood to adulthood, sawed the bone and aged bamboo, spliced the pieces through an interlocking anvil-shaped notch, and sanded the sharp pieces into a smooth, pleasing object. After passing through each stage of construction, assembly, carving, and painting, the tiles were wrapped and packed into cardboard boxes for future arrangement in wooden cabinet boxes, themselves decorated with brass corners and handles, each stacked drawer to be filled with different suits of tiles. After their steamer voyage across the Pacific, Americans of all walks of life would eagerly scoop up the sets that had been seemingly transformed by marketers' rhetoric into ivory rather than bone.

FIGURE 3.1 Craftsmen for the Mah-Jongg Manufacturing Company of China put the finishing touches on mahjong tiles by painting the engraved bone faces and wiping off the excess pigment. The multiple hanging lamps indicate the importance of light to this detailed work and would have created significant heat in the interior spaces. Parker Brothers Archive.

As the American market developed a voracious appetite for the game, in 1923 Chinese and Western merchants launched new kinds of large-scale factories in Shanghai that standardized production with artisanal workmanship. Mahjong factories encompassed multiple paradoxes, implementing old-world aesthetics and "primitive" techniques in a factory model that advertised its modernity. They produced hand-carved items out of variable natural materials, yet each piece needed to be nearly identical so that game players could not distinguish facedown tiles. Factories demanded machine-like precision and consistency while effectively recognizing individual skills in labor negotiation and marketing that emphasized handmade "authenticity." The result was an industrialized commodity whose value increased through association with an artisanal human touch, even as the sets lost individuality and production capacity maximized profits.

The mahjong craze sparked the development of hybrid forms of production and helped shape a key period in the evolving economic and cultural relationship between China and the United States. Demand for the game put great pressure on sourcing materials and labor to make the tiles. The mahjong industry, based primarily in Shanghai and involving transpacific flows of raw materials and capital, built on long-established consumer patterns of Western markets for Eastern goods. However, mahjong marked a significant change in Americans' increasingly direct economic and cultural engagement with China. For the first time, Americans jumped on a Chinese good on their own, rather than in response to European tastemakers.

The materiality of mahjong was a fundamental part of its "new-old" appeal, signifying authenticity, exoticism, sensory satisfaction, and the excitement of something different from cards. Although most mahjong consumers understood themselves to be at a remove from their sets' origins, the production of the game sets and their consumption were in fact intertwined. Manufacturing mahjong presented one of the troubling challenges of modernity: how to translate the sensory and class-based satisfactions of artisanal and natural materials while still fulfilling modern promises of cleanliness, safety, and efficiency.

"To fads, civilization owes much"

The exploding consumer market for mahjong drove meaningful growth in Shanghai's expanding American export industry in the early 1920s. It provided a desperately needed bump for a Chinese economy foundering over a falling silver standard, war indemnities, and a widening disparity between imports and exports.[1] Economists in the Chinese government credited "modern enterprise" with the dramatic spike in exports to foreign ports from Shanghai for "creating a demand for the game that is apparently insatiable, particularly in America."[2] A meteoric rise in mahjong exports occurred between 1922 and 1924. In 1921, Shanghai exports of "sundries," the miscellaneous category that included mahjong, went primarily to other Chinese ports, with the value of exports to foreign ports less than a quarter that of domestic Chinese shipping. The following year, sundry exports to foreign countries exploded to thirty-three times those of the year before. Exports continued to skyrocket through 1923. By October, the Shanghai sundry trade to the United States alone increased tenfold over the total foreign exports of the previous year. The American mahjong market eclipsed all others, with Hong Kong ranking a distant second as it was simultaneously building its own mahjong industry.[3]

The mahjong rush was so powerful that it caused a bump in the total China trade. Mahjong dominated the pages of the January 1924 issue of *The Chinese Economic Monthly*, the English-language periodical published by the Chinese

Government Bureau of Economic Information; the previous year had proven that the game could not be ignored.[4] Congress would soon pass a new tax specifically on mahjong sets, one of only two new taxes in a year that saw an overall reduction in taxes.[5] In 1923, mahjong sets had surged to become the sixth largest export to the United States from Shanghai, worth $1.5 million.[6] Total exports from China to the United States increased about 22 percent over 1922 totals, with a pre-holiday export trade of 47.5 million dollars.[7] While much of the increase was driven by the enormous and growing market for raw Chinese silk, mahjong was the single dominant consumer good export, particularly during the holiday season. "Mah Jongg sets are more in demand by Christmas shoppers than any other novelty on the market," announced the *Los Angeles Times* in 1922. This favored gift was given across the nation the following year, nearly doubling mahjong exports in the final three months of the year.[8] And these were only the recorded exports. Many other sets crossed the Pacific as part of the "vast amount of tourist traffic," explained the *Chinese Economic Monthly*; "if there is one thing that tourists generally stow away in their trunks nowadays," it had to be "a souvenir of China in the shape of a set of mahjongg."[9] Linking mahjong with a longer history of popular Chinese goods "from willow ware [china] to Pekingese pups," the *Boston Daily Globe* posited, "To fads, civilization owes much, for they, rather than necessaries, often have been the first springs of international trade."[10]

China Weekly Review editor and Shanghai American John B. Powell poked fun at the hypothetical imperialist response such an enormous trade generated: " 'But we must have Ma Chang even though it leads to foreign intervention and the scrapping of the Washington treaties,' said the buyer for the American department stores, the novelty shops and the high-class dealers in up-to-the-minute goods." Pro-business but critical of Western aggression, Powell satirized American hubris in light of the game's lure.[11] "America has always been the friend of China and countless as the sands of the sea-shores are the lowly Chinese who have been uplifted through the efforts of self-sacrificing sons of Uncle Sam," whined his fictional American merchant, "but we must have Mah Chang sets and by the thousands." Threatening aggression but actually dependent on Chinese knowledge and skill, the fictional buyer was helpless in the face of mahjong shortages.[12]

Americans had long followed Europe's lead in importing specific Chinese goods as markers of refinement, but it was American consumers who led the way for a European mahjong craze. Although the game had already entered various European markets through independent routes and imperialist connections, England and the Continent would not embrace mahjong en masse until after the American craze.[13] In England, bridge posed an even greater barrier to mahjong among the established moneyed class than in the United States. *Vogue*, usually tasked with keeping Americans up to speed on European fashions, emphasized the hesitancy of the wealthy British, who saw "the game as an interloper."[14] Nonetheless, mahjong spread throughout the British empire.[15] An Australian store that prided itself on "Always Being First with the Latest" advertised its "special effort" to acquire sets, complaining that the game's popularity in London and the United States absorbed Chinese output.[16]

By 1924, mahjong entered the circles of European royalty, Parisian fashionistas, and trendy Londoners.[17] Some European elites picked up the craze in America.[18] For those seeking to create a new society after the Great War and embrace "sudden, dazzling chance," mahjong held special appeal. "Games, like women's fashions, are better clues to an epoch than its laws and statesmen," wrote British journalist William Bolitho. "To-day the unmistakable marks of post-war Europe are shingled hair and Mah Jongg.... Out of this jumble of Relativism, Communism, Reparations, and ruined Exchanges, is a vivid mental picture of thin, elegant women with close-cropped hair, playing a Chinese game, by shaded electric light, just out of hearing of the throb of saxophones, to while away the revolution."[19] In Europe as in America, the association of mahjong with chic modernity—embodied by stylized young women wearing bobbed hair and cosmetics—fueled the booming international market.[20]

"A very difficult business"

Almost overnight, demand for mahjong sets far outpaced production. The international fad simultaneously fueled further growth in China itself. "One thing is certain," the *Economic Monthly* reported, mahjong "flared into popularity almost as suddenly in China as abroad."[21] Seattle importer Andrew Kan reported to *Time* magazine in 1923 that he had returned to China "to place orders for a half a million sets, but was only able to obtain a fraction of that number, owing to the enormous demand. The price of the game has been increased 100% during the past few months, and Mr. Kan thinks that the price will continue on its upward flight until the American public stops buying."[22] Kan was not alone. Frantic purchasers meant unmet orders, shoddy and inconsistent products, and outrageous prices.[23] Observant economists expressed concern over what they saw as a mahjong bubble.[24] Demand, however, only continued to grow.

The craze seemed to catch everyone off guard. In shipping records, mahjong remained obscured in the "sundry" category for things too unimportant to merit individual listing, despite its outsized presence. Exporters hesitated to devote their resources to what appeared to be a transient frivolity, and producers resisted transforming existing, time-intensive manufacturing methods. "Mahjongg is a very difficult business to handle," explained the *Economic Monthly*. "It requires specialised knowledge and long experience, if it is to be treated as a legitimate trade."[25] By 1924 the market began to stabilize as importers grew convinced of its durability. Exporters began incorporating manufacturing into their businesses—usually purchasing rough tiles from "jobbers" who cut, spliced, and joined the bamboo and bone elements of the tiles for the manufacturer's craftsmen to sand, carve, and paint.

Resource shortages caused major bottlenecks in mahjong set production. Bamboo and bone, as well as the skilled labor necessary to procure and process the components to careful specifications, were all in short supply. Manufacturers needed to buy "dried and seasoned" bamboo from specific bamboo experts because its quality was central to a successful product.[26] Bamboo expertise tracked back to the very moment of harvest, as cutting had to be timed to avoid worm egg deposits. Links to the profitable export trade could be severed if manufacturers and exporters lost their reputations for providing reliable products. Indeed, "leaping larvae" wriggling in imported mahjong tiles made front-page news in San Francisco in 1924.[27] It took special skills for craftsmen to splice the bamboo, sourced mostly from a broad swath of territory around Shanghai in the Yangtze River Delta, with the shinbones of American cattle.

American demand for mahjong exports created a new Chinese market for one specific American export: cow bone. In a twist that echoed early trade between the new American nation sending raw materials such as ginseng and furs in exchange for finished goods like porcelain and silk, in the 1920s American ships carried cow bones as building blocks for handcrafted mahjong tiles, thus bringing the Pacific into closer contact with the American interior.[28] Bovine bones were an essential component for the most common form of tiles, and China simply did not produce the huge numbers of bones necessary to churn out thousands of sets overnight.[29] The shortage was exacerbated by the small percentage of bone equipped for mahjong tiles: joiners could only use sections of several inches taken specifically from shinbones. Front leg bones furnished fewer but also thicker and more valuable pieces; bone thickness directly determined the value of the sets and the cost of customs duties.[30] American packinghouses benefited from the shortage of bones, with steamships like the

Patrick Henry carrying bones from Chicago slaughterhouses out of Galveston, Texas, to Japan, where they were re-exported to China.[31] Skyrocketing prices of bone paralleled the value of mahjong exports: bone prices in 1923 were two to four times greater than in 1922, and in China the value of bone imports in 1923 jumped to two thousand times the 1921 total.[32] The United States already enjoyed the world's greatest trade surplus, and the Department of Commerce happily reported that the American market for imported mahjong sets had "a beneficial effect on business at home" by fueling bone exports.[33]

Unpredictable supply prices and a rapidly shifting global market made mahjong an alluring but vexing investment. Distributors in the United States like Andrew Kan complained of late shipments as material shortages and price spikes made it difficult for exporters to make scheduled deliveries.[34] Yet, even with the high cost of bone, the vagaries of bamboo quality, and scarce skilled labor, mahjong could provide a tidy profit.

"Gentlemen with iron chisels in hand"

Although small-scale workshops proliferated in Shanghai and the surrounding areas, thousands of American consumers played with sets coming from two specific large-scale mahjong factories: Mei Ren and Joseph Babcock's Mah-Jongg Manufacturing Company of China.[35] These factories were photographed extensively, and the similarities between them are striking. Both demonstrate the consistency of large-scale work environments and structures fueled by the massive mahjong export industry. Despite their differences, the fundamental steps of handmade production remained the same in large factories and small workshops. Examining the processes of large-scale—yet handcrafted—manufacturing highlights the paradoxes in these new transnational factories. Photographs of laborers also illustrate the complex power dynamics inherent in the making of mahjong.

For *China Weekly Review* editor J. B. Powell, the Mei Ren Company represented an inspiring example "of what Western ingenuity can accomplish in China when it really wants to." It started in 1923 as a joint venture between American and British businessmen. Within the first several months the company employed 400 craftsmen from numerous Lower Yangtze Delta provinces, who churned out 2,500 sets each month of 148 tiles and accoutrement such as small bone sticks used to tally points. Operating both under the American name "Mei Ren" and the British brand "Pung Wo," the company eventually ran the largest mahjong factory in China and employed 1,100 people.[36] In June 1923, *The China Weekly Review* included a special insert featuring an eight-page illustrated article about the Mei Ren Company and its mahjong manufacturing. The Shanghai publication was a powerful voice for American interests in China and enjoyed international circulation. The mahjong feature was widely excerpted and disseminated to an American readership.[37]

For Powell and other industrialists, Mei Ren's example encouraged further investment. Its name directly translated to "American friendship" and represented the unequal partnership of traditional Chinese skill and capitalist Western oversight that American business representatives viewed as a positive good.[38] A longtime Shanghai resident, Powell positioned himself as an authority on both the West and China. He believed strongly in the capacity of Western investment to improve China, but he also critiqued the Shanghai Municipal Council's discriminatory policies and the imperial powers' roughshod treatment of China. Mahjong inspired Powell's gentle ridicule of both "crazy foreigners" who urgently demanded their sets and also of tradition-bound Chinese craftsmen who refused to consider new methods. In contrast, Powell praised the ingenuity of Mei Ren's Western chairmen as well as the Chinese "gentlemen with iron chisels in hand" who worked for them.

Mahjong factories embodied the synthesis of Western early industrial techniques in a Chinese city. In the Mei Ren factory, craftsmen labored in exterior courtyards or three-walled rooms, in task-specific areas. In a step toward vertical integration, the mahjong "factory" consisted of workshop-style hand labor housed under one roof. The bricked areas opened through a tall wood door into a Shanghai alleyway.[39] Workers at the Mah-Jongg Manufacturing Company factory crowded into rooms with brick floors and mixed architecture. As opposed to the small-scale workshops in which craftsmen also sold the tiles to the next workshop, the factories separated labor from commerce. In the well-lit Mah-Jongg business office and showroom, American businessmen conferred at dark wood desks, speaking into a dictaphone while smoking cigars. Chinese employees filed papers and wrote in ledgers. Despite the variation in spatial details, more united than differentiated the two factories.

In some key ways, the factory environments, workers, and methods contrasted with "modern" industrial methods emerging in the United States. Unlike the plastic mahjong factories that would soon open in both the United States and China, bone-and-bamboo tile fabrication for Mei Ren and the Mah-Jongg Manufacturing Company was based entirely on labor-intensive handwork.[40] Also, a significant minority of Shanghai's general laboring population were children, many of whom worked in the factories as apprentices.[41]

Yet, what made the factories "modern" in the eyes of Powell and Chinese economists was the combination of Chinese skill, international exchange of materials, and the influx of Western capital. The American business owners attempted to combine a "primitive" process with streamlined production to maximize output and profit, and they expected a long-term and growing market for mahjong.[42] While they assumed a progressive idea of modernization based on Western models, the reality of the mahjong factories, with their hybrid environments, created instead a different kind of paradoxically artisanal factory.

The factories were places where Chinese craftsmen both lived and labored, making the rooms simultaneously workplaces and residences. Workers sawed cow bone into pieces in a room lined with shelves that held essential personal belongings. Bedrolls and cigarette boxes leaned haphazardly against each other, punctuated by hanging clothing and the occasional framed image. Lines of laundry dried in rooms and courtyards as their wearers daubed pigment on carved tile faces. Tile painters worked at a table likely used for eating as well, dipping brushes into small porcelain bowls, while nearby shelves held rice bowls stacked with soup spoons.

Shards of bone, bamboo, and wood littered the floors. What workers wore or did not wear—shoes, shirts, fabrics, hats—marked their status within the factory. When Mei Ren factory workers gathered for a group portrait, hundreds of workers poured from the factory's entryway.[43] Their clothing was distinct from that of the factory's "Executive Staff" of overseers and proprietors. The color white, particularly on shoes, and the tailoring of fabrics marked the upper levels of management and could distinguish both Westerners and Chinese elites. In contrast, each worker wore loose pants of woven fabric, tightened around the waist by folding the top of the fabric over a tied sash. Only very rarely did a worker wear a leather belt; no laborer wore laced leather shoes.

The Chinese business partners' involvement in the Mei Ren and Mah-Jongg factories illustrate the narrow but growing zone of elite Chinese and American interactions and contested alliances. Both Western and Chinese elites sought to exclude the lowest classes of laborers and beggars from rarefied public spaces, but toiling workers were integrated into all aspects of the city, including mahjong factories.[44] After passing through the hands of shirtless craftsmen and collared inspectors, crated mahjong sets were ready for transport to ship or shop by a "wheel barrow man," whose shoeless feet wrapped in strips of cloth revealed his struggling existence.[45] Pausing for a photograph in an alley outside the Mah-Jongg Sales Company factory, a young man balanced

FIGURE 3.2 The Mei Ren/Pung Wo Company's promotional photograph of its mahjong factory, titled "A Few of Our Skilled Workers," featured a glimpse of their company's workforce, from overseers to craftsmen. Prints and Photographs, Library of Congress.

a load of mahjong sets bound for export across the Pacific.[46] Lashed onto the cart, large wooden crates bore stamps informing English readers that the boxes held "MAH JONGG" sets "MADE IN CHINA," which the recipient should "HANDLE WITH CARE." Packed inside crates like these were fifty mahjong sets, shipped as wrapped tiles and accessories in tin cartons, with the wood cabinets sent separately.[47] The person propelling this simple machine peered from behind the crates, his unbuttoned shirt allowing some cooling air while providing slight protection from the cart's balancing straps pulling on his shoulders. He, too, wore a hat, though not the fashionable

FIGURE 3.3 A wheelbarrow worker pauses en route from the Mah-Jongg Manufacturing Company of China Shanghai factory to loading docks, with crates of mahjong sets soon to be exported to the United States. Parker Brothers Archive.

and fragile boater hats of the factory bosses. Near the bottom of Shanghai's social hierarchy, the wheelbarrow man nonetheless curled his mouth in a slight smile.

The photos captured not only the lines of machine-like precision and exposed workers' bodies, but also the persistent individuality of the wheelbarrow man and the workers in the factory. In one image, five shirtless workmen arranged in rows carefully held tiles against tree-log worktables while pounding them with mallets and chisels to shave off the surfaces.[48] A basket of finished tiles gathered at their feet. In a classic image of racialized power, two white factory owners leaned over the workers to supervise the product. The craftsmen's naked torsos show off their biceps as their hands work; their varied hairstyles and bodies disrupt the uniformity. Dressed in suits and with pomaded hair, the white men posed for the camera as diligent managers: exempt from the labor happening on their behalf, but working hard nonetheless. Yet, complicating the image, behind them a group of laborers pause their work to stare back at the camera. In this image and in several others, the resting bodies of workers who gaze at the camera with curiosity belie the image of colonized worker as efficient machine.

FIGURE 3.4 In the Mei Ren/Pung Wo factory, American and British investors posed as overseers examining workers splitting cow shin bones in preparation to make mahjong tiles. Splitting the bone was one of the first steps in creating a smooth white surface for carving the tile faces, which would be spliced to backs of bamboo. Prints and Photographs, Library of Congress.

Although the balance of power tilted decisively in favor of employers and investors with capital, especially the Western businessmen with geopolitical advantage, mahjong production could not be reduced to simply one-sided exploitation. Those who skillfully wielded physical tools could use their knowledge as a negotiating tool. The skilled nature of the work, which manufacturers valued because of the corresponding increase in the selling price of the sets, and the mahjong labor shortage meant that craftsmen had some bargaining power. The Mei Ren Company recruited most of its initial 400 workers from areas bordering Shanghai and acquiesced to workers' demands in order to entice them to join the large-scale Western factories.[49] Otherwise vulnerable to the vagaries of piecework, workers gained a guaranteed base income, a healthy bonus, round-trip railroad fare to Shanghai, and food and lodging at the factory.[50] *China Weekly Review* editor J. B. Powell noted approvingly that successful negotiations with labor meant "this modern Ma Chang factory is an accomplished fact in spite of the grumblings of the reactionaries who said it couldn't be done."[51] While the average wages of mahjong craftsmen are unknown, the American Commercial Attaché to the Department of Commerce cited reports that expert mahjong workers in Shanghai earned $70 to $100 per month.[52] In contrast, most skilled urban workers in the engraving, hat-making, or clay figurine industries earned the equivalent of 10 to 20 cents a day with board.[53] Mahjong businessmen felt confident that an American public eager to purchase mahjong tiles "engraved in quaint, gay-colored Chinese characters and symbols" would repay their investment.[54]

Mahjong craftsmen made sets simultaneously for foreign and Chinese audiences. The small numerals and letters in the corners of their respective tiles required for an English-speaking customer were unnecessary but not cumbersome for Chinese players, so manufacturers did not need to strictly segregate products for export. The most ornate and beautiful tiles were the eight "flower" tiles that had become widely used by the 1920s.[55] The flowers consisted of two sets of four tiles and provided the most artistic variation between sets. Their name stemmed from the fact that one tile quartet often represented flowers (with the name of the traditionally associated season carved in Chinese).[56] Even the cheapest relatively unadorned sets required some kind of imagery for the flower tiles. These tiles accentuated the game's aesthetic appeal for audiences on both sides of the Pacific, though their meaning registered on different levels. Most Americans' understanding of the images remained more superficial, and the commonly engraved scenes of flowers or Chinese transportation styles (wheelbarrow, sedan chair, rickshaw, boat) and architecture (bridge, gate, pavilion, pagoda) easily fit with *chinoiserie* designs and Orientalist ideas of Chinese culture. Foreign-made sets in the United States and Europe often replicated these pictures on pressed plastic or stamped wood.

For Chinese audiences, the images drew from a deep and widely known well of cultural references. They would recognize the iconic tools on another common set of four "flowers" as representing the traditional "Four Noble Professions" of Fisherman, Woodcutter, Farmer, and Scholar. Although many sets made in China for both domestic use and export bore the same consistent standardized designs, others communicated a wide variety of advertisements, images, and words. These were the same aesthetic possibilities that had allowed reformers to see mahjong as a tool for instructing the masses.[57] Finely carved sets often illustrated idioms, folktales, and acts from popular operas, so that the tiles recreated complete scenes when lined up in a row.[58] Tile suits beyond the flowers also provided opportunities for additional carvings: the first tile in the "circle" or "dot" suit was a large circle, which often included more words in Chinese characters carved inside the center.[59] Manufacturers with less literary orientations adapted tile designs and the wood covers of mahjong cabinet boxes to promote their business names.[60] Carved characters on the original Mah-Jongg Company flower tiles spelled out "Manufactured Under Company Supervision."[61] Even as its popularity in the United States was predicated on new modes of mass advertising, the game's surface also served as a marketing platform to readers of Chinese.

The rich visual culture of mahjong tiles, and how its players interpreted their images, helped make the game adaptable across divergent contexts. The tiles' carved designs were an essential component of their multifaceted sensory appeal. For the American public, the Chinese imagery and writing added to the mystique of the game and created an utterly new experience.

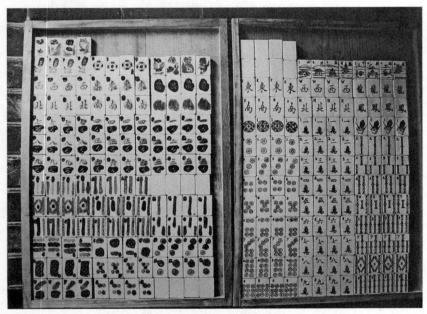

FIGURE 3.5 These two trays demonstrate the final stages of painting and polishing tiles for the Mah-Jongg Manufacturing Company of China. The tiles from a standard 1920s set are all visible in the tray on the right. At the top is a row of eight "flower" tiles with pictorial scenes. Below them are the "honor" tiles of cardinal directions and colors, known as "dragon" tiles. Four of the blank tiles at the top left are included as spares, in case a tile needed to be replaced, while the remaining four are "white dragon" tiles. Underneath, the main suits are organized in three columns. Circles are on the left, characters are in the center, and bamboo are on the right. Parker Brothers Archive.

"Game of Iv'ries" and Artisanal Mass Consumerism

Despite its use of cow bone, mahjong became deeply identified with ivory, a valuable natural material that was, in fact, rarely involved. As an American writer mused, "there is something delightful in the fact that it is a costly little outfit, with its bamboo and ivory pieces, its ornate box and generally Oriental and mysterious aspect."[62] The mahjong fad was created in large part by linking the game to elite status and exotic materials. "Ivory and bamboo" became shorthand for the game.[63]

High-end mahjong sets could, in fact, be made of ivory, but they were extremely rare and the objects of envy and social competition.[64] Tusks from Asian elephants came to China through South Asia, while Japan distributed ivory from East Africa to the world.[65] As the ivory vogue decimated elephant populations, traders struck out "for the Siberian Coast and Alaskan Arctic waters" for new sources. In 1924, the *Boston Daily Globe* warned: "Walrus May Be Wiped Out: Enormous Demand for Ivory for Mah Jong Sets and Cigarette Holders Has Spurred Hunters," as buyers offered "unheard-of prices to walrus hunters, natives and whalers."[66] Fortunately for elephants and walrus the world over, ivory was never a predominant mahjong material, despite popular belief.

Consumers often mistook bone for ivory, likely because of a combination of similar appearances, an association with luxury and class, and intentional confusion created by marketers. Bone and ivory have smooth, lined surfaces well suited for fine carving, and both give a warm off-white natural appearance. They feel nearly identical in players' hands. Before the American fad, mahjong craftsmen likely chose bone to evoke the elite traditions of carved ivory for their Chinese customers. By the twentieth century, ivory's association with class was thoroughly international.

The game's reputation soon indelibly linked mahjong with ivory and seemed to justify the high prices.[67] Joseph Park Babcock subtly conflated his company's bone sets with ivory when he urged customers "to secure a set in which the attractiveness of the colored design carved on the ivory-white face is really an object of beauty," with tiles made by expert "Chinese ivory carvers."[68] A few wry commentators pointed out the inconsistencies. When Babcock arrived in Los Angeles on a steamer with "170 tons of Mah Jongg sets, 'all made of ivory and bamboo,'" a journalist asked, "Ivory? Well, yes, in a way of speaking it might be called ivory. But that is where all those [cattle] shinbones have gone—into the making of ivory Mah Jongg sets."[69] Many who purchased sets likely preferred to believe Babcock's allusions to exclusive ivory instead of this ironic commentary pointing out prosaic bone, happily believing that they had bought "ivory" sets at bone prices.

The natural materials that helped build the game's appeal also posed challenges for manufacturers, and some turned to alternatives. By spring of 1923, factories in the northeastern United States as well as around Shanghai began producing celluloid and plastic tiles that could be either stamped or carved with designs. They used a plastic that had been developed in the late nineteenth century as an affordable ivory alternative, commonly known as "French ivory."[70] The majority of sets during the initial fad were still made in China from bone and bamboo, but plastic factories made up supply shortages and allowed stateside manufacturers to use cheaper, less skilled American labor.[71] Under the heavy-handed trade name "The Ancient Game of the Mandarins," an American producer of celluloid novelties, the Piroxloid Products Corporation, "turned its vast plant over to the manufacture of Mah Jong sets" in 1923. Advertising a fusion of modern and traditional, "a modern fire-proof building, with volume-producing American machinery and massive engraving processes, a touch of the Old World has been added in this latest effort to produce by machine what has hitherto been an exclusive product of Chinese handiwork."[72] In their rendering, artisanship could transfer to machine-made mass production, thanks in part to association with the "ancient mandarins" in their name.

Soon after Parker Brothers bought the Mah-Jongg Company's trademark and copyright in 1923, they announced a new line of "domestic sets of Mah-Jongg in low and moderate priced editions to supplement the production of Mah-Jongg by the Mah-Jongg Company of China."[73] The tiles of these cheaper sets were machine-cut wood with stamped or painted faces, with the nicer tiles topped with a smooth white plastic "ivoroid" face.[74] Their "Country Club Set" advertisement linked ivory, Chinese design, and modern convenience for only ten dollars, compared to the imported bone-and-bamboo set that sold for forty dollars and up.[75] By 1924, cheaper sets reigned. Parker Brothers abandoned Babcock's "Chinese art craftsman" and the Mah-Jongg Manufacturing Company of China factory in Shanghai in favor of domestic sets to reach the mainstream market.

American commentators who assumed that "cheap and patient Chinese labor" precluded American competition neglected to consider that Chinese sets were in fact made by scarce skilled laborers and retailed for much higher prices than American tiles.[76] Made by machine rather than by hand, from wood and plastic rather than bone and bamboo, American sets were in fact simpler to make and cheaper to buy. Similar economic factors led to mahjong manufacturing in cash-strapped Europe as well.[77] Some companies even created low-end sets from cardboard (requiring the purchaser to cut apart the "tiles") and thin strips of wood, while Parker Brothers also continued plugging their playing-card version of the game.[78] In both hand-carved and machine-made versions, aesthetics and craftsmanship were reduced as the price lowered. Some of the sets made in the United States and Europe featured crudely mimicked Chinese characters; maintaining an air of Chinese culture was vital to the game's appeal abroad, but as with other *chinoiserie* goods most foreigners could not discern the inaccuracies.[79] As the fad wore on and the "crooning East Wind has found its way into humble cottage and brown-stone mansion alike," alternative materials made the sets more accessible but less artisanal, even though "ivory and bamboo" remained a shorthand for the game.[80]

Once they adopted American-made plastics and stamped wood, Parker Brothers, along with other American manufacturers of mahjong sets, faced a marketing dilemma over perceived authenticity. In naming specific lines of sets for sale, Parker Brothers chose to emphasize two elements of mahjong's social cache: "Newport," "Tuxedo," and "Country Club" suggested elite milieus, while "Ning-Po" signaled Chinese origins.[81] Using terms like "ivory pyralin," by plastic-tile manufacturers, and "ivoroid," by those making painted wood, helped manufacturers build upon ivory associations. It also avoided the resource bottlenecks of bone and bamboo and enabled them to tap into lower-cost markets.[82]

Unlike other mass advertising in the 1920s that aimed to promote machine-made factory-produced goods as scientific and modern, most mahjong advertisements focused on mahjong as an artisanal object. Although even handmade sets were still churned out on a mass scale, advertisers sought to avoid any indication of industrial production. In an ad for individual consumers and wholesalers, one Chicago store drew directly from the text of the Mah-Jongg Sales Company catalog to proclaim "Mah-Jongg—with its weird characters, beautiful ivories, hand carved and hand painted tiles, counters, ming boxes, dice and cabinets, hand made by skilled Chinese workmen in China" combined with "the rapid action of play that mystifies, fascinates and baffles, **creates a desire to buy**."[83] Notably, the advertisement dropped a reference in the original text to the American-supervised "efficient" Chinese factory.

Marketers of Chinese-made sets faced different challenges. They sought simultaneously to heighten the handcrafted aesthetic and Eastern origins of the pieces and to remove the taint of racialized Chinese labor—a negative association that their American-made competitors hoped to highlight. Since the late nineteenth century, Americans had labeled Chinese laborers as low-skilled and exploited. In California, labor leaders decried Chinese workers as capable of subsisting in subhuman living conditions, which drove down the wages of white workers.[84] Politicians and popular media targeted Chinese bodies as inherently toxic and dangerous to public health.[85] US-based manufacturer L. L. Harr tried to exploit these fears when he smeared his competitors' Chinese workshops as unskilled "gangs of coolies gathered in conditions that would make our old-time 'sweatshops' a sanitary Paradise," in contrast to his own American factories for plastic mahjong tiles.[86]

Popular humor from comic strips to newspapers already linked mahjong with Chinese labor stereotypes, particularly laundrymen. The Chinese script that was an essential and widely displayed aspect of the different tile suits of mahjong evoked a specific kind of caricatured Chinese labor. Most Americans interacted with Chinese language and writing only through laundry tickets, and they were quick to associate Chinese culture with laundries. As a Massachusetts writer quipped in a column entirely devoted to mahjong jokes, "The only Chinese gambling game we know anything about is taking a pink check to a laundry and having Jong Jong guess which bundle is ours."[87] While the service interactions happened in English, the language barriers and unfamiliarity of Chinese writing provided low-hanging fruit for humorists trading on caricatured Chinese workers.[88]

Thus, marketers faced a challenge in tying the game exclusively to selective and elite aspects of Chinese culture. Although economic commentators praised the Mah-Jongg Company's "modern" large-scale production, advertisements emphasized instead "skilled ivory carvers" and workshop artisans.[89] The one and only depiction of mahjong manufacturing and individual craftsmen featured "Wong Liang Zung. The Maker of the first set of Mah-Jongg," complete with photographs of Zung and a group of Chinese men and boys in a village setting. In an interview, Norma Babcock described Zung as the first craftsman Joseph Babcock convinced to add "strange English numbers and letters" to mahjong tiles.[90] Everything in the advertisement, from the workers' clothing to their environment, contrasts sharply with the Mah-Jongg factory in Shanghai, just as the factory's "modern" efficiency contrasted with the advertisement's description of slow artisans. While heralding Joseph Babcock's leadership and vision "to make the game more practical for modern use," the text emphasized Zung's "careful work" while making "the ancient Chinese game." In fact, when the advertisement ran, not only had Babcock been relying on the Mah-Jongg factory in Shanghai, but Parker Brothers had already purchased the Mah-Jongg Sales Company and begun moving to domestic production of machine-made wooden tiles.[91] Highlighting craftsmen such as Zung, whether real or staged, emphasized the artisanal appeal of the object and encouraged consumers to conflate prized hand-carved bone-and-bamboo sets with more affordable domestic wooden tiles.

Images of actual Chinese craftsmen were kept at a distance in marketing mahjong, but they were not invisible in the production process. Their individual tastes and skills indelibly shaped the tiles they carved, despite routinized work and uniform sets. Even in the large-scale standardized Western factories, workmen were not anonymous. Beside each tray of finished tiles, a bilingual "job ticket" recorded the names of the workmen who completed the final stages of polishing, carving, and coloring, and the foremen who oversaw each stage.[92]

However, the marketers' strategy worked. Chinese workmen were not a part of popular imagery about the game, despite the emphasis on handcrafted tiles. While newspapers featured photographs and drawings of white players, and cartoons depicted Chinese mandarins and laundrymen, the craftsmen themselves were virtually absent. To the limited extent that visual representations of tile manufacture existed, they portrayed white women as tile artists.[93] A far cry from the rigorous hand labor of half-clothed men in Shanghai factories, these imaginary artists exuded leisured creativity. In one image, artist and author Marietta Minnigerode Andrews posed in a long evening gown.[94] Larger-than-life painted replicas of mahjong tiles lay scattered on the floor and hung on the walls all around her. The photograph utterly disrupts the game's association with premodern materiality and Chinese culture, yet its link with elite luxuries, feminine beauty, and white America was also an essential part of the game's meaning and appeal in the United States.

Mahjong's materiality, from the origins of its components to the tiles' creation, illuminate the importance of both senses and perception in understanding how the game achieved such resonance. The way the tiles looked, how they felt in players' hands, and how they sounded on game tables were essential to its appeal. Playing-card versions of the game never found a robust audience despite the rules remaining identical. In a basic sense, the physical tiles and the money that exchanged hands were quantifiable. Yet how the tiles were interpreted added layers of meaning to the images and gameplay, which brought mahjong into an international Orientalist marketplace and contemporary Chinese political debates. Specific physical components evoked cultural meanings. Even something as seemingly objective and observable as the composition of mahjong tiles was always filtered through perception.

Examining the economic story of mahjong's production and the factories that made the sets reveals the contradiction between the traditional and the modern that animated much of 1920s culture. In American understandings of the expanding relationship between the United States and China, the West embodied the modern but desired the traditional, symbolized by the East. By moving the rapidly growing sector of low-end set manufacturing to the United States, American companies sought to resolve some of the economic challenges of making mahjong while retaining a commodified sense of authenticity, craftsmanship, and natural materials.

4

Moderns and Mandarins

AT THE MEI REN mahjong factory in Shanghai, a quartet of young and old Chinese men posed for a photo later titled "As Mah Jong 'is played in China.'" They dressed in long fine silk robes with stiff mandarin collars, a 1920s version of traditional clothing worn by many wealthy Chinese men like the Mei Ren Chinese business partners. This contemporary grouping, playing with tiles made in a mahjong factory famous for its "modern" large-scale manufacturing and British-American backers, was dramatically recast on the cover of "Pung Wo Junior," a cheap bamboo mahjong set that sold for $6 in Gimbel's department store. On the game's cardboard box, a color-tinted image of the players was placed front and center above the words "The Royal Game of China Played for Thousands of Years in the Land of Confucius." Modern businessmen no more, these men transformed into mandarins in the ancient royal court, endowing the game within their cardboard vessel with premodern grandeur.[1]

Rather than the actual laborers and craftsmen who created the sets, the Chinese individuals most widely represented with mahjong were figures of the ancient Chinese court. Origin stories of mahjong's creation abound throughout the literature of mahjong, from rulebooks to short stories. Manufacturers and importers of the game repeatedly relied on Orientalist elements to generate an impression of cultural authenticity: myths that linked the game to Confucius and ancient Chinese "mandarins," images hand-carved on natural materials, and references to assumed Chinese cultural characteristics.

Authenticity, or the idea of some untarnished Chinese essence, was at the heart of American mahjong culture. On the surface, "authenticity" simply means real or genuine. However, authenticity is hardly neutral or objective. Ideas of what defines the realness of a particular place and time are created

FIGURE 4.1 Mahjong manufacturers frequently made "junior" sets that were cheaper and made of stamped or painted wood, as opposed to the spliced tiles of bone and bamboo. This cardboard box cover features the designs that replicate the hand-carved tiles. The font used in the trademarked Pung Wo title closely mimics their competitor's Mah-Jongg Sales Company font. Photograph by James Shanks Photography. Courtesy the Museum of Jewish Heritage—A Living Memorial to the Holocaust.

and inherited, often based on hierarchical ideas of tradition, modernity, and progress. Authenticity rests on an idea of stable cultural origins, and groups assumed to have static traditional cultures have been closely associated with authenticity. As a rich scholarly literature argues, the "authentic" has been defined as a connection to the "primitive," to what has been lost in industrialized modern society.[2] Authenticity as it has been imagined in the modern West is especially informed by the legacies of colonialism. In the United States, Native Americans have frequently been referenced either as a positive symbol of authentic Americanness and liberty or as a savage foil to white civilization. In either case, they are ineffably linked to the past.[3] Orientalism overlapped with this larger pattern: European colonization informed understandings of the Islamic World and Asia that defined the East in oppositional terms to the West.[4] The East was cast as passive, traditional, and despotic, in contrast to the West as active, modern, and enlightened. Some of these oppositions were appealing—after all, the "authentic" was also desirable—especially when it connoted some lost connection to a more mystical or natural past presumably lost in the modern world.

China existed in a unique position in the American search for authenticity. Unlike Native Americans, Chinese culture did not serve as a symbol of a core national essence. Long-held understandings of China painted the national character as fundamentally opposite to the United States: backward-looking and unfathomable. In some ways, China was the ultimate Other. Yet Americans also held contradictory views of China. Chinese people could simultaneously signify ancient advancement and modern stagnation, innocence and treachery, passivity and cunning. Unlike colonized people who were imagined to be authentically uncivilized, the China of yore had long been admired as an advanced civilization. By stressing the game's connection to ancient China, mahjong marketers emphasized China's early advanced status "when our own ancestors were living in caves."[5] Despite being mahjong's actual birthplace, modern China was irrelevant in this conception.[6]

The mahjong fad, with its constant evocations of a mystical Chinese past, evidenced a larger reaction to change in the 1920s. Americans during this decade self-consciously spoke of themselves as "moderns" in new and newly consistent ways. American modernity emerged from rapid, often overwhelming change: a more pluralistic culture; individual and community dislocation in the face of urbanization, a bureaucratic state, and growing corporate power; the reorganization of work; mass consumer culture embedded in global economic trends; and changing social values.[7] Many Americans felt deeply ambivalent about the changes that came with increasing bureaucracy and urban anonymity, and they sought a connection to an ancient authenticity. To be clear, people played mahjong for the challenges and delights of the game, as well as its sensory satisfactions. But Americans encountered mahjong in the context of claims to a mystical elite Chinese past, which also helps explain why the game spread so rapidly.

A range of individuals understood the stakes involved in promoting mahjong as a truly ancient Chinese game. In particular, marketers of the game shaped mahjong's image and fought for turf over its authenticity. Members of the group being described as "authentic" or "inauthentic"—in this case Chinese Americans—asserted their own vision of Chinese authenticity. Although other voices often drowned them out, they too shaped the cultural meaning of mahjong.[8] Some of these attempts were conscious, some were likely not, but all participated in creating what would become a dominant understanding of mahjong as an ancient, courtly (and thereby authentic) Chinese game. Mahjong's strengthening association with the ancient Chinese court had implications for how the game would be understood as either a gambling game or a respectable form of leisure—understandings that could have material consequences for groups targeted by police as potential gamblers. As in the larger history of authenticity, race and class were at the heart of these developments.

"The ancient game of the mandarins"

Two main themes emerge in the apocryphal anecdotes that spread across newspaper articles and advertisements: that the game was played exclusively among the Chinese mandarins, and that these elites held despotic control over the game until the 1911 Republican Revolution (or some unspecific rebellion of varying earlier dates) and its recent explosion into the West.[9] In some ways, the game's history seemed to confirm this narrative: mahjong did indeed emerge after the mid-nineteenth century Taiping Rebellion, it was played in the last years of the Qing court, and it came on the international scene after World War I. However, these origin myths explained the recent developments in terms of the Orientalist assumptions of Chinese backwardness, passivity, and despotism and ignored the fad's actual origins in the very modern and international milieu of Shanghai.[10]

The mandarin—a Chinese court official—was the single most prevalent figure in mahjong marketing. The stereotypical mandarin was instantly recognizable by his luxuriant robes and button hat; he often sported long fingernails and a Fu Manchu mustache. Fu Manchu, the evil genius introduced by novelist Sax Rohmer in the 1910s, became a powerful caricature that plagued Chinese Americans for decades.[11] The Fu Manchu aesthetic often blended with mandarins as representative of Chinese culture. One mahjong company directly evoked "that accursed Chinaman" with the title "Fu-Manchu Ancient Chinese Game."[12]

Again and again, marketers and commentators created the sense of ancient timelessness by blending depictions of Fu Manchu–styled mandarins with the single Chinese figure Americans would know: Confucius.[13] The cover of *How to Play Ma Jong: Played by Confucius 2200 Years Ago the Rage of Today* features a solitary Confucius-as-mandarin in complete regalia: necklace over a coat embroidered with a dragon, topped with a mustache and button hat. Playing mahjong in front of pagodas, he is separated in time and space by the Great Wall from a table of elegantly dressed Western players.[14] Confucius himself was often used as a stand-in for Chinese culture marked by hierarchy and unchanging tradition. In 1923, columnist Anne Rittenhouse asserted that the "very fact that the game comes from China gives it a charm. It is said to be as old as Confucius. At any rate, it was played there thousands of years ago, but only by the emperor and his favored courtiers."[15] Accompanying the text is an image of a mustachioed mandarin unpacking a set, highlighting his long nails. Confucius' constant presence in the game's marketing swirled together American concepts of Chinese tradition, aesthetics, and character to help make mahjong embody China in a commodified, consumable form. Consistent with Orientalist renditions, what was most important—and authentic—about China was not its contemporary political experiments and intellectual debates, but unchanging tradition.

These depictions characterized the Chinese court as from approximately "thirty centuries" ago and as despotic.[16] In *Vogue's* introductory article on mahjong, an imagined Chinese court takes center stage. After claiming that the game's exact origins remain "lost in the saffron mists of Oriental court history," *Vogue* confidently described how "centuries ago, only those of royal or mandarin birth were permitted to touch with their pale jewelled fingers the little disks of bamboo and deerhorn."[17] When promoters insisted that "anybody outside this class who played the game was beheaded," their assertions incorporated long-held Western associations of ancient Oriental traditions with cruel punishment and untouchable rulers.[18] Several American writers explained that the game escaped into the broader populace as a later imperial move to appease the restless masses.[19]

Within American marketing discourse, the combination of ancient stasis and draconian abuses of power worked to position China outside modernity,

FIGURE 4.2 Philip Naftaly's instruction manual illustrates the ubiquitous depictions of Confucius and mandarins juxtaposed with modern players. The title sparked a lawsuit by Joseph Babcock and the Mah-Jongg Sales Company, who claimed Mah-Jongg and related terms as proprietary. Author's Collection.

while highlighting the game's exclusivity and thereby its elite appeal. The idea that modern Chinese game players developed the rules and engaged in the cosmopolitan, profoundly capitalist society of Shanghai simply never entered the realm of possibility for most Americans. Indeed, mahjong's presupposed ancient presence initially discouraged George Parker of the Parker Brothers from investing in the Mah-Jongg Company because he believed any marketable Chinese innovation would have already been found by American importers centuries earlier.[20] In a self-reinforcing cycle of assumption, a *Washington Post* humorist tied together mahjong's ancient origins with China's perceived passivity: "We understand now why the Chinese have never built a powerful nation. All their brain power has been concentrated on learning how to play Mah Jongg."[21] Similar articles repeatedly explained that the game was isolated in China for thousands of years because, as opposed to "amusement-seeking" and "alert" Americans, the pre-capitalist Chinese sat on the mahjong gold mine "in their usual calm stolidity, not recognizing its commercial value."[22]

In contrast, Chinese mahjong origin stories (perhaps equally apocryphal) involved recent invention. One story widely circulated in China told of a starving scholar who sold his idea for the game in the late 1800s. "This is a version that is not popular abroad," explained the Chinese Government Bureau of Economic Information. "Even in these republican days, it is difficult to persuade the great buying public that products are coming out of Far Cathay that are without the labels of hoary age and intriguing romance."[23]

The importance of desirable authenticity presented both challenges and opportunities for marketers. The Pung Chow Company faced a particularly severe marketing dilemma. Opened in conjunction with DuPont as makers of the early plastic Pyralin, Pung Chow needed to convince customers to purchase their plastic tiles made in East Coast factories, sold under the unfamiliar brand name of "Pung Chow." In short, they lacked both the geographic and material markers of authenticity that had been emphasized in advertising and articles about the game. Nonetheless, Pung Chow founder Lew Lysle Harr sought to dominate the market by aggressively claiming to be more authentic than even its Chinese-made competitors.

To bolster its credibility, the Pung Chow Company relied on a standardizing set of images and references for Chinese elite authenticity and divorced them from the production process. Within book covers graced with a fearsome gilt dragon, Harr introduced the Pung Chow game through all the elements of courtly associations, Confucius, and exclusivity. He generated an origin myth revolving around languid courtesans in "the Court of the King of Wu, now known as Ning-Po, during the year of 472 B.C." Lest readers not recognize the import of this strangely specific year, Harr added: "This was about the time of Confucius." Designs on Pung Chow sets added physical reminders of Chinese cultural elements, filtered through a foreign lens. Tiles widely known as "dragons" in American play had the serpentine beasts engraved on them, even though they had nothing to do with dragons in the Chinese game. Pung Chow then advertised their additions as "the set with the Real Dragons." The tiles marking geographic directions were graced with simple "mandarin" figures rather than the Chinese words for East and West.

"Flower tiles" closely matched the images of pagodas and bridges on Mah-Jongg Company sets, but with stamped Chinese characters clearly designed in imitation, without knowledge of correct Chinese writing technique.[24]

Pung Chow also sought endorsements from people who could lend an air of authenticity. The company leaped on the opportunity to hire Marion Angeline Howlett, who had already publicized her early mastery of the game learned in China, as general manager for their New England division and instructor-promoter of Pung Chow. Her new business card prominently featured "Shanghai, China" directly under her name, though she had only traveled through the city.[25] Even after she left the company, Howlett continued to be an asset for Pung Chow, perhaps because she genuinely believed Harr's manufactured tale of lost authenticity. For example, Howlett made no explicit sales pitch on behalf of the Pung Chow Company at her enormous mahjong lesson for 300 attendees in Massachusetts. Instead, she simply retold Harr's version of the game's origin and dismissed "Mah-Jongg" as merely the trademarked modernized and degraded version of the game, a story bolstered by her advertised authority about China.[26]

One of the ironies of the claims to exclusive knowledge of China touted by returned expat instructors and by marketers was that these foreign communities were themselves embedded in a transpacific cycle of information and misinformation. Hangzhou teacher Thyra Pedersen could sell an authoritative account of mahjong to American readers by virtue of her residence in China, explaining "Mah Jong: The Game de Luxe of China," using Harr's widely circulated fabricated Court of Wu.[27] In fact, her primary community in China was among other foreigners. The rapid circulation of stories created an air of established fact around key tropes in mahjong myths, particularly its courtly origins.

Emphasizing an exaggerated authenticity was not enough to defeat the competition, who trumpeted similar rhetoric. Harr understood the popular view of modern China as inauthentic. Commentators such as Louise Jordan Miln drew a sharp and hierarchical distinction between Chinese past and present, asserting that contemporary urban China was not truly "*Chinese*" thanks to modernization efforts by "Christendom and Japan."[28] Rather, authentic Chinese culture could be found in the misty past and "a version [of mahjong] nearer the original played in unchanged corners of China."

By reinforcing negative associations with contemporary China, Harr could make the potential liability of American-made plastic sets an ironic asset. In Harr's apocryphal version, the ancient game sadly lost its way after it was democratized. Mah-Jongg was thus one of many "corruptions," and the very name smacked of vulgar gambling games. Harr insisted that, despite being physically manufactured in the States, Pung Chow was "the true and original Chinese game."[29] Indeed, he asserted, Pung Chow factories could make a superior set to those coming out of China of "modern coolie" origins. The result would be simultaneously more authentic than his competitors' by virtue of its supposed unsullied elite lineage, while modern plastic and American production made it "clean, durable, and disease-proof."[30] Impervious to contradictions between claims to mandarins and modernity, he asserted that "Pung Chow is the real Chinese game, with classic designs in finest American workmanship."[31]

The imagined ancient scholars and court officials peopled an elite realm of exoticism and Chinese culture where Americans could venture without associating with the despised image of "the coolie." A politically loaded term that originally referenced semi-enslaved Chinese laborers in South America and the Caribbean, coolie came to be a catchall and generally degrading term for Chinese laborers in the United States.[32] Emerging as the predominant Chinese stereotype in American popular and political discourse by the late nineteenth century, the coolie embodied white American working-class fears of unskilled Chinese labor competition, particularly on the Pacific Coast. In vitriol such as that spewed in the 1870s by *The Wasp* magazine published in San Francisco, coolies were literally subhuman.[33] Even without these extremes, for decades Americans considered coolies drudges of low intelligence and extremely low class. They often applied the same association to Chinese migrants more broadly, despite the range of wealth, education, and occupation represented in the population. Mainland Americans looked to those who had spent time abroad to inform and confirm their assumptions. The hierarchical worlds of Shanghai and other treaty ports encouraged coolie stereotypes. There, imperialist structures reinforced racialized boundaries that separated European, American, and Japanese foreign residents from Chinese "natives," and class-based boundaries between elite Chinese and the thousands of impoverished laborers.

As competition heated up over the summer of 1923, the Pung Chow and Mah-Jongg Companies went toe-to-toe with aggressive marketing techniques in print and over the airwaves. Pung-Chow Associations cropped up to declare the superiority of Pung Chow's elite roots in China over "coolie" Mah-Jongg and introduced radio listeners to Pung Chow.[34] In an apt if exaggerated depiction, a cartoon policeman in the *Boston Herald* ran toward a vicious brawl between white men in bowler hats and cried, "Oh, another tong war, between the Mah Jong and Pung Chow factions!," parodying the infamous

Chinatown gang wars.[35] The Mah-Jongg Company, meanwhile, tried to shut Pung Chow out of popular discourse entirely. Babcock wasted no time intervening when a cartoon of "Pung Chow" players began making the newspaper rounds. Babcock lobbied to have the seemingly innocuous comic strip edited to subsume Harr's brand name as merely the moves called "pung" and "chow" that were used to create winning hands in "Mah-Jongg"—Babcock's game.[36]

Joseph Park Babcock faced his own acute marketing dilemma over authenticity. Mah-Jongg's fortunes rested upon a public view of the game as emblematic of the exotic Chinese. Yet therein lay the dilemma. No single trademark could copyright Chinese culture. Dozens of competitors used the power of authenticity to market their versions of the game. Babcock sought to market two overlapping but distinct aspects of authenticity: not only was mahjong authentically Chinese, but only the Mah-Jongg brand could be authentic mahjong. The catalog promised that a genuine Mah-Jongg set breathed "the very soul of the Orient, in which lurks the mysterious game that can only be unlocked by Babcock's Red Book of Rules."[37] In October 1923, Babcock decided to adopt the bold strategy of attaching authenticity to himself. Announcing that the game was in fact "foreign to China," he proclaimed himself to be the sole inventor of the game.[38] He risked killing the golden goose by severing the link between his game and the ancient cultural aura that surrounded it. He likely hoped that the Mah-Jongg Sales Company's marketing blitz had cemented the link between himself and the game in the public's mind, and that the game had thoroughly embedded itself in society. If he proved correct, the game's popularity could continue, but then players would indeed require the Mah-Jongg Company's "GENUINE" sets. His attempts went nowhere, however, and he soon returned to a more nuanced emphasis on his adaptation of the game with "all the age-old mystery of China" as "the one authentic source."[39] However, he did succeed in incensing young Chinese Americans invested in their own evolving sense of Chinese cultural authenticity.

Cultural Authority

When Harr and Babcock overreached their claims, they faced the angry reactions of Chinese Americans. Harr's claims proved particularly galling. In a public argument with transpacific coverage, the *China Review* published a cover-page editorial devoted to debunking Harr's claims that contemporary Chinese people knew only the "modern coolie" game, and that he had the sole ancient and aristocratic version. The *Review*, a journal published by the China

Trade Bureau based in New York, angrily refuted Harr: "The misrepresentation of China and things Chinese in this country, particularly if it serves any selfish commercial purpose, is something which all fair-minded Americans deplore and justly condemn." Further, the editorial asserted, "It is something which the Chinese have the right to resent and the privilege to correct."[40] The *Review* used mahjong controversies to address the broader issue of the simultaneous commodification and denigration of Chinese culture. It also appealed directly to Americans' self-concept as "fair-minded" while asserting a uniquely authoritative platform for Chinese Americans.

Politically aware Chinese Americans understood mahjong to be an opportunity to improve the image of China and the position of Chinese people in the United States. Because Americans perceived the game as authentic, it could potentially represent Chinese culture in positive ways. The Chinese American advocacy group the Native Sons of the Golden State used mahjong as a form of cultural diplomacy. This fraternal organization for California-born Chinese American men had intentionally appropriated a name similar to the influential anti-Asian group, the Native Sons of the Golden West. When President and First Lady Harding visited San Francisco in 1923, the (Chinese) Native Sons of the Golden State sent them an elegant mahjong set, with hand-carved tiles made in Shanghai.[41] Mahjong fit nicely into the group's stated goals of "the promotion of friendship between the two races."[42] An article in the Shanghai newspaper *Shenbao* argued in 1934 that "other than [opera star] Mei Lanfang, perhaps the best thing we have to promote Chinese civilization is none other than mahjong," as it "encompassed the philosophy of life of the Chinese people."[43] Mei Lanfang might have agreed with such a comparison, as he was already the proud owner of a custom mahjong set.[44]

Eleanor Chan, the "bobbed-hair spokesman" of the Chinese Students' Club at the University of Southern California, sparred publicly with Babcock when he claimed that he was the sole inventor of mahjong. "We have not only played Mah Jongg years before Mr. Babcock ever visited China, but our Chinese ancestors also have played the same game," Chan argued. Drawing directly from the game's mystique, Chan went on: "Furthermore, this same game provided entertainments for the royal courts of China 1100 years ago."[45] Mahjong was one of the few arenas in which a young Chinese American woman could directly challenge a wealthy white businessman and have her expertise be taken seriously by mainstream media.

Chan's references to ancient China, which echoed the game's marketers, may have also reflected her personal belief in and attachment to an esteemed Chinese culture. Chinese Americans could genuinely hold many of the same romantic and Orientalist ideas of the East held by white Americans. After all, they were surrounded by the same American discourses and had their own reasons for holding fast to positive portrayals of Asia, however reductive.[46] Actress Anna May Wong, for example, held preconceptions of timeless Eastern simplicity and spirituality until she traveled to China, where the modern cities surprised her.[47]

Amid the explosion of mahjong rulebooks, many of which echoed advertisers' Orientalist visions of "a delicious magic world" of Chinese culture, a few notable Chinese American voices attempted to claim both timeless authenticity for the game and their own authority in modern transpacific discourse.[48] Chinese Americans generally avoided use of the derogatory term "coolie," and one rulebook author specifically criticized the court versus coolie debate as a marketing ploy.[49] Instead, they asserted the possibility of a modern China and relied on class-based appeals to the "classic" game's respectability. Unlike most of the white rulebook authors, the Chinese authors listed their credentials and degrees on the inside covers to establish themselves as educated experts. Julius Su Tow, secretary of the Chinese Consulate General at New York, was already engaged in attempts to educate Americans about Chinese culture and ameliorate anti-Chinese prejudice in the United States when he wrote a mahjong instruction manual. In *The Outline of Mah Jong: How to Play and How to Win, the Real Chinese Methods,* Tow asserted the genuine Chinese origins of the game and rejected the idea that Americans came up with the name. Drawing from Chinese publications and "friends from different parts of China," Tow positioned himself as a source of authoritative knowledge.[50]

Chinese American commentators consistently linked the game to authentic Chinese culture while also situating it in a modern society. In doing so they countered the strong assumptions fostered by people like Harr who separated an authentic and ancient Chinese past from a degraded Chinese present. Instead, via mahjong the writers asserted Chinese inclusion in a modernity marked, like the West, by rationality and power, while retaining Chinese character and history. A modern Chinese authenticity steeped in philosophical wisdom and ancient roots indicated both a positive contribution to the world and a position of authority from which to speak specifically as Chinese Americans. When Ly Yu Sang wrote his book *Sparrow,* he linked the game to philosophical symbolism from the *I Ching,* the ancient book of divination.[51] He also asserted the rational and mathematical elements of the game. While lacking in historical and philosophical accuracy, Sang's argument appealed to both white and Chinese American readers in its reinforcement of lofty Chinese culture.[52] When the *New York Times* intimated that the game was not actually Chinese, a Chinese American reader wrote in protest and cited the popular rulebook by Ly Yu Sang.[53]

Sang was not alone in combining Chinese authenticity with modernity. W. Lock Wei, who identified himself as "Captain of China's Davis Cup Tennis Team, 1924," wrote *The Theory of Mah Jong* with the help of Lam Ping Leung of Columbia University; the authors' credentials demonstrated their inclusion in educated elite Anglo-American circles.[54] *The Theory of Mah Jong* included a chapter devoted to "Mah Jong Psychology," in which Wei asserted the superiority of the classical Chinese method of play over American changes not by references to premodern authenticity but rather through modern intellectual categories like psychology. Importer Andrew Kan also used Chinese merchants' involvement in the mahjong trade to counter stereotypes. "China is often called a nation of sleepy people, or one that has been asleep for hundreds of years, but here is one case in which they are not asleep," he told *Time* magazine. "Instead, they are awake to the profits that may be made from Mah Jongg, and for the time being they are reaping a good harvest."[55]

"Fascinating New-Old Game"

The supposedly ancient game was closely tied to notions of modernity. "New-old" was a frequent refrain in descriptions of the game.[56] A Los Angeles store advertised "Mah-Jongg, that fascinating new-old game that is sweeping the country by storm! It is as old as the rains of Hong Kong and the murky waters of the Yangtze River. It is as new and as popular—in its Occidental form—as radio—and it smacks of that same alluring mystery-of-origin."[57] Commentators frequently compared the game to radio, the epitome of modern technology, but steeped in ancient mystique. New technology also seemed mysterious in similar ways, and mahjong united both fantastical ideas of time: the ancient and the futuristic. Western Electric, an American company in England, produced a set of mahjong playing cards as a 1924 British Empire Exhibition souvenir that featured symbols of modern technology, from telephones to light bulbs and cables.[58] Mahjong, electricity, and international corporations were connecting the world.

In part, China acted as a foil for a narrative in which Americans modernized the game by capitalizing on it. Mah-Jongg Company of China partner Albert Hager explained in oft-repeated terms that "the little yellow men with their usual stolidity did not trouble themselves to spread this native game" of supposedly ancient origin, requiring "one Joseph Babcock, a clever

American" to spread English rules among the Shanghai social clubs.[59] Players enamored with Orientalist fantasies resisted the "disillusioning thought" that "some bright [Western] modernist threw the thing together."[60] It seemed natural, however, that an American would be required to streamline the game and bring it to the modern Western world, where it would leap into profitable success.

Mahjong's entree to the West, then, represented Eastern backwardness and American entrepreneurial ingenuity. The Mah-Jongg Company linked its founder with American military and economic interests, claiming "as America opened the commercial gates of China after years of knocking, knocking, so did one Joseph Babcock realize with what eagerness our game loving Americans would grasp this interesting game of skill."[61] In this version, American imperialism not only took center stage over British and European involvement, but was also part of a mutually beneficial exchange. Americans did not perceive themselves as imperialists, but rather as enlightened leaders, protecting China both against aggressive foreign powers and its own ignorance.[62] Whether advocating for the supremacy of the "modernised" American version of the game like Babcock, or the supposedly recovered ancient version like Harr, marketers could paint American players as potential saviors of the game over its degeneration in modern-day China.[63] Louise Jordan Miln, a well-known weaver of Chinese-inspired tales including a particularly fanciful story of mahjong's origins, explained to a reporter: "though mah jongg is Chinese, it is greatly doctored for the western market. The English have unbound its feet and cut its queue, so to speak."[64] A belief in the values of Western modernity, marked by technological improvements, increased material comforts, and a democratic individualism, justified American power and intervention in Chinese politics and economics. Consumers were able to have the best of both worlds: imagining the glories of royal luxury in ancient China while congratulating themselves as "moderns."[65]

The fascination with the ancient Chinese court also related to strains of antimodernism, wherein Americans sought escape from the social and economic transformations of industrialism. Yet, this form of consumerist escapism was a distant relative to antimodernist quests for natural experiences such as tourism to Niagara Falls, or the artistic turn toward medieval imagery.[66] Mahjong served as a symbol of the past for Americans acculturating to the rapid pace of change, not opting out of the modern results. Modern contraptions like motorcars could become, ironically, vehicles for premodern imaginings when made over with mahjong. "Indeed, Mah Jong seems to have brought back into our lives a little of the romance and play of imagination which our modern commercial tendencies have done their best to throttle," wrote a promoter of "Mah Jong cars."[67] Drawing inspiration from a luxury vehicle with "strong Oriental flavor" commissioned for an East Indian prince, an imagined American Mah Jong car might have "upholstery and carpet in Chinese design, the exterior painted in carefully selected hues to suggest some of the colorful tiles." Not only would riders enjoy a game on a folding table in colorful mobile luxury, but "to give a final dash of verity," the car would have "a Chinese chauffeur and footman." Overt displays of wealth and reliance on servants was part and parcel of 1920s glamour, as was the luxury of Eastern royalty.

Imagining a spectrum of modernity, with the United States at the pioneering modern end and China as hopelessly premodern, helped protect Americans from uncomfortable anti-democratic contradictions in American society. *Vogue's Book of Etiquette* singled out "mah jong and the mandarins because only the elect were allowed to play" in order to contrast the past, when recreation was only accessible to the elites, with the present. Now, the guide explained, everyone needed to know how to demonstrate "fine breeding, temperament, and character in the playing of games."[68] The rhetorical separation of present-day Chinese and Chinese American laborers from the vaunted ancient Chinese court allayed potential conflict between the widespread American fascination with a quintessentially Chinese game and anti-immigrant sentiment. As one writer assumed, "Of course, a Chinese laundryman doesn't really know anything about Mah Jong. If he had played it in his youth in the old home town his head would have been cut off."[69]

The distinction between ancient court and contemporary coolie helps explain why white Americans embraced the idea of traditional Chinese culture as commodified in an "elite" game, while simultaneously advocating for increased immigration restrictions on "Asiatics." Even *The Wasp* and the anti-Asian group Native Daughters of the Golden West promoted mahjong as *au courant* among white "society."[70] If working-class Chinese Americans conceptualized only as laundrymen, cooks, and domestic servants could not have known the game because it was supposedly the province of mandarins, they had no claim to the class-based respectability accorded the game. Americans could thus be simultaneously pro-mahjong and anti-immigrant, democratic and imperial. The mythology of the ancient Chinese court and the American entrepreneur created distance between the modern self and the anachronistic other.

Mahjong was not the first nor the only time the contradiction between an embrace of Chinese culture and the rejection of people associated with it coexisted in early twentieth-century American culture. For at least two decades, Chinese food—especially the famous Americanized dish of "chop suey"—had become increasingly integrated into American culture and desired by a diverse range of diners. As opposed to mahjong's advertised misty mandarins, Chinese food became known as cheap comfort food. Until Chinese American celebrity restaurateurs like Johnny Kan and Cecilia Chiang in San Francisco elevated the image of Chinese food in the 1950s, American consumers expected Chinese restaurants (or "chop suey joints") to charge only rock-bottom prices. Accessing Chinese culture through consuming either mahjong or chop suey could remain largely relegated to superficial exoticism or sensory pleasures without a meaningful engagement with Chinese culture or individuals. Going to Chinese restaurants or "slumming" in Chinatown, however, positioned Chinese culture differently than did dressing up in imagined costumes of an esteemed and far-off royal past. The popularity of both mahjong and Chinese food reflected the slowly changing position of Chinese people in the early twentieth century, when, despite persistent and vicious stereotypes from Fu Manchu to the idea of rats and cats in Chinese food, fears of a Chinese immigrant "invasion" had significantly cooled. Cultural integration helped lay the groundwork for conditional and selective inclusion of Chinese Americans, but nonetheless remained largely in a consumerist and stereotyped realm.[71]

Authentic Dangers

As news of the game's wild popularity in the United States spread around the world, in 1924 missionaries in China began writing increasingly insistent pleas to Americans to stop setting a bad example as a supposedly Christian nation of mahjong players. For these missionaries, questions of cultural authenticity were not their first concern; instead, they were invested in changing Chinese culture to bring it in line with Protestant values. American missionary Dr. Watts O. Pye described three social evils among the social changes sweeping the northern Chinese interior, spreading along with what he saw as the positive Westernization of business and religion. Lumping mahjong in with smoking and drinking, he complained, "the demoralizing gambling game of Mah Jongg is being taken over by the West. Christians in China are becoming confused over the participation of Western Christians in Mah Jongg."[72] Meanwhile, the Canton Christian College requested that their faculty not play mahjong on campus, and the Beijing YMCA prohibited mahjong as a gambling game.[73] Instead, they hoped their Chinese patrons would absorb messages from posters on their walls proclaiming "No Work, No Money," and "You can't satisfy an automobile appetite on a ricksha income."[74] For those who believed Western influence should focus on Christianity and capitalism, Anglo-American consumption of the game risked the opposite deleterious effect.

Arguments for mahjong as an "innocent and long suffering" pastime, versus those against mahjong as a dangerous "disease," spawned debates in national publications from the *New York Times* to the *Christian Science Monitor.* The argument hinged on whether the game was ancient and aristocratic, or a modern corruption. For some, Harr's fabricated difference between respectable Pung Chow and degraded Mah-Jongg provided a useful defense, as they argued that Pung Chow was an upright game inhospitable to gambling.[75] Mahjong's modernization, its defenders claimed, had transformed it in the American context to unite its esteemed ancient roots with modern domestic entertainment. The dispute raged in columns and letters mailed from the middle of the country and across both the Atlantic and Pacific.[76]

Although voices of white American missionaries dominated opposition in the American and transpacific press, Chinese Americans spoke up too. With both sides of the mahjong gambling debate referencing Chinese culture and, as usual, the game's supposed Confucian origins, Chinese and Chinese American commentators once again used cultural authority to weigh in on the debate. In his influential rulebook, mahjong importer Ly Yu Sang urged readers to spare the game from association with the gambling that he agreed had overtaken the game in China by asking that "the players of America, true to their high ideals, will remember the history and purpose of Ma-ch'iau, and will keep this beautiful and intellectual game unsullied by corruption and unimpaired by abuse."[77] In contrast to Harr, in Sang's version the core ancient characteristics still remained in the contemporary Chinese game, which would fit especially well in a modern American milieu.

Newspapers paid particular attention to Chinese Christians and Chinese Americans who objected to the game's embarrassing association with Chinese culture and gambling. Y. P. Wang, a Chinese student at the Columbia University School of Journalism, wrote a lengthy screed against mahjong in the *New York Tribune.*[78] Likening gambling in China to American bootleggers as problems of corrupt policing, Wang worried that the American "habit" of mahjong would both encourage its use as a high-stakes game in China and reinforce the American association of Chinese culture with gambling. He was particularly alarmed by the "intolerable" claims that Confucius would have invented such a thing. Subtly challenging American moral superiority, Wang opined, "It is very unfortunate for the Chinese to be considered by many American writers as being possessed of gambling instinct. It would be even more unfortunate for our American friends to acquire this unfortunate habit through the exercising [of] this unfortunate game prohibited in China and yet tolerated in America."

Despite appeals to "Christian Endeavored America," moral arguments against mahjong fell mostly on deaf ears.[79] Though the comparison was rarely made in popular discourse, American culture had its own long and rich—albeit conflicted and contested—gambling history, and the modern American economy was, after all, based on stock market speculation.[80] On the heels of 1910s Progressive reforms, including campaigns against gambling and the passage of Prohibition, 1920s popular discourse about gaming was often contradictory.[81] A get-rich-quick mentality pervaded popular culture in the 1920s.[82] Prohibition era workarounds from urban speakeasies to sailing jaunts to Cuba for the wealthy meant that gambling was never eliminated.[83]

Not only were cultural mores changing quickly around traditionally suspect entertainments, but the American version of mahjong was also not widely played as a high-stakes gambling game. Certainly some played mahjong for money, particularly early on in the fad in 1922, when it supplanted poker in middle-class men's clubs like the Elks Lodge.[84] However, it quickly became predominantly a mixed-sex and female parlor game played for little or no money.[85] As they did in China, players could choose to score according to points that translated into money or play a non-gambling version that simply involved completing hands. Its status as a social game meant that mahjong fit into a respectable modern parlor more than the Wild West saloons and Chinatown dens of the American imagination, or even contemporary illicit speakeasies. In short, mahjong in the United States soon became more akin to bridge than to poker or dice games. As a humorist explained in 1923, "Mah Jongg is different from dice. If you want to you can pay $100 for a set of Mah Jongg and then lose nothing. If you want to you can pay nothing for a set of dice and then lose $100."[86]

At least as important, it simply did not make sense to most Americans that they could possibly harm China's social progress by encouraging gambling, let alone with an ostensibly authentic Chinese game. Long-held American views of Chinese people assumed them to be instinctive "born gamblers."[87] Gambling dominated Americans' impressions of contemporary Chinatowns as steeped in vice.[88] For most Americans, because mahjong was Chinese, the game as played in China was automatically presumed to be not only a gambling game, but also one played for enormous stakes. They were unaware both of anti-gambling Chinese reformers and of mahjong's own evolution. While Chinese culture had a long and rich history of game development, and mahjong did indeed have roots as a male gambling game in urban centers, other Chinese voices saw gambling in general as detrimental to social progress, and mahjong had long been played for both low and high stakes.

Yet American discourse, whether missionary or mainland, did not engage with the nuances of mahjong in China. For fans of the game, this meant that far-off mahjong addicts had little to do with them.[89] "In taking its place at the family fireside it must have been purged of the native grossness," the *Tribune* responded to Y. P. Wang's critique.[90] "If not, and the missionaries were right, there would certainly by this time be an Anti-Mah Jong Society." Alluding to Prohibition, the *Tribune* went on, "Addicts would be advised to pung with 'careful discretion,' and constitutional amendments would be preparing. In the absence of these infallible symptoms of depravity we must reject Mr. Wang as a moral expert for America, while accepting with appreciation, if not with enthusiasm, his dark portrait of Ma Chiang at home." Echoing many white Americans, the *Tribune* had no trouble believing that mahjong gambling was a major social problem in China, but it simply did not agree with the comparison between the need to regulate alcohol, especially in working-class and immigrant communities, and mahjong, whose most visible players were elite and middle-class white women.

Race and class determined which players would be suspected of engaging in mahjong's illicit function as a form of gambling, resulting in occasional arrests of working-class African American and Chinese players. Stereotypes of Black and Chinese people held them as definitively outside respectable white and middle-class leisure associated with bridge games, and closer to impulsive games of chance. Assumptions of retrograde behavior brought working-class and minority communities under greater scrutiny, while also shaping how law enforcement viewed their gaming. A midnight police raid targeting "a negro gambling house" in Pittsburgh discovered instead "a group of negroes intently manipulating little rectangular tiles bearing queer Oriental figures."[91] Despite the fact that "so far as the policemen knew, Mah Jong tiles did not come under the category of gambling paraphernalia," the men were arrested and fined. In 1924, the police banned "Mah Jong gambling" in Philadelphia's Chinatown.[92] Citing cases that "had come to his attention where Chinese had been fleeced of all their belongings through the game," Captain of Detectives Alfred Souder resisted "a delegation of Chinese" who petitioned him to lift the ban. At the same time, well-founded fears of arrest made a group of Chinese laundrymen vulnerable to "two unmasked white bandits" in Atlanta. While the resting workers sat at their mahjong table, two armed men launched a fake police raid. After showing the players false badges and brandishing their weapons, the robbers stole their money while "condemning them for gambling."[93] Race profoundly shaped mahjong players' de facto relationship to the game as a respectable and legal activity.

However, mahjong's emergence as a respectable activity could sometimes cross racial designations. A group of Chinese student mahjong players arrested in New York were lucky to find a mahjong fan presiding on the bench. Judge Joseph Corrigan ignored the common conflation of Chinese with vice and declared "Playing Mah Jong is not a crime; almost everybody is playing it."[94] The article reporting the decision betrayed a note of surprise with its title, "Rules Mah Jong Is No Crime, Even When Played by Chinese." Although racial profiling likely heightened their surveillance, Orientalist cultural conflation nearly protected a group of Japanese poker players in Washington State. Police officers first assumed they "were playing Mah Jongg, this new society game," as they were surrounded by incense described as "scorched chop suey" by the officers who "listened for a time to the soft Oriental conversation of the dark skinned Japanese."[95] Mahjong would have been fine, but the jig was up when the "the mystic Oriental atmosphere was punctured with a very American expression. 'Yama Yama. Three johns and a brace of queens.'" Poker may have been American, but it was still an illegal gambling game, especially when played by non-white people already targeted for illicit behavior.

During its national heyday, mahjong helped translate both modern progress and an imagined past into an American future. Players could participate in a pastime shared with the mansions of the Vanderbilts and the ghosts of mandarins—both figures equally distant and impossibly alluring to most Americans. The mahjong mythology presented an ancient court improved and made accessible by American intervention, out of "coolie" hands. Mahjong served to construct a self-consciously modern identity, one marked both by cosmopolitan worldliness and exclusions of class and race. Americans imagined mahjong as a symbol not to resist modernity, but to enter into the cultural changes and global power of modern America while retaining a sense of authenticity and primitive artisanship: to gain the sophisticated capitalist metropolis but to imbue it with privilege, beauty, and mystery.

5

White Women and a Chinese Game

IN NOVEMBER 1922, two months after the grand Mah Jongg Blues "fantasie" at the Granada movie palace in San Francisco, the elite women's Ebell Club of Los Angeles hosted a high-profile philanthropic mahjong party. The club members posed in advance for pictures in the *Los Angeles Times* and the *Los Angeles Examiner* dressed in complete "Chinese costume," wearing elaborate beaded headdresses and embroidered silk robes. In an article titled "Dragons Clash at Mah-Jongg," the Ebell Club's women-only gala was heralded as "a great event, a sort of official coming-out party for mahjong in Los Angeles, where the elite of the city will gather to shake a wicked dice to help Ebell Rest Cottage Scholarship Fund." The female attendees, the press observed, were "determined to be desperately Chinese in action and dress," and so were "plotting to lay hold of their husbands' pajamas for the occasion."[1] While some purchased fine embroidered "mandarin" robes, others simply used pajamas to evoke the loose silk Chinese trousers familiar to Americans.

Thanks in part to women like these costumed club members, soon after mahjong's debut the game became increasingly associated with women—specifically wealthy and middle-class white women. The process of gendering mahjong as feminine was not instantaneous. Game experts and business leaders, all disproportionately male, continued to publicly play, promote, and discuss the game. Yet by the time the fad ended in the mid-1920s, mahjong was thoroughly feminized in American culture.

Orientalist notions of China informed why white women embraced the game and how they used it to play with the boundaries of self-presentation. Mahjong was quite obviously—even desirably—Chinese, in an era when Chinese bodies were alien, exotic, and sexualized. In the 1920s, mahjong—sold by costumed salesgirls, played by often-costumed socialites—allowed

FIGURE 5.1 Participants in the Ebell Club's "Mah-Jongg Tea" starred in the society pages of Los Angeles newspapers with their "costumes of the Orient." Club members like Mrs. Harris Robertson (pictured here) displayed ornately embroidered silk robes and headdresses reminiscent of Chinese opera singers and ornately embroidered silk robes. *Los Angeles Examiner.* Parker Brothers Archive.

middle-class and elite white Americans to imagine, appropriate, or reject an exotic Asian sexuality while maintaining their own respectability. Gendered ideas of race, specifically of Asian cultures as feminine, also encouraged Americans to understand the game as a feminine pastime. Orientalist consumerism was not unidirectional, however. While white women experimented with new boundaries of respectable femininity, Chinese Americans leveraged mahjong's popularity for economic opportunities. The choices that these Chinese Americans faced, however, were fraught with pitfalls and contributed to sexualized stereotypes of the seductive power of the game and of Chinese instructors.

On one hand, the association with fashionable "smart women" helped drive the fad. On the other hand, the fact that white women became iconic consumers of this Chinese game posed multiple troubling implications. One consequence mattered primarily to game experts who wanted the game to remain an esteemed intellectual pursuit, in contrast to supposed female frivolity. On a societal level, game-focused mahjong matrons symbolized social changes that destabilized traditional notions of the patriarchal home.

As the game spread across the nation, mahjong unleashed criticisms of Chinese influence and women's leisure that linked female mahjong players with neglectful and self-centered domesticity. The ways in which mahjong symbolized modern American culture, buttressed by Orientalist ideas of race and gender, allowed the game to stand in for debates over white femininity. Rather than merely a temporary foray into the exotic, mahjong came to represent the threats posed by changing gender, sexual, and racial norms during the 1920s.

Gender and Mahjong

In 1923, a comic strip subtitled "The only way you can force your husband to learn mah jong" depicted a frantic man trussed up in a torture device while his elegantly dressed wife calmly explained the game's seemingly endless rules.[2] The cartoon's humor relied upon the presumably widespread assumption that only women would want to learn such a convoluted game, complete with strange symbols and words. What began as the game's advertised appeal had become a silly feminine exercise and inappropriate display of wifely power imposed upon victimized husbands.

As the game evolved, the cultural associations of women with mahjong's "flowery" aesthetic encouraged a higher percentage of women to join the ranks of mahjong players. Oblivious to the Chinese association of carved plums and chrysanthemums with men, Westerners associated these flower tiles with women.[3] American players created a heated controversy by using flower tiles as wild cards, heightening the element of luck and promoting quick, high-point games. Soon primarily male experts blamed social clubs and women players for delegitimizing the reputation of mahjong as a game of skill.[4] In his lighthearted rulebook, *White Dragons Wild and How to Win at Ma Jong*, Elmer Dwiggins devoted a section to "Experts versus Flowers."[5] Though flowers added "nothing to the skills of the play," he wrote, "the

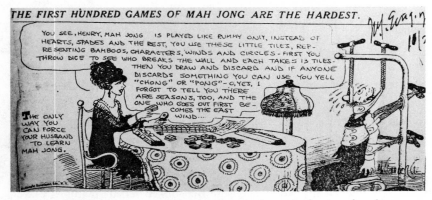

FIGURE 5.2 As this comic indicates, Americans increasingly viewed mahjong as a women's game while the fad roared along in 1923. In addition to the obvious humor about wives forcing their husbands to learn the game, the cartoon included more subtle jokes, as the woman's speech includes errors and a meandering, convoluted explanation. *New York Evening Mail.* Parker Brothers Archive.

ladies enjoy picking flowers. They find them beautiful in design; they are complimented by receiving them, and they are duly jealous when the men draw them." Writing soon after women gained constitutional voting rights in the United States, Dwiggins approved of an end to male gallantry because "the ladies relinquished that when they acquired equal rights," but recognized that in mahjong, "flowers are here to stay." In his rendition, archetypal white male experts banged their heads against the increasingly powerful world of female flowers, bedecked with Oriental accoutrement.

Because the game became a stand-in for Chinese culture, the gender and sexual stereotypes that underwrote American ideas of "Orientals" shaped understandings of the game as well. Fueled by the growth of anti-Asian sentiments in the nineteenth century and building on Orientalist frameworks that projected a feminine character on "the East," stereotypes of Chinese men characterized them as lacking in masculinity.[6] Notably, in contrast to the legions of white society women portrayed in Chinese costume, very few white men were ever pictured in Chinese "mandarin" dress.[7] The few exceptions featured a wrestling star, a World Heavyweight Champion, and an internationally renowned billiards professional: all icons of white masculinity.[8] One of Joseph Babcock's rulebooks featured a full-page portrait. In it he displayed a costume, albeit of a different sort from the ladies' Chinese dress. He posed with a safari hat and suit reminiscent of the colonial British Raj, indicating both his intrepid imperialism and his expert knowledge of foreign lands.[9]

The most ostentatious mahjong players and the philanthropists who took on the public role of organizing and hosting mahjong charity balls were women, but men played in single-sex as well as mixed gatherings and dominated as self-described experts and rule makers.[10] The elite bachelor's club in Newport decorated its walls with mahjong hands, while "experts in the game had great sport looking over the various hands and contemplating their worth in a game."[11] The growing popularity of mahjong spawned a multitude of books that purported to explain the real or "authentic" rules of play, with slightly varied and competing rulebooks.[12] In an attempt to standardize the American version of the game, in 1924 five noted mahjong "experts," including J. P. Babcock, created the Standardization Committee of the American Official Laws of Mah-Jongg. The Committee determined that their laws "should be logical" and "in accordance with American ideas."[13] These American ideas were closer to characteristics of rational strategy associated with bridge than with the high-yield "lucky" play of flower tiles actually evolving in the United States and associated with women. The few women who published mahjong instruction guides generally joined the chorus of male experts in decrying the Americanized game. Bridge expert Florence Irwin, however, rejected all the ostensibly authoritative changes as well, including the rules promoted by the Standardization Committee, not simply those driven by players.[14]

One unique group of white women and Chinese men attempted to reshape the American game, but they faced resistance from white men who claimed naming rights and expertise. In the fall of 1923, mahjong purveyors Elisabeth Godey Kohl and Sang M. Ho convened dozens of mahjong instructors in Manhattan's temples of wealth, the Ritz Carlton and the Waldorf-Astoria.[15] They met to create an official body for standardization of game rules and the name of the game itself, creating the International Ma Chiang Players' Association to stem the tide of proliferating styles of play.[16] They attempted to combine the forms of authority available to white female and Chinese male authors of mahjong texts: wealthy women who already had reputations as bridge players advertised their group's "access to the most authentic Chinese sources of information."[17] Two Chinese Oxford graduates and one Stanford University alumnus, Mr. W. C. Meh, who had been a member of the Chinese Students' Club while at college, joined Kohl and Ho at the inaugural meetings.[18] Newspaper accounts of the meeting reveal the acrimonious debates behind the association's naming process. While merchants Ho and Kohl advocated for the use of "mah jong" on the pragmatic grounds that "Mah jongg is the name under which it is being played all over the country, and people will never take up the name of ma chiang," the two guest experts (both white men), R. F. Foster and British diplomat to China C. G. Anderson, wielded their authority to advocate for "ma chiang" as closest to the "pure Chinese" spoken in Beijing.[19] The Ma Chiang Players Association succeeded in briefly getting Macy's department store in Manhattan to advertise its wares as Ma Chiang, but as Kohl predicted, the rest of the nation kept "mah jongg" as generic even as Parker Brothers tried to insist on its trademark of the Mah-Jongg name.[20] As a member of the other Standardization Committee, Milton C. Work published his own rulebook dismissing Ma Chiang as "fathered by a committee composed of American ladies and Chinese gentlemen who held a christening bee in New York," painting a picture of demure triviality despite newspaper accounts of the inaugural Ma Chiang meeting as raucous and contentious.[21] By their own measure, in contrast, the Standardization Committee was "authoritative" and they certainly did not hold effeminate "christening bees."[22]

Mahjong Masquerade

Disapproving experts did little to discourage women from continuing to play mahjong in growing numbers—and to take the opportunity to embrace an immersive performative approach to the game. In cities across the country, elites flocked to mahjong galas involving ballets where wealthy young ladies danced as mahjong pieces.[23] Wealthy hostesses held garden parties with elaborate mahjong plays on the grass.[24] Stages were not always needed; for society matrons, performance often took the form of elaborate costumes. Like those worn by the Ebell Club members, these outfits were divorced from actual Chinese fashions but reminiscent of Chinese opera costumes: feathered, embroidered, or beaded head-dresses and embroidered jackets, pantaloons, and slippers. Middle-class white women dressed in mandarin coats and served Chinese-themed treats for smaller mahjong parties.[25] A photograph of four fashionable young Seattle women sitting around a mahjong table made the rounds of Pacific Northwest newspapers in the fall of 1922, from Portland, Oregon, to Walla Walla, Washington.[26] They did not wear conventional flapper dress; rather, they were covered with variations of elaborate "mandarin" costumes.

The racial performance of white women and the smaller numbers of men dressed in Chinese costumes related to a much longer and pernicious history of white actors dressing as caricatured African Americans, Asians, and Native Americans.[27] Over the previous decades, these performances appealed to white Americans as a way to distance themselves from denigrated groups—which was especially appealing for marginalized European groups such as the Irish—while still accessing the ostensibly uncivilized freedoms, primitive authenticity, or boundary-crossing behaviors that Anglo-American social norms discouraged. By the 1920s, blackface had grown past its early roots with working-class and immigrant vaudevillians to become ubiquitous and mainstream entertainment and an easy form of humor. Meanwhile, Orientalist experts posed for portraits in turbans and Arab clothing, and male fraternities like the Shriners created elaborate pseudo-Arabic worlds on a grand scale.[28] Chinese costuming was less pervasive in American culture, but "yellowface" was still standard practice in Hollywood. Dressing as Chinese at mahjong parties rarely involved changing physical appearance through face-altering makeup, but it shared some of the allure of accessing exotic freedoms as did other forms of racial performance.

FIGURE 5.3 The original caption of this photograph read, "These Seattle girls are enjoying the absorbing game that is made more entrancing by the Chinese costumes and the Oriental setting." Their hairstyles of double buns also evoked imagery of Chinese women. *Seattle Times*. Parker Brothers Archive.

Chinese costuming at mahjong parties built off two other trends: the "Oriental" style in women's clothing and the 1920s vogue of masquerade. For the more independent and publicly engaged "New Woman," looser-fitting fabrics inspired by "the East," especially Japan, offered a reprieve from corseted clothing in the early twentieth century.[29] Kimonos worn in public evoked new sexual boundaries, in part because of Orientalist ideas of the East as feminine and sensuous. Soon mandarin coats joined kimonos—and mahjong sets—in import stores. Masquerade balls were wildly popular, as Americans dressed as a wide variety of people imagined to be far from the modern world, from Dutch peasants to harem girls.[30]

Dressing in Chinese costume, eating "Oriental" treats, and watching staged mahjong-inspired dance revues were all ways in which individuals—particularly middle-class and elite white women—transformed mahjong into a means of experimenting with different personae and demonstrating modern worldliness.[31] Chinese costuming appears to have been primarily, if not exclusively, a phenomenon among white mahjong enthusiasts. African American clubwomen in the urban North and Midwest created the "newest elite clubs" to play the game, but there is no mention of costumes or particularly Oriental atmosphere.[32] Ethnic groups on the margins of whiteness, such as upwardly mobile German Jews, were more integrated into mainstream white mahjong culture.[33] The Vanderbilts' elaborate "Ma-Jung Fete" and ballet served as a fundraiser for the Catholic, Protestant, and Jewish Big Sisters Organizations.[34] To the very limited extent that there is any record of ethnic-specific costumed events, they are virtually indistinguishable from the broader white American culture.[35] For white women, racial performance remained always an obvious masquerade. At a time when fashion magazines frequently featured primitive masks, white female models encouraged readers to consume products like cosmetics and Asian-infused clothing that allowed them to put on, and necessarily remove, a racial mask.[36]

Matrons as well as modern girls participated in Orientalist performances that evoked sexuality and cosmopolitanism. The magazines, films, and popular fiction that promoted self-expression by "the modern girl" of the 1920s—distinguished by "bobbed hair, painted lips, provocative clothing, elongated body, and open, easy smile"—also made sexualized portrayals of mahjong available for mass consumption.[37] While urban youth engaged in petting parties and went dancing at jazz clubs, their parents' generation and their elite counterparts performed sexual and gender subversion through the more respectable route of mahjong.[38] "Many a timorous lady," described the Los Angeles *Herald,* "still quakes a little" at the thought of joining the "illusive atmosphere of the Chinese game."[39] Elite New Yorkers could participate in an elaborate genteel mahjong ballet at the Plaza Hotel and still attend the risqué 1924 *George White Scandals* revue "Mah Jongg." Renowned Art Deco artist Erté designed extravagant and revealing costumes for the dancers embodying mahjong pieces.[40] In lustrous prints of red, gold, and black, his set design imagined a towering dragon folding screen, in front of which a dancing "Mah Jongg," clothed mostly in beaded mesh, was to cavort as the winning move.

The language of mahjong itself became a form of access to titillating boundary crossing. Players could feel "deliciously Oriental when uttering Chows and Pungs," words necessary to snatch discarded tiles and complete hands.[41] For a few bridge and mahjong experts like Robert Foster and Florence Irwin who were focused on the methods of play, the exoticism and popular frivolity surrounding the game was vulgar and distracting, but they were in the distinct minority. "Why must we do violence to such beauty?," Irwin pleaded, ending an irritated rant against the proliferation of slang words used to describe various tiles.[42] The "cheapening" language she described were a result of players relishing in the inside knowledge and innuendo of nicknames like "The Red Lady" for the red dragon tile. In a cartoon by iconic Jazz Age artist John Held Jr., "The Ancient Chinese Game According to the More Modern Generation," a white American couple lustily illustrates mahjong terms. A game that begins with a "pung is a kiss on the cheek" climaxes with a full embrace: "Ah! My friends to Mah Jong, is to Mah Jong."[43] In game parlance, to "pung" was to take a discarded tile to complete a hand, and to "Mah Jong" meant to make it, to go all the way and win the game. As depicted in the comic, the "modern generation" ascribed an erotic meaning to the very name of the game. Introducing its readers to mahjong, the *New York Times* compared the name to "a novel swear word" with its "emotional twang."[44]

Held's cartoons revealed the range of consumer goods that mahjong inspired, such as clothes and jewelry, as well as how race, gender, and sexuality were connected in the culture of the game. In one illustration, a bobbed blond flapper looks askance at a Confucius-cum-samurai-mandarin, with long fingernails and elaborate armor, who seems to have appeared in her dressing room.[45] "If Confucius should return," the comic asks, "What would his reaction be to the new Mah-Jongg underthings?" The décolleté flapper displayed her mahjong-inspired lingerie with faux Chinese writing hemming the slip to the martial Confucius, as well as to the magazine reader.[46] Other figures displayed dragon-adorned bathers sharing a cigarette with a young man in a distinctly suggestive manner.

The new cultural lore of mahjong was infused with racial connotations that were themselves predicated on notions of gender and sexuality. When authors and marketers created characters named "Mah Jongg," they were consistently female, literally objectifying Chinese women. The *New York Times* dedicated a lengthy article to a new type of womanhood embodied by the young Chinese American flapper, whom the article dubbed "Miss Mah Jong."[47] "She has charm, allure. There is nothing as saucy on the face of the earth," the

FIGURE 5.4 John Held Jr.'s comic mahjong art frequently featured his iconic images of flappers. In addition to the sexual undertones of most of the images in this feature, Held references another 1920s fad, golf, with a joke that satirizes ubiquitous mahjong-inspired fashions through a dig at Chinese laundries. *Auction Bridge and Mah Jong Magazine.* Library of Congress.

article went on: "The Chinese flapper, American-born, is the East and the West in one, and so eternally exotic." Even George Gershwin spun a tune he named "Mah-Jongg," full of musical tokens that evoke ideas of Chinese music to a non-Chinese audience (such as the high, rapid chords in the well-known piano ditty "Chopsticks").[48] In the humorous song the lovesick gentlemen "Pung" and "Chow" serenade the "charming maid, who answered to the name, Mah Jongg." With the opening line, "From the sly Chinee, many years B.C.," lyricist B. G. DeSylva began the story by referencing the ancient mahjong origin myths. He also joined other mahjong descriptions in echoing popular perceptions of the Chinese as wily and inscrutable, as in Bret Harte's long-lasting 1870 poem known as "the Heathen Chinee."[49] The earnest Pung and Chow cap their plea to Mah Jongg by calling to her, "Lovely little Oriental witch, in the boxes down at Abercrombie and Fitch! Mah Jongg! Mah Jongg! From Tibetan ridges, you're as nice as Bridge is, my Mah Jongg!" Thus, Mah Jongg, the imagined Chinese woman, is directly commodified into the game and sold for mass consumption.

Stereotypes of Chinese women built on assumptions of exploitable sexuality, from the passive "lotus blossom" to the elite concubine and the Chinatown prostitute.[50] Images of sexually vulnerable and available Chinese women could have particular appeal as white women's sexuality became more public, advertised, and independent. Whether white women imagined themselves as "deliciously Oriental," or male writers merely assumed they did, dressing in Chinese costume may have normalized mahjong matrons' tamer forays into the erotic. Respectable consumers did not need to engage explicitly in such sordid matters; contextual allure was enough.

This process of mainstreaming marginal behavior happened at specific sites, often places where mahjong itself helped incorporate new behaviors and made new boundaries respectable. The Marcel Café in downtown Los Angeles was one such place. Above the title "Some Girl—Some Game!" an unusually alluring photograph of the young white mahjong "instructress" Alice Troxler advertised mahjong's presence at the Marcel Café, which had "engaged Chinese to instruct other patrons."[51] The café was on the cutting edge of the mahjong fad, introducing the "Mah Jongg teas" to Los Angeles that found "much favor with local society folk" who crowded in on Wednesday and Saturday afternoons.[52] Located near Hamburger's department store, which advertised the "game of a thousand wonders," the café was also targeted by a prohibition raid before the café's owner was arrested for joining in the dancing after midnight—something café proprietors were expressly forbidden from doing.[53] It was not a disreputable place per se, since its brushes with the law were for relatively minor infractions that highlighted how society had changed: sociable drinkers, late-night dancers, and alluring mahjong instructors were all rubbing shoulders in middle-class environments.[54] Anti-vice ordinances were no longer "up-to-date." In contrast to outdated laws, mahjong was a hallmark of cosmopolitan consumerist modernity, distinguished in large part by public sexuality. Women played a key role in the transition, as players, purveyors, and teachers of the game.

Selling Authenticity

In July 1922, white Angelenos flocked to the Ville de Paris department store to watch and learn how to play, and to buy sets. The *Los Angeles Evening Herald* described the growing numbers of customers who came to see "William Wong, a Chinese expert teaching Los Angeles girls how to play Mah-Jongg" in the store's basement, while daily "throngs" congregated before the store's window "to watch three wrinkled Chinese play the game to which they became devoted when lads in China."[55] Literally on display along with goods for sale, the players in the window became just as commodified as the game, both merged in *chinoiserie* consumption. Inside the store, Wong wore a Western suit, while his teaching partner from the "Far East" wore his "working costume" of a mandarin button hat and coat.

For a brief period during the mahjong vogue, mahjong instruction and demonstration provided real economic opportunities for Chinese Americans. "Teaching society folk how to play 'Mah Jong' is helping Chinese students in Columbia University defray college expense," the *New York Times* reported as the craze took off in 1923. As the *Times* explained, "The Chinese game, which is rapidly superseding bridge, has proved a veritable godsend to some of the students." While other students found work "in a score of other ways," Chinese American students could rarely gain access to jobs open to whites, and mahjong instruction enabled them to earn money for school through the fad years.[56]

Many Chinese American mahjong demonstrators and instructors were of the second generation, who came of age in the 1920s. In the late nineteenth century, severe anti-Chinese immigration restrictions had initially targeted women as potential sex workers and then banned the entry of Chinese laborers, while exempting merchants and close family relations of citizens by birth.[57] By 1920, the majority of Chinese youths had been born in the United States.[58] The stereotyped characters in popular fiction dogged these young Chinese Americans as they sought to break out of racialized low status and labor-intensive occupations. Their presumed mahjong skills were more marketable than their individual academic and professional skills honed in American universities, just as their assumed authentic selves remained stereotypically Chinese: foreign and homogenous.[59]

Being marked as Asian and foreign was both a liability and, within a constrained set of options, a possible advantage in service work and entertainment designed to appeal to a white customer base.[60] Individuals navigated a slippery and often painful path in trading on cultural commodification. Non-Chinese Americans rarely hired Chinese American graduates, who were then pushed into nearly the same low-paid jobs their parents occupied, working in family businesses such as restaurants or laundries, or hiring out their services in Chinatown curio shops. A social worker in Hawaii described the lack of opportunities for young Chinese women; instead they had to "find positions in the American community as 'figure-heads' as the girls themselves say, where they wear their Chinese costumes. And oh, how they hate to wear them! But they know they would not be wanted except for the costume." As a young Chinese American woman on the mainland protested, "As a senior in college, I have no intention of clerking in a curio shop, or of hiring myself out as atmosphere in a would-be Oriental establishment, not that I feel above such work, but the advantages of a college education have brought obligations as well. . . . I must accomplish something; I must find a worthwhile place in the world."[61] Despite their education, fluent English, and career goals, second-generation college graduates faced a grim economic landscape.[62]

More often than "wrinkled" men, Chinese women were displayed as emblematic of the game's Oriental beauty and exotic appeal. The *Los Angeles Examiner* featured three Asian American young women dressed in "Oriental garb" gathered around their mahjong student, a famous Italian wrestler, with the suggestive caption "Wrestling Training!"[63] In San Francisco, two "belles of the Chinese quarter" worked as in-store instructors while dressed in elaborate silken robes with jade bracelets.[64] Behind their photograph, the newspaper layout artist added paper cutouts of lanterns and cherry blossoms. Commanding more respect than the usual anonymity or caricatured names of "John Chinaman" or "Lotus Blossom," however, these instructors were named respectfully as Miss Tue Tom and Miss Tsuey Ha. Notably, white salesgirls could still market the exotic when dressed in appropriately Chinese costume, though they were perhaps less of a draw.[65] In contrast, Chinese Americans could not advertise standard American or Western qualities. Both white and Chinese Americans could perform "Chineseness," but only whites could pass back into the privileges of whiteness.

By combining elements of Chinese "authenticity" and Western fashion or American speech within a modern moment, Chinese Americans inherently challenged a bifurcation of Eastern traditionalism and Western modernity.[66] They thereby occupied a gray zone of cultural commodification and resistance.[67] An American context defined Chinese authenticity as outside Western modernity in either a degraded present or an esteemed past. It thus becomes a significant choice that the Ville de Paris instructor William Wong marketed himself as an expert in a Chinese game while wearing a Western suit. Notably, his unnamed fellow instructor more closely played the part of "authentic"

FIGURE 5.5 Tue Tom and Tsuey Ha taught customers mahjong in San Francisco's Aladdin Studio Tiffin Room. The two young women were from the city's Chinatown and may have been among the many local Chinese American college students recruited to teach the game. The costumes they wore matched the tea room's decorations of Chinese lanterns, dragons, and elaborately carved performance stage. *The San Francisco Call.* Parker Brothers Archive.

Chinese with a robe and button hat. Regardless of how strategic their paired presentations, both men would certainly have been aware of the expectations for demonstrated authenticity on the part of their white customers. Whether they could subvert such expectations would have depended upon their own economic vulnerability and their ability to claim authority and authenticity by other means.[68] Additionally, incorporating Western clothing may have held some appeal for white customers as a way of crossing boundaries rather than erasing them.[69]

Even as popular media represented them as quaint and foreign, in practice Chinese American instructors were closely affiliated with the American marketplace and directly facilitated the game's marketing and distribution. For white customers, they could prove authenticating and alluring but remain in the store's safe remove. Yet Americans continued to look askance at those who destabilized neat categories, particularly at Chinese men who entered, or who were imagined to enter, the white American home. In practice, instructors frequently positioned themselves in public: at department stores, galas, and large events, but the other main locale of learning—in the home with individual instruction—was a frequent focus in popular culture.[70]

Mahjong's Dangers

In reality, the vast majority of independent mahjong instructors were white women, but an emerging fictional archetype cast them as predominately Chinese. Sexualized depictions of mahjong could be enticing or lighthearted when associated with white men accessing "Oriental" women, but Chinese men became the representative mahjong instructors. With white women as the most closely associated consumers of the game, in popular fiction and commentary mahjong instruction became a site of Chinese cultural—and potentially sexual—encroachment.

As mahjong instructors developed an outsized cultural presence, fears of both boundary-crossing Chinese men and a backlash against white women embracing non-domestic pursuits combined in darker depictions of mahjong. In the process, a new stereotype of a faux-assimilated Chinese charlatan emerged, as did depictions of a threatening aspect of Orientalist consumerism: cultural seduction. Rather than donning a racial mask such as costuming that she could play with, consume, and discard at will, the woman exposed to cultural seduction risked transforming on a more intimate, physical, and lasting basis. Without outside intervention on the part of a stronger white man, a white woman might lose her ability to remove Oriental features. The mask would then become fundamentally transformative.[71]

When embodied by a Chinese woman encountering a white man, mahjong's transgressions were humorous and appealing. John Held Jr.'s comic series inverted Rudyard Kipling's oft-quoted "East is East, and West is West, and never the twain shall meet" with a sexually aggressive instructor in his illustration titled ". . . and the Twain Shall Meet." "Yes, me Miss Plum Blossom would be welly glad to teach Clistian [Christian] gentleman to play the Honorable Chinese game," the headdress-adorned woman says in typical caricatured speech. "I will teach you the Seasons," Plum Blossom continues, holding a tile as she lures her white male student to lean across the mahjong table, "If you Clistian gentleman will teach me the esteemed American game of Necking."[72] She embraces the unsuspecting young man and joins Held's iconic American flappers in revealing her garter. At the same time, the popular short instructional film of 1924, "Mysteries of Mah Jong," also offered a tempting warning.[73] In explaining the romantic possibilities of the somewhat unorthodox two-person style of play, scenes showed a young couple, "hands in center holding discarded tile. Business with fingers," as described by the film notes. Text in the silent film cautioned, "Should you be fond of the two handed game take no chances with a real Chinese Flapper." Between scenes featuring the Eurasian actress Princess Nai Tai Tai batting her eyes, the film explained, "In the age old game of Goo-Goo Eyes the oriental expert can give cards and spades and win."[74] These depictions reinforced not only a sexualized image of Asian women, but also demonstrated the relative lack of concern over white men overcome by their flirtations.

In contrast, long-held American beliefs about Chinese men assumed that they posed various sexual and gender threats.[75] Neutered by the feminized economic niches such as laundry and domestic servitude that male Chinese labor dominated, often living outside traditional family structures in predominantly male Chinatowns, and associated with non-Western masculine dress and food, Chinese men existed outside the dominant American framework of civilized gender roles.[76] By the 1920s, Chinese American society largely appeared more recognizably American as the second generation came of age and as the Chinese Republic wrestled with Western-style modernization, but the stereotypes had barely shifted. With less violent expression than the horrific massacres and beatings of the late nineteenth century, by the 1920s previous Sinophobic stereotypes were joined by images of the evil Dr. Fu Manchu, who specialized in capturing white women.[77]

Mahjong highlights the development of a new Chinese stereotype that focused on potential Chinese mobility. Fears of cultural seduction echoed earlier concerns about physical contagion, but they applied more to social than to bodily mobility. Earlier twentieth-century public health officials decried the supposed predatory spread of syphilis among white men and boys by Chinese sex workers, and newspaper commentators cautioned against white female missionaries entrapped by wily Chinamen.[78] The predominant fear centered on opium. Political cartoons, sensationalistic postcards, and popular representations of opium featured white women lying amid men, insensate at the pipe.[79] When associated with a specific urban geography, insidious Chinese influence could be contained in Chinatown, and white women warned away or actively prevented from entering.[80] However, by the early 1920s, a growing population of second-generation Chinese Americans disrupted easy containment and categorization. Indeed, a sizable number were of mixed-race heritage as Chinese men had partnered with and married, where legally allowed, women of other ethnicities, often European immigrants.[81] At the same time, more white women were entering Chinatown as "slummers" and tourists out for a thrilling time. They were also bringing mahjong and the people associated with it into their homes.[82]

Mahjong provided a new entree for Chinese culture and male instructors into the sacrosanct feminized white American domestic space. In response, popular literature sought to maintain racial boundaries by identifying male mahjong instructors as tricksters. Whether harmful or merely exploitative, they were depicted as snakes in the grass.[83] Chinese servants cut absurd figures among the gullible white elite, as a fashionable matron in *Harper's* invites a caricatured laundryman into her home to "join us for a game."[84] In an article subtitled "Cooks Have Been Lured from Kitchens to Instruct in Native Game That Has Reaped Fortune," the writer described "certain soft-footed, slant-eyed denizens of the kitchen have for the first time in their American career been introduced to the parlors, where, garbed in brocades, they have presided as teachers of the game." The "exorbitant rates paid for lessons" only added "to the popularity of the ancient game." In one short story, even a white male mahjong instructor used a manufactured Eastern mysticism to seduce a woman described as the "loveliest of morons." Women—ostensibly impressionable and superficial—were vulnerable to men under the guise of mahjong.[85]

In mahjong-inspired popular fiction such as *The Green Dragon Emerald*, a mystery play performed in California high schools, and in the comic *Saturday Evening Post* story *Punk Pungs*, the Chinese villains are marked as dangerous

FIGURE 5.6 The sheet music cover for "They Call It Mah-Jongg" depicts a stereotyped Chinese man, including an anachronistic queue, teaching two white women who appear smitten with his charms. Above them, a cloud of smoke from a Buddhist statue evokes the opium smoke widely associated with the seduction of white women by Chinese men. Courtesy of The Strong, Rochester, New York.

because of their ability to perform smooth, fluent English.[86] The portrayal of Westernized Chinese men as nefarious tricksters echoed fears from the 1910s of supposedly Christianized Chinese men seducing, murdering, or otherwise ruining naïve female missionaries.[87] Signs of assimilation were seen as a dangerous masquerade.

Mahjong never sparked any recorded instance of actual violence, but popular media frequently deployed dark humor in portrayals of Chinese mahjong instructors. Sometimes it ended in fictional anti-Chinese violence, superficially rendered innocuous by humor or a narrative sense of justice. In *Punk Pungs*, racial violence was justified as a defense against a Chinese mahjong instructor who attempted to seduce the white narrator's wife.[88] Written in faux urban working-class dialect and malapropisms, the novel portrays Dink O'Day and his wife Kate as they learn bridge, engage in domestic power struggles through the game, and then almost abandon it in favor of mahjong. Mahjong enters their life through Kate's female friend, who enthuses, "all the swells is taking up [mahjong] and so is we."[89] Although Dink resists learning the new amusement, he is pulled in by his headstrong wife. Dink, as someone knowledgeable of Chinatown's vice, rails against learning "something invented by a heathen Chink. . . . [Y]ou don't understand these slant-eyed babies. They is a crafty lot. First they'll get everybody to playing this mahjong, after the which they'll ease in other Chinese costumes, like hitting the pipe and the such, and before you knows it you'll be burning josh-sticks and praying to this lad Confusion them yeller kids is all so cuckoo about."[90] Much like Negro dialect and blackface minstrelsy, the powerful combination of stereotypes taps into anti-Chinese tropes while simultaneously inviting the audience to laugh at Dink's clownish mistakes. Although Dink calls his rant "hop," the story affirms his ostensibly facetious tirade. Dink goes on to demonstrate his need to accompany his wife to the mahjong lesson conducted by a genuine "mandolin" (mandarin) because "I ain't the sorta guy that'd let his woman go alone to a place where they is a Chinaman."[91]

In the end, Sing High Lee, the wily Chinese instructor, justifies Dink's fears by attempting to seduce Kate. She and her friend buy into the instructor's supposed elite pedigree, as his high-bred pretensions and kowtowing obsequiousness overcome white female—but not white male—defenses. In reality, the "swell naboob" Sing High Lee is Charlie Bang, a San Francisco–born gambling tough from Chinatown's underbelly. His flowery and literary English gives way to his apparently more true and authentic pidgin English, explaining that "Cheap Chinamen get ten dollars hour. Twenty for mandolin with mandolin talk." Charlie Bang embodies numerous Chinese stereotypes: groveling coolie,

poetic mandarin, violent vice lord, and—most important—insidious sexual
threat. Dink convinces Charlie to pretend to seduce Kate's friend, but Charlie
actually manages to begin seducing two white women at once—Kate genuinely and the friend as yet another form of subterfuge. Charlie is dangerous
because his racial performance is that of a Westernized non-threatening elite.
Ironically, despite being born in the United States, his "true" self is *more* foreign. His trickiness relies on an assimilated cloak that covers a perpetually
alien core. In pursuing Kate, Charlie tricks the trickster Dink, but meets his
"just deserts" at the hands of the other husband. *Low Bridge and Punk Pungs*
ends with the jealous husband dragging in showing signs of a fight. " 'That
Chink,' " he reports, " 'ain't never coming back here to bother no more white
women against their wills.' 'Ain't Jim brave?' " gushes his wife.[92]

Not every Chinese presence in the household seemed threatening. Instead,
morality was predicated upon fitting into the established niches of economic
and cultural hierarchy. In other words, an impotent Chinese servant could be
morally good. American notions of contemporary Chinese authenticity drew
on caricatured depictions of working-class laundrymen, cooks, or servants;
thus, an alternative persona, especially if powerful or Westernized, became a
de facto malicious ruse.[93] In the *Green Dragon Emerald*, the faithful servants
demonstrate through their overdrawn dialects, lack of worldliness, humble
carriage, and anti-modern sentiments that they are exactly what they seem.
The servants' non-threatening sexuality is only present as an innocent affec-
tion between Ty Lee and his "sweetheart" and the childlike vulnerability of a
giggling female servant who "drops her little Chinese trousers" on stage to try
on a "Melican" (American) "little flapper dress."[94]

The Green Dragon Emerald perfectly encapsulates the thrilling and haz-
ardous exoticism associated with Chinese culture transported into American
homes via Chinese men and mahjong sets.[95] The thriller revolves around an
American family living in late-1920s Beijing. A shadow hangs over the family
as unwilling possessors of a cursed ancient mahjong set that emits ghostly
specters to lure the father into touching a poisoned emerald tile, the "green
dragon." The daughter Corinne, engaged to an upright young American
man, is nearly seduced and eventually captured by a suave and Westernized
Fu Manchu–style sinister genius Sang Wu, who seeks to transform her into
a "Manchu princess." After venturing into the Chinese city with Sang Wu
and possibly enjoying opium, Corinne drinks a potion that brings out her secret heritage as the product of a white American father and deceased Chinese
mother. Reflecting ideas of race that conflated biology and culture, the elixir
draws out her latent tendencies to make her physically and mentally Oriental.

She feels a "yellow devil that's feeding upon my soul." With narrowed eyes, she develops stealth, cunning, and cruelty.

Not surprisingly, Wu is behind the whole creepy business, as the dramatic ending reveals his scientific capabilities to manipulate the mahjong set through "some very clever electrical experimenting," radio, and his own fantastical contribution to science: projecting "thought vibrations." A Harvard psychologist-cum-scientist saves the day, and the stalwart young fiancé gets a rehabilitated, re-whitened Corinne. Sang Wu kills himself by clutching the poisoned tile after praising "my illustrious ancestors, and the Green Dragon Mah Jong set!" Although two loyal Chinese servants lose their lives in the hubbub, their sacrifice is all part of a happy ending. The "Mah Jong game is ended," the psychologist tells the father in the play's closing line, "and *you* have won!"[96]

The character of Sang Wu epitomized the risk posed by Oriental power cloaked in seductive people or goods that promised unwary white consumers, especially women, luxury and pleasure. For a white woman to become Oriental meant degradation. Because of long-held sexual stereotypes of non-white women, and because of associations of smooth-talking Chinese men as sexual predators, becoming Oriental for a white woman meant becoming more sensual and sexually available. After Corinne drinks the potion, Sang Wu croons, "tonight, my lovely one, you are wholly of the orient. Yes, you are as beautiful as one of my own Manchu ancestresses; green eyes glittering like serpents; red, wanton lips, begging for kisses."[97] In the ultimate sign of her transformation, Corinne allows Sang Wu to kiss her. In *The Green Dragon*, the pairing of a Chinese man with a white woman suggested a sexual availability far more threatening than the interracial union of Corinne's own parents.

Mahjong did not require the presence of a Chinese man to pose a threat to American women, however. The long-held associations of Oriental luxury tinged with depravity imbued goods themselves with symbolic power.[98] Media described legions of mahjong-addled "addicts" in terms that smacked of opium.[99] The ways in which white women engaged with the game, emphasizing costumes, Chinese-inspired food, and a "Chinesey" atmosphere through carved furniture and hanging lanterns, highlighted the spectacle of female domestic luxury.[100] The Oriental goods enabled displays of women's consumerism, sensuousness, and non-productive labor.

Mahjong itself could possess seductive powers that, overlaid with Oriental luxury, could transform a white woman in fundamental ways that destabilized the mahjong player's home. Biting critiques of white female victims of cultural seduction reacted not only to Chinese mobility but also to white women's leisure: Chinese culture was the vehicle, but the result meant disrupted white American homes. As portrayed in the popular press, when women developed "mah-jong-itis," or an "excessive tendency" for the game, they disrupted the household through becoming "Chinese" in certain imagined ways, neglecting domestic duties, and providing an entry point for the subversive foreign element: Chinese men.[101] Newspaper articles across the social spectrum linked mahjong to women's frivolity and excessive consumption, emphasizing female lack of self-control as "naturally lazy."[102] Although couched in often-humorous song lyrics or prose about a seemingly superfluous topic, the anxieties expressed about mahjong reflect more generalized anxieties over changing gender roles, immigration, and race.

A hit song, "Since Ma Is Playing Mah Jong," popularized by performer Eddie Cantor, depicted how a mother's infatuation with mahjong dramatically disrupted her family.[103] The song's narrative focuses on familial upheaval through gender disorder, and the father's attempt to remove the outside threat of the "Chink," using a racial slur common at the time. The bouncy and disturbing refrain cries:

> Since Ma is playing Mah Jong
> Pa wants all "Chinks" hung.
> We get rice chop suey each night,
> Chinese cooking you should see how Pa is looking.
> Ma wears a kimona
> She yells "Pung" and "Chow."
> Ma left dishes in the sink
> Pa went out and killed a "Chink"
> Ma plays Mah Jong now.

The many encroachments of stereotypical Chinese elements encourage the audience to sympathize with long-suffering Pa. Significantly, while he desires the eradication of all "Chinks," it is not until Ma actually neglects dish washing that he is pushed over the edge into lethal violence. As in other popular literature, the song's comedic frame defused the real violence that plagued Chinese Americans by transforming it into a reassuringly humorous enactment of white patriarchal authority.[104]

In cultural seduction, consumption of luxury goods associated with the Oriental preyed upon a white woman's assumed desire for consumer goods. After becoming too close to mahjong and its trappings, a woman could actually shed certain gendered features of whiteness—specifically related to domesticity. Rather than transgressing racial boundaries in urban geographies through slumming or temporary costuming, which reaffirmed the individual's whiteness, these domestic transgressions risked more permanent (and inevitably disastrous) racial crossings.[105] Like many white mahjong players who engaged in masquerade with Chinese costuming, "Ma wears a kimona [*sic*]," as does the woman illustrated on the sheet music cover who holds a wooden mahjong case. The woman's image clearly drew from traditional Japanese portraiture; it is unclear if she was supposed to be an "Oriental" woman (who would not be Chinese in any case) or if Ma had actually become Oriental, even down to the cartoonish slanted eye lines. The song portrayed the results of adopting stereotypical foreign characteristics, from cooking chop suey to growing long fingernails, as potentially dangerous in gendered ways. Eddie Cantor sung, "China you're poison to me, / You broke up my whole family," as Ma succumbs to the game's temptations.[106]

Cultural commentators across the political spectrum decried women's focus on the game over their familial responsibilities. Social reformer Miriam Van Waters critiqued women's distracted self-absorption when she attributed juvenile delinquency to "the modern phenomenon of groups of women playing bridge and mah jongg while groups of boys and girls have 'petting parties,' or expeditions to steal automobiles," she admonished.[107] Her concerns were echoed more facetiously in the press coverage of Vancouver men who advocated for a Husbands Protective League "as a means of protecting themselves and of asserting their authority over their fair partners" because "mah jongg parties are cutting in on wives' time so seriously." Poor hardworking husbands, the article complained, "expecting a hot supper and a little human companionship" were met instead by a tardy wife with her head still in the mahjong game, a cold meal of convenience foods, and an obligatory mahjong game with another couple. Early in the fad, women bringing the game into the home could be seen in a positive light of domesticating husbands, as a California man described, "It beats anything I know of to keep father and the boys home nights." Increasingly played among women at its peak popularity, however, the game risked drawing their focus away from the domestic to pleasure and peer-oriented unproductive leisure.[108]

Critiques of women's self-focused pursuits and desires reflected discomfort with increasing female independence and a broader social ethic of individualism. The new ideal of companionate marriage was one way to contain the search for personal and sexual fulfillment within heterosexual marriage. Yet companionate marriage also involved a renegotiation of the power dynamics within marriage. In 1920s popular media, men often depicted themselves as at the mercy of their strong-willed wives. In 1923, a *San Francisco Chronicle* headline wailed, "Divorce Wrecks 148,554 Homes in One Year! Yearning for 'Self Expression' Brings Menace to Institutions of Civilization." Meanwhile, mahjong humor often poked fun at women who irresponsibly spent their husbands' money on mahjong sets or forced them to play the game.[109]

Humorists frequently depicted mahjong as disrupting the white American household and its patriarchal privileges, with Chinese people as its crafty creators. Widely published columnist James Montague put these views into verse that made mahjong the scheme of "A heathen Chinee who was angered to see / The civilized races supreme," who succeeded in laying a trap: "For the people who play at Mah Jong night and day / Are rapidly going insane!"[110] The Husbands Protective League advocates warned of "total eclipse at the hands of the malignant inventor who perfected that devilish device known as mah jongg and sent it forth into the world to perplex and confound the male sex for ever and ever."[111] Such accusations echoed more serious endorsements of violent expulsion that blamed Chinese launderers and servants for making white women forget how "to do their own housework."[112] In a remarkably similar albeit more facetious warning, the comic strip "The Gumps" cautioned that mahjong's popularity could mean that "all the Chinamen will close their laundries and open Mah-Jongg schools. Then we'll all have to wash our own shirts."[113]

Imported Dangers

Cultural seduction could trigger physical and bodily transformations, causing mahjong players to become "Oriental" in certain stereotyped ways. Yet in discourse both humorous and serious, the game itself also seemed to pose a direct physical threat. Physical ailments joined anxieties over gender disruption and female obligations to home and race. Emphasizing ideas of racial difference, the theme of hidden dangers associated with the game echoed fears of Chinese mobility as well as cultural changes wrought in American households. Tongue-in-cheek rumors from the Shanghai English-language press of the "Mahjongg neck" as a special strength for "bending over the table playing for an hour or more," later shifted in the American press to more harmful effects.[114] Commonly referenced as "the Yellow Peril," as an invasion or addiction, the mahjong craze was discussed with enough pathological undertone to lead one misinformed woman to believe mahjong to be a "germ."[115] Advertisers promoted the nearly dangerous excitement of mahjong, tapping into long-held associations of Chinese people with physical and social contagion. Demonstrating the simultaneous alluring and ominous tones that marked the mahjong fad, a department store ironically sang the praises of "this wonderful game" in a full-page spread by describing it as "not a game— it's a disease."[116]

In 1924, the *San Francisco Examiner* made room on its front page to alert the reading public to the "new American malady" of "Mah Jongg Eyes."[117] Shortly after, the *Los Angeles Times* described on its front page the California State Association of Optometrists' committee to investigate the "'morning after' headaches disturbing the peace of thousands of devotees of the Chinese game."[118] The *Los Angeles Times* acknowledged the supposedly well-known psychological danger that "Mah Jongg more or less unsettled the intellects of those fanatically devoted to it, and unfitted them for any other avocation, but," the writer added indignantly, "it was not supposed to cause physical injury as well."[119] "The new malady has become so general," reported an optometrist in Sacramento, "that special glasses have been devised." The cause of "Mah Jongg Eyes" was apparently Americans' inability to read Chinese, which forced players to rely on the tiles' small numerals that had been added to the tiles' bright surface for Western consumers. After the initial *Chronicle* article "set San Francisco a-talking," a humorous follow-up article posited a different explanation for Mah Jongg eyes through a uniquely bizarre (and terribly punned) origin myth.[120] Since "Mah Jongg emanated from a Chink of powerful light, the indelible refraction of which has been left in every set, [it will] blind one's vision a priori." Such brightness, the author concluded, could still not illuminate the dark confusion of calculating the score.

Although much of the negative press coverage of mahjong was couched in humor, it expressed genuine underlying anxieties about Chinese influences. The *Examiner* once again featured a front-page story on mahjong's unexpected consequences with an article about "athletic Chinese insects lodged in the tiles" that "required the ministrations of a state plant quarantine official."[121] It is not surprising that the West Coast media covered mahjong's imported dangers more emphatically than elsewhere. As a border region with seaports where Asian bodies and goods landed first, the Pacific Coast maintained a frontline mentality and hostile suspicion toward an Asian presence.

More serious concern over mahjong-induced dermatitis emerged from the medical community. Medical scares, regardless of their factuality or fabrication, indicated that mahjong carried dangers to the eyes and skin of white Americans that did not affect the Chinese, reinforcing the logic of cultural and biological difference. In a rush to produce boxes for the seemingly insatiable American market, shoddy mahjong workshops were prematurely packing insufficiently dried cases. Blaming "an epidemic of skin rashes" on the lacquer variously attributed to Japanese and Chinese mahjong box makers, the *Journal of the American Medical Association* and the *British Medical Journal* engaged in a transatlantic warning "that the beautiful imported Mah Jongg boxes covered with Japanese lacquer should be regarded with some suspicion."[122] A medical missionary in China's Hunan Province wrote in to affirm the concern, identifying "the famous Ningpo varnish" as "a potent source of trouble to foreigners here."[123] The Chinese, she explained, had already acquired immunity.

For all the hubbub and warnings, both serious and flippant, Americans eagerly purchased hundreds of thousands of mahjong sets and devoted many evenings to playing with friends and spouses. Mahjong's edginess, its attractive flirtation with imagined dangers, and its exotic performativity helped Americans transition through profoundly consequential social changes during the Jazz Age. If mahjong-obsessed women were not, in fact, becoming "Oriental" like Eddie Cantor's Ma, then perhaps the song helped release anxieties and normalize racially transgressive entertainment at least as much as it humorously advertised its dangers.

Despite the many cultural forms it inspired, the mahjong fad only lasted a few years. As early as 1924, newspapers began reporting its demise.[124] Though overdrawn and premature, these claims charted a roughly accurate boom-and-bust story. L. L. Harr's Pung Chow Company declared bankruptcy in 1925; the inventory that had sparked such heated rhetoric was sold at auction.[125] After Parker Brothers moved to cheaper American-made sets and the fad slowed, Joseph Babcock quietly left the mahjong industry, divorced his wife Norma, and turned his attention to a career in law.[126] The wild sales of mahjong had provided a much-needed bump to Parker Brothers' slowing sales, and George Parker used the profits for seafaring vacations as well as to invest in the company's factory and the next generation of new products.[127] With the collapse of the American mahjong market, Chinese import shops first slashed prices and then were left with a glut of stock.[128] By 1928, the Chinese mahjong industry had shrunk to one-third of its peak size of 1923, sustained by domestic orders and small export streams to Japan and Europe.[129]

There was no single or simple reason for the fad's decline, though commentators frequently blamed the proliferation of contradictory and ostensibly authoritative rules—and ensuing conflict.[130] Early efforts by Babcock to control the game may have ironically hastened its undoing by encouraging superficial differentiation to avoid trademark infringement.[131] Each competitor promoted opposing claims on a single, supposedly correct and authentic style of play. In addition, mahjong faced competition from other games. Contract bridge, crossword puzzles, and charades all sprung up to take mahjong's place in evening parlors.[132] The American craze ended well before the stock market crashed in 1929.

Cultural reasons likely explain the drop in popularity as well. In the early 1920s, mahjong allowed white American women to try on alternative "Oriental" personae and thereby access new boundary-crossing forms of self-presentation. Once this fresh cultural territory had been normalized, however, such ventures were no longer titillating and mahjong-related costuming lost much of its cultural utility. In addition, fads by their nature dwindle with time. For mahjong, the sparkling newness and smoky exoticism that carried excitement and status and cosmopolitan modernism wore off as the game became part of everyday American life. Mahjong no longer made society column headlines.[133]

Although the incandescent brightness of the early 1920s craze dimmed, it never entirely burned out. For many enthusiasts, mahjong retained its enduring appeal of sensory satisfaction, mental stimulation, and conversational rhythms. Without a clear pattern, pockets of elite players continued playing the game throughout the worsening economic crisis of the 1930s, often alongside bridge, in disparate communities—including DC political circles and African American clubwomen in Chicago.[134] Working- and middle-class Chinese Americans also continued playing the game in stores, homes, and family association halls.[135] In its enduring albeit diminished presence, mahjong became increasingly associated with a comfortable and domestic American culture, and references to mahjong eventually shifted from visions of ancient China to those of a shared American past.[136]

6

Inside and Outside Chinese America

IN THE LATE years of the Depression, a young Frank Eng and his nine siblings crowded into a makeshift loft above the family store in San Francisco's Chinatown. In the evenings they would fall asleep to the familiar rattling of tiles, laughter, and voices echoing at the mahjong tables below. After long days of working at the store in the building they rented, Frank's father hosted extended family members and friends who had come to pass the time by helping out at the store, breaking at night for drinks and mahjong. The children slept through the noise of people coming and going through the night, sometimes stopping only a few hours before the long workday began anew. A few years later Frank would join his friends at the Chinatown YMCA, where they played basketball and soccer, when they weren't playing cards on the mahjong tables in the back of the family store.[1]

Beginning in the 1920s, in Chinatowns across the United States, the rumble of shuffling mahjong tiles could be heard in apartments, association halls, and the back rooms of general stores as the game became a fixture in Chinese American communities. Mahjong's cultural meaning emerged in the context of the global 1920s fad; by the 1930s, mahjong stood in both China and abroad as "the national game of China." Over the following decade, mahjong became embedded in a built landscape of Chinatown spaces that served dual purposes—facing outward to white consumers and facing inward to Chinese Americans. In the process, the game became established in the tension between inclusion and exclusion that would define the experience of Chinese American ethnicity in the early twentieth century.

For Chinese Americans, as for other players, mahjong was a way to gather around an enjoyable and stimulating game. But the game's particular history as a Chinese game that also became enormously popular in the United States shaped its meaning, helping to spread its popularity as many Chinese

Americans embraced mahjong for both its perceived Chineseness *and* its perceived Americanness. Chinese Americans interacted with mahjong in ways that in effect helped navigate tensions associated with Americanization. Chinatown residents participated in commodifying and marketing mahjong as an aspect of Chinese culture for outsiders, while also using it to create separate ethnic spaces for Chinese Americans to engage with each other. The presence of mahjong—through the noises of the tiles and the language of game-play, through its visual presence in public spaces and in private homes—helped mark geographic spaces of ethnic community. For Chinese Americans, playing mahjong was not about assimilation in contrast to cultural continuity or vice versa. Rather, it was a versatile pastime that helped create spaces for a shared Chinese American experience.

Mahjong could serve as a point of commonality across generations during the 1920s and 1930s because it was both Chinese and American: a Chinese game whose cultural meaning transformed because of American consumption. It was simultaneously a gambling game among men in hometown association halls and a low-stakes parlor game for women to play in homes. Its associations with gambling endured among Chinese Americans longer than in white society, so that some Chinese Christians avoided mahjong even after its social evolution made it a more malleable game. Chinese Americans fostered social ties in and through particular built environments, during an era when American attitudes toward diversity and Chinese Americans in particular were shifting.

In the interwar era, Chinese immigrants and second-generation Chinese Americans navigated tenuous possibilities of inclusion in American society. Having been legally excluded as laboring immigrants, their numbers were no longer seen as threatening to white American workers or to Christian society. Americans also viewed China with increasing sympathy as a nation facing famine and Japanese invasion, and the Nationalist government of Chiang Kai-shek won favor with American officials and media.[2] Anti-Asian discourse shifted to focus increasingly on the perceived threat of Japanese, particularly among powerful agricultural interests and landholders in California. Yet Chinese Americans—a term that here includes both citizens by birth and long-term residents—continued to face exclusion from equality.[3] Seen as perpetual foreigners, they were barred from most forms of employment and routes to upward mobility, even after many in the second generation attained higher education. Exclusion from American society contributed to a rising sense of allegiance—including among second-generation Chinese Americans—to a Chinese homeland desperately in need during the famine, war, and invasion of the 1930s. As the "national game of China," mahjong served as a symbol in transpacific debates over the nation's identity and future.

By the early twentieth century, Chinatown boosters broadcast shops and architecture to white tourists. Many came to purchase mahjong sets, but mahjong was never just an outsider's game nor Chinatowns primarily outward-facing tourist destinations. From inside, Chinatowns were homes or cultural and economic hubs to return to. The game provided one ritual of connection, unique in its ability to cross boundaries of gender and generation into diverse (non-Christian) spaces. It was also part of a complex dynamic for Chinese Americans facing China, crossing between China and the United States, and building connections across the Pacific.

It would be easy to assume that Chinese Americans were already familiar with mahjong by the time of the American fad, but just the opposite is true. In the 1920s, many Chinese Americans began playing the game along with the broader American public. When white Americans noticed that mahjong had not been among laborers' gambling games in "Old Chinatown," they wrongly asserted its absence as evidence that mahjong was not a working-class "coolie" game. In fact, mahjong was missing not because it was the sole province of mandarins in the court, but because it was simply not a widespread part of Chinese culture before the early twentieth century.[4] For most Chinese American players at the time, it was not yet rooted in family traditions or memories of the homeland. But it represented a tie to Chinese heritage nonetheless, and it was rapidly spreading in popularity in China as well. During the 1920s, as one observer noted, the mahjong craze "obsessed all Chinatown."[5]

Chinese Americans often purchased their sets from the same wholesale shipments advertised for sale to "Americans from all walks of life," complete with Arabic numerals and English letters on the tiles.[6] However they heard about it—whether through its growing profile in China as the mahjong export boom took off, through rumors of the demand for Chinese mahjong instructors, or through other Chinese friends and visiting students who already knew the game—mahjong spread quickly among Chinese Americans amid the widespread American fad.[7] Over the ensuing decades, Chinese migrants would continue to bring different regional styles of playing the game with them to American shores. Before immigration reform in the 1960s increased and broadened Chinese immigration, many Chinatown residents played styles that reflected their Cantonese origins.

Ironically, while marketers advertised the game as an exclusive pastime of the Imperial court, if Chinese immigrants had heard of mahjong at all in the early days of the fad they often approached it with some suspicion as a gambling game associated with women of ill repute.[8] In the 1920s, however, the sudden and massive American market spurred the spread of the game in China and changed its image there and in the United States.[9] Soon even respectable and relatively well-off merchant families welcomed mahjong into their homes. "The fact that all America was taking up the fad also gave the game an aura of respectability," explained sociologist Pardee Lowe in his 1943 groundbreaking family biography, *Father and Glorious Descendant*.[10] For most Chinese Americans, the game evolved from its urban nightlife roots to become more domestic even as white Americans engaged with the game for, ironically, its exotic appeal.

In China, a similar transformation occurred as the game spread and gained popularity, along with awareness of the American mahjong love affair. By the 1930s, men—and more notably, women—across social classes played the game along a broad spectrum of stakes.[11] Crackdowns on public gambling under the Nationalist government of Chiang Kai-shek meant that authorities had to negotiate when mahjong would be considered a vice, which was not straightforward. Within the Chinese press, news circulated in 1936 that "the famous Chinese game of Mah Jong (Ma Chiang) has been pronounced a legal form of amusement when played in the home and not in public places" or shops.[12] Such a decree further encouraged a realm of respectable mahjong play and its integration into homes and domestic life. As in the United States, the privileges of privacy were most accessible to those with the means and family structures to create recognizably private homes, as opposed to the living spaces occupied by transient or single laborers.

Ethnicity at Play

Iconic representations of Chinatown featured curving pagoda rooflines, bright colors, and neon chop suey signs. Behind and around those external-facing commercial facades, however, were private spaces for living and for a Chinese American public life. Chinatowns also drew immigrants and Chinese Americans from the surrounding regions as economic and cultural hubs. Chinatowns' significance as cultural nodes extended beyond their geographic limits. Despite regional distinctions, Chinatowns along the West Coast, in Chicago, and in New York also shared core commonalities. San Francisco's Chinatown remained the primary import center and was influential nationally. In the Bay Area, the Chinese population increasingly dispersed after the 1906 San Francisco earthquake and fire—though, like Chinese Americans across the nation, most remained urban.[13] Many Chinese residents

moved south and east of the city as prejudicial relief policies made recovery
more difficult for Chinese San Franciscans, who also encountered housing
discrimination.[14] Their economic opportunities, however, remained largely
in Chinatown. Those who regularly commuted into the district were thoroughly enmeshed in local personal, economic, and political networks.[15]

In the national seat of anti-Asian sentiment, San Francisco, Chinese
residents faced severe residential segregation and restrictive covenants.
Chinatown was effectively a ghetto and, as such, contained a diverse array of
people living in close quarters with each other. Single men squeezed together
in crowded rooms and leased beds in shifts between those who worked nights
or days.[16] In New York's Chinatown working-class men also faced similarly severe crowding. "For a dollar a month a member can sleep on a cot in the *fong*,"
or the family association headquarters, which could be in tenement buildings.
"On Saturday night sleepers and *mah-jong* players take turns."[17] Although a
leisure activity, mahjong was present among those whose lives were hardly
leisured. For laborers, games provided relaxation, male bonding, or the addictive escapism of gambling.

In some ways mahjong functioned like other kinds of cultural connections
such as gambling with dominoes, consuming medicinal herbs, or watching
Cantonese opera. Yet the game's strategies and rhythms, and its small groups
of four players, created unique and consistent cultural patterns. In addition,
its meaning as a game that could be simultaneously American and Chinese,
and its unusual ability to bridge multiple kinds of social spaces across gender
and generational divides, meant that it served unique purposes in creating a
larger sense of Chinese American ethnicity. Chinatown's homes, shops, and
association halls became communal mahjong spaces. The game's tiles created a
particularly resonant sense of a Chinese cultural space. When players shuffled
the tiles, the clattering rumble could echo down alleyways. Walking along
Chinatown's sidewalks, one observer noted, a visitor could hear flowing from
the windows "Dominos and mah jongg pieces click crisply and the voluble
conversation of the excited players."[18]

Conversely, bringing mahjong outside those boundaries risked raising the
residents' racial profile. Trailblazing Chinese American reporter Louise Leung
Larson wrote about how her father, who was a successful Los Angeles herb-
alist, once brought a mahjong set along on his family's outing to the beach.
Although his daughter was an avid mahjong player with her friends, she later
explained that "We didn't want to play—we got stared at enough, without
playing mah jongg in public."[19] Her fears were well founded: the *Chicago
Tribune* published word of "real Chinese actually playing Mah-Jongg" spotted

outside of Chinatown.[20] As an area marked by the racialized people who lived in it, Chinatown was a socially constructed space.[21] Within its safe spaces, mahjong could help build community, while outside it could be viewed as reinforcing a sense of difference and exclusion.

General stores, where crisscrossing streams of Chinese Americans met, became central places for mahjong.[22] In communities large and small, these stores operated as post offices, immigrant remittance banks, import shops, and groceries.[23] On Sunday market days the stores were alive with people from far and wide who came to have political discussions, "lunch in the tea houses, meet their friends and relatives, shop, gamble, and then go home."[24] Gambling and storytelling provided a much-needed antidote to loneliness.[25] In more rural Chinese communities, on their last legs as area populations shrank and aged, mahjong also provided a refuge for older residents and a small revenue stream for shops.[26]

Shopkeepers kept mahjong most often in the back of stores to maintain the outward facing image of a business-oriented environment.[27] A 1930 *Los Angeles Times* article encouraged visitors to Chinatown "to look through the doorway of a store after night has fallen. Always in the rear of the shop will be gathered eight or ten Chinamen about a table. The inevitable game of mah jongg or dominoes will be in progress."[28] Mahjong played by "Chinamen" in their native habitat became another exotic experience to be consumed by outside tourists, but it was a genuine community experience as well. It built upon an older tradition of gambling in the back of Chinatown shops where bettors could quickly escape from police vice squads.[29] Mahjong's location in the back of shops illustrated its enduring connection to older practices, but its status as the "new society game" and its distance from illegal gambling as a low-stakes friendly game created a new association and could sometimes protect mahjong players from police arrest.[30]

In public spaces, men were the predominant players of mahjong, but stores were often family enterprises.[31] Emma Hoo Tom of Oakland lived with her family behind their shop, where they worked as laundry middlemen and advocates for Chinese American political rights. Her son remembered, "She was always at the store," which had a little room where "people came to play mah-jongg. A lot of single men came in, and my mother cooked and sewed for them. She helped out in any way she could."[32] Like the stores themselves, mahjong's presence in them likely highlighted the shared experience of being Chinese in America.[33] Although families and friends played the game in mixed contexts, men and women also developed separate mahjong cultures that varied according to the spaces they occupied and their social roles.

FIGURE 6.1 Photographed in 1942 in New York City's Chinatown, this general store and many others offered a range of products, services, and opportunities to socialize. No mahjong set is visible here, but one was very possibly out of the camera's reach behind the counter or in the back of the store. Photograph by Marjory Collins. Library of Congress.

Men played mahjong in another cornerstone Chinatown social institution: the family association halls for men who shared places of origin in Southern China. These spaces, which span Chinese American history, served a diverse set of social functions. They were highly gendered institutions, largely run by and for men, and their buildings provided safe gathering places.[34] Such spaces had been invaluable in the late nineteenth century, when extreme violence against Chinese people was commonplace. Under oppressive and unstable conditions (in China as well as in the United States), gambling held a long-established social niche, promising luck, entertainment, and male bonding. Mahjong in family association halls tapped into this older history of gambling games.[35] Fantan (wherein players bet on the number of hidden buttons or coins) and pai gow (a domino scoring game) were the two games that primarily coexisted with mahjong in gambling spaces.[36] Unlike many of the gambling games based heavily on chance and guesswork, mahjong also held intellectual appeal because of its advanced strategy and the importance of skill as well as luck.

Despite mahjong's increased stature and integration into a variety of community spaces, it remained a gambling game in Chinese American communities and could be destructive. It was acceptable for men to socialize at gambling halls as well as family association halls. In contrast to family associations, Chinatown gambling halls functioned only for gaming purposes and their addictive appeal crossed social boundaries of kin group and tong membership. Nevertheless, men could still lose distressing sums at the ostensibly more community-oriented family association halls. Growing up in San Francisco's Chinatown in the 1950s, Joyce Lee remembered her mother coming upon Lee's stepfather, who regularly lost large sums at the mahjong table, playing once again at a family association hall.[37] Outraged, she sent the mahjong table flying. At the time, Lee felt confused by her mother's apparent hypocrisy because she, too, played mahjong. In contrast to her husband, however, Lee's mother played for negligible sums in the homes of family friends.

Women played mahjong primarily in low-stakes female gatherings, where it provided a vital thread of connection. In part because many older immigrant women retained traditional standards of respectability by staying indoors much of the time, older women in Chinatown played mahjong with relatives or other women in shared and crowded home spaces in each other's apartments.[38] Mahjong also spread into houses outside Chinatown that had more room for privacy and entertainment.[39] The games provided another network to disseminate community information. For older women, mahjong served as "a medium for parlor conversation and gossip. Not only does this game aid in promoting good fellowship," Pardee Lowe explained, "but it also includes many kinds of tidbits," ranging from melon seeds and spiced dried fruits to doughnuts and popcorn.[40] Games often ended on a delicious note with a late-night supper "known as 'siu yeh.' Food, usually fried noodles, fried raviolis, waffles, are sent up from a restaurant."[41] These rituals could be lifelines for widows and other isolated elderly, for women as well as men.[42]

For women, having sex-segregated but age-integrated games provided a key opportunity to socialize the younger generation. While Joyce Lee's

FIGURE 6.2 A recreated exhibit of a family association hall centers the mahjong tables that had for decades been filled with men playing mahjong in Seattle's International District. The building first housed the Gee How Oak Tin Family Association until the 1930s, followed by the Hoy Sun Ning Young Association until the 1970s. The Wing Luke Museum.

first memory involved watching her siblings so that her mother could play mahjong, young women sometimes played with their elders. As Lowe described, the "ma jong table becomes the training-school, as it were, where the older generation of women pass on the traditional lore by word of mouth to the younger Americanized women."[43] Amy Tan's 1989 novel *The Joy Luck Club* portrays a similar dynamic when a daughter takes her mother's place at the mahjong table.[44]

The structure and pacing of the game also provided an opportunity for socializing that worked around intergenerational language barriers or points of conflict. More than many other games, mahjong incorporates natural pauses between rounds, and, in less competitive play, allows for staccato conversations as people take turns. Because the game's tempo facilitates a comfortable space for brief dialogue, mahjong games have become a long-lasting cross-generational activity.[45] Present-day families in China gather to play mahjong during the Lunar New Year as a form of togetherness that does not require extensive conversation. Pardee Lowe's father initially disapproved of younger family members playing mahjong, but "in the end even Father agreed that games of chance had their social value. It was one activity, Father admitted, which kept our family home together and appealed equally to young and old alike."[46] Such activities were not easy to come by.

The lack of cross-generation pleasure and recreation was compounded by the scarcity of leisure time experienced both by adults struggling to make ends meet as well as by children shuttling between American and Chinese school. When not in school, the young who did not have to work participated in a range of clubs and activities, including those through Christian organizations like the YMCA and YWCA, as well as sports teams and community service groups.[47] Older generations gravitated toward Chinese theaters, gambling, chatting while performing other productive activities, and mahjong. As sociologist Rose Hum Lee found, "The most common form of recreation for sojourners, other than feasting together, is Mah Jongg." Games could be squeezed into off-duty hours, "quickly organized as soon as four players are gathered, or a telephone call brings the 'fourth leg' when three are present. The nights for playing are chosen to suit the schedule of the laundry workers," enjoyed after days of washing, drying, and ironing, "and Saturday evenings when the week's work is complete."[48] While middle-class family members experienced some time outside of school for recreation, children in family businesses later remembered long hours of work, when "Only in the evenings, when relatives or friends dropped by for long chats and games of mahjong, did the business oriented effort of the family relax."[49]

Chinese American communities faced wrenching changes during the 1920s and 1930s. The generational conflict that marked society more generally during this time was experienced en masse in Chinese American families because of a demographic shift shaped by immigration policy. By 1920, the older population had begun to decline due to the long-term effects of exclusion laws, so young adults who were American by birth formed a larger proportion of the community.[50] In addition to the broader American youth rebellion of the 1920s, across the Pacific young progressive reformers sought to remake Chinese society. In the United States, both young and old faced conflicting pressures as Chinese Americans, and they responded with a broad spectrum of accommodation, resistance, and negotiation. Meanwhile, integration into American society seemed to demand assimilation. Many, especially 1920s youth, felt pressured to choose between being Chinese or being American.[51]

As an au courant game, mahjong meshed with a youth culture that was also forging new territory. Young Chinese American women in particular pushed the boundaries of respectability by playing sports, working, and moving freely in public space. After 1915, Lowe wrote, there was "a revolutionary change in the freedom of the young girl." Most scandalous of all, "girls now entertain their boys friends [sic] in their home, even when going to high school. Some boys do likewise. Ma jong parties, bridge parties are constantly arranged on the spur of the moment."[52] A *New York Times* article described an iconoclastic San Francisco Chinese flapper dubbed "Miss Mah Jong." Although it was clearly written from a white perspective that objectified the "saucy" young woman as a kind of fashion-print fantasy of "the East and the West in one, and so eternally exotic," Miss Mah Jong had real-life counterparts. Flora Belle Jan, a self-described flapper who chafed against Chinese traditions in her Central California upbringing, published newspaper articles satirizing both mainstream and Chinese American culture.[53] Such shocking behavior, though it corresponded with "the clamoring for women's equality with men" happening simultaneously in China, was often scorned by the older generation as degenerative American influence.[54] Young women found themselves consistently circumscribed by race outside Chinatown and by gender inside.[55]

Mahjong as a symbol of chic modernity *and* of Chinese identity appealed strongly to young Chinese Americans. It did not place American and Chinese ways of being in conflict. A young man whom Pardee Lowe described as "the epitome of a small group of Chinese who believe that assimilation consists in shouting in action and in deed, 'We're Americans,'" nonetheless played mahjong without hesitation. In his sociological notes, Lowe titled this man's description as "Assimilation: Pathetic Features: Over-assimilation, 1934," and listed his habits as "smokes cigars, drinks heavily, loves to fish, play poker and ma jong, and drives medium priced, rakish looking automobile."[56] As the only Chinese pastime in the list, mahjong stands out for being a marker of "over-assimilation" despite its Chinese origins. College students also played the game with friends, at parties, as a fundraiser for future events, and at conferences designed to build social ties and a sense of Chinese patriotism among Chinese American students.[57]

Both young and old quickly adopted mahjong. The age of mahjong players still held specific associations, however. Just as the game's new status as a family entertainment did not preclude its ongoing use as a gambling game, mahjong's divergent generational cultures also formed a Venn diagram of coexistence. Louise Leung contrasted "us American-born Chinese" with an older man "playing mah-jongg with his Chinatown cronies."[58] Here, mahjong's meaning was dependent upon the "Old Chinatown" context, despite Leung's own earlier feverish playing "day and night" with her college friends.[59]

New Year's celebrations provide a particularly clear example of how mahjong could be both generationally specific and a possible bridge between generations. During Chinese New Year, gambling is traditionally seen as bringing good luck. As a family game, and as a gambling game, mahjong was played everywhere in homes across generations at this time of year. It is also a time of homecoming, and dispersed Chinese Americans came for visits to Chinatowns. For younger Chinese Americans who struggled with the rigidity of Chinese school and traditional rituals of observance, New Year's "was the one thing on the Chinese side of our existence that appealed to us children."[60] On Chinese New Year, older men gathered from around the region, "some coming in from the country—any point outside of San Francisco is called the country in Chinatown. Mah jongg was played everywhere."[61]

In contrast, American New Year was a time of peer celebrations. Although these parties tended to be less family focused for Chinese Americans, they were often still centered in Chinatown.[62] Second-generation adults would throw mahjong and dance parties, where "the conversation is practically conducted in nothing but English, usually slang of the cheapest variety," Lowe described. "If games are played, the betting tends to be steep. Liquor flows freely, some man inevitably gets drunk, and the party waxes merry loud, ending only around dawn."[63] Older Chinatown residents attended Chinese theater or stayed inside to play mahjong or Chinese dominoes—but those games often lasted all night.[64] These scenes of generational difference and similarity on American New Year's provide a clear picture of how Chinatowns were places of concurrent Americanization and the creation of Chinese American ethnicity.[65]

Not all members of the community, however, found common ground over a mahjong game. While mahjong successfully made the transition into class-based respectability, it did not gain Christian approval as a moral activity. Despite American preconceptions that an anti-gambling Chinese person was oxymoronic, the game's 1920s popular sweep did not successfully penetrate strongly Christian Chinese American communities. Unlike missionaries in China, Chinese American Christian leaders did not launch publicity campaigns against mahjong as a corrupting force. Rather, the game was simply absent from community events and activities of Chinese Christian groups. Recreation in clubs with roots in the YMCA or other Christian affiliations, even for second- and third-generation youth, would involve American sports such as baseball and basketball, philanthropic events, or the ever-respectable Western game of bridge.[66]

Christian concerns over mahjong as an immoral gambling game did not halt its spread among the Chinese American community in part because by the 1920s and 1930s, secular Chinese nationalism and a growing sense of Chinese American group identity increasingly provided an alternative basis for organization. In 1922, the students and intellectuals of the reformist May Fourth Movement in China launched an Antireligious (also known as Anti-Christian) Movement. Although the Chinese YMCA and the YWCA both remained crucial social service organizations well integrated into the community, some anti-missionary sentiment rubbed off on them as well.[67]

Anti-missionary feeling deflected Christian critiques of mahjong as a gambling activity, as the criticism could be read as evidence of imperialism. Religious rejection of gambling, and mahjong by association, entirely stemmed from the Western origins of Christianity and its long-held associations of gambling with immorality. Chinese religious traditions generally did not prohibit gambling.[68] As mahjong gained social mobility it also gained strength as a marker of Chinese culture. Chinese nationalists linked missionaries' admonitions against mahjong with foreign chauvinism and misguided "modernization" that sought to erase Chinese culture in favor of a Western model. A communist writer in the *Chinese Students' Monthly* criticized missionaries who "live in the Middle Kingdom without realizing that it is just as much the 20th Century in China as elsewhere. They want the Chinese to drink coffee instead of tea, to play bridge instead of Mah Jong."[69] In other words, they argued, mahjong should be considered part of a simultaneously modern and timeless Chinese identity.

The National Game of China

During the 1920s and 1930s, mahjong became "the national game of China," on the heels of the creation of a coherent modern Chinese nationalism. The game became emblematic of debates happening in and about China that sought to define what it meant to be Chinese.[70] Nationalists envisioned transforming the country from a past traditional self to a strong and modern nation that would retain an essential Chinese identity. Since the early twentieth century, a movement led initially by urban Chinese intellectuals grew to define China in national terms that transcended home regions and placed Chinese oppression by foreign powers in a transnational context.[71] Five years after Sun Yatsen's revolution in 1911, which was strongly supported with financial and material help from Chinese abroad, the nascent Chinese Republic devolved into regional warlord rule. In the 1920s, increasing violence raged between the Chinese Communists and the Kuomintang Nationalists under Chiang Kai-shek. The Japanese military marched toward war in the early 1930s by first carving off northern territories and establishing the sham government of Manchukuo. In 1937 a bloody full-scale Japanese invasion of China that captured Beijing and Shanghai rapidly unified Chinese Americans—students, Christians, old, and young—and prioritized a shared nationalism.[72] The groundwork, however, was laid earlier. As historian Yong Chen has argued, Chinese transnationalism "manifests itself in the everyday material world in which Chinese Americans have lived and continue to live."[73] Although overtly political discussions and actions defined Chinese nationalism, mahjong was one of many objects that reinforced a shared sense of what it meant to be Chinese.

Even as the game's reputation as "the national game of China" solidified, Chinese discourse indicated acute awareness of mahjong's enormous popularity in the West, as well as how marketers' visions of an essentially Chinese game equated it with a quaint and mystical China.[74] However, within China, links to Chinese culture did not always necessitate stories of ancient origins and timeless Chinese courts. Chinese commentators could reference mahjong's "ancient roots" in the context of the game's predecessors, as opposed to American beliefs in an unchanging premodern Chinese culture.[75]

Searching for ancient roots to create a modern national identity meshed nicely with Chinese nationalist discourse that married the true Chinese nation with a Han ethnic identity and blamed China's weakness on the 300 years of "barbarian Manchus" under the Qing.[76] Intellectuals in China were eager to grab on to symbols of China's "character" as they engaged in vigorous debate over how China ended up as the "sick man of Asia," how to get it out of its predicament, and how to hold on to Chinese identity while doing so. For them, mahjong indicated ancient Chinese wisdom gaining strength on a global stage.[77] Many Chinese commentators embraced the image of the game as "a national treasure," particularly after the global mahjong explosion.[78]

For some commentators, mahjong's status as a national game was far more negative—but they, too, shared the assumption that mahjong said something meaningful about Chinese "essence." In the 1920s, preeminent intellectuals who blamed the collapse of the Chinese Republic on traditional Chinese culture saw mahjong as indicative of supposed negative national characteristics like indulging in leisure and an "'all for me' attitude."[79] In China, mahjong also retained a strong association with its roots in gambling and sexual entertainment, which some critiqued as degenerate. Japan reinforced the game's association with weakening China in 1932 when the Japanese puppet state of Manchukuo used mahjong in its gambling form as a wedge for demoralization, creating a vice-ridden zone in the segregated Chinese quarter while banning gambling and prostitution in the Japanese section.[80]

Ultimately, the root of critiques of mahjong was that it emphasized individual gain rather than group progress, was imbued with a sense of "feudal" pre-Republican China, and thereby hurt the struggling nation.[81] This criticism could be levied against men as well as women.[82] However, it had particular meaning for women because conservative nationalist social reformers in China portrayed women as safeguarding Chinese traditions while still engaging in modern reforms by "redirecting the virtue of self-sacrifice to the nation."[83] In the United States, one line of criticism against female mahjong players engaged Christian Chinese communities as well as the growing push for women's civic activism. Writing from Shanghai to Westerners and Chinese Christians, Roberta Chang addressed what she saw as the problems of women.[84] Chang was an advocate for General and Madame Chiang Kai-shek's New Life Movement, which blended Confucian ideology with Protestantism and nationalism to dictate a set of rules for self-improvement, loyalty, cleanliness, education, and, above all, work on behalf of the nation. In a strong critique of middle-class women, Chang argued that both mahjong-playing women who focused on pleasure and family-focused homemakers neglected their highest duty as nationalists. Recreation, if carefully chosen to enhance women's intellectual and societal engagement, could be "one of the strongest curative measures possible."[85] Assuming that mahjong would only serve petty desires for entertainment or solidify narrow localized bonds, she castigated women who played mahjong.

Chang reflected old and new ideas about women and leisure. As historian Joan Judge contends, across a variety of forms of Chinese nationalisms, the "new woman" ironically recast the old idiom that "'only a woman without talent is virtuous' with the unspoken dictum that only a woman who did not indulge her private talents was patriotic."[86] Educated women were to demonstrate their rejection of individualism through obedience to "a moralistic regime of patriotic virtue."[87] Yet, Chang also reflected a new and bold claim

by and for women as legitimate political actors and as needing "a larger acquaintance with the outside world through education and travel."[88] The New
Life Movement was part of a conservative-inflected effort to prove women as
deserving of equality through their patriotic activities. As Los Angeles branch
president Lily Chan explained, they aimed to "churn the wheel of progress
without jeopardizing the family."[89] Selfish mahjong playing thus not only undercut women's obligation to the national family, but also furthered their exclusion from progress and civic engagement.

As mahjong became ever more established in the fabric of Chinese life,
it was drafted into nationalist discourse and increasingly insistent calls for
Chinese self-determination. Shanghai's stratified semi-colonial society was a
primary target of Chinese nationalists. Resistance increased after the May 30,
1925 massacre of Chinese by British police during a mass protest after a Chinese
union leader was killed while striking against a Japanese factory in Shanghai's
foreign settlement. In 1933, Shanghai residents spoke against the illegal confiscation of a mahjong set and $4 in funds by two officers of the foreign-run
Shanghai municipal police "accompanied by a foreign dressed Chinese,"
linking the game with a rising tide of resistance against foreign dominance.[90]
The complaints were filed by both a merchant and a laborer who were gambling
together in a home, showing the game's cross-class possibilities. In the midst
of warlordism, mahjong sets themselves conveyed nationalist messages of
"Unifying the Land" and "Cultured World" through engravings on the pictorial bone and bamboo "flower" tiles. Rather than chrysanthemums, these
tiles depicted scenes of national modernization and uplift through new technology like electrical poles.[91] By the late 1930s, mahjong craftsmen celebrated
military resistance against the Japanese, featuring early forms of plastic tiles
with finely carved fighter pilots and armed soldiers in uniform.[92]

"Unity" was a call that rang throughout Chinese American student groups
as well. These student organizations mixed Chinese nationals and Chinese
American students in a shared patriotic effort on behalf of China.[93] Chinese
Americans coming of age in the late 1920s and 1930s experienced numerous
push-and-pull factors to Chinese nationalism. For young adults who grew up
strongly identifying as American, entering the adult world of discriminatory
college admissions, economic barriers, and status as perpetual aliens felt like
a betrayal of the American promise.[94] Racism could push them to identify as
Chinese instead, even potentially moving to China altogether, "returning"
to a nation many of them had never seen.[95] Young Chinese American college graduates were already angry at the lack of opportunity that forced them
into wearing costumes in curio shops, as they did during the mahjong craze

of the 1920s.[96] When the Great Depression hit in the 1930s, discrimination exacerbated Chinese Americans' economic marginalization and pushed many into severe poverty. Meanwhile, an embattled China called for engineers and American-trained professionals, promising a meaningful and remunerative future for educated Chinese Americans. In the 1930s, America held the least promise for Chinese Americans at the very moment their "native land" seemed to need them most.[97] By the end of the decade, roughly 20 percent of Chinese Americans born in the United States had "returned" to China.[98]

The growing nationalism shared between students motivated them to meet the challenge of building a diasporic Chinese identity. Students responded to Chinese strife caused by natural disasters and famines, warring factions, and foreign imperialism with a fervent call for unity and support. After the shared experiences of growing up Chinese American, native-born Chinese Americans urged divided Chinese student groups (whose rancor reflected regional hostilities raging in China) to come together. Student associations relied on mahjong and other forms of recreation to create this intra-group unity by bringing young people together in both informal and structured settings. During the fad years of the early 1920s, the game "was the rage with the Chinese USC students; they were at our house playing day and night," remembered Louise Leung.[99] As student nationalism developed, it was also integrated in a more official capacity. Reflecting the religious fervor of nationalism as war with Japan loomed in 1936, the San Francisco Bay Region Chinese Students' Association met "to lay down a foundation for our national salvation activities," as well as create an action plan for the domestic concerns of Chinese Americans. Socializing was part of the program, as "we urgently hope to bring the Chinese students of each school in the bay area to closer contact so that we can be of better acquaintance with one another." Mahjong was one of the activities at the 1936 conference meant to bring students together "in this holy struggle for national existence."[100] Long after the broader American public had shelved their mahjong sets, the game continued to develop a transpacific following as the national Chinese game.

Chinese Americans and transpacific communities like Chinese student associations debated questions of nationalism and identity, but these conversations remained invisible to most Americans. Instead, Orientalist consumerism shaped interactions between Chinatown residents and outsiders amid a changing economic landscape.

Retailing Chinatown

In the early 1930s, the song-and-dance trio "The Three Mah Jongs" performed their way through Los Angeles. Dressed in brocaded "mandarin" robes and pantaloons, the small group heralded a wave of nightclubs with more risqué shows than theirs. These clubs capitalized on the recent repeal of Prohibition to bring white American dollars into Chinese American communities and served as a cultural flashpoint. "The Three Mah Jongs" consisted of two Japanese American sisters, Dorothy and Helen Toy, and Paul Wing, a Chinese American man. Over the following decade this kind of grouping would become increasingly rare as anti-Japanese sentiment reached fever pitch in Chinese communities and, especially after Pearl Harbor, among white Americans as well. Dorothy and Helen had already changed their longer Japanese surname of Takahashi to the "easier," diminutive, and less ethnically marked name of "Toy."[101] Soon the sisters split up their act and Dorothy joined Paul as "Toy and Wing." He later recalled, "the name itself implies we're Chinese, and your costume is all-Chinese and your music is all-Chinese." The nightclubs were utterly American, but they marketed an exotic foreignness through sexualized displays of Asian women's bodies, and a faux-Chinese aesthetic reminiscent of the Chinese opera-style costumes worn by 1920s mahjong matrons.[102]

Many community members objected to the Chinatown nightclubs and rejected the women who danced in them. However, promoters like Charlie Low of San Francisco's famed Forbidden City later argued that "old fashioned" propriety was "backwards." Instead, the revealing dance numbers at his club demonstrated "that we're on an equal basis. Why, Chinese have limbs just as pretty as anyone else!"[103] The clubs asserted Chinese inclusion in the increasing public sexuality that was part of modern American culture while also capitalizing on the novelty of difference and the long-standing sexualization of Asian women. No longer explicitly racialized as Chinatown sex workers, however, this sexual economy merged with a burgeoning mainstream American aesthetic of dancing girls. Despite their initial resistance, by the mid-1940s many middle-class Chinese Americans joined the thousands of white nightclub customers.[104] In the late 1930s, newspapers also featured young Chinese American women urging readers to boycott Japanese silk stockings, to prevent the lucrative silk trade from funneling American consumer dollars to the Japanese military as it committed atrocities against Chinese civilians.[105] They posed like showgirls, displaying their legs clad in US-made lisle cotton stockings. Whether for personal profit or consumer politics, Chinese women's bodies were part of appealing to white Americans'

FIGURE 6.3 Dorothy [Takahashi] Toy, Paul Wing, and Helen [Takahashi] Toy, as they appeared as "The Three Mah Jongs" in the 1930s. Their embroidered costumes and button hat echoed the long-established image of traditional Chinese clothing in the United States, while the women's hairstyles, makeup, and their song-and-dance act situated them squarely in modern American culture. Estate of Dorothy Toy Fong.

pocketbooks through marketing Chinese culture as of the modern West and exotic East simultaneously. Because strategies for economic survival and for promoting inclusion as Americans both involved reaching out to white Americans, the line between the two often blurred.[106]

Chinatowns had long been spaces of interaction with non-Chinese outsiders. They stood in the popular imagination as exotic districts. That imaginative power could be an economic and cultural asset. It also reinforced stereotypes of Chinese Americans as perpetually foreign or inherently different from Americans, ideas that fostered social, legal, and economic exclusion. Slumming, whereby middle-class outsiders journeyed through urban areas like Chinatowns that were known for illicit behavior and racially marked as non-white, had grown as an industry since the late nineteenth century.[107] A 1926 guidebook for New York Chinatown slummers described the souvenirs for sale to "satisfy the folks back home in Skeneateles or Saginaw City that the possessor has actually been among the joss houses and opium joints of the Manhattan home of the Celestials."[108] A visitor might even get to glimpse "a place where Mah Jong, or Pa Cheuk, is played, with utter seriousness, by these stolid faces." Although white slummers would have already known mahjong as a pastime of American society, the sensationalized Chinatown milieu rendered the game foreign—and would hopefully impress the "folks back home" with the traveler's worldliness.

Merchants and civic leaders led the efforts to optimize the double-edged exoticism of Chinatown by drawing in outside customers, first as an economic survival strategy and increasingly as an appeal for relief efforts in China as Japanese aggression escalated. As a respectable Chinese game, mahjong would be welcomed as one of many imported goods bringing white shoppers to Chinatown. Although the bulk of mahjong sets were distributed through large department stores, major Chinese American and transpacific importers like Andrew Kan and the Nanyang Brothers sold sets as part of larger shipments of Chinese goods, with their own international connections.[109] When Washington society became all aflutter in the winter of 1922 for the hot new game, they ordered sets from China as well as from curio dealers in San Francisco and New York, and reported "Chinatown is being carefully searched for the markers."[110] The Mah-Jongg Sales Company had also looked to expand their market to Chinese American retailers by advertising wholesale prices and a Chinese representative in the major Chinese-language San Francisco newspaper *Chung Sai Yat Po*.[111] Mahjong could be both familiar and exotic, contributing to a larger effort to foster inclusion into American society through a sense of appealing and commodified difference as opposed to assimilation.

In the 1930s, Chinatown merchants hoped that "picturesque" redevelopment would foster more profitable and positive tourism. The push for "Oriental atmosphere" built on earlier redevelopment campaigns.[112] After the devastating 1906 San Francisco earthquake and fire razed "Old Chinatown," the rebuilt Chinatown incorporated urban planning to "clean up" the area and added architectural elements inspired by the popular Chinese Village pagodas first exhibited at the 1904 St. Louis World's Fair.[113] Bazaars owned by native-born merchants soon hired white architects to create "emphatically Oriental" structures, crowning Chinatown's main shopping street with pagoda-topped beacons of exotic consumerism.[114] Later, a Depression-stricken Chinatown looked toward the 1939 International Exposition in San Francisco as a chance to draw much-needed tourist dollars. In Los Angeles, redevelopment meant that a declining "Old Chinatown" was demolished to make way for the new Union Station, with its residents evicted and its businesses relocated to a "New Chinatown," complete with a neon entry sign, pagoda rooflines, and restaurants hosting mahjong and cocktail parties.[115] Although designed for tourist traffic, it was also intended to be a place for Chinese residents.

As the Depression lengthened and Japanese aggression increased overseas, Chinese American civic leaders and citizens felt compelled to present a respectable front as a way to combat discrimination and facilitate inclusion. A family-friendly Chinatown environment also encouraged tourism and shoppers, providing money for survival in the United States as well as much-needed remittances to family and political causes in China.[116] "To some, Chinatown holds all the glamour, the mysticism, the exotic lure of the Far East," the *Chinese Digest* editor Chingwah Lee reminded Chinatown merchants. "They who come will want to remember Chinatown. They will want to BUY."[117]

Mahjong embodied the proud links to China that Chinese Americans sought to promote in familiar and attractive form for white American consumers. In 1936, a short film created by the progressive Harmon Foundation and the American Council of the Institute of Pacific Relations promoted a nonthreatening vision of interracial friendship.[118] In it, a Chinese American boy enters a white boy's home and fills him in on the history of "many things, some so well known to us that their origin is forgotten. In your own home," the narrator instructed viewers, "you daily use and enjoy China's gifts." Among them were "Chinese playing cards, ancient ancestors of modern cards, dominoes, and mahjong." The film, which was still promoted a decade later to promote "intercultural understanding" in schools, thus portrayed "China's gifts" as utterly familiar everyday objects, lumping mahjong in with American playing cards.[119] The vision of happy integration and innocent childhood provided a sharp contrast to representations a decade earlier of mahjong as an entry point for a disruptive Chinese influence.

Representations of China reflected a reorientation in the 1930s toward what historian Karen Leong has called "the China Mystique," a romantic vision of a stoic and quaint people, which would later gain strength through the wartime alliance between the United States and China against Japan.[120] The tremendous popularity of Pearl S. Buck's Pulitzer Prize–winning 1931 novel *The Good Earth* and its on-screen portrayal six years later promoted and exemplified this shift. Meanwhile, Fu Manchu as an evil abductor of white women found a more benevolent counterpart in the fictional detective Charlie Chan. The new portrayals still involved two-dimensional stereotypes and feminized "Orientals," however. White actors in what would later be called "yellowface" played the key film roles. Nonetheless, the shift was unmistakable and promised inclusion, though not equality, in an increasingly important vision of the United States as a multiracial democracy.[121] Mahjong was one piece of larger efforts by Chinese Americans to foster inclusion and economic survival through commodified cultural outreach.[122]

7

Asian Exclusion and Enforced Leisure

MEN CROWDED AROUND the table where the mahjong game was in full swing. Others gathered near the phonograph spinning Cantonese opera records. Domino players shuffled Chinese coins nearby; the mahjong players had smaller piles of their own. The high window of this former bathroom let in enough light to play but offered no view of the ocean. Just as well, since the men could not venture past the fences anyway. Stuck indefinitely in the immigration detention center at Angel Island just offshore San Francisco, they waited for their interrogations to begin, end, or be decided. The hours were long and the company changed from one week to the next as young and old came and went through the detention center's locked doors. Rumors lingered in the air about a man whom they deported, a food riot, a woman who hanged herself in the bathroom. All over the Chinese barracks, the walls sang silently with poems of longing and frustration carved into the wooden boards. The players focused for the moment on the game. It was 1930.

Twelve years later, a father and teenage daughter sat at a mahjong game held on a plain wooden table. They invited the neighboring couple who had recently taught them the game to join them; they had heard the couple arguing the night before through the thin wooden walls. The room in the hastily erected barracks at the Tanforan racetrack was a far cry from their 1920s bungalow home in Berkeley, and they dreaded having to use the shared latrines, but they considered themselves luckier than the hundreds of other Japanese American families who had to move into the stink and filth of converted horse stalls. The girl's mother, working in the camp vegetable garden, had carefully swept the threshold, hung pots on the wall, and drawn curtains over the plate glass window. No coins appeared with the mahjong tiles.

Between rounds they discussed the results of the camp baseball game, the spate of diarrhea caused by a mess hall dinner and the old woman who died from it, and the latest news about when and where officials might move them next. The players focused for the moment on the game. It was 1942.

For the first half of the twentieth century, Asians in America encountered an acute tension between inclusion and exclusion. Individuals of Chinese and Japanese heritage, resident by migration or American by birth, shared experiences of segregation and incarceration. Their positions were indelibly shaped by the twists and turns of geopolitics between the United States and China or Japan, as well as American domestic politics around economic competition felt or feared by white Americans. Geopolitical relationships had profound consequences for policies that targeted one national group or another, particularly those focused on movement—whether migration across borders or residence during wartime. American concepts of race and ethnicity dynamically fractured and solidified—sometimes hardening distinctions between the meaning of Chinese and Japanese descent while offering more inclusion to one or another, and sometimes unifying them under a racial understanding of essential difference that could never be assimilated. Chinese and Japanese Americans and immigrants also positioned themselves in opposition to each other for reasons beyond American politics, related especially to China's relative weakness and vulnerability to Western and Japanese aggression, and Japan's rising militarism and invasions of China.

The detention of Chinese Americans at the Pacific border and Japanese American incarceration in World War II camps were the physical manifestations of exclusion. Immigration exclusions that initially targeted Chinese laborers in particular hardened national borders and crystallized Chinese migrants' tenuous position in the country. Immigration policy and enforcement mandated that their claims for inclusion were inherently suspect. The place that enacted American policy for the majority of would-be migrants on the Pacific Coast was Angel Island Immigration Station, where thousands of Chinese applicants for entry were detained and interrogated in the early twentieth century. Detained male migrants played mahjong to carve out social spaces in a dehumanizing context, though women found themselves with far fewer options. Tracing mahjong at the Angel Island Immigration Station reveals overlooked and diverse survival strategies among Chinese migrants. Their experiences redefine the particular difficulties posed, ironically, by leisure. Far from relaxation or frivolity, the enforced leisure of detention between borders was a crushing psychological experience of anxiety and boredom.

Although the strength of the modernizing Japanese state had protected Japanese migrants relative to the subjects of the crumbling Chinese empire, in the early twentieth century fear of the rising military threat posed by Japan combined with California agriculturalist resentments against Japanese immigrant farmers and their American children. Japanese Americans became a new target of immigration exclusion and legal disadvantage. When war broke out between the United States and Japan with the bombing of Pearl Harbor in 1941, American sympathies already lay with Chinese victims of Japanese imperialism. Japanese Americans felt exclusion most intensely when the US government forcibly removed from the West Coast all persons of Japanese descent—two-thirds of them American citizens by birth—and incarcerated them in confinement facilities inaccurately dubbed "internment camps."[1] In a history that echoes the experiences of Chinese detainees on Angel Island in previous decades, incarcerated first- and second-generation Japanese Americans played mahjong during the war as a release from the pressures of disruption and anxiety, both to build community and to gamble. These two roles did not always easily coexist, as community concerns over gambling sometimes resulted in attempts to curtail mahjong.

Despite their differences, Chinese and Japanese migrants and their American children occupied a shared location in an American racial framework that placed them outside the possibility of inclusion through cultural and political assimilation, regardless of long residence or native birth. Even as social scientists challenged earlier fears about cultural and biological blending, most Americans consistently held Asian people apart as inherently foreign and often threatening. Detention as a measure of national defense, enacted at Angel Island and in incarceration camps, separated detainees from the norms of work, family, and sociability. Even as the United States screened working-class immigrants for their risk of becoming "public charges," the government enforced leisure on those incarcerated. Unchosen leisure thus became a problem to be solved.

Mahjong in Detention

The design of the Angel Island Immigration Station in San Francisco Bay accentuated migrants' marginal status in the United States. At the administration building, applicants were slowly shuffled through semi-public medical exams, then into literally caged areas where they waited to apply for admittance. Migrants were assigned beds in rooms crowded with rows of metal bunks; each row had narrow berths stacked two or three high and two across. It was a place of tentative waiting punctuated by a bureaucratic dance of verbal interrogations. As historian Adam McKeown has described, detention thrust migrants into "a betwixt-and-between period of invisibility, unfamiliarity, and the suspension of normal relationships and responsibilities."[2] It was a period of isolation generally without, McKeown argues, "relaxation or game-playing." Yet the history of mahjong shows that playfulness could in fact be underwritten by otherwise intolerable conditions. It could be an element of survival. Further, following who could access such strategies reveals social positions that differentiated the shared experience of detention.

Over the history of the immigration station's existence from 1910 to 1940, approximately 100,000 mostly Chinese men and boys experienced life in detention there. This number represented nearly two-thirds of the Chinese-descent population who were admitted to the United States as "new immigrants, returning residents, and US citizens" during the same three decades.[3] The station's creation evolved from the administrative apparatus that sprang initially from a series of laws targeting Chinese immigrants as the first "illegal aliens."[4] Severe anti-Chinese immigration restrictions passed in the late nineteenth century, first as a ten-year ban on laborers signed into federal law in 1882, had foreclosed legal possibilities for most migrants.

The ban was never as airtight as it appeared. Over the seven decades of the "exclusion era," more Chinese people entered the United States than in the forty years of immigration before exclusion.[5] The initial ban made exceptions for "exempt classes" of merchants and close family relations of citizens by birth. Determined immigrants, lured by often overinflated hopes of wealth and pushed by ongoing turmoil in China, continued to enter by establishing themselves as merchants (such as by purchasing shares in a restaurant) or through genuine or fabricated family connections.[6] Of course, no migrants arrived as an abstract "class." Rather, they arrived as individuals, scrutinized by officials to identify their accurate categorization.[7] Even students or merchants exempt from exclusion could not simply pass through. In 1924, however, the Johnson-Reed Act curtailed all "Asiatics" along with the Chinese and blocked previous exempt classes. It sought to also reduce numbers of Mexican and Russian (especially Jewish) immigrants, while specifically strengthening restrictions against aliens ineligible for naturalized citizenship, a condition that applied solely to Asians.

Geopolitics and class shaped the treatment of migrants. Housed, sometimes for months at a time in the island's prison-like barracks, they came from varied ethnicities and from all over the world. Racial segregation between Asians and whites remained a priority, implemented through the detention

center's design and administration. Barracks separated residents by nationality and gender, with Japanese, South Asian, and Korean men grouped together and Chinese men kept separate. Japanese and Chinese women (far
fewer in number than the men) were soon housed in a separate building with
a supervisory matron. The Chinese formed the largest single group and were
also the most likely to be detained the longest and scrutinized most closely.
Though subject to similar racial bias and segregation, Japanese migrants
moved through Angel Island expeditiously because they were associated
with a strong and militaristic government that helped the process by issuing
identifying documents.[8]

Among the detained Chinese were American-born citizens seeking to
return home after time abroad, foreign-born wives of citizens or merchants
(before the increased restrictions of 1924), and children of established
migrants, as well as the immigration officials' worst fear: "paper sons,"
or those posing as blood relatives through an elaborate procedure of
purchased documents and assumed identity. The 1906 San Francisco earthquake and fire that destroyed public documents, including birth records,
had made falsification more possible. Many resident immigrants claimed
that they had been born in San Francisco and were thereby citizens; "paper
sons" crossed the border by purchasing a familial identity connecting them
with an American citizen. After the 1924 Immigration Act foreclosed
other possibilities, the pressure to masquerade as direct family members of
American citizens by birth increased.

A logic of exclusion animated the procedures at Angel Island, but in
fact most migrants made it through to the United States. The immigration
halls' plaster walls held a complex reality wherein individuals experienced a
maddeningly cryptic process of interrogation and examination. Because the
results had little to do with the actual identity of the detainee, and everything to do with his ability to navigate the rituals of interrogation and formal
interactions, an individual's best hope was to rely on information networks
of preparation for interviews and then endure a soul-deadening wait for
an uncertain outcome.[9] In 1923, in the midst of mahjong's rapid spread, a
Chinese American merchant familiar with navigating Angel Island warned
a relative: "I hear there is new equipment at the immigration station. There
are some wooden pieces like majiang [tiles] that the officers will ask you to
use to demonstrate the layout of your village and what your house is like."[10]
Detainees needed to produce minute details of their homes and families: how
many steps led to the front door, what cardinal directions their doors faced.[11]

Accuracy could not be measured and thus was not effective—only consistency mattered. The uncertainty and apparent capriciousness of it all stoked the anxiety of waiting.

From the earliest days of Angel Island, men turned to gambling as something to do during their hours of boredom. With enormous variability, gambling could encompass a range of stakes and games. Most immigrants had very little money, and their empty pockets and economic motivations for immigrating kept some from gambling at all.[12] However, games of luck and skill could also be played for low stakes, and they were an entrenched activity to pass the time and build social bonds among Chinese men. The dynamic and shifting nature of the population meant that social groups were never static. "You gambled with what you had," one detainee remembered, "even one cent if that's what you had."[13] Before the 1920s, the predominant games were pai gow and fantan, betting games played with dominoes, coins, and other small objects.[14] By 1921, however, the surging popularity of mahjong brought it into the men's quarters at Angel Island. Officers stationed at Angel Island were primarily concerned with preventing interviewees from accessing "coaching notes" and in ensuring detainees peacefully followed their prescribed schedule of mealtime movement. They generally did not intervene in gambling groups.[15]

The fact that migrants had mahjong sets at all indicated the networks and organizations male detainees created, even in the midst of constant flux. It is unlikely that many migrants would have had the means and desire to devote a portion of their one allotted bag at detention to a bulky, heavy mahjong set. Rather, they purchased sets with pooled funds transferred in turn to contacts on shore by the Angel Island Liberty Association, a self-governing organization (*zizhihui* 自治會) that detainees formed in 1922 out of frustration with substandard and discriminatory conditions.[16] They successfully negotiated to have officials provide Chinese detainees with toilet paper and soap, which all other groups had already been receiving.[17] The Association officers also played a key role in passing coaching notes to detainees, often smuggled in through food served by the kitchen staff. The zizhihui emerged from a longer tradition of gendered public leadership in which countrymen would create a modicum of fellowship, order, and enforcement.[18]

The mahjong sets joined other resources available for men to pass the time in a recreation room that had been converted from a bathroom, including Chinese-language newspapers from San Francisco and Cantonese opera gramophone records.[19] "Down there on Angel Island . . . we were all very depress[ed] and worried," Mr. Mock told an interviewer nearly five decades after his experience as an eighteen-year-old detainee in 1937. Asked how he tried, as he said, "to forget some of the frustration and depression," Mock remembered, "Well, there was music, a library, and we play mah-jong."[20] Although sources are limited, it seems possible that some men may have encountered mahjong for the first time on Angel Island in the early 1920s, though the game was also spreading very quickly in China.

Coordination did not necessarily mean consensus about socially accept-able activities. While betting games such as pai gow were censured by the Angel Island men's self-governing association in the early 1930s, mahjong could also stand as a non-gambling game, depending on how it was played. "The conditions [at Angel Island] were very bad," the 1932 Association pres-ident remembered. "Many Chinese immigrants gambled—fan tan, pai gow. As chairman, I didn't like it because a lot of people lost with all kinds of ad-verse results. We talked it over and decided to forbid gambling. No fan tan or pai gow, but mahjong was alright. And even mahjong had its limits."[21] Mahjong could allow for a lower monetary bar for entry, as "most of us had no money, we play[ed] mah-jong for fun or for very little money," another

FIGURE 7.1 In the Angel Island Immigration Center museum exhibit, the recreated rec-reation room holds a range of entertainments that detained Chinese men relied upon to pass anxious days of waiting. A record player indicates the Cantonese opera music detainees listened to while reading, smoking, and playing games. A *weiqi* board and dominoes lay on the table next to mahjong tiles. Angel Island State Park, CA.

migrant explained.[22] With the transient nature of detainee leadership, no consistent Association policy remained.

As indicated by its exemption from regulated gambling games, mahjong developed a unique ability to cross into a potentially respectable genre. Although it was still a game of luck and skill that could siphon away valuable resources from its players, mahjong was granted the possibility of respectability—at least for men. (Younger boys were not always welcome to enter the smoky rooms and gray zone of gambling mahjong occupied.[23]) Women, however, did not have access to the game at Angel Island. Lee Puey You was detained for an unusually long period of almost two years before being deported in 1940 when she was twenty-four years old. She later described, "Day in and day out, eat and sleep. Many people cried. Everyone there cried at least once." When asked if the women had options like gambling and music as did the men, Lee's answer was clear: "No, no mah jongg, no recreation."[24]

Through the physical space, the nature of immigration restrictions, and the related interrogations, detention was as much a gendered experience as a racialized one.[25] Men and women were rigidly segregated. Officials did not want husbands and wives to be able to communicate during their detentions and interrogations. Even older boys traveling with their mothers could be separated. Residential restrictions and regimented schedules created a bizarre and prison-like existence.[26] Times when detainees were allowed to move around the grounds were tightly controlled, with each group traveling under guard to dining areas. Women and children were allowed occasional supervised walks around the island, but Chinese men never passed beyond the fences. Men could access a (racially segregated) recreation yard, but Chinese women were not allowed to spend time there.

Their status as female filtered women's entire relationship to the immigration process.[27] Because Chinese women at the time generally lacked the educational and professional identities to claim the pre-1924 exempt category of merchants or students, their immigration rights depended upon male relatives; after the 1924 Immigration Act their opportunities shrunk further.[28] Immigration barriers combined with economic and cultural patterns in China resulted in far fewer women making the trip than men. Women needed to convince interrogators that the relationships they claimed were genuine and that the men involved were legitimate (American-born) citizens or merchants. Interrogators targeted men as potential laborers and fraudulent sons, and women as false wives and possible prostitutes.[29] Grueling immigration interrogations, which could last many hours and extend over days, questioned women based on the details of their alleged husbands' families rather than their own.[30]

Perhaps the biggest challenges of daily life at Angel Island were psychological, and they created a painful, insidious burden. Detainees emphasized again and again the difficulties of simply passing the time. For women, the toll of waiting and worrying was borne without the distraction of recreation. Echoing many others, Mrs. Jew remembered that in 1922 the women had "Nothing. You had to preoccupy yourself anyway you could."[31] The reasons for this discrepancy were partly logistical. There was no self-governing association among the women, likely due in part to fewer opportunities to develop leadership skills, as well as barriers to accessing necessary resources. Women were not traditionally involved in family or hometown associations. The male zizhihui maintained itself through funds collected from immigrants. While many had little to give, returning migrants familiar with Angel Island often were able to give more and understood the importance of the Association.[32] They were able to perform the important functions of contacting attorneys, facilitating the delivery of interrogation coaching notes, and acquiring goods and news from Chinatown through their contacts in San Francisco.[33] Female migrants generally lacked direct access to the financial and social capital inherent in the Association's success, and they were only a small percentage of the migrants coming through Angel Island. Cultural barriers for female participation in gambling also overlapped with lack of funds. Though many migrants were too poor to engage in serious gambling, on Angel Island some men had wealth they brought with them from working in Mexico, while others had "tea money" sent to them from stateside relatives and clansmen.[34]

In addition, Protestant ideas of moral recreation for women, which did not include games, filtered available resources. Besides family members, female detainees had access to contacts outside Angel Island via the white American women who provided humanitarian relief along with Christian teachings. Female recreation was not high on the list of social or moral values for either Chinese or Christian American traditions. An old Chinese saying declared that women who could not embroider were unfit for marriage, for "if poor she cannot contribute to the support of the family; if wealthy, she does not know what to do with her leisure."[35] Similarly, middle-class Americans and Protestants assumed the necessity and importance of women's time channeled into productive labor like handcrafts.[36] Sewing and knitting fit within ideas of Christian respectability and could still facilitate personal relationships, at least when the scarce materials were available.[37] Mahjong would not have fit the criteria of productive and ladylike behavior. Christians also associated mahjong with gambling longer than did American society at large; Protestant missionaries would certainly not have brought in anything of questionable morality like a gambling game. When asked if the women had "any games like mah jong" in 1928, Mrs. Leong replied incredulously: "Are you kidding?" and emphasized the lack of options to pass the time.[38]

Mahjong's absence from the women's quarters throughout the 1920s also demonstrates women's enhanced need to appear respectable while on Angel Island. Respectability had enormous consequences for them, influencing their social position within the Chinese immigrant community as well as their legal position in the eyes of the American government.[39] Working-class women from any nationality faced scrutiny by immigration inspectors for "moral turpitude," and women suspected of immorality met a barrage of extremely intimate questions about their sexual behavior. Deeply held suspicions of Chinese prostitution compounded the issue for Chinese women, who could be suspected of being a prostitute "just by appearance."[40] Immigration commissioners could directly ask Angel Island employees and interrogation interpreters if they had observed whether a migrant woman had, during her stay, "behaved in a manner that might lead you to believe she was a respectable family woman."[41] Between immigrants, as well, respectability denoted class standing and social power. Both American and Chinese elite assumptions reinforced the logic that the legitimate ability to pass through national boundaries was embedded in and expressed through intrinsic individual traits.[42] Before the 1924 restrictions, merchants highlighted their own privileged position within immigration exclusions by complaining that their wives and children were housed in the same dormitory room as prostitutes.[43] Because mahjong had been strongly associated with courtesan culture in the urban centers of China, its illicit reputation may have lingered longer in the conservative environment of Angel Island.[44]

Chinese men also faced social consequences for their reputations, but their reputations were built more upon reliability in business dealings and fulfillment of filial duties than sexual or social propriety.[45] Gambling held a nebulous position in regard to masculine respectability and was a long-established male social activity. At Angel Island, that meant there were lower social stakes for men to associate with others who might be extreme or reckless gamblers, as opposed to women's potential guilt by association with shady characters.

Not until the late 1930s would some women enjoy games of mahjong on Angel Island, over a decade after the men. There would never be a smoky gambling room off-limits to children, as there was for the male detainees. Instead, mahjong entered the women's shared and crowded mixed-use space.

Only a few years before the end of Angel Island's role as a detention center, women could finally play mahjong and receive a single Chinese-language newspaper, though even then both were sporadic and inconsistent.[46] Although Chinese women's roles were changing quickly amid a transpacific movement for women's rights and participation in the modern world, on Angel Island they remained sidelined by their relatively small numbers and constrained by the heightened need to communicate a conservative respectability in order to gain access to the United States.

In 1940, fire destroyed part of the detention center at Angel Island and the government moved the facilities inland to San Francisco.[47] By then, Chinese migrants faced a different and less hostile set of American stereotypes of Chinese people than they had in the 1920s, but their legal ability to cross borders was just as restricted. A few years later, in the midst of the new wartime alliance with China, Franklin Roosevelt signed the 1943 Chinese Exclusion Repeal Act. The symbolism was significant. Although the number of Chinese immigrants allowed under the quota was tiny, the new law allowed for the naturalized citizenship of Chinese immigrants.[48] The rules of exclusion and conditional inclusion that had underwritten Angel Island's maze of detention and interrogation had loosened for Chinese Americans.[49] Yet the racial ideas that drove it endured, even as the homogenizing idea of Asiatics fractured in the face of wartime Chinese allies and Japanese enemies.

Mahjong in Incarceration

The improving position of Chinese Americans in the United States during World War II stood in direct contrast to the effect that wartime geopolitics had on Japanese Americans. After Japan bombed Pearl Harbor on December 7, 1941, Japanese Americans were thrust into years of great uncertainty and anxiety over their future, with periods of episodic stability and makeshift community life in incarceration. In 1942, virtually all individuals of Japanese ancestry who lived on the West Coast—as over 80 percent of Japanese Americans did—were forcibly expelled from the "Potential Military Zone," a decision based upon long-held beliefs of the inherent unassimilability of Asian people. As a public brochure by the War Relocation Authority (WRA) explained, "military considerations can not permit the risk of putting an un-assimilated or partly assimilated people to an unpredictable test during an invasion by an army of their own race."[50] The WRA pushed neighborhoods, families, and individuals first into makeshift assembly centers, where they were held for months en route to hastily erected long-term incarceration "camps" (which the authorities preferred to call "relocation centers"), and then between different camps. In the midst of it all, mahjong played a relatively minor but unique role among multiple sources of recreation.

Mahjong functioned for Japanese Americans as a way to pass the time amid anxiety and enforced leisure. Through play, it served to build cohesion within families, forced communities, and between camps in the face of massive disruption. In short-term assembly centers and in long-term camps, officials went on periodic campaigns to confiscate potentially subversive items, but mahjong was not flagged. For the American government, the priority was evaluating and restricting activities and materials deemed political, with the goal of preventing support for Japan or subversive activities. Their determination was often capricious and usually targeted items with Japanese language, screened with the help of second-generation Nisei interpreters.[51] In this context, mahjong was deemed apolitical as a game that was solidly within an Allied landscape of American and Chinese cultural contexts.[52] Americans did not associate mahjong with Japanese culture, even though mahjong had also been in Japan since the early twentieth century.[53]

Wartime was not the first time Japanese Americans played mahjong. Richard Nishimoto, one of a handful of researchers who studied their own imprisoned communities, chronicled mahjong's earlier ebbs and flows in the large Japanese American community in Los Angeles.[54] He described how in the late 1920s, after the broader American fad waned, mahjong was especially popular as a middle-class parlor game among the Issei, or immigrant generation. It then "deteriorated into a device of gambling" for " 'bums' and 'Nisei [second-generation] undesirables' " in mahjong clubs in the early Depression, before it eventually returned to the middle class as a low-stakes game, albeit in diminished popularity.[55] Before the war, then, Japanese American mahjong players had developed patterns that embedded the game in a specifically American context. Across the ocean, although mahjong players had been developing their own culture in Japan since the 1920s, for some Japanese nationalists like Colonel Saburo Aizawa the "fad of mahjong" was part of a "Westernism which was 'corrupting the youth of the country.' "[56] Interestingly, Aizawa associated mahjong with Western degeneration, not with Chinese targets of imperialist expansion.

Confinement inspired a reengagement with mahjong among Japanese Americans. In the rush of packing for their forced removal, Japanese Americans dusted off their mahjong sets and cleared the stock in stores in Little Tokyo. "On the eve of departure with the army escort the Japanese packed the paraphernalia of 'go', of 'shogi', of Mah Jong, of poker, and of hana," Nishimoto wrote: "They knew then what they were going to do when they arrived at these assembly or relocation centers."[57] Their forethought may have been for naught in the end, since in the severe space constraints posed by transporting and housing thousands of forced migrants almost overnight, individuals were only permitted to bring to the assembly centers what they could carry.[58] Nonetheless, individuals found ways to access mahjong sets. At least one player painstakingly carved his own tiles at Rohwer in Arkansas.[59] Others had mahjong sets sent to them from relatives at other camps.[60]

Those who did not already know the game often learned it in the camps. Doris Hayashi's family "had been quite isolated from the Japanese community throughout the pre-evacuation period," choosing to associate primarily with their white neighbors in Berkeley, California.[61] Once thrust into the horse stalls and makeshift barracks at the nearby Tanforan Racetrack assembly center to await their fates, Hayashi's parents socialized with their new church community and through activities such as mahjong. Notably, Hayashi's Nisei mother held prejudices against the Chinese (as well as Jews and African Americans), but played mahjong with other Japanese Americans seemingly without association.[62] Her father, an elite Japanese immigrant, learned mahjong from a neighbor, and eventually helped teach their children's friends how to play as well.[63] Mahjong crossed class lines in the forced communities of "relocation."

Both inmates and WRA authorities saw organized recreation as a way to make camp life "livable," and they encouraged peaceable community building while the usual parental and social controls were in upheaval.[64] Once they arrived at the camps, strained living conditions and disrupted lives demanded extensive work. At Poston in Arizona, for example, dust constantly bedeviled residents, while at Rohwer in Arkansas the rainy season brought mud and mosquitoes.[65] Unlike detainees on Angel Island, incarcerated Japanese Americans had significant demands on their time, from cultivating gardens to creating newspapers to teaching school and running for office. Most camp jobs were dedicated to feeding thousands of mouths on a strict government budget that aimed below the forty-five cents a day allotted for soldiers.[66] Committees needed to be formed, ground prepared, and produce planted. One task of the committees was to address the problem of leisure.

Mahjong provided one answer. Recreation departments at Tanforan and Tule Lake in California, Jerome and Rohwer in Arkansas, and Granada in Colorado all sponsored official tournaments joined by both men and women.[67] These bouts, played without stakes but for small amounts of prize money or merchandise, built on the tournament culture that thrived in

Japanese American communities a decade earlier. Outside of tournaments, Japanese-language pages in the camp newspapers advertised "mahjong meets" at Tule Lake, while the Issei recreation group at Topaz debated whether to host "discussions and talent shows," or "just games, such as checkers, mah-jong, cards, ping-pong, baseball, etc."[68] Nisei advocated for retaining the mahjong club at Gila amid funding cuts in 1943, "realizing the importance of recreation for Isseis in the relocation life."[69] Peer socialization became the norm as cramped quarters made domestic space less conducive to family togetherness.[70] Young adult organizations also sought "to create fellowship" with "card games, mah jong and tete a tete."[71] The Young Buddhist Association at Heart Mountain in Wyoming organized a "get-together and fellowship" with games including mahjong, while mahjong entertained the "Working Girls" group at Gila in Arizona.[72]

Although observers often described mahjong as primarily an older Issei men's game, sources including diaries and records from tournaments and meets depict a much more diverse following. In a classic formulation, a brochure about the Amache camp in Colorado listed mahjong as an activity of "elder men," along with Japanese games and reading. Women, the brochure described, were occupied with productive leisure activities like dressmaking and knitting.[73] Certainly, women were likely a minority in tournaments and gambling halls. Yet at the same camp, a woman nonetheless ranked among the top five mahjong tournament competitors.[74] Issei women found themselves with less domestic work in the context of cafeteria meals and small living quarters, so, in addition to the many tasks of making a new life and community, they turned to adult education and various forms of recreation.[75] Both young and old who did not enter the camps knowing how to play mahjong learned the game during their stay. Particularly among the younger, American-born Nisei generation, mahjong was part of an esteemed set of social skills. The Topaz camp newspaper profiled one young woman as "ne plus ultra in a wife, companion, and mother."[76] Her "social poise and grace" was marked by her accomplishments in "mah jong, business, karuta [a Japanese card game], horseback riding, dancing, homemaking, handicrafts, and domestic arts," along with the Japanese fluency valued by Issei. In this rendition, mahjong was part of a modern Japanese American ethos in which even respectable young women could combine American and Japanese values and win the admiration of both immigrant and American-born generations.

In incarceration, mahjong's dual roles as community builder and as a gambling game coexisted, sometimes in tension. After Pearl Harbor, Japanese Americans faced property damage, loss of jobs and wealth, harassment, and

terrifying rumors of murders and rape. In this time of uncertainty and upheaval, Japanese Americans first experienced what would become an ongoing period of enormous anxiety. Mahjong became one form of recreation
that helped pass the hours, sometimes returning to the adrenaline-stoked
gambling table. "In effect," Nishimoto explained, "the revival of gambling was
an escape on one hand and a means of 'killing time' on the other hand."[77]
The temporary (and especially miserable) assembly centers like Tanforan saw
an increase in high-stakes mahjong games and resurgent gambling bosses.
During the contentious first year at Poston in Arizona, one of the most populous camps, gambling was on the rise again.

Camp communities at Tanforan and Poston responded to what they
saw as an outbreak of gambling. Residents felt little control over their lives,
from the prescribed cafeteria meals to rules over shared clotheslines, and
communities debated what norms to establish and how to enforce them.[78]
At Tanforan, although the chief of police did not regulate any games, the
residents' council advocated the prohibition of "certain games that are conducive to gambling," including mahjong along with poker.[79] Within the de facto
regulatory structures that corresponded to the shared barracks and camp
regions, Issei and Nisei leadership could assert some internal regulations.
Despite the localized prohibition, however, families and friends continued
playing mahjong for little or no stakes, without hesitation.[80]

At Poston, concern over gambling erupted in conjunction with the camp's
burst of violence, particularly the severe beating of a suspected informant by
fellow prisoners. Suspicion, fear, a breakdown of family life, and the relocation of those previously involved in underworld activity combined to foster
a dark underbelly, which included gambling with mahjong. After the attack,
the elected Temporary Community Council of Poston wrote a penal code
focused on gambling, assault, extortion, forgery, and prostitution. It prohibited mahjong along with a list of gambling games. "It is very significant,"
wrote Nishimoto, "that the final draft begins with the sections on gambling
on its very first page, indicating where the utmost concern of the committee
had been and how much they were worried about gambling in the future."[81]
Mahjong remained both a part of gambling culture and a social game, but
local contexts shaped the spectrum.

If gambling became disruptive to the status quo, camp officials got more
involved. WRA administrators lent their authority to Poston's community
leadership in their objection to gambling.[82] More generally, officials promoted
American and Christian organizations such as the YMCA and physical recreation such as baseball as tools of Americanization over parlor games of any

kind.[83] Among Japanese Americans, however, Christian identification was perhaps less likely to inspire a rejection of mahjong than it did for Chinese Christians. Families like Doris Hayashi's went to church and played mahjong later the same day, without note.[84]

Despite its gambling association, mahjong as a way to pass the time extended beyond monetary stakes. In a particularly extreme example during the later years of the camps, a Nisei prisoner remembered turning to mahjong in a military stockade. It was one of the few modes of relief available while he was imprisoned at Tule Lake in California, where he was subject to brutal treatment for resistance to the War Relocation Authority regime.[85] In less exigent circumstances, Issei and Nisei relied on multiple forms of recreation as part of constructing community life.

Mahjong spread within the context of the upheavals of incarceration, as it facilitated connections across generations and between individuals who were repeatedly thrust into new environments and communities. In addition to being forced from their homes into the horse stalls and fairgrounds of assembly centers, then into quickly erected barracks in remote relocation camps in foreign and harsh landscapes, individuals were also moved between camps according to the logic of administrators. Mahjong emerged as one thread shared between camps.

In the long process of "resettlement" after camp life ended, finding common ground among a population whose previous geography had been utterly shuffled and remixed was equally important. In Philadelphia, "relocation hostels" sponsored by humanitarian groups and those opposed to the government's actions provided community space for Japanese Americans experiencing the disruption of trying to establish new lives outside the camps in the summer of 1944.[86] In the face of widespread hostility to potential Japanese American residents, photographs promoted a vision of happy and peaceable new Philadelphians who came to play mahjong, "see friends and catch up with their reading of project newspapers."[87] Gathered around the mahjong table were men and women from camps across the country, from California to Utah and Arkansas. These photographs were the only example of a kind of performative mahjong designed to demonstrate the assimilability of Japanese Americans into urban middle-class society. Though a rare event, the gathering reflected broader trends. A coherent mahjong culture helped create new connections among a people trying to survive ongoing community fracture.

A different photograph captures a more frequent scene. Cameras were rare and regulated in incarceration, but photographer Walter Muramoto

FIGURE 7.2 Most of the players of this mahjong game in a "relocation hostel" were recently incarcerated in wartime camps. Left to right are Masao Yabuki, Mrs. Arnold Nakajima, Naomi Sakaguchi, June Amamoto, and Arnold Nakajima. While the Nakajimas resided in New Jersey, the others had been incarcerated in Utah, Arkansas, and California. Looking over their shoulders is Jennett C. Walker, a War Relocation Authority employee. Images like this one promoted a non-threatening image of Japanese Americans as they sought new homes after incarceration. War Relocation Authority Photographs of Japanese-American Evacuation and Resettlement. Bancroft Library, University of California, Berkeley.

shot moments of daily life at Rohwer in Arkansas with the help of a camera borrowed from a Buddhist priest.[88] In the photograph, four men, most likely Nisei, sit at a square table in the autumn heat to casually smoke and play mahjong. Just as in the Philadelphia hostel and akin to other American mahjong sets, but in contrast to both China and Japan, players organize their tiles on wooden racks. They play in a building with rough wood walls, near a door marked "Supply Room." No money or chips are on the table. It was 1944, and Rohwer's existence would continue for another year. In the months since 1942, Japanese Americans' lives had been forever changed. Mahjong games played a role, both minor and pervasive in its commonplace presence, in making and remaking social lives.

Mahjong serves as a surprising way to understand suffering and survival in incarceration. Enforced leisure highlights what is not immediately obvious from the outside, but which is profoundly evident to those who experience it: the painful burden of waiting an indefinite period of time for an uncertain outcome over which they have little to no control. Luck and the games that promise to harness it hold particular appeal when the winds of fortune are stormiest. The circumstances of their incarceration differed in significant ways—detained Chinese migrants were primarily foreign-born men crossing national borders, while incarcerated Japanese Americans were primarily American-born citizens imprisoned with their families in the United States— but the logic of racial exclusion and provisional inclusion underpinned both.

The challenges posed by enforced leisure in immigration detention and wartime incarceration reveal gender's shaping role as well. Yet the gendered meanings of leisure, and of mahjong specifically, were inconsistent. Detainment exacerbated the inequalities of Chinese society for women, and American officials scrutinized them in a sexualized frame while trying to cross the border. Their heightened need to communicate respectability and their lack of institutional resources prevented them from accessing most forms of recreation. The opposite was true for Japanese American women. In wartime camps, incarcerated women experienced a breakdown of society, which was damaging in many ways but also rearranged their domestic responsibilities and increased their opportunities for (regulated) recreation.

In these contexts, mahjong provided for those who could access it one activity to ease anxiety as well as to form relationships within new and shifting communities. Although mahjong's role as a gambling game could grow in these uncertain and stressful environments, it also remained a game of skill played for negligible stakes. At Angel Island and in wartime incarceration camps, not government officials but community leaders attempted to regulate gambling; they often exempted mahjong, depending on how and where it was played. Though it played a minor role in the history of incarceration, mahjong provides a powerful lens on enforced leisure.

8

The Americanization of Mahjong

IN THE FALL of 1937, nearly four hundred women (twice the expected number) crowded into the sumptuous hall of the Essex House hotel, its gilded Art Deco doors opening directly onto Central Park's bright foliage.[1] Ladies from across the New York region gathered to answer the call by Viola Cecil, president of the newly formed National Mah Jongg League and a resident of Essex House, to standardize the rules of the game. Many, though not all, were Jewish, including Cecil herself. The wealthier among them came from established families and lived either near the Essex, close to Columbus Circle, or in Midtown and the Upper East Side. Others came from more modest but upwardly mobile communities in Brooklyn, the Bronx, or Long Island.

The packed hall vibrated with excitement as the attendees urged the League to make decisions that would unify a game that they felt had fractured over small differences from group to group. One impassioned speaker targeted a conflict over how groups collected the small betting amounts: "If you don't standardize the rolling kitty, you'll be caught with your pants down!" she cried.[2] The League's decisions would take the first steps toward creating a unique version of mahjong that set what they called "National Mah Jongg" on its own path, away from the Chinese game. In so doing, they created a consumer base that would drive the Americanization of mahjong manufacturing for decades to come.

The women who founded the National Mah Jongg League (NMJL) in 1937 aimed to standardize the game and thereby revitalize its popularity. Mahjong had never died out entirely, but by the 1930s its popularity in the United States was a pale shadow of the craze years a decade previous. During the years of depression, war, and postwar expansion, however, the game evolved in the United States and abroad, creating discrete national, regional, and community forms.[3] In the 1940s, the wives of Air Force officers created their own version, which continued to spread across postwar bases. The most influential community adaptation by far was driven by the National Mah Jongg League. Although aiming for universality in their bid for success, their new game grew primarily through Jewish women's networks, and, as with other versions of mahjong, it created new boundaries around communities of play. The League's membership rolls quickly mushroomed to more than 35,000 by 1941.[4] Over the ensuing decades, eventually hundreds of thousands of players, mostly but not exclusively Jewish American women, played their "National" version of the international Chinese game.

In creating a National version of mahjong, the League took a shared reference point from mahjong's American past and transformed it into something new. When the League codified the first uniquely American style of play in the 1930s, it marked the cultural and physical Americanization of the game—a process that continued through the following decades as the American game became increasingly differentiated in rule and form. By the 1960s, their repeated changes had transformed the game enough that it required a different set of tiles. The changes to the game that the League initiated were enabled by their proximity to the small factories making the tiles, as one kind of Americanization helped enable another. After World War II the locus of mahjong manufacturing for the American market moved from China to plastic fabricating shops in New York City. The materiality of the game reflected its changing social meaning, as the plastic tiles lost their much-discussed "exotic" and artisanal materials even as they retained clear aesthetic markers of the game's Chinese origins.

The Birth of the League

The League's game initially solidified as a "simplified, faster, and more enticing" variant that built upon the earlier American rules.[5] This new version was "streamlined," a fashionable word borrowed from the curves of Art Moderne.[6] These words of speed and sleekness revealed what the founders of the League considered the biggest obstacles of the original game: inconsistent variations dragged down by cumbersome scoring systems. Standardization around a simplified scoring system and fewer choices for winning hands, the League's founders believed, could unite American players around their new "National" game and thereby regain widespread popularity.

One of the founders of the League, Dorothy Meyerson, laid an important foundation for the game's development and its eventual spread among Jewish women in particular. The oldest daughter of a German American

Jewish mother and a Russian immigrant father, the indefatigable Dorothy Meyerson exuded energy and was a natural performer. After marriage and motherhood, she focused on mahjong as a vehicle for creativity and public leadership, without jeopardizing her class status by engaging in paid work.[7]

By the time she helped found the League in 1937, Meyerson had been promoting her "streamlined" form of the game for more than a year. Viola Cecil, another mahjong enthusiast, contacted her to help found the League in order to restore mahjong from social decline and fracture.[8] Cecil, the wealthiest among the founders, became president and Meyerson vice-president, a position she held for years. Meyerson already had a network of traveling agents for her rulebook *That's It!* (named to evoke the exclamation of an excited winner). Her business's growth coincided with—and certainly encouraged—a slow but more widespread renewal of interest in the game.[9] Meyerson herself was a particularly skilled teacher, distributor, and promoter. Although she admitted, "No one person created the new way to play," her version of the game was nearly identical to the form that the League adopted.[10] She advertised it as an heir to the familiar "ancient game of the Mandarins," as a "new American game made up of representative suggestions from different groups."[11] The independent but League-approved rulebooks written by Meyerson and Cecil would soon compete with each other for market share and would both promote the League's official version as the "National" and "American" form.[12]

Meyerson helped build an infrastructure for the game's resurgence, particularly among middle-class and upper-middle-class women. Frequent patrons of department stores like Macy's, these consumers not only shopped but also learned "the new way to play mah jong" at Meyerson's free in-store lessons, which she conducted both before and after the founding of the League.[13] Meyerson may not have needed additional income, but her agents, among the many women who worked as the foot soldiers of mass consumerism and distribution, did.[14] As they had in the 1920s, department stores such as the Stearn Company in Cleveland and Bamberger's in New Jersey hosted "clinics" where agents simultaneously taught customers Meyerson's (and then the League's) version, sold her rulebook *That's It!* and the stores' sets, and promoted an image of the game's resurrection.[15] "You ought to get around," agent Mrs. Lee Goldman chastised a *Cleveland News* reporter who mistakenly viewed the game as "obsolete." "I'll bet everyone I know is playing mah jong again," she told him.[16]

While economic need did not drive Meyerson and other League founders, status aspirations did. As Meyerson's daughter later explained, "Money was important, but it wasn't the thing that was going to elevate her in society. She was in society in her own field"—a social arena she created through her public leadership of mahjong. Meyerson loved the spotlight; within the constraints of her social position as an affluent woman, she maximized media coverage and appeared on radio programs and even very early television.[17] On Sunday evenings in the early 1940s, New York households that were part of the nation's first experimental residential television systems could watch Meyerson teach the game with a "specially-enlarged Mah Jongg set."[18] An experienced teacher, she developed numerous techniques for effective instruction that also promoted sales of new products, including a "Practice While Learning" set of perforated cardboard tiles to accompany her instruction book.[19]

In a key distinction from her entrepreneurial mahjong predecessors, Meyerson was a married mother of means. Lack of financial necessity provided a cloak of genteel femininity while she developed her business. Similarly, Viola Cecil veiled her extensive business-minded efforts, claiming that the League "just sprang up spontaneously."[20] Even as Meyerson aggressively marketed the game and wrote advertising copy in which she called herself the "world's greatest authority on mahjong," she deliberately presented herself as a devoted mother and, initially, as an accidental entrepreneur.[21] "It seemed a shame to give it up," she told a reporter in 1937, who described her as a "young, good-looking housewife" and a "careful mother" who was already teaching music and painting, volunteering with her synagogue sisterhood, serving as president of the Parent-Teacher Association, and making sure her children had a good lunch each day.[22] The article did not discuss the live-in nanny who helped enable Meyerson's expansive commitments.[23] Unlike the original experts, Meyerson's authority as a mahjong expert did not rest on any connection to China, nor on an established reputation with games such as bridge. Instead, her role as mother and PTA president took the place of familiarity with China that Babcock and Howlett had featured in their promotional media. After five years of successful growth in her mahjong company, however, Meyerson began to portray herself as the successful head of a "serious business enterprise" and included herself among "people with ambition," who "can always make jobs for themselves."[24] Indeed, she argued that having interests outside the home made women better able to "face their family problems with steady nerves and a clear head." Meyerson skillfully negotiated the image and duties of a housewife while operating as an entrepreneur.

In her own life, Meyerson participated in the upward mobility available to many second-generation Jewish Americans even before the more widespread postwar prosperity.[25] After growing up as one of six children in an established Jewish community in New Brunswick, New Jersey, she married Perry Meyerson, whose widowed Russian immigrant mother had raised five children in poverty. Perry and his brothers ran a lucrative clothing factory in New York's Garment District. By the early 1930s, Dorothy and Perry, with their two children, participated in an early wave of suburbanization by moving to "the country" from the elegant Ocean Parkway in Brooklyn to the desirable Forest Hills development in Queens (connected to Manhattan by a trolley line and soon subway). Dorothy hired a series of German "Fräuleins" to serve as nannies who walked to the neighborhood school each day in full German dress and veils, much to the children's embarrassment. Although Dorothy thus emphasized her higher-status German roots over her family's more extensive Russian heritage, the game she helped create would prove especially popular among middle-class children of East European Jewish immigrants. The League's game spread along the lines of networks of its leaders and members, the majority of whom were Jewish women, and it eventually became a cultural marker for them.

Creating the National Game

Unlike other forms of the game (and other games more generally), National mahjong was not a standalone activity but was integrated into an organization that directed the game, controlled its distribution, and distributed the profits. The League increasingly differentiated the National game from other variants, so players formed communities with others who played the same style, one regulated by the National Mah Jongg League. The League brought what was otherwise an essentially individual leisure activity in line with the culture of clubs and associations through their organizational bureaucracy and their philanthropy. With their success, the NMJL bucked the trend of declining American club membership and associational culture in the dark years of the 1930s.[26]

Their National style instituted a new model that changed the standard number of tiles and rhythms of the game. Over time, their changes created an entirely new version, even changing the set itself. One key area of experimentation and evolution revolved around the question of luck and "wild card" tiles, which had been a point of debate in the 1920s. The League initially counted the eight formerly controversial "flower" tiles as wild. The number of flowers fluctuated over the first few decades, peaking at a whopping twenty-four tiles in the mid-1950s.[27] In 1960, the League unveiled a momentous development: they added new tiles as "jokers," which took over the flower tiles' role as a wild card. The number of jokers and flowers also fluctuated over the ensuing decade, but by 1971 the American set had stabilized to eight jokers, matching the restored number of eight flowers. The National rules also codified a game ritual not present in the imported 1920s form but which had likely been evolving among American players: after the initial shuffle and draw, players exchanged tiles in a standardized passing motion that they named after the 1920s popular dance, "The Charleston." These passes provided an opportunity for players to improve their hands and learn about other players' early positioning, and became an essential part of the rhythm and strategy of the game.[28]

In a major change from Chinese mahjong—one that would have multifaceted repercussions for the development of the League and their National game—winning combinations of tiles were legitimate only if they completed a relatively small set of official hands. The League set forth roughly sixty acceptable hands. Additionally, the combinations in these hands did not necessarily correspond to the same rules used as the basis for winning hands in the Chinese game. The base of challenge thus shifted: in Chinese mahjong, the intricate scoring system structured the strategy necessary to win. (Without scoring, the game could be played in a simple form akin to gin rummy, but scoring was essential to the challenge and interest of the Chinese game.) Although there were many possibilities for winning hands, the combination of patterns of those hands determined the ultimate value of each. In contrast, in National mahjong the challenge lay in securing one of far fewer hands—and in defensive play, or "dogging" one's opponents to prevent them from acquiring their needed tiles.[29] Each hand had an easily identifiable point value that primarily depended on difficulty.[30]

In order to keep the game interesting despite the restricted possibilities, the official hands needed to change fairly frequently. By the early 1940s, the League changed the hands every year. Creating a consistently quality game accessible to beginners and still enjoyable for veterans became an annual experiment for the League's rule committee. A yearly cycle evolved in which the board of directors met for at least two months to play test games and design the next year's hands. It was a process in which members were eager to participate (canasta players had urged for the successful addition of jokers, for example), hinting at the intellectual stimulus many women found through mahjong and which distinguished it from other popular games of pure luck.[31] Players were so eager to sign up for the new annual rule card that the line for memberships stretched out the League's office door when it was due to be released.[32]

Having invested in the importance of this evolving list, the League faced the question of how to distribute the hands while maintaining the central goal of standardization and consistency. Although the League began as a members-only organization, it soon added an "over-the-counter" option of buying "lists," or rule cards, for non-members. The League explained to its members that, although they were hesitant to "commercialize" their game, adding the list option was necessary to combat the "unfair competition" they faced from those who plagiarized and sold their lists of hands.[33] Thus, players necessarily had to pay a yearly fee of at least ten cents for the card, if not the fifty-cent membership, in order to keep playing with their groups, which all followed the League's "National" version. The League urged their members to "assist this organization by playing only with members" and to recruit new ones among their acquaintances.[34] This practice of selling official hands in the form of a rule card became a defining feature of "National" mahjong and quickly served an economic purpose. When the hands changed every year, buying a new card was essential.

The innovation of an annually revised rule card had lasting consequences on multiple fronts. Not only did the League use it to develop a dynamic and enduring game, but the yearly card also helped the League enforce its own authority in standardization and ensured a regular source of funds. In practice, this also meant that players could only play with others who shared the same card. League leadership defended the annual changes to disgruntled members on the grounds that a majority of members preferred to keep the game fresh and admitted that this encouraged a steady renewal of memberships—though they denied any profit motive.[35] At the time, the League's board donated their time, so any profits after basic operating expenses fueled the League's philanthropic donation program. They appealed to their members' sense of loyalty to the hard-working League, as well as moral superiority of charity over the personal profit enjoyed by competitors who sold "bootleg" versions of their rules.[36]

The League succeeded where previous standardization efforts had failed. Its founders were not bridge experts, but they were entrepreneurial women who saw the opportunity to develop a public presence, revitalize an overlooked game, and fundraise. After unsuccessful attempts in both the United States and England, standardization remained an enduring goal because of the difficulties of playing across idiosyncratic differences, even if those differences were relatively minor.[37] By the late 1930s, there was no longer a wealth of competitors vying for authority and market share. The League's success inspired a few imitators who advertised knock-off names and rule cards, but its appeal rested in large part on a consistent game, which it spread through a critical mass of players who stayed connected to the League.[38] As one League loyalist wrote, "the pleasure of the game has been greatly increased since standardization has eliminated the lengthy discussions. We want constructive improvements but we do not want this pleasure hampered by erratic innovations."[39] Although the League's game was also a result of "innovations," it positioned itself as regulated and uniform against "erratic" and disruptive interlopers. With their success, they transferred American mahjong authority from male to female voices and the financial orientation from company profit to charity, during a generation when these ambitious women remained identified with family and community, not commerce and career.

Legitimate Leisure

In 1939 the League first confronted a challenge of success: surplus proceeds. Since its officers donated their time, the money they generated through memberships, rule cards, and sales of mahjong sets more than covered their operating costs.[40] They decided to funnel the money toward specific causes, informed both by patriotism and their predominantly Jewish communities of players.[41] Mahjong tournaments had long been used as fundraisers, including the glitzy mahjong galas of the 1920s. Dorothy Meyerson published her first book of mahjong rules to raise funds for her local synagogue.[42] Through in-person lessons and mahjong tournaments, she had also helped support the PTA and Jewish refugee relief.[43] The women who led the League participated in the established norm of philanthropic volunteerism by elite women as a form of public engagement that demonstrated their class position and also benefited the community. As the League grew and subsidiary branches cropped up in states around the nation, they too used surplus funds to donate according to their constituency's votes.[44] Whether for civic or tax-motivated reasons, philanthropy became an important way the League marketed itself.[45]

During the League's early years, promoting mahjong as a philanthropic and civic-oriented activity helped legitimize a leisure pastime during depression and war. Social scientists and philosophers had recently identified the "problem of leisure" exacerbated by Depression-era unemployment.[46] Social scientists advocated for government intervention to direct the masses toward wholesome and enriching activities. Gendered concerns specifically targeted women's irresponsible use of leisure time, while also fretting over weakened men as subject to, in one historian's apt phrase, a "new matriarchy of leisured consumers."[47] Anxieties about leisure built on a longer cultural ethos in which, historian Foster Rhea Dulles explained in 1940, "the American tradition still insists that amusements should at least make some pretense of serving socially useful ends."[48] As the NMJL Massachusetts Branch president wrote, "It is gratifying to know one can be doing good even while indulging in a game."[49]

Even within the American ideological valuation of work and discomfort with leisure, some social scientists and officials advocated certain forms of recreation. When war broke out, the government promoted "home play" as an opportunity for family togetherness in a time of disruption and rationing.[50] However, along with most other adult parlor games, mahjong did not exist within the Depression-era vision of state-sponsored healthful recreation, nor was it a part of the family-focused recreation endorsed by the government during the war. The League had an uphill battle in asserting mahjong's role in women's productive and appropriate use of time. Even before the American entry into World War II, League leadership vigorously promoted mahjong as not a frivolous pastime, but instead as a way that women were providing war relief. In 1941, the NMJL convention theme proclaimed: "The Vital Part Which Mah Jongg Can Play in Giving Women a Greater Role in Democracy."[51]

After Pearl Harbor, the League sought to convince not only the public but also its players of the game's patriotic value.[52] Wartime placed extra demands on women's time with both paid and unpaid labor and further discouraged them from taking part in activities that did not actively further the war effort. The Pennsylvania Chapter went "inactive for the duration" when its president joined the armed forces, and "most of the other women are all doing some kind of War Work." But, they reported, "women are playing in their spare time. After Victory we hope to continue our Tournaments and other activities."[53] Despite their reduced activity, their charitable donations continued without interruption. In an audacious move during wartime rationing, the League even encouraged further membership drives. One enthusiast wrote that she "had no trouble at all" recruiting new members eager to subscribe "so that they could feel that they are helping in their little way to do something for our Fighting Boys."[54] Further, League publications exhorted their female members to uphold conduct that would help the nation, urging them to avoid gossip and devote their time to "real work."[55] Implicit in this statement was the assumption that mahjong (especially as a vehicle for fundraising) was a worthy use of time.

Embedded in a nation focused on the war, the League promoted its maternal efforts to provide recreation to the armed forces.[56] In 1942, League officers posed in elegant hats, dresses, and fur coats in front of a mobile canteen they had purchased and outfitted to provide relief to servicemen and women on sentry duty on the waterfront and anti-aircraft bases of Manhattan.[57] The following year, the radio program "Women Can Take It" asserted that "women who can supply furniture for recreation rooms in camps and service clubs, donate a Mobile Canteen, completely equipped, and sponsor relief benefits for China and Russia through playing a game, are proof enough" that women could indeed "take it" and add their strength to victory. In the radio skit, soldiers admired the recreation room at their training camp, provided for them by the National Mah Jongg League. Notably, mahjong sets were not among the listed games—but the League did provide a set to the female WAC (Women's Army Corps) in training.[58] In the broadcast and in League newsletters, Viola Cecil emphasized the maternal touches of the "little picture or ornament that reminds them of home, the home for which they are fighting. It is a morale booster."[59]

The League intentionally donated to nonsectarian charities that affirmed an all-American image, though with strong New York loyalties.[60] Although Jewish women led the game, their history of marginalization and experiences with ongoing anti-Semitism likely inspired their desire to prevent mahjong from being pigeonholed as a Jewish game. The League's first official donations in 1940 went to the American Red Cross, the Greater New York Fund, the Hundred Neediest Cases (in New York), and to unnamed "New York and Brooklyn Charities."[61] Once the war began, the League advertised their "patriotic and charitable causes" on the cover of their rule cards.[62] Only after the number of charitable recipients grew did Jewish organizations join the list. Congress Defense Houses, the Jewish-run hospitality centers for all servicemen in New York, gratefully responded by emphasizing both the League's patriotism and the way its work inherently helped "to break down anti-Semitism." Visitors left Congress Defense Houses "with an entirely different view-point concerning the Jewish people."[63]

The shift to Jewish charities accelerated after the war. The League had developed a system to harness their members' desire to contribute, one that also encouraged the growth of their membership. Individuals who sold extra memberships and rule cards, known as "collectors," could request that their portion of the League's donation go to a specific charity. Once they could earmark the recipient groups, individual donations tended to flow toward local Jewish organizations as well as more general funds.[64] In contrast to wartime donations, which dispersed to a range of local, national, and Jewish-specific

FIGURE 8.1 In November 1942, board members of the National Mah Jongg League proudly presented a mobile canteen sponsored by the League. It joined a fleet of wartime relief vehicles organized by volunteer women. Dorothy Meyerson stands at the far left and Viola Cecil at the far right. Courtesy Marjorie Meyerson Troum.

organizations focused on war mobilization and refugee relief, postwar recipients of mahjong philanthropy were strongly Jewish and consistent across regions.[65] The 1950 rule card was the last time American patriotic causes were advertised on the cover—thereafter, it read simply "Proceeds donated to charitable causes."[66] Many combined a local and global effect by donating to their neighborhood Hadassah or B'nai B'rith chapter and related projects such as Hadassah's Youth Aliyah, a project begun to relocate European Jewish orphans and young refugees to Palestine and, later, Israel.[67]

An Allied Game

When the soldiers' scripted dialogue on "Women Can Take It" encountered the National Mah Jongg League's foreign-sounding name on the recreation room donation plaque, one commented warily, "Mah sounds kind of Chinese." The other soldier cheerily replied, "Yes, it's a Chinese game all right, and that 'sets' it with me. Only a lot of swell American women are playing it right now, and contributing their proceeds to furnish rooms like this all over."

The broadcast thus domesticated the game by connecting the game's foreign origins to its homey American form and emphasized mahjong as an Allied cultural link.[68]

Wartime alliances accelerated the shift to positive portrayals of China begun in the 1930s. Mahjong made rare appearances as a wholesome, even healing recreation in popular fiction. In a 1934 novel, the camaraderie of a daily mahjong game breathes life back into a World War I veteran suffering from long-term physical and psychic wounds. After dusting off the mahjong box that had been ignored for years, the narrator reflected, "there must have been some small Chinese elf with kindness in his slant eyes shut up in that lacquer box."[69] As in the 1920s, the text personified Chinese culture through the game and did so in language that highlighted racial difference and caricatured exoticism. However, this was a far more benevolent spirit of mahjong than the "heathen Chinee" and "evil" tricksters who peopled earlier representations.[70] Not long after the book's publication, the League gathered at the grand Ruby Foo's Den in Manhattan to play, dine, and fundraise for United China Relief. Speaking to them were Lee Ya-Ching, a pathbreaking female aviator who solicited support across the Americas for United China Relief, and author Carl Glick, who helped Americans reconceptualize Chinese American tongs as mutual aid societies rather than violent gangs.[71] With its red lanterns and ornate wallpaper mimicking Chinese painting, the restaurant exemplified an aesthetic of carefully marketed Americanized Oriental exoticism.[72] The League's newsletter featured a photograph of the organization's officers, all white women, smiling in front of the restaurant's life-sized statue of Buddha topped with a pagoda-style bower.[73] Although the League generally emphasized the game's Chinese origins far less than did the 1920s fad culture, the Allied connection became another link to patriotism. Viola Cecil hosted mahjong dinners in her home to support United China Relief. The League's newsletter encouraged readers to host their own, as "Linked to America, as China is, by the bonds of a common cause, her need becomes our responsibility."[74]

Once the United States joined the alliance against Japan, popular media began in earnest to promote an image of a noble and long-suffering Chinese people.[75] Less than two months after Pearl Harbor, San Francisco columnist Herb Caen emphasized the unifying patriotism found in Chinatown. "The American-born Chinese are still bewildered by the traditions of their elders, the Chinese from the old country are shocked by the antics of the young generation—and yet everywhere you'll find true Americanism, true contempt for fascism, and a true determination to stick to the weary fight till the Axis is ground to bits," Caen wrote. "That is Chinatown."[76] In Caen's rendition, what brought the divided generations together was not Chinese culture, but "true Americanism." In contrast to the League's recreation rooms at Army training camps, the "hospitality centers" run by the Chinese unit of the American Women's Voluntary Services provided Chinese American soldiers with mahjong sets.[77] As portrayed in the *Chicago Daily Tribune*, mahjong was evidence of how the San Francisco–born troops were nonetheless "Chinese all the way thru." Due to wartime alliances, mainstream American media could present Chinese Americans as fighting for both the Chinese and American causes without conflict. Racial logic that previously lumped together all "Orientals" fractured—just slightly—in a wartime context that allowed for limited inclusion of Chinese Americans, while still promoting the exclusion of Japanese Americans as inexorably foreign.

Mahjong served as one building block in creating a bridge between the United States and China. Many among the rising generation viewed commodified Chinese culture as profitable for both domestic coffers and war relief abroad.[78] Attendees of a fundraising supper aboard a "crimson-sailed Chinese junk" anchored off Manhattan played mahjong while enjoying a "Chinese costume party."[79] American film star Anna May Wong hosted a mahjong luncheon in Beverly Hills complete with "Chinese waitresses."[80] Such events were part of a longer history of Chinese Americans making opportunities within limitations, which often involved marketing commercialized Orientalist fantasies of Chinese culture.[81] Mahjong had provided an economic opportunity for individual instructors in the 1920s and enabled fundraising in the late 1930s and early 1940s. Because the game was a well-known American pastime that was simultaneously foreign, it could be used to create a sense of cultural commonality and sympathy.

From the Heartland

Mahjong's meaning as a Chinese game endured, but in its Americanized forms it was increasingly used to create communities demarcated in part by specific forms of the game and less through associations with an imagined elite Chinese past. In 1938, shortly after the founding of the National Mah Jongg League, one Oklahoma City fan proclaimed, "Now we can play mahjong in New Orleans or Omaha, for this will set national rules and do away with the old complexity of different cities having individual rules which they held to be secret affairs."[82] In fact, Oklahoma City was one of the few places where she would be proven wrong. The regional variations and individual experimentation that led to the League's founding also resulted in other long-lasting American variants of the game. Although none would approach the scale of the National Mah Jongg League, regional communities oriented around specific types of mahjong play endured.

One influential form was codified and promoted by, unusually, an Oklahoma bank. The Federal Savings and Loan of Oklahoma City began publishing a booklet of mahjong hands with regional flair as a form of advertising.[83] Through their banks it spread across the region among women players well into the late twentieth century.[84] It is possible it was influenced by Dorothy Meyerson's marketing efforts in the region in the late 1930s, or that the similarities in approach co-evolved out of variations of play that had developed from the dominant 1920s version. Along with a ritualized passing of tiles called the "Exchange" instead of the "Charleston," the bank's version also based the game on a restricted list of winning hands—but the number of possibilities was far greater than the League's. The list of over one hundred winning hands generated names for the various combinations of tiles based on popular culture and local references, including the bank's own motto: "The Home Folks." The tiles required to compose a winning hand entitled "TV NEWS" featured the numbers of local television stations, 4-5-9.[85] The bank's rules helped further mahjong's longevity in the region, but there remained more room for minor differences in how individual groups passed tiles before the game, or even the names they used for elements of play, than in the League's more strictly standardized National game. Although little known outside the region, the bank's game influenced another American version of the game, borne out of the Midwest, which would become a hallmark of social life on American Air Force bases around the world.

In 1941, four officers' wives who were "tired of all the emphasis on bridge" set up a mahjong club of their own.[86] What became known as "Wright-Patterson Mah Jongg," after an Ohio Air Force base, went on to flourish in the postwar era. Although military life also repeatedly brought American troops in contact with Asian styles of play during the war—involving male players as well—the style of mahjong that became uniquely associated with the American military grew out of an Air Force Officers' Wives' Club and was influenced by changes to the game happening in the United States, not abroad.

The Wright-Patterson rules were initially created by Sylva Bauer, herself a trained pilot and colonel's wife, and Helene Morris, a longtime mahjong player and wife of a general. Although Bauer was new to the game, Morris had first learned it as a young woman in California twenty years earlier, in the fad years.[87] When she returned to the game with her fellow officers' wives in 1941, Morris integrated some of the winning hands from booklets circulated by the Oklahoma City Federal Savings and Loan.[88] Similar to the bank's approach, Morris and Bauer created pithy monikers for their list of around eighty winning hands. Some referenced those who created them, like "Helene's Gate," while others drew from military or patriotic references. By 1970, players could win with hands named "Pearl Harbor" and "Moon Landing."[89]

As these American variants evolved, they became increasingly differentiated from each other. In contrast to the National game, there were no "wild" tiles in Wright-Patterson mahjong. They incorporated flower tiles but with specific rules that differentiated flowers from other tiles. The hands changed less frequently and on a more irregular schedule than did the National Mah Jongg League's game. Bases could also make their own slightly different variations, in a base-wide version of "table rules"—even eventually integrating jokers if players voted to do so, as influenced by the National game and its growing popularity.[90] In contrast to the League, leadership of the group depended in part on shifting residency patterns.

The roots of what became a hallmark of Air Force base life among officers' wives were planted during the war years, when husbands were away and the Air Force was still within the Army. In 1944, *Good Housekeeping* asked its readers to imagine "If You Were Mrs. Eisenhower."[91] "Pooling ration books," the article described, "you frequently dine with other lone wives. Afterward you play Mah Jongg," as Mamie Eisenhower famously did with other Army wives. Although General Eisenhower's household had a maid, portrayals of Mamie Eisenhower emphasized how mahjong fit within housewife duties, from working within a rationed wartime household economy to—in a move both domestic and democratic—washing dishes after her mahjong friends cooked a meal to share.[92]

Women's relationship to the military and base life structured how the game's culture evolved. Officers' wives often came to see playing the game with the wives of their husbands' superiors and peers—not with the enlisted—as part of their political responsibilities. "One of the unwritten rules" that shaped an officer's chance for promotion was to have a wife who was involved in the club.[93] The Mah Jongg Club did not officially begin as part of the Officers' Wives Club, but the two were socially integrated: the OWC promoted it as an activity and the Mah Jongg Club donated to the OWC welfare fund with the rulebook sales proceeds.[94]

After the war, mahjong became a useful part of base camp life, which demanded frequent introductions to new communities who were sharing similar experiences. Unable to work outside the home due to repeated uprooting and foreign residence, as well as social expectations, officers' wives faced the challenges both of repeatedly building community and of domestic responsibilities. Officers' wives' clubs held sign-ups for various activities shortly after families arrived at the bases in the summer, in part to address those needs. "So pack the young'uns off to school or the Base Nursery and take advantage of the lessons, which are only given in September and October," a 1967 bulletin advertisement called. "Enjoy each Tuesday 'out' from 9:30 a.m. until 3:00 p.m."[95] In some ways, the women's culture that emerged on war-time Army bases foreshadowed the culture that emerged not only on postwar Air Force bases, but also in Jewish neighborhoods after the war. Although base life forced much more rapid turnover, in both contexts the game was rooted in communities of women who shared strong (though not uniform) commonalities of life stage.[96]

The development of Wright-Pat mahjong connected more to the 1920s American legacy of the game than to the Air Force's international context. However, the Asian associations of the game still shaped the way the mostly white players interacted with it. (The Air Force had racially integrated in the decade after the war, but the majority of officers' wives remained white.) In the early 1960s, and possibly earlier, the Wright-Patterson base club directly echoed the game's early American history by dressing in "Oriental costumes," generally simple homemade kimono-style outfits, on a weekly basis.[97] In 1964, the costumes at Wright-Patterson aimed to "set the mood" and paired with a festive "Oriental Coffee" that marked the activity sign-up season opening.[98] Kimono-clad women taught the new arrivals a six-week course on the game. The costuming stopped by the late 1960s, perhaps because it was too hard to keep up with making them, or perhaps due to changing cultural norms. The outfits were the Wright-Pat club's most significant revival of the Orientalist consumerism and racial imagination that surrounded the game in the 1920s. No tales of Confucius or faux-Chinese font populated the rulebooks that were the most widespread materials of the game.[99]

During the war and afterward, servicemen and their families also learned and played Asian forms of mahjong while stationed in Japan, China, Taiwan, and the Philippines.[100] Denice Wisniewski, a trained nurse married to an Air Force doctor, played Japanese mahjong with Japanese military medical wives and Wright-Pat mahjong with the wives of other Air Force officers, which is the form she returned to when she came back to the United States. Although members of the Air Force sometimes played Asian forms of the game, Wright-Patterson mahjong created a foundation of shared rules and

FIGURE 8.2 In October 1964, officers' wives at Wright-Patterson Air Force Base gathered to play mahjong to kick off the season's recreation schedule. Sylva Bauer, one of the writers of the original Wright-Patterson mahjong rule book, stands to explain the players' moves to newcomer Winnie Pangburn, who is the only one without Chinese-inspired clothing. Seated at the table, left to right, are Lois Potter, Lucy Hallock, Margaret Crenshaw, and Ra Hansen. The women's Chinese costumes ranged from simple homemade loose robes to embroidered finery. Courtesy of Wright-Patterson Officers' Spouses Club.

winning hands that marked commonalities for newly relocated wives to enter a community. As the rulebook reminded its readers, standardization "allows you to transfer from Base to Post to Port and still play the same game."[101]

Both the regional Oklahoma market and Wright-Patterson players could play with older mahjong sets, but as they grew new suppliers linked them to the resurgent American market that was driven by the League's rising numbers. When Sylva Bauer and Helene Morris first started the Wright-Patterson group, they had to find resold sets and rummage through estate sales for them.[102] Soon, however, Dorothy Meyerson supplied Wright-Patterson players with American-made plastic sets.[103] All American forms shared a physical connection to one piece of the set that was far less common in other parts of the world: the racks used to hold players' tiles, which were tangible evidence of the Americanization of mahjong.

Manufacturing an American Game

The changes that the National Mah Jongg League initiated demanded new tiles—first with the expanding numbers of flowers, then the fluctuating numbers of new joker tiles in the early 1960s. The localized production of the game enabled the New York–based League to change the form of American mahjong. Along the way, mahjong tiles shed their exotic "ivory and bamboo" aura steeped in artisanal production and natural materials to retain their Chinese imagery as embossed in American plastic.[104] Nonetheless, amid changes to the rules of the game, the physical tiles and their accompanying sensory appeal remained one of the core unifying elements that kept mahjong recognizable.

New York became the center not only of National mahjong culture, but also its American manufacture. In the 1930s, a smaller but sustained stream of imported hand-engraved plastic Chinese sets had replaced the bone-and-bamboo sets from the mahjong craze of the 1920s. However, Shanghai essentially stopped being an exporter of mahjong to the United States once Japan occupied the city in 1937. While other mahjong manufacturing centers remained in Hong Kong and Japan, the epicenter of mahjong distribution to the American market moved from the Pacific to New York City. The additional tiles that the League's game required encouraged the growth of a local manufacturing base that could respond to these changes.

Two factories offer a window onto the Americanization of mahjong manufacturing. Like many other entrepreneurs in the small but growing plastic industry, the founders of these two factories were working-class men whose small-scale shops joined an increasingly crowded field of plastic-related businesses growing in the industrial centers of the mid-twentieth century.[105] These family-based factories were part of the upward mobility of recently immigrated groups from Eastern and Southern Europe—Italians and East European Jews. Although the work of the Lodatos and Silvermans was in factories, as owners and managers they were part of the rise among "white ethnics" in white-collar positions over industrial labor or petty shopkeepers.[106]

In the early 1940s—only a few years after the creation of the League and before the postwar mahjong boom—the A&L Manufacturing Company began adding mahjong to their line of small plastic products. Founded just a few years earlier by an Italian immigrant and his family, A&L would become one of the most prolific American makers of mahjong. In the late 1930s, Alfonso Lodato (known to all as "Al") launched a small shop in his basement that he christened A&L Manufacturing Company after his parents' family names,

Adami and Lodato. He began by fabricating and delivering small plastic tubes for use in scientific laboratories before branching out to mahjong. Within a few years the business moved into a Brooklyn storefront. As the orders kept coming in, the profits were invested back into the business—particularly in the form of expensive raw plastic material that had to be purchased from manufacturing plants. By the time the war was over, A&L was on its way to supplying thousands of Americans, mostly Jewish women, with brand-new plastic tiles.[107]

After the war, the new mahjong market was poised for its largest growth. At the same time, returning soldiers needed to find work, and many turned to the promising plastics industry.[108] One such hopeful veteran was Seymour Silverman, who had gone from his family's dairy business in upstate New York to paratrooping in the Army.[109] He returned to live in Brooklyn and quickly needed to find a job. He joined with a business partner who had significant experience with games manufacturing, and in 1947 they set up shop as "Empire Games" in a loft on the edge of Soho in Manhattan, near Chinatown. They shared the building with a printer and a maker of another plastic novelty: Juggle Head toys.

Over the next four years, Empire Games' shoestring operation fabricated dominoes, mahjong, and poker chips—ingredients for America's surging love affair with parlor games—while Silverman traveled across the country to drum up business. Along with New York, the biggest markets for mahjong were Chicago and Los Angeles. Not unlike their 1920s predecessors who struggled with fallout from competitors' worm-invested bamboo tiles, Empire Games fought to maintain an association with quality when competitors used substandard plastic that quickly discolored, thereby tainting the reputation of all plastic mahjong sets. However, a building fire in 1951 left the valuable raw plastic material melted into a giant ball. The insurance representative refused to compensate their losses because the plastic still technically existed, thereby destroying Empire Games.

The disastrously melted material demonstrated a larger development in the evolution of plastic itself: the discovery of thermosetting plastic, which irreversibly hardened under heat and pressure. The type of plastic that composed mahjong tiles made by A&L, Empire Games, and the handful of other American mahjong factories after 1940, such as Cardinal and TYL, was a cast phenolic plastic known by the trade name Catalin. This material significantly differed from the first celluloid plastic mahjong tiles made in the 1920s. As the first plastic, celluloid was developed in the nineteenth century out of plant-based cellulose and camphor and was widely used as an imitative replacement for natural materials such as ivory and tortoiseshell. Celluloid "French ivory" mahjong tiles had carefully constructed layers that mimicked the light brown lines of elephant ivory.[110] However, in the 1920s customers preferred bone-and-bamboo engraved tiles coming out of workshops and factories in China over American stamped plastic tiles.

By World War II, celluloid had been eclipsed by the superior new forms of phenolic plastic first heralded by Bakelite in the early twentieth century.[111] Despite the combustible origins of its ingredients, Bakelite was inflammable and solved one of the explosive dangers of making celluloid. Aesthetically, however, the early formula was ill suited to replace celluloid in ivory-colored combs, jewelry, and mahjong tiles. Made initially for industrial use, Bakelite came only in black or brown. The problem of devising a stable, colorfast plastic remained an intractable challenge until 1928, when the American Catalin Corporation imported a process from Germany heralded as the "gem of modern industry."[112] Cast phenolic—resin poured in liquid form to cool and harden in lead molds of varying shapes—could display vivid colors that retained their hue for years, with a depth far surpassing surface-level paint. Fabricating shops purchased these raw materials. As the resins dropped in price, plastic could be integrated into even inexpensive novelties and game pieces. Within a decade, the second-generation phenolic plastic that later collectors would call "Bakelite" dominated the costume jewelry shops of New York and was celebrated as a democratizing material.[113] End-use mahjong fabricators like A&L and Empire Games purchased the bars of Catalin produced by the chemical brewers at the Marblette Corporation factory in the neighboring borough of Queens.

Despite the postwar zeitgeist of an iconoclastic American orientation toward the future and the apparent modernity of the materials involved, strong threads of past economic patterns remained. Although fabricating the plastic tiles was more machine-driven than creating the bone-and-bamboo tiles had been, much of the process was still labor-intensive. Workers first cut the bars of Catalin into tile-sized pieces. The blade-sharp edges needed to be smoothed, so the tiles were tumbled in a barrel-like machine. Although the tumbler did the work, managing the process required skill and precision: if the timing was off, thousands of dollars' worth of Catalin could be lost.[114] Not unlike the Mei Ren factories of the 1920s, A&L workers specialized in particular tasks and created mahjong sets (along with their other products such as dominoes) along a rough assembly line.

In addition to the tiles themselves, American mahjong factories also made racks—a game accoutrement that had first been popularized during the

1920s. Then made of wood and often sold separately, since neither Chinese players nor manufacturers used them, by the late 1940s racks were regularly included in sets.[115] Marbled swirls of color—a hallmark of Catalin's aesthetic possibilities—provided bright contrast to the creamy white of the tiles. The raw material for racks came to the factories already formed into their basic slanted shape, but each subsequent step in their assembly: beveling, polishing, and screwing in the small brass pieces that held betting chips was done by hand.[116] Some specialty racks even had metal ashtrays affixed to the metal ends. No longer were points counted on the bone counting-sticks included with Chinese-made sets; players instead used small colored plastic chips.[117] Each element dovetailed with the American social fabric developing around the game, with groups of women smoking and counting points for their small-scale wins and losses.

These small factories continued longer traditions of family economies. Unlike the plastic mahjong factories of the 1920s attached to chemical companies, or the Shanghai-based factories of Mei Ren and Mah-Jongg Manufacturing with their hybrid systems of large-scale artisanal production and international financing, A&L and Empire Games were typical of many fabricating shops in the evolving plastics industry.[118] Their owners were independent businessmen of humble origins who relied heavily on family members. Scrappy by necessity, they frequently put in hours on evenings and weekends. Al was joined by his brother, Anthony "Lucky" Lodato, in the business. Not only did their sisters provide essential early funds, but nearly everyone in their large extended family worked in some capacity on the factory floor or delivering products to New York retailers.[119] The family matriarch Maria, along with sisters Anna and Jo, painted and cleaned the embossed tiles in their home amid the heavy chemical fumes of paint thinner. Other female employees painted the tiles on the top floor of the factory, where the light was best.[120] This detail-oriented handwork task was consistently done by women in the A&L and Empire Games factories, including Seymour's wife, Edith Silverman.[121] Although officially a "two-man operation," Edith was a hidden force behind Empire Games. Despite the men's best efforts, the games factory was not paying the bills and Edith's part-time secretarial work supported them. After work, Edith came to the factory to paint the tiles along with doing typing and paperwork. Another woman began painting as well and was soon joined by her sister and brother. In Seymour's words, "It was a family affair."[122]

Empire Games and A&L were also places where older patterns of ethnic mutual aid and family-based upward mobility persisted. The Lodato brothers hired nearly everyone in their large extended family to help put nephews, nieces, and cousins through school. In patterns similar to a "moral" version of capitalism more commonplace before the Depression years, Lucky Lodato emphasized welfare policies such as paid vacation and time for family care, Thanksgiving turkeys for employees, and attentiveness to female workers' needs to leave work on time for childcare and household duties.[123] Lodato's policies paid off when the workers declined union representation. Whenever a new baby was born in the neighborhood, the parents received a box of rejected mahjong tiles to use as building blocks. The boundaries of family, neighborhood, and ethnic communities overlapped and bled into each other.

Ironically, plastic fabrication provided a space for traditional economic forms in a modern industry. It combined the growth markets of leisure goods and a new arena for manufacturing with the scales of family businesses and artisanal craftsmanship. Although growing, plastic was still a small economic sector and, unlike the corporate ownership over the production of plastic material itself, was not dominated by the large corporations that manufactured automobiles, cotton textiles, iron, and steel.[124] While other sectors of the economy such as restaurants and small retail shops had traditionally been more feasible for working-class and immigrant entrepreneurs to enter, this new sector temporarily provided entry into family-based manufacturing.

As Italians and Jews in Brooklyn, the Lodatos and Silvermans were part of the communities that were developing the playing of American mahjong, and their proximity shaped how they understood the manufacturing. Members of the extended Lodato family were among the Italian Catholics in Brooklyn who played the game alongside Jewish Brooklynites. Seymour Silverman also observed his aunts playing the game and investigated what worked for them and what did not. He adjusted the tile dimensions accordingly to avoid bulky tiles that could be hard for them to hold. In contrast to her sisters and other friends, Edith never learned the game she helped produce. "I really didn't have much interest in it, especially [from] working on it," she admitted. Not much of a games enthusiast, Edith did not turn to other amusements either, but for her mahjong meant work, not leisure. The separation of the two was less possible for those who manufactured it.

Piece by piece, American mahjong sets became materially distinct. With the addition of racks as a standard set component came new boxes to house them. The new cases were long and rectangular, resembling backgammon or attaché cases. As with the tiles, instead of the natural material of wood, the cases were covered with a plastic vinyl, most often "leatherette" or faux-alligator, considered an elegant and modern finish for the times.[125] A&L

began by purchasing the mahjong cases already made, but when prices became prohibitive, Al and Lucky brought a third brother, skilled with handwork, into the fold to make the cases in-house. Compared to wooden boxes, these cases were made less for show and more for portability, and they facilitated women taking their sets outside their homes.

The material changes that the National game required were only possible because of the League's proximity to factories. Manufacturers and the League built mutually beneficial relationships with each other, which enabled the factories to insert the League's annual rule cards into the boxes of tiles, as well as to change tiles according to League specifications. One year, Seymour Silverman remembered, the League decided to send the necessary additional flowers as a gift to members; they placed an order of thousands of tiles from Empire Games. After 1960, the factories changed the production of sets to incorporate jokers as well. Not everyone bought the necessary joker tiles—many who had pre-joker sets took matters into their own hands and painted over some of the now-extraneous flower tiles with red nail polish, or covered them with specialty red "joker" stickers.

FIGURE 8.3 This 1948 advertisement in *Playthings Magazine* illustrates defining elements of American mahjong sets. Here, A&L Manufacturing promotes their plastic tiles in either all-white "ivory" or with colored backing. The elongated leatherette travel case displays Catalin racks with attached coin-chip holders while the text heralds the surging postwar popularity of mahjong. Published in New York, the magazine reached a national audience. Courtesy of Katherine Hartman.

Because they were new, Joker tiles offered the first blank slate for American designers to institute a new look. With few exceptions, the American die manufacturers created designs that represented caricatured and friendly elements of Chinese culture: rotund Buddhas, smiling Confucius-esque faces, or simply the words "Big Joker" in stylized Chinesey font. Notably, one grinning joker with a Fu Manchu mustache and red mandarin cap had a double-edged cultural reference: the mandarin-style Joker was renamed "Kibitzer," a Yiddish term also common in bridge that referred to an onlooker who offered unwanted commentary. (No kibitzing, warned the League newsletter in 1960.[126]) These choices underlined the continuing salience of references to China in the game's appeal and cultural meaning.

The Americanization of mahjong sets did not entail an erasure of their Chinese origins. Nor, apart from the caricatured Jokers, did they represent an overall distortion of the original designs. In contrast to other sets made in the 1920s in the United States and Europe, which often featured crudely mimicked Chinese characters, the standard tile designs demonstrated legible machine-embossed Chinese writing and images that, though evoking scenes that could easily be associated with American stereotypes such as pagodas and rickshaws, nonetheless had origins in Chinese designs of the 1920s. The Chinese references literally embedded in the tiles, as well as in certain phrases of game play, remained an essential part of the experience. Unlike a deck of cards, this physical presence helped demarcate the game's recognizable foreign heritage.

The materiality—what the tiles were made of—had, however, declined in cultural importance. The American public's warm reception of these new American-made mahjong sets reveals the domestication both of plastic and of mahjong. No longer did advertisers emphasize mahjong's evocation of the ancient Chinese court through the bone-and-bamboo tiles. Yet neither did they proclaim the plastic tiles as particularly modern or notable; by the mid-1950s plastic had become an everyday material.[127] Instead, advertisements emphasized the quality of non-fading Catalin plastic.[128] Most of the tiles remained a creamy white color—still referred to as ivory in some advertisements—but tiles also incorporated new colors to fit with the fashions of the times.[129] In 1954, Macy's demonstrated the duality between celebrating newness and maintaining an association with the marketable "Orient" when it advertised the new "Chinese pink" set—a color far more associated with suburban bathroom tiles than with Chinese culture or the red, green, and blue of the traditional sets. In short, the materiality did not hold the same import as it did in the 1920s, but the retention of the Chinese and Chinese-inspired designs remained central to the game and its cultural meanings.[130]

As factories developed in concert with distinctive regional and community-based forms of the game, American mahjong grew into a domestic industry. The ability to adapt the rules of mahjong while keeping key shared elements—including the aesthetic and feel of the tiles—meant that there was room for constant creation and iteration. The organizations that standardized their own versions capitalized upon and sought to channel this potential for change. Yet mahjong also became a vehicle for continuity, including the economics of family-run fabricators.

Because most Americans did not return to mahjong nationwide after the fad years, the new varieties spread along and reinforced various community lines, from Oklahoma to Air Force bases to Jewish women's networks. Women's cultures shaped the game, too, since groups of women led the two most significant uniquely American games of the National Mah Jongg League and Wright-Patterson. Both organizations integrated philanthropy into their structure and attracted players who turned to the game to build community amid mass mobility. The growth of American mahjong in the postwar period demonstrated the importance of these connections and the pressures that drew players to it.

Despite the growth of the League's game in particular, it did not make many inroads into broader American society. By the early 1950s, mainstream media rarely mentioned mahjong, though it occasionally served to reference an outmoded fad of the 1920s.[131] Apart from Chinese and Japanese Americans, the largest pockets of the game's survival were among Air Force officers' wives playing by Wright-Patterson rules, and—especially—the rapidly growing numbers of primarily Jewish women playing according to the National Mah Jongg League standard. The Americanization of this Chinese game set the stage for Jewish women to claim a unique place in American leisure culture.

9

Suburban Migrations and Summer Bungalows

WHEN RITA GREENSTEIN moved to Long Island in 1955, her new home felt much further away than the geographical distance from her tight-knit community in the Bronx. Greenstein had been raised in a large artist colony born out of a Socialist and Communist housing cooperative. The community had a strong Jewish identity, rooted more in cultural and political norms than in religion. On Long Island, Greenstein strove to replace her displaced network by turning to the Conservative Temple and to mahjong on Long Island.[1] She was already familiar with the game from childhood summer visits to a Far Rockaway beach club, for mahjong had spread among Jewish women's places of leisure on the eve of World War II. Her neighbors in the brand-new subdivision included other women who all shared the experience of raising young children there. While the Jewish families in the mixed community joined the same temple, some Italian women joined the mahjong group as well. "We became not only very good friends," she remembered; "we became mahjong players."[2]

It is an inherently American story to explain how mahjong became known as a Jewish game by virtue of it being Chinese. The game provided a way to belong to the nation and to retain their distinctiveness as Jews. This was not only a psychic process: it was tied to changes in housing, manufacturing, gender, and leisure. This ethnic identity was thus produced in the physical world. Without even meaning to do so, Jewish women effectively created a new cultural marker of a midcentury Jewish ethnicity—with a Chinese game played in an evolving residential and residentially segregated geography of increasingly suburban homes and summer vacationing landscapes.

FIGURE 9.1 In 1954, this model home advertised a new development in Hicksville,
Long Island. Rita Greenstein moved into a nearly identical split-level ranch house in the
community the following year. The empty landscape surrounding the model was soon
filled with similar suburban houses. Library of Congress.

Mahjong helped women meet new neighbors and form localized Jewish
communities in a period of massive residential disruption and atomization. In
retrospect, it also illuminates the complexity of ethnic cultural formation amid
middle-class assimilation. "Moving up" in the postwar era meant a dramatic
reorganization of Jewish American culture and social networks. Greenstein's
trajectory is revealing: from a secular, Socialist, arts-oriented, strongly Jewish
immigrant community, which bumped up against Orthodox enclaves and was
at a remove from mostly integrated third-generation Reform communities,
she moved as an adult to a second-generation middle-class neighborhood
knit together through a socially oriented suburban Conservative Temple and
weekly mahjong games.

    In the years between the world wars, the Jewish population tilted from
majority Eastern European immigrants to majority native-born Americans.
Accordingly, the divisions that marked national origin and religious practice
receded. The generation before World War II built more secular forms of mass
culture and ethnically based associations.[3] Divisions remained, particularly

along lines of class and denomination, but a dominant American Jewish culture emerged that was relevant even for those who did not fully identify with it. No longer rooted in a racial identity, nor defined solely by theology or religious commitments, Jewish American ethnicity became located in a new nexus of culture, class, Jewish education, and perceptions of whiteness.[4] As for minority identities more generally, ethnic identity was shaped by a core tension between the external designation of a group (horrifically highlighted by the Holocaust) intersecting with internal cultural norms, identities, and rituals among group members. Even for those who did not participate in these shared experiences, like mahjong, they became widely recognized as cultural markers by Jewish Americans as well as outsiders.

Many of the trappings of middle-class midcentury life were indistinguishable from mainstream "Christian" norms, but mahjong was different. By the 1950s, Jewish Americans across the country recognized mahjong as "our game."[5] In part, National mahjong became known as "a Jewish game" because Jewish women were primarily the ones who were playing it—and teaching it to each other, meeting to play, and building communities around it. Some women very consciously connected mahjong and Jewishness, often in playful but meaningful ways, such as interspersing Yiddish words during play or visualizing a menorah in spilled mahjong tiles.[6] Others eventually resisted the association, wary of being pigeonholed as an ethnic stereotype. For many, however, the game's Jewishness was part of its broad and generally unobserved context, Jewish by virtue of the neighborhoods where it happened to be played.[7] The League's game had become naturalized, most easily explained in matter-of-fact terms: "That's what Jewish women did."[8] Children who grew up in strongly Jewish communities like the Flatbush area of Brooklyn could simply assume that everyone was Jewish and everyone played mahjong.[9] Husbands or children who were around the game but did not themselves closely interact with the tiles often believed that the game was in fact a game brought from the "old country," its name a Yiddish word.[10]

It was more than just coincidence, however, that caused the game to spread within these neighborhoods.[11] The formation of mid-twentieth-century Jewish identity was beset by contradictions about the relationship with the past and the assimilative drive in the present. Straddling modernization and a received identity handed down over generations, Americanization took form in the development of an ethnic identity at the same time American ideas about race were changing alongside new concepts of ethnicity. American mahjong resulted from the material, residential, and social elements that made up an increasingly coherent Jewish American culture—and helped create it.

"Our Game"

Mahjong's rituals and material culture did not stem from a sense of connection to an ancestral homeland, nor did it serve as a sign of Americanization into homogeneity—or even a "hybrid" culture that combined the two.[12] Instead, mahjong offers an example of a process of triangulation. For Jewish women, in effect this Americanized Chinese game fostered careful entry into the mainstream while still maintaining group distinctiveness by using a third reference point, China, to remain both outside and inside "domestic" American culture. In the matrix of American racial thought, Asia had a particular symbolic power to indicate the foreign. Its outsider status was accentuated by the fact that mahjong was no longer played by most Americans. By tapping into an American Orientalist tradition, Jewish women participated in mainstream white American culture, but through a marginal activity no longer engaged in by most Americans. In doing so, they exemplified the insider/outsider tension that their upward mobility into the privileges of white America provoked, and which mahjong culture (in unintentional ways) helped resolve. Ironically, Jewish women used an explicitly Chinese game to help create modern Jewish American culture.

Although mahjong did not evoke for Jewish Americans a sense of heritage as it did for second-generation Chinese Americans, it similarly provided a useful demarcation of safe and shared space. Suburban Jewish Americans interviewed by sociologists in the 1950s described feeling more comfortable with fellow Jews, even if they lived in mixed areas and frequently interacted with other groups.[13] Their words echo those of other minorities past and present, who have felt the constant pressure of representing their group and being aware of their perceived difference. Chinese Americans in the 1920s were careful not to play mahjong in public because of fear of being "stared at," but relished being able to "drop a disguise" when entering Chinatown.[14] So too could mahjong serve as a de facto community marker for Jews who were sometimes "less comfortable with non-Jews because you feel that they think of you as a Jew. Jews don't really think of you as a Jew."[15] Although a distinct minority of National mahjong players were not Jewish, they were joining majority Jewish groups and invited into a shared environment to play what had become a predominantly Jewish game. On a broader group level, the game became rooted in Jewish women's recreational rhythms, philanthropic networks, and domestic spaces. Mahjong was part of a proliferation of cultural rather than theological markers of Jewishness that grew and changed in postwar America.[16]

The link between postwar Jewish women and a nineteenth-century Chinese game was not an obvious one. Mahjong joined a narrow zone of Chinese and Jewish cultural overlap. Most notably, the widely practiced twentieth-century "tradition" of family meals at Chinese restaurants on Christmas and often on Sundays relates to a shared position outside Christianity in a predominantly Protestant nation.[17] Commentators in both popular culture and scholarly literature have highlighted shared cultural characteristics, from the importance of historical memory in diaspora to an emphasis on education and financial acuity.[18] It is tempting to assume that Jewish and Chinese Americans crossed paths in the shared geography of New York City, or even that World War II Jewish refugees in Shanghai brought the game with them to America. But direct cross-cultural exchange was not the seedbed of Jewish American mahjong culture; only in rare cases did Jewish individuals learn about mahjong from Chinese players.[19] Instead, the National Mah Jongg League became the source of the game's spread among Jewish women.

Nonetheless, it still mattered that mahjong was a Chinese game—though in often nuanced ways that changed over time. Historically, Jews and Asians had been loosely grouped together in the Orientalist imagination as people from the East; Western Orientalism had originally focused in the late nineteenth century on the "Near East."[20] Arguably, then, Jewish Americans may have sought to differentiate themselves from the non-European "Orientals" and assimilate into white society by appropriating a Chinese game.[21] However, it is more likely that the appeal was of a subtle affiliation with difference rather than assimilation. The 1920s socialites whose mahjong culture helped them step into a new kind of self—in their case a modern and cosmopolitan whiteness—engaged much more explicitly with Chinese personae, costuming, and stereotypes than did the largely Jewish players of the National game who followed them. To be sure, some stereotypical representations of Chinese culture persisted, as it did in American culture at large—such as the faux-Chinese font on the cover of National Mah Jongg League President Viola Cecil's 1938 rulebook *Maajh* and conical straw "coolie hats" occasionally worn by summertime players in the Catskills—but it was no longer pervasive nor a focus of the game's appeal.[22] Also in contrast to the League's wartime gestures toward Sino-American alliance, the Jewish postwar game culture ignored, for the most part, the Chinese association. Cold War suspicion of newly Communist China may have contributed to the silence, though Chinese Americans were navigating their own conditional inclusion and emerging "model minority" status in the shifting racial landscape of the Cold War.[23] After the brief explicit engagement with its Chinese origins during World War II, American mahjong culture reverted to an understated familiar current of Orientalism. League publications maintained the same misty terms of Confucius-era timelessness that had characterized the exotic 1920s fad.[24] Unlike a game played with a deck of cards, mahjong retained its Chinese markers through the tiles' physical appearance and nomenclature.

No other recreational activity had such a strong association specifically with Jewish women, but mahjong also represented national leisure trends. Since World War I, leisure time had become increasingly accessible to the middle class and the middle-income working class. Hostesses could entertain friends without hired help by relying on prepared and purchased foods, and various card and board games surged in popularity.[25] Young people frequented dance halls, couples played bridge, and men played poker.[26] The South American card game canasta swept the nation in the 1940s, and many Americans enthusiastically continued playing it into the 1950s—including Jewish American women who also played bridge and mahjong.[27] "The normal social pattern," according to *New York Times* games columnist Albert Morehead, was for married couples to entertain each other with dinner and a card game, preferably a partnership game like bridge "so that husband and wife need not play against each other." In his estimation, such routines increased once couples were reunited after the war. Visiting friends who lived further away became easier with the end of gasoline rations, and rising prosperity along with economic policy meant that "[w]ives left the factories and returned to their kitchens."[28] In the 1950s, games of Scrabble were played in family rooms across the country, while living rooms were the site of informal bridge parties with friends.[29] By the 1960s, the family room was a major feature of new suburban construction, marking the era's emphasis on informal and family-centered recreation.[30] Mahjong players participated in these dominant dynamics of the "normal social pattern," but they also carved out new territory that was fundamentally different.

For Jewish Americans, mahjong was strictly a women's game. Jewish men did not touch the game, at least "never in front of strangers."[31] A son of a player in Texas explained his understanding in terms analogous to childbirth: "It's not for men to know, it's a secret. It's a mystery."[32] American mahjong culture created a specifically female community organized not around the productive labor of work parties, volunteerism, sewing circles, or children's education, but instead on women's social recreation. This gendered culture differed significantly from Chinese mahjong players, who still played mahjong in all-male gambling halls alongside low-stakes games in homes and among women. It also differed from 1920s American predecessors for whom there was little distinction between bridge and mahjong circles, and who played both games in mixed- or single-sex groups. In the national culture, men played games like poker defined as "masculine" due to their inherent gambling purposes, while men and women played bridge and other games together. Jewish men often played pinochle. Non-Jewish women played games in single-sex groups, such as afternoon bridge or canasta parties (which Jewish women did as well), but no game became so uniform and so exclusively female as mahjong was for Jewish women.

Though not all elements of ethnicity need be as strongly gendered, ideas about the proper roles and relationships between men and women structured both traditional and new sources of identity. The family home had emerged over the early twentieth century as the locus for the growth of "American Jewishness" marked by culture and shared rituals more than traditional theology.[33] With home as feminized space, women took an increasing role in shaping family traditions and in claiming time and space for unique forms of leisure. However, unlike other common rituals like the Americanization of Hanukkah or the development of bat mitzvah ceremonies for girls, which still held intrinsic religious meaning, mahjong developed a Jewish resonance because Jewish women created a culture around it in the spaces and rhythms of their everyday lives.

Playing Mahjong in the Suburbs

For Jewish Americans, participating in the postwar push to increasingly suburban homes was a powerful symbol of new levels of integration into the American middle class. In Rita Greenstein's life, the severe anti-Semitism she experienced as a child during the 1930s from the neighboring Catholic community in the Bronx contrasted sharply with the mixed suburb of Italian Catholics and Jews on Long Island in the 1950s.[34] In the early twentieth century, waves of East European immigrants had refueled the Lower East Side world of Yiddish culture and crowded tenements, of radical politics and theological diversity.[35] For this previous generation, ongoing outmigration to other New York City boroughs and Northeastern cities complemented a slow but steady upward mobility, despite the obstacles of anti-Semitic quotas and other forms of discrimination in housing, education, and professional employment.[36] American anti-Semitism peaked during the nativist 1920s, when immigration restrictions curtailed Jews from entering the United States. After the war, when the horrors of the Holocaust became public and the United States increasingly positioned itself as the "leader of the free world" against

Soviet Communism, blatant racism and anti-Semitism became less culturally acceptable.[37] This shift affirmed religious diversity as democratic and
American, even as the fundamental color line between white and Black was
further strengthened.[38]

While the scales of class mobility had long been teetering, amid postwar
prosperity the second-generation children of the earlier wave of East European
immigrants gained increased access to the middle class en masse.[39] Anti-
Semitic quotas in education and employment dwindled; restrictive policies in
housing persisted but declined. Building on affordable public education, the
growth in the service economy boosted professions Jewish families had traditionally invested in, such as education, law, medicine, and management.[40]
Economic mobility for Jewish men and national cultural norms led to the
explosive growth of Jewish suburban domesticity, marked by a newly dominant middle-class ethos, increased affiliation with Conservative Judaism, and
support for the new state of Israel.[41]

The Jewish suburban population doubled in the 1950s, as second- and
third-generation Jewish Americans were four times more likely than their
non-Jewish peers to move away from urban centers.[42] This movement was
not without class distinctions: the most upwardly mobile were the first to
move, and the particular developments they moved to often had strong
boundaries of wealth and prestige.[43] Soon Los Angeles, Miami, and Detroit
joined New York, Chicago, and a cluster of northeastern cities to become
major centers in the Jewish landscape; each had attendant suburbs that grew
alongside them—and both cities and suburbs became nodes in the mahjong
landscape.[44] Suburban synagogues became major neighborhood institutions,
largely through the efforts of women, many of whom in turn connected with
other congregants at the mahjong table.[45] Conservative synagogues spread
particularly quickly as the second generation gravitated toward this middle
ground between the liberal American Reform tradition popular with an
earlier German Jewish population and the Orthodoxy of Eastern European
immigrants. Jews joined with other Americans in creating a peak period of
religious affiliation in the postwar era as "Catholic, Protestant, Jew" came
to mark a triumvirate of American civic religions, a hallmark of national
belonging and postwar pluralism.[46]

Differences between Reform, Conservative, Orthodox, and secular Jews,
as well as political alliances with the Civil Rights Movement and support for
Israel, all knit Jews further into the American fabric even as they could drive
individuals apart. But they were not significant for the kind of ethnic formation that mahjong facilitated, which was based more on local networks.

Women who played mahjong were bound together through a shared ritual, not based on older patterns of theology, or even on the newer cultural "Jewishness" that was rooted in Judaism or Eastern European culture.[47] Instead, these friends and neighbors who came together to play a weekly game of mahjong prioritized proximity and localized communities over other boundaries.

Not all Jewish women played mahjong—and some did so only grudgingly as a social obligation. Although class lines could be blurred and many women outside the middle class played mahjong, class provided the most common fault lines for dissent. Some among the working class or lower-middle class felt excluded from the dominant upwardly mobile milieu, or wealthy women sometimes felt it smacked of middle-class strivers. When one affluent mahjong group in Detroit "played mahj they would *dress* so that they showed they had pearls on and necklaces"; a neighbor felt she did not have the money to belong, despite her friendship with one of the members.[48] Hosts might put out their best plates and silverware, which could communicate both an honoring of the mahjong group guests, as well as financial means.[49]

As Jewish Americans achieved new rates of upward mobility, the American cultural desire to preserve a positive vision of an egalitarian and meritocratic nation created pressures for previously marginalized or conditionally accepted groups like Jews to identify unambiguously with the white "mainstream."[50] By the mid-twentieth century, "whiteness" appeared to be such a consolidated, self-evident category that the fractured and racial history *within* whiteness was erased for most groups, even those particularly denigrated and differentiated as the Irish had been. Yet lingering vestiges of "the Jewish race" remained, even as the perception of Jews as white became commonplace and the focus on ethnicity grew. With the long history of European racism informing an American landscape organized along different racial axes, Jewish immigrants and Jewish Americans occupied a position that reflected the contours of American racial thought but with their own unique position as "both white and Other."[51]

Yet the full Americanization of Jews brought its own unsettling tensions over the precariousness of their social position, the fear of cultural loss, and the meaning of success for a group whose outsider status had been central to their identity. Jewish intellectuals and commentators explicitly asked each other how to be both American and Jewish.[52] Cold War pressures for cultural homogeneity meant that many American Jews felt their differences simultaneously highlighted, making them vulnerable, and eclipsed, robbing them of their cultural heritage. The vigorous and vocal assertions of belonging in and

FIGURE 9.2 A 1962 mahjong group enjoys a game in Valdosta, a small city in southern Georgia. From left to right, they are: Ida Broomberg, Lillian Miller, Annie Lee Esterman, and Frieda Spieler. Although the candelabra is unusual, many hosts would put out the "good dishes." The formal table setting is belied by Spieler's casual bare feet. Courtesy of the Cuba Family Archives for Southern Jewish History at the Breman Museum.

to America reflected Jews' "spectacular arrival in the American mainstream coupled with lingering fears of anti-Semitism and doubts about Jewish acculturation," explains historian Joyce Antler.[53] Jews in postwar America found themselves haltingly entering the privileges of whiteness, while maintaining their own ethnic identities.[54] In rapidly growing developments farther off the historical Jewish grid, such as California and Florida, Jewish Americans often felt newly self-conscious of their difference from the dominant culture, heightened by associations of Jews with communism, particularly in the first decade after the war.[55] Suburban developments further inscribed racial and economic segregation. While some neighborhoods brought Catholics and Jews together, realtors often enforced religious and ethnic homogeneity, a practice some new residents resisted and others welcomed.[56] Both through choice and through hostility and segregation, regional Jewish communities tended to have a common identity; despite significant migration, most Jews clustered in a handful of cities and states rather than dispersing into non-Jewish areas.[57]

Not all families jumped to the more stereotypical suburban neighborhood, at least not right away. In New York City, they built upon earlier migration patterns as many moved to apartment complexes in less dense outer boroughs like Brooklyn and the Bronx.[58] As the generations before them had successively moved out of the Lower East Side, so their children moved to housing in nearby boroughs. These were stair-step migrations akin to Rita Greenstein's, which often began in more urban boroughs and ended in suburbs on Long Island or in New Jersey. Each New York City borough and neighboring region would become a major center for mahjong culture.[59]

Part of the image sold with suburban life was one where leisure and everyday life would be more intertwined, resulting in an upsurge in the market for leisure goods. A 1959 Macy's ad for mahjong, for example, sat right next to one for the "Suburbia chair," a patio chair "for summer living."[60] This growth corresponded with a larger boom in consumer society after the war. Marketers, government officials, and consumers worked together to make consumption the engine of growth in a demilitarized economy. Houses themselves became consumer goods, as well as all the things to fill them—including board games, dominoes, and mahjong. Suburban developments advertised new kinds of temples to consumerism—the shopping mall—which would also serve as entertainment centers for the young families that surrounded them.[61] Leisure became a way for the rising middle class to step into the modern future, and new materials like plastics facilitated the proliferation of family-oriented accumulation.[62]

Bungalow Colonies and Mahjong Summers

The Catskills Mountain region became an iconic place for upwardly striving Jewish Americans to grab hold of the American good life in a distinctly Jewish environment. "The Borscht Belt," as it was commonly known, was not only the largest Jewish resort area, but also the world's largest community of contiguous resorts.[63] The core of the "Jewish Alps" covered 250 square miles of hills and farmland about 100 miles northwest of New York City. Having evolved in the first half of the twentieth century, the Catskills region hosted an unprecedented efflorescence of Jewish leisure culture after World War II. At its peak in the 1950s and 1960s, vacation communities dotted the land-scape, with hundreds of options for lodging available, from cramped rooming houses to cozy bungalow colonies to luxurious hotels. Millions of Americans spent time in the area, often returning summer after summer, and the hotels created an entertainment circuit that honed Jewish humor into a national art. From the war years through the early 1960s, the middle-class milieu of bun-galow colonies in particular created a venue for female leisure with its daily rhythms of eased domesticity.

During the early twentieth century, accommodations slowly evolved to be-come more comfortable as growing numbers of New Yorkers escaped summer heat and overcrowding by going to the mountains. By the 1930s, a kind of hy-brid accommodation of small outbuildings or rooms with a shared farmhouse kitchen provided an affordable and increasingly popular option during the Depression.[64] The cottages were known by their Yiddish name *kuchalayn*, lit-erally meaning cook-alone—or more accurately for these crowded kitchens, cook-for-yourself.[65]

Going to the country was simply "what women did."[66] It was also a dem-onstration of status that became increasingly pronounced as accommodations continued to diversify. By the 1940s, those who could afford it generally pre-ferred to stay at a bungalow colony, a structural cousin to the kuchalayn. (To add confusion, the bungalow colonies could also be referred to as kuchalayn.) A bungalow colony generally provided small fully equipped cottages with a recreation building known as "the casino"—home to mahjong games during the week and couples' dancing on the weekends. One commentator opined that the bungalow colonies were effectively training ground for suburbanites, highlighting neighborhood committees as the exemplary feature of suburbia. Colonies could host "a great stir of activity, even organizing committees during the first few weeks to adjudicate disputes among the children and plan soft-ball and mah-jongg tournaments."[67] Women provided much of the labor necessary to keep the community infrastructure and their families going, but there was still more time for relaxation.

During the early 1950s through the mid-1960s, the Catskills experienced enormous growth. The end of wartime shortages brought an explosion of ren-ovation to meet pent-up demand. Each year, legions of visitors descended on the region, with estimates ranging from one to over two million guests.[68] The traffic spurred new expressway construction, easing the driving commute and replacing the train.[69] Class was a significant, though not clear-cut, distinction between the increasingly luxurious hotels and the more communal bungalow colonies. The "big hotels" were in a class of their own, though they were far outnumbered by small family hotels. Among the trendsetters, Grossinger's and the Concord led the pack. Both hotels advertised mahjong tournaments as part of their highly organized schedule of activities, with visiting experts from the National Mah Jongg League.[70] This "supernova period" in the Catskills, as historian Phil Brown dubbed it, directly coincided with the flourishing of mahjong culture.[71]

Each kind of environment developed its own tempo of leisure. The "pleasure dome" hotels catered more frequently to couples' short-term stays and mahjong was present more at the pools and tournaments than scattered everywhere as it was on the lawns between bungalows.[72] Small hotels shared the colonies' culture of weekend-commuting husbands. To commentators like David Boroff, who decried women's influence on modern Jewish culture, the Catskills could appear to provide women with "total leisure" and regression to an adolescent "camaraderie-of-the-girls"—acquired on the backs of their poor working husbands, whom he likened to slaves.[73] From a different perspective, the summers apart provided both parents some respite from cramped quarters and family demands amid ongoing, though reduced, labor.[74] Across the board, the resort communities allowed family members to pursue independent recreation, for women to play hours of mahjong while children were otherwise occupied. By the 1950s and 1960s, women playing mahjong and cards dotted the resort terrain. "Everywhere! They were like, everywhere," a former Catskills hotel waiter remembered.[75]

One family's story maps the patterns of these vacation communities. For over a decade, the Feinstein family joined thousands of other mostly middle-class Jewish families on an annual summer migration to the Catskills. Beginning in 1958 with a very small bungalow colony with neighbors from their apartment building, they joined a larger community two years later. Their move up in Catskills accommodations mirrored their moves to larger city apartments and, in 1963, to a suburban house near the coveted "shul with a pool."[76] After traveling a couple of hours north by car with her husband, Martin, and two children from their home in Queens, Gloria Feinstein set up their cottage, one of a group of twenty-four bungalows, where she would spend the summer with her children, away from the sweltering heat of the city. Martin Feinstein then went back to Queens, continuing his work as an attorney during the week and returning to the cottage to join his family on the weekends. With her husband away and their children at day camp, Gloria's household responsibilities relaxed. Meals became simpler. She could assume

FIGURE 9.3 At an outdoor mahjong game in 1955, these players and their friends met and vacationed every summer at Green's Lakeside Hotel, Port Jervis, New York, near the influential Catskills region. Games took place on the lawn between the families' bungalows. The women's swimwear and hairpins speak to the leisured tempo of summertime vacation communities. Courtesy of Lorna Drake, Freudy Photos Archives, LLC.

her children were safe and entertained. She was surrounded by acquaintances whom she saw only at the bungalow colony, all following their own similar rhythms. Although there were constraints—the twenty-four bungalows shared one washing machine—domestic expectations were lower there than at home. In the afternoons, circulating games at mahjong tables filled the small patches of lawn between the cottages. The clicking of mahjong tiles was one of the sounds of summer. Families ate according to the same established dinnertime and, after Gloria had made a simple supper and the children were in bed, she joined her neighbors in the colony's "casino," and played mahjong every weeknight. Gloria's daughter Barbara later remembered women playing mahjong "all the time. Really all the time"—except, however, when the husbands returned. "When the men were there," Barbara recalled, the wives "were there for their men."[77] This would be an important distinction from how mahjong functioned in the home.

Playing mahjong in the Catskills became a signature part of growing up as Jewish and female in 1950s New York. One woman fondly described her kuchalayn as "the shtetl revisited or, more accurately, transformed and transported to a cleaner, safer, place."[78] In this remembered idyllic and specifically Jewish context, she "learned how to swim, find Indian arrowheads, dance, play Mah Jongg, kibitz, and had my first real crush and my first real heartbreak there." Rooted in a sheltered culture of the 1950s, the Catskills helped many baby boomers come of age.[79]

The Catskills profoundly shaped an evolving American Jewish culture, but the region hosted diversity among Jews, too. Amid the dominant culture of second-generation middle-class Conservative suburbanizing urbanites was a significant minority of working-class kuchalayn residents and Orthodox bungalow colonies. In the late 1940s, Ruth Milch seasonally left her full-time work as a keypunch operator in Brooklyn, while her husband drove back and forth from his job as a grocer middleman.[80] Refugees from the Holocaust brought their families, too.[81] Just as mahjong players counted neighborhood Catholic women among their ranks, not all Catskills visitors were Jewish. However, in both cases, they were participating in a distinctly Jewish milieu.[82] "Even without an explicit agenda or ideology, many forms of American Jewish vacationing have encouraged a sense of group cohesion and distinctiveness against the backdrop of American pluralism," explained historian Avi Decter.[83]

Where Jewish women relaxed together, mahjong was very often present, both among those who traveled to the Catskills and those who did not. As part of the growing middle-class ethos, a leisured domesticity spread and diversified. Women played mahjong at beach clubs on Long Island, at community swimming pools in the Bronx and New Jersey, at Jewish country clubs in Atlanta, and resorts by Lake Michigan.[84] In the late 1950s, a new landscape of leisure developed through beach clubs, particularly on Long Island. Influenced by Catskills culture, beach clubs were closer to home and therefore more amenable to the family life that 1950s culture celebrated.[85] Families could pay a summer membership for a living-room style cabana to stay in or a more affordable locker for their belongings. At $200 to $800 for three months, the cost was comparable to that of a bungalow colony but allowed for husbands to join their families on weekday evenings. Although most went back and forth to their homes overnight, women's culture still flourished during the day as children attended day camps. As the *New York Times* described it, the "heart of the clubs is the card game, the mah-jongg, the chit-chat in front of the cabanas."[86] Barbara Dellon's nuclear family relished their summers in the Catskills, but her grandmother played at a Long Island beach club and avoided what she saw as dreary bungalow colonies.[87] Mahjong was her daily beachside activity, despite the sand that eventually encrusted her set.

Summer communities were the epicenters of mahjong's ripples into neighborhoods. Women could learn the game over one or two summers and return to their new communities with skills to share. Ruth Unger, who would later serve for over three decades as president of the National Mah Jongg League, "really learned" the game at "a bunch of little places" in the Catskills after the war and brought her knowledge to her Brooklyn apartment building with other young mothers.[88] The New Yorkers who came to the Catskills, along with smaller numbers from Detroit, Boston, and Baltimore, used neighborhood networks to build summer communities and took some elements of Catskills culture with them when they returned home. In 1960 the League responded to players' desires for more time to practice the year's new rule card before the summer vacationing months of mahjong by bumping up the release date from the end to the beginning of April.[89]

In the context of what scholars call "postwar pluralism," marked by a newly popularized support for the integration of distinct groups rather than absorption, Jewish Americans created an upwardly mobile middle-class group identification with shared religious and cultural markers.[90] For the first time in American culture, these distinctions would not be seen as threatening to the national polity or as barriers to group success. Although no one stated this intention explicitly at the time, for Jewish Americans mahjong served to demarcate an ethnic identity in the midst of the newly possible and still tenuous zone of integration. As with other ethnic identities, the tension between the loss of group identity and access to the benefits of the Christian white majority was resolved unevenly and temporarily within specific social contexts.

Mahjong helped create cultural patterns in Jewish American communities across the nation, connecting women who were substantively dislocated from the original core areas of Jewish settlement. Regional patterns in table rules and nomenclature emerged, but from Atlanta to Philadelphia and from Los Angeles to Detroit, groups across the country played the same game, at parallel places and times, while noshing on similar snacks.[91] The rituals that mahjong players forged around these plastic tiles represents one important piece of postwar Jewish American culture—and it proved particularly vital for the young mothers who made mahjong a ubiquitous presence in their homes.

10

The Paradoxes of Postwar Domesticity

IN 1959, FOUR women in Brooklyn, New York, gathered in an apartment dinette for their Wednesday night ritual. Coffee steamed near a plate of danish, and cigarette smoke curled from dark glass ashtrays. The quick "click click" of plastic tiles sounded against the hard surface, a staccato background to the women's voices announcing their discards. "One bam." "Three dot." "Call!" one cried and snatched the tile, displaying her tiles atop a bright green plastic rack to reveal her winning hand: "Mahjong!" A fifth woman standing nearby celebrated as well, for her successful bet on the winning player. Laughter and cries of lament joined the drifting smoke as her compatriots handed over plastic coins (placeholders for the final payment). Red lacquered fingernails pushed the tiles into a swirling shuffle; the clacking rumble joined the women's discussion about the Parent Teacher Association meeting, a toddler's ailment, and a nephew's bar mitzvah. Betty Friedan later cast mahjong as a stifling symptom of trapped housewives. Philip Roth painted scenes such as this as a horror story of Jewish mothers' self-absorption. These oversimplified characterizations nonetheless reveal the pervasiveness of mahjong as a symbol of postwar domesticity and its specifically Jewish resonances. For most of its participants, the game became a pleasurable hallmark of postwar Jewish American culture, ritualized by women who made space and time for autonomous leisure in their family homes.

At the height of the postwar domestic revival, middle-class Jewish women created forms of leisured domesticity, marked by temporary female-only recreational spaces in their otherwise family-centered homes. In contrast to school-hour kaffeeklatsches or couples' games of bridge, with mahjong second-generation Jewish women gained an entitlement to peer-oriented leisure in the very site of domestic labor, at a time when society expected mothers to be focused on their domestic roles when husbands and children

FIGURE 10.1 Taken in 1963, this photo captures a weekly mahjong group after a decade of playing together in Brackenridge, Pennsylvania. Closest to the front sits Millie Sparks, with Jan Wikes to the left, Mary Wikes (Jan's mother-in-law) center, and Selma Schwartz on the right. Boots Hersh stands behind them. The group's families belonged to a local Orthodox synagogue and rotated between each other's homes to play, from living rooms above grocery and meat markets to suburban dens and dining rooms. The tiles shown here are from a Royal Depth Control set made by A&L Manufacturing Company in Brooklyn; Hersh continued playing with the set for more than fifty years. Courtesy of Bernice "Boots" Hersh.

were present. Although the culture of mahjong could reinforce their domestic roles as much as undermine them, the weekly mahjong ritual explicitly came at the expense of both household labor and their family members' comfort.[1]

Early Cold War culture has carried special weight in shaping popular images of the American home. Then and now, Americans have incorrectly viewed the iconic "June Cleaver" image as a return to the traditional family, when in fact the opposite was true: the generation that rushed into early marriage, child-rearing, and racially segregated suburban homes embarked on an aberrant family-building spree that disrupted a century of declining birthrates. As historian Elaine Tyler May has argued, the domestic culture they co-created and celebrated with the government and media was born of Cold War anxieties about the need to contain both communist infiltration and non-normative sexuality.[2] American leadership, most famously Vice President Richard Nixon in his "kitchen debate" with Soviet premier Nikita Khrushchev, promoted housewives as emblematic of the American promise of the good life, in contrast to ostensibly mannish Soviet workers.

This postwar version of the American dream echoed the long-standing hallmarks of domesticity that emerged in the industrializing United States of the mid-nineteenth century: a separation of home and work, middle-class comforts and material objects provided by a breadwinning father, with gentle patriarchal leadership and maternal care in a harmonious child-centered home. Central to the historical evolution of domestic ideology was the question of wifely labor, and specifically the reimagining of a housewife's work from labor to love.[3]

Contrasts between devoted mothers in family-centered middle-class homes and the ways in which women resisted or were excluded from these norms have dominated understandings of postwar domestic culture. In the background loom one-dimensional stereotypes popularized by voices like Friedan's and Roth's. In contrast, examining how women constructed their domestic lives—including shaping men's behavior—in homes as physical spaces with social meanings paints a fuller picture.[4] Mahjong-playing mothers neither overthrew nor fully acquiesced to the powerful norms of postwar American "model" domesticity. This new recreational rhythm made domesticity more livable for women by enabling them to create patterns of leisure within it.

A subset of women who fully participated in the culture of domesticity nonetheless claimed a unique space for leisure with their peers in the form of a weekly evening mahjong game. For the majority of mahjong players, husbands temporarily took over childcare duties (granted, often after the children were ready for bed). In the twentieth century, middle-class fathers faced increasing expectations regarding their parental involvement, but clearly in terms of family togetherness or gender-specific paternal roles, certainly not childcare in place of mothers.[5] Perhaps similar overlooked traditions of leisured domesticity existed among other groups. Many individual non-Jewish women experienced community and recreation through other means, including games like bridge and canasta. However, there has yet to be evidence of another widely held cultural norm of women's leisure involving a regular activity that required a temporary exemption from domestic work. That may speak more to the need for future research than to the uniqueness of Jewish women. Everyone experienced domesticity through the intersecting social and economic contexts they inhabited. In doing so, Jewish women forged a particularly widespread and consistent set of rituals through mahjong.

Jewish American women participated in the postwar domestic revival even as they broke the mold. In the 1950s, nearly two-thirds of young adult Jewish women worked outside the home, but for women of childbearing age, those rates dropped to only one in five, half the national level of mothers with school-age children.[6] Yet Jewish women also earned bachelor's degrees at nearly twice the rate of their non-Jewish counterparts, and they bore fewer children.[7] Jewish women capitalized on their relatively high rates of education and small family size to engage in politics, philanthropy, and religious activities outside the home.[8] Many of these women also sought intellectual stimulation that they could integrate into their domestic lives, including through the competitive challenges of a game of skill like mahjong.

Young mothers in particular established the rhythms of a weekly mahjong game. These game-playing groups helped women build female-focused networks in new family-focused communities. Along with living in new communities with young children, many women had recently left the workforce. Mahjong proved one way to mitigate their risks of isolation. They sought to create support networks and space for themselves while still fulfilling their domestic roles. They used the game to make their circumstances work for them, not to radically change those circumstances.

Because the home was a place of work, not of rest, for women, wives risked being seen as shirking their duties by engaging in a leisure activity that was disruptive to the household. Mahjong became a socially accepted form of group recreation for Jewish women that did not rely on associations with "productivity." Mahjong groups were not sewing circles, political meetings, or auxiliaries: they played a game. They could (and did) serve as a tool for fundraising and often overlapped with Jewish women's volunteer organizations—the National Mah Jongg League has long advertised its role in charitable giving—but the widespread popularity of the game did not primarily rest upon associations with productivity, nor did weekly rituals focus on its philanthropic possibilities. Instead, it was about the female community that formed around mahjong and the pleasures of the game itself.[9]

Mahjong-playing women also developed a specific and widespread culture around the game. Hosting rituals took the form of broadly consistent patterns of types of food ("You've got to have a nosh!" one woman explained) and rhythms of circulating among players' homes.[10] A shared material culture extended beyond the Catalin sets and their leatherette cases to include personalized coin purses and the fabric table covers sometimes teasingly called *schmatte*, Yiddish for "rag." The integration of small bets added another layer of opportunity to increase a player's spending money, to share resources with their mahjong group, and to support philanthropic causes.

Examining the many factors that undergirded middle-class Jewish women's leisured domesticity highlights the beliefs that enabled women's—and specifically mothers'—labor to be understood not as work but instead as a natural and necessary expression of love. Domestic ideologies remained resilient in the face of challenges: leisured domesticity did not necessarily undermine larger constraints of gender and class. It is telling that mahjong players could be critiqued both as narcissistic mothers by Roth and as confined housewives by Friedan; they existed within domesticity and also temporarily subverted its key tenets of motherly devotion.

Despite their claims on autonomous domestic leisure, mahjong-playing women became emblematic of the trappings of stereotypical postwar domesticity. As Jewish mahjong players established their strong cultural norms in the 1950s and 1960s, they became embedded in the evolving stereotype of the domineering Jewish mother.[11] This association signaled the waning of both postwar domestic norms and the patterns of leisured domesticity that thrived within them, as economic changes and generational shifts transformed middle-class home life.

Leisured Domesticity

In 1963, Charlotte Levy and a close-knit group of friends took turns hosting weekly mahjong games in their West Philadelphia neighborhood. The group of five, sometimes four, women gathered in the small living room of Charlotte's row house, eating dessert and shuffling tiles. Charlotte taught the game to her two young daughters, who watched their mother's group and then played with their own (cheaper) children's mahjong set. Charlotte's husband Art was a social fellow and chatted with the ladies when they arrived or visited with the group's husbands on the front steps on warm summer nights. On summer weekends, Charlotte and Art drove their children to the swim club, where she played mahjong with friends she knew from her role as an officer for the local chapter of the Jewish charitable organization B'nai B'rith.[12]

The Levys had moved into their home with the help of the GI Bill around 1950 after living with Charlotte's parents, Russian immigrants who lived twenty minutes away in Philadelphia. Overbrook Park was a strongly Jewish residential neighborhood that had been transformed after World War II from

FIGURE 10.2 Charlotte Levy, second from the left, pauses during a mahjong game in the Overbrook Park section of Philadelphia around 1963. These neighbors rotated between each other's row houses on mahjong night. Here they are playing in their usual spot in the living room, using a table cover to soften the noise of clacking tiles as the player on the right considers the "one bam" tile in her hand. Courtesy of Beth Lean.

farmland to affordable housing for returning servicemen and their families, backed by federal financing. Art had served in the army in England before becoming a carpet salesman. Charlotte worked as a legal secretary during the war, before her marriage.[13] In 1965, Charlotte's family "moved up" to Wynnewood, a nearby suburb in a desirable school district. Although they were not observant in their previous, heavily Jewish neighborhood, in the new suburb they joined a Conservative synagogue. However, Charlotte retained a more religious regularity with her mahjong group than the family's occasional attendance at services. Every week she drove the ten minutes back to her old neighborhood, or her friends would carpool to the Levys' new home and play in her more spacious living room. In many ways, Charlotte Levy exemplifies pervasive patterns that shaped thousands of postwar Jewish women's lives. An upwardly mobile, middle-class, second-generation housewife and mother of two children, passionately involved in a Jewish women's charitable organization and somewhat involved in her suburban synagogue, she redirected her energies from family to friends once a week at the game table and, through mahjong, built long-lasting friendships with other women.

Compared with the game of bridge, which many mahjong players also enjoyed, during mahjong "people can spill out all their family history and problems," Leeds described.[14] The difference between bridge and mahjong cultures was due in part to the frequently mixed-sex and couples-based bridge games. But even in all-female bridge groups the culture of talk was still different, in part because of the longer pauses between rounds when shuffling tiles instead of cards. Players could briefly raise issues in their lives and then return to them at the next break, Ruth Unger explained. "It's not that you've left those problems behind. It's that everybody has time to think about them and come up with solutions!"[15] Especially in less competitive play, the game allows for staccato conversations as people take turns.[16] Groups could shuffle with different combinations of compatible players, with slower groups chatting throughout, and others preferring fast-paced competitive—and quieter—games. The intellectual challenge of the game was part of its utility, but within mahjong circles players also critiqued each other for being either too social or too competitive.

Groups could develop a rare intimacy over many years, something deeply valued by those who experienced it. Many felt "we needed a support group because we were going in untested waters with young children that we had to find the patience for and the right answers for. And this was our support: 'Don't worry about it, it's okay, I went through this already, it'll be fine.' "[17] When meeting with the same group every week for years, players often grew close in unexpected ways, supporting each other through births, bar and bat mitzvahs, deaths, and divorce. A great many women found mahjong to be a lifeline amid the ambivalence of postwar domesticity, with its unfamiliar territory of new families and new neighborhoods and the limitations women faced. More than one player described her mahjong group as "therapy."[18] Another remembered that it "was more than a game, it was like life itself."[19] Their words capture not only the centrality of these relationships, but how mahjong groups intertwined with the rhythms of their lives. Addressing the tensions they experienced as women also meant creating physical spaces inside their homes into which the rhythms of vacation bungalows could temporarily transfer.

The designs of homes helped make the dynamics of domesticity, from finances to leisure time, more concrete. Postwar housing structures physically reinforced the importance of family and of women's roles as mothers. Since the nineteenth century, home recreation spaces had moved from masculine game rooms to the family-oriented rec room.[20] In the 1950s, socially valued recreation changed to focus on family togetherness, and time together increasingly became the norm.[21] Spaces in the home marked as female were oriented to domestic work, not leisure. During mahjong play, however, family-oriented workspaces like kitchens could become no-children zones. This remapping did not occur only in classically suburban tracts. Square mahjong tables occupied entryways in Philadelphia row houses, dinettes in Brooklyn apartments, and living rooms in Atlanta houses.[22]

Space for women's leisure was not designed into homes; it had to be marked out. Mahjong players claimed territory through the game table, the clatter of the tiles, the rules and phrases of game play that were unknown to male members of the household, and the accompanying rituals of food and hosting.[23] This space made possible a certain time away from family duties, more akin to the rhythms of bungalows or beach clubs. Mahjong hostesses temporarily reallocated their energies when it was their turn to host the weekly group. Food that was normally prepared or purchased for family consumption was held apart for the players. Some players taught their daughters or nieces to play, but often mothers "exacted" silence from family members, and others sent their children—and husbands—to their rooms after an early supper. One player infamously temporarily abandoned her role as nurse to her husband with acute pneumonia while she held a particularly advantageous position in a round of mahjong.[24]

It mattered too that players rotated hosting duties and thereby left their own homes to play the game. Postwar Jewish women differed from a previous immigrant generation, the more conservative of whom rarely left the house without their husbands, but purpose, time of day, and location still circumscribed women's independent time outside the home. For mahjong, women circulated among each other's homes—in apartment buildings, row houses, and suburban streets—at night. As one daughter remembered, even her lower-middle-class mother who worked full-time as a bookkeeper never left the house at night without her husband "for *anything* other than mahjong."[25]

In order for women to feel entitled to temporarily set aside their domestic duties, they had to reallocate household labor. Unlike daytime television, mahjong games were not something that women could enjoy while also giving their attention to household tasks.[26] Both non-Jewish and Jewish women met for daytime coffee or cards, and husbands were involved in nighttime couples' games of bridge.[27] In contrast, until the 1970s, mahjong groups nearly always met at night. When the weekly mahjong gatherings drew mothers to other homes, childcare was required. The late hour made it easier for fathers to look after the children and enabled working women to participate after hours, as those who worked part-time and full-time as bookkeepers, teachers, and keypunch operators joined housewives at the table.[28] Although husbands of players might refer to themselves in joking complaints as "mahjong widowers" to other men, their cooperation was often essential for a mother's participation.[29] Dorene Beller's father owned a cleaning store but would arrange to be home on the night his wife left for mahjong; another father brought home sandwiches and the unusual treat of soda pop before playing cards with his daughters while their mother was at mahjong.[30] However, most players mitigated the heavy lifting for fathers by generally still preparing dinner for their children. In some households grandmothers instead of fathers watched the children the nights players were out.[31]

The labor dynamics of women's relaxation versus domestic work could be explicit. In one New Jersey suburb, Thursdays were mahjong nights—or as the locals called it, "the maid's day off." It was the night that husbands agreed to be home so that their wives (humorously but revealingly referred to as servants) "could fly the coop."[32] In 1959, the front page of the *Los Angeles Times* featured a "shaky dad" who took on the "tough baby-sitting job" of parenting his own children for an afternoon. The profiled father's resulting ineptitude "explains why Arlene doesn't take more evenings off for mah-jongg and kindred hen parties."[33] The cultural acceptance of a night off was notable, but was constrained by the expectations that surrounded it, which assumed a mother's care to be both natural and necessary. So closely did identities as mother and mahjong player merge that mahjong sets became common Mother's Day gifts.[34]

For many, mahjong marked adult womanhood and married life. When Marilyn Starr married, she had already been playing mahjong since she was a girl in Brooklyn. She informed her husband that there were two essential and immediate purchases for their new home in Queens: a shopping cart and a bridge table with four chairs to play mahjong. One would be used to fulfill her domestic duties, the other to offer reprieve. When they later adopted an infant daughter, the newborn slept in a bassinet right next to that mahjong table.[35] As Marilyn Starr demonstrated, women took individual approaches to balancing their ongoing domestic responsibilities.

Mahjong did not challenge the fundamental underpinnings of domestic life and obligation because it represented only a temporary break from a wife's household duties.[36] Even for couples experiencing marital discord, mahjong did not prove to be a notable flash point. If anything, their children would later surmise, fractious marriages enjoyed the break a single-sex game culture provided. "If she was busy, all the better," one daughter recalled.[37] Husbands who would otherwise object to wives' activities that disrupted their domestic obligations accepted mahjong. Marjorie Meyerson Troum had grown up watching the mahjong games of her mother, Dorothy Meyerson, a founder of the National Mah Jongg League. After her own marriage in 1949, Troum played with friends "once a week. That was the limit, once a week." That cap was set by her husband, who liked to have dinner on the table when he came home; he accepted a once-a-week mahjong night but no more than that. Another woman did not rely on her husband for childcare; instead, she hired a babysitter for mahjong nights and played until the wee hours of the morning. "As long as I got up in the morning and I fed those kids breakfast and got them off to school, it was okay," she explained.[38]

A Shared Culture

In an era of widespread relocation and suburbanization, many women like Charlotte Levy uprooted themselves repeatedly to move to new communities, and their neighbors had, too. Mahjong became a social imperative for newcomers. As Sylvia Leeds frequently moved with her husband's work, in each town from Texas to Oklahoma and Kansas the first question between women was the same: "Do you play mahjong?" A negative answer was met with "You've got to play!"[39] Reva Salk started playing when she moved from Manhattan to a strongly Jewish suburban neighborhood on Long Island in the 1950s. Her mother had actually worked as a mahjong instructor in up-state New York in the 1920s. In contrast to her mother, among Reva's generation it was young mothers playing in their homes who fueled the surge. "We all moved from different places, so we were all new, all had little kids," she remembered.[40] Members of her mahjong group quickly learned how to drive "the minute they came out here" to Long Island and then drove to each other's homes for nighttime mahjong games. When her group needed new players, they posted "Anyone for Mah Jongg?" advertisements in laundromats and supermarkets.

Many women at the time did not know how to drive, and within dispersed suburban neighborhoods, carpools shortened longer distances. Shirley Greenfield submitted her "ode to the chauffeur" to the National Mah Jongg League's 1965 annual bulletin. Living in the Bronx, she wrote, "In rain or shine, in sleet or snow / Georgia and Janet are ready to go. / Like the mail, we must get through / 'cause in this car is the Mah Jongg crew. / In reverence I speak with head that's bowed / I cannot sing her praises too loud."[41] Carpools could also cut off their services if a player became an undesirable member. One woman who was "a sore loser and a crowing winner" found herself without a mahjong group when the carpool eventually stopped picking her up.[42] Group members helped each other participate in their weekly ritual, but without broader community norms that shaped husbands' expectations, ad-hoc support would not have been enough.

The mahjong table became a place to share "housewife talk" of children, schools, clothes, and groceries, and domesticity suffused mahjong culture.[43] Players literally stitched the game into the fabric of daily life, sewing mahjong tiles onto tablecloths and celebrating its aesthetic with the emblem of domestic labor: mahjong-print aprons.[44] In 1951, Dorothy Meyerson broadcast televised mahjong instruction to a New York audience.[45] The show she guest-starred on aimed to reach housewives and featured as a soundstage an idealized feminine 1950s domestic space. Meyerson explained mahjong to the aproned hostess in a reconstructed kitchen, with a 1920s mahjong set and the modern NMJL playing-card version displayed in front of the stove.

Because members of a mahjong group took turns hosting "the ladies," games involved hosting rituals that developed a remarkable level of consistency across many different households and regions, including maraschino-studded pineapple slices and bowls of the popular new hosting snack of bridge mix.[46] Hosts often tasked their children with spearing the cherries to the pineapple with little red plastic swords.[47] Children indirectly benefited from the special preparations with bites of pineapple or bowls of forbidden candies that they discreetly nabbed before being shooed away. Dorene Beller's mother made lasagna and cheesecake just for the players; although the children were not allowed to touch the food before the game, they looked forward to leftovers the next day.[48] Sour cream coffee cake was a staple at one Detroit table, and cookies from Ebinger's bakery in Brooklyn graced another in Queens.[49] Hilda Schaffer remembered the standard mahjong evening coffee and danish served in the dinette of her Bronx apartment as simply a given: "We served in those days," she said—the "we" meaning women.[50]

Because mahjong culture created women's communities along ethnic lines, they also engaged women who did not fit the suburban housewife mold. Working women, although less likely to participate in weekly mahjong games, did play, including bookkeepers, teachers, department store clerks, theater managers, keypunch operators, and storekeepers.[51] Groups included those did not work outside the home and the minority who did; some accommodated more restricted schedules by meeting monthly rather than weekly. Working

FIGURE 10.3 A mahjong game in full swing in Hilda Schaffer's Bronx, New York, dinette in 1955. At the time, Schaffer had two evening mahjong groups: one with older women and family members, another with fellow young mothers in neighboring apartments. During the summers she also played at a Bronx beach club while the children played or napped. Ubiquitous elements visible here, including cigarettes, a pineapple refreshment, the plastic tiles with embossed Chinese designs, and the National Mah Jongg League rule cards in front of the players' tile racks, helped create the shared sensory and cultural experiences of mahjong groups. Author's collection; courtesy of Hilda Schaffer.

women juggled domestic duties as well, working part-time to be sure to be home when children got home from school. They participated in similar mahjong hosting rituals, too. And although middle-class homes were the primary venues for mahjong games, finances did not necessarily exclude working-class players: some groups pooled funds to buy shared sets. Or only one member of the group might own a set to share. The group dynamics of mahjong could provide an entry point to activities inaccessible within one's own limited means.[52]

Although never a major gambling game, American mahjong involved money in ways that shaped how players formed community through the game. The rule cards produced every year by the National Mah Jongg League had always marked the value of each hand: first in points for small plastic chips to be traded in for cash, later in denominations of dimes and quarters.[53] Nearly every regular American mahjong group agreed on an unofficial loss cap called "pie."[54] As an unwritten rule, pie meant that individuals would arrive to the game with a set agreed-upon amount of cash in their coin purses. (Coin purses became part of the personalized and beloved ritual accoutrement.[55]) Even after losing all her money, a player could keep going and simply resume paying up if she won. The pie limit and small stakes allowed games to remain relatively accessible; they also allowed players to not perceive themselves as gamblers. No debtor sheets trailed American mahjong. In the 1950s and 1960s, pie often capped the cost of the evening's entertainment at two dollars.

The structure of betting also generated opportunities for women to use their mahjong winnings to carve out more time for themselves apart from domestic labor. A Catskills regular later remembered that a "harried and hurried mom could purchase an entire Friday dinner with some mah-jongg winnings" from the food truck knishman at the bungalow colony, "and save Friday afternoon for sunning at the pool."[56] Many groups played with a communal pot of money called the kitty, which accumulated funds when games ended without a winner.[57] The kitty could serve as a kind of community piggy bank, especially if players chose to supplement it with weekly dues. After they collected enough money, players could share the reward by going out for a night on the town as "just girls" or they might take their menfolk out.[58] After pooling their money over several months, Arlene Revitz and Martha Lustbader's group would take their husbands for a weekend at the Nevele resort hotel in the Catskills.[59]

Mahjong games offered a venue where women could gain money of their own. Many mahjong players controlled household expenses, including those who helped to financially support their families by working outside the home. Others, however, were part of a midcentury household economy wherein the husband "took care" of the money and gave his wife an allowance.[60] Mothers expected to provide for children's expenses out of their own funds, which mahjong could help to supplement: one mother's mahjong winnings, kept as a pile of coins, paid for her daughter's school supplies.[61]

Despite minimal personal winnings, money remained essential to one key aspect of the game's spread: philanthropy. As Jewish women left the workforce and built family-centered communities, their organizational commitments grew as well.[62] In particular, Hadassah's postwar networks overlapped with the mahjong landscape, targeting young housewives to fill their ranks with energetic fundraisers and organizers, and offering educational talks and camaraderie. In more than one local group, a player recalled, "if you belonged to Hadassah, you played mahjong."[63] Women's organizations like Hadassah maintained their strength even after other American Zionist organizations waned, due to their remarkable success uniting American patriotism with a sense of global Jewish community and duty, and to their successful recruitment of suburban women.[64] Martha Lustbader led her Hadassah chapter in Newburgh, a small city between Manhattan and Albany, and also had a regular mahjong group formed from newly resident young mothers in her garden apartment complex. She relied on mahjong parties to fundraise with ticket and raffle sales, with revenue going to build a hospital in Israel, a cause she passionately supported. She made sure her mahjong group supported the parties. "Everybody had to go," she remembered, or "I'd let them have it."[65]

Philanthropic and neighborhood organizations were one important way of creating women's networks, but they were not the only way. Although mahjong groups overlapped with other groups, they were essentially neighborhood based. That locality facilitated a social glue that, when built on the structure and tempo of the game itself, formed a powerful norm that was both of the family-centered home and outside it. The strong cultural rhythms that players built were part of why the game would come to symbolize postwar domestic femininity and its limitations.

The Jewish Mother

By the late 1960s, mahjong became part of an emerging harsh critique of the excesses of postwar culture: the ever-consuming, overbearing Jewish mother. This stereotype co-evolved with the spread and solidification of Jewish women's mahjong-centered patterns of leisured domesticity.[66] The caricatured Jewish mother found broad cultural resonance because she effectively combined class, ethnic, and gender elements to symbolize an exaggerated provincial and upwardly striving domesticity. Within Jewish circles, she built on longer-standing tropes, while for the broader American public, the image resonated with established stereotypes that associated Jews with insular acquisitiveness. Jewish mothers faced a double bind: pressured to perpetuate their families' upward mobility and scapegoated for Jewish Americans' concerns about assimilation and materialism.[67] At the same time, the dominant American culture also broadcast contradictory messages about prototypical mothers. Women faced significant pressure to serve their families above all else, yet they were also blamed for "smothering" their children, particularly their sons.[68] In an era of mother-blaming in popular psychology, the overall positive image of white Protestant domesticity contrasted with the parodied Jewish mother.

When Philip Roth popularized a version of this negative stereotype in his 1969 novel *Portnoy's Complaint*, he painted a portrait of an aggressively overbearing and manipulative mahjong-playing mother. The novel mocks Sophie Portnoy and her friends not only for embodying suburban family life, but also for daring to proclaim themselves the center of it. References to mahjong scattered throughout the text include a misogynistic screed by the narrator, Alexander Portnoy, against "these Jewish women who raised us up as children," who would be better described as "cows, who have been given the twin miracles of speech and mah-jongg."[69] In his retelling, women's speech, particularly at the mahjong table, was illegitimate and reinforced inappropriate parenting. "From my bed," Alexander describes, "I hear her babbling about her problems to the women around the mah-jongg game."[70] In Roth's influential picture, mahjong became a weapon used by domineering women to take even more control within the home and to force their sons to undertake feminizing supportive domestic labor.[71] The novel characterized Sophie Portnoy as a sore loser, a tableside gossip, a status-oriented poseur, and a nightmare mother. After the success of Roth's book, mainstream media references to mahjong increased, but nearly always in the context of Sophie Portnoy's egregious behavior.[72]

By the time that *Portnoy's Complaint* became required reading, the children of those who had created this rich mahjong culture had come to reject it and the domestic sphere it represented as part of their politicized youthful rebellion. In the late 1960s, the bungalow colonies and Catskills milieu declined in the face of generational change, increasing air travel, and residential air conditioning. Jewish sons and daughters disproportionately led a growing cultural critique of the 1950s suburban scene.[73] Hailing from the same neighborhood as Philip Roth, Stephanie Grossman remembered that when she was going through "that rebellious stage when I wanted to do anything but be a Jewish housewife, the things I avoided were a) going to Miami and b) playing mahjong."[74] In other words, she sought to avoid all those things that were just "what women did." The cultural script was clear, as was her desire to avoid being typecast. Grossman explained, "I would never play mahjong because that was, like, so Jewish. I never denied my Judaism, I just didn't want to do the same get married, have children—you know, that kind of thing." Mahjong's powerful role in creating a gendered Jewish identity had become a double-edged sword. With the emergence of second-wave feminism and Jewish feminism, commentators debated whether mahjong helped Jewish women socialize "as self-willed, self-sufficient individualists," or whether, as Betty Friedan recalled in 1981, "endless games of bridge and mah-jongg" were symptomatic of women's trapped energies and simmering discontent.[75]

Some daughters later described feminist inspiration from their mothers' mahjong nights, which encouraged children to view their mothers as individuals with their own desires for companionship outside the family circle. "I loved what Mah-Jongg did for my mother," author and Yonkers native Rolaine Hochstein wrote in *Ms. Magazine* in 1977, prompting another woman to recall the unique place of mahjong in creating community on "a woman-to woman basis," without husbands and children.[76] Not all feminists agreed, including one who later reflected that the fleeting claim of space for a female community that ended with an evening's round of mahjong actually acculturated women to a circumscribed domestic world.[77]

Feminist critics were not wrong to link mahjong to domestic culture, but they oversimplified its role. What they missed was that domestic spaces did not simply represent oppression or resistance; their meaning had to be created by the people who lived in them, shaped by the expectations that surrounded them but sometimes creating new expectations as well. The patterns of leisured domesticity underscore the importance of labor, while revealing the possibility of men's gender-bending domestic labor—looking after children, not mowing the lawn—in certain circumstances. When the postwar domestic norms that supported and necessitated patterns of leisured domesticity crumbled in the late 1960s, the mocking stereotype popularized in *Portnoy's Complaint* helped obscure the legacies and possibilities that mahjong-playing women created.

The world that mahjong-playing women responded to and helped create remained just as relevant to some among the next generation as it was to their parents, but it was no longer consistent. Part of what ended in the late 1960s was the coherence of the cultural script that presumed all the things that were just "what women did" (and did not do). The strong norms pervasive in midcentury America, which took particular form for most Jewish Americans, fractured.

The dynamics of domesticity have also changed over the ensuing decades. The promise of reduced working hours inside and outside the home began evaporating by the late 1960s. Combined with the decline of leisure once heralded by 1950s visions of work, life, and home, by the 1970s postwar domesticity and its paradoxes were no longer the norm.[78] Alongside the liberating trends of increased public authority and social options for middle-class women have come an onslaught of new pressures: increased work hours, bleeding of outside work into home spaces, a shrinking middle class amid a growing economic divide, and parenting philosophies that emphasize mothers' constant attention to their children and their safety.[79] Combined, these recent developments have contributed to a loss of the possibilities mahjong culture represented, when mothers' social leisure and women's communities, enabled by some of the same conditions that limited their options, temporarily remapped domestic space.

Epilogue

READING THE TILES

TODAY A DAUGHTER who grew up going to a Catskills bungalow colony hosts a group in her San Francisco living room. Two non-Jewish men, life partners and singers in the San Francisco opera, join two Jewish women at the table. The host turns on a kettle for tea. Placed around the four edges of the table are the newest rule cards from the National Mah Jongg League; two are the large-print versions. It is the host's turn to rotate out for this round, and she walks slowly behind the players' chairs, examining their combinations of tiles. Her fingers jot a note on a pad of paper to place her secret bet on a winner, then linger near a cookie plate before swerving to the bowl of carrot sticks on the granite kitchen counter. The players moan in turn as they pluck tiles from the wall, complaining about their luck. "It's just a game," says one. "If only that were true," another replies.[1]

Voices calling, "One bam! Six dot!" still waft out of New York apartments, and the clatter of mahjong tiles still echo down the alleys of San Francisco's Chinatown. Now, however, the smells of bustling cafés, the intense quiet of tournament halls, and the clicking of computer keys join these more familiar mahjong sights and sounds. From the twentieth century into the twenty-first, mahjong's cultural meaning continued to evolve and diversify along with the social, demographic, and technological changes that marked each era. Today mahjong is once again rising in popularity.[2] Even film star Julia Roberts celebrated the joy of her weekly women's mahjong game on the *Late Show with Stephen Colbert*, as the audience cheered in response.[3] The game's adaptability continues to undergird its evolving social meanings, from ongoing ethnic and gendered resonances to a new digital world and increasing diversification. Collectors interested in the game's aesthetics and materiality, nostalgic baby boomers recalling their mothers' forms of play and community, and younger generations looking for ethnic roots and undeterred by gendered stigmas are all fueling a mahjong revival, as an American gaze increasingly fixates on a China seen as, once again, both alluring and ominous.

Over the past decades, mahjong retained its resonance for building ethnic identity. In the early 1960s, a group of mothers started the Chinese American Women's Club in San Jose, California. The club was borne out of a weekly mahjong game held as its founders waited to pick up their children from Chinese school. They pooled their small winnings with the goal of promoting Chinese culture to a broader American audience and to the next generation through public events like cooking demonstrations and food booths. It is perhaps unsurprising that mahjong should have facilitated this connection, both because of its history in building ethnic communities, and its use as a way to raise funds for philanthropy. For adherents to the National Mah Jongg League's game, mahjong has also continued as a fundraising activity, facilitated by the League's ongoing rule card sales.[4]

Since the 1990s, the game has seen a steady rise in American popular consciousness, sparked first by Amy Tan's 1989 novel *The Joy Luck Club* and its film adaptation in 1993.[5] Tan's story begins when a daughter takes her deceased mother's place in a long-standing mahjong game. Their game facilitated friendships among a generation of immigrant Chinese women and structures the telling of their complicated relationships with their American-born daughters. In a relative dearth of popular representations of Chinese American culture, *The Joy Luck Club* shaped white Americans' perceptions of Chinese American family relationships and women's experiences. It also inspired the president of the Foster City Chinese Club, Joyce Chan, to organize *Joy Luck Club*-themed mahjong events, complete with movie theater posters for decoration. Media coverage of the game spiked as readers desired to learn more. A line in the film compared the National Mah Jongg League's game, which they called "Jewish mahjong," unfavorably to Chinese mahjong and thereby informed some viewers of a link they had not known about. When a young Jewish woman in Arizona heard the reference to her identity from this surprising source, it motivated her—and her baby-boomer mother—to then learn the game; meanwhile in West Los Angeles, Carol Kaiserman launched a "Jewish Joy Luck Club."[6]

In 2018, the blockbuster film *Crazy Rich Asians* became the first Hollywood English-language film to feature an all-Asian main cast since the *Joy Luck Club* twenty-five years earlier.[7] Its enormous commercial success made headlines, while a pivotal mahjong scene brought the game back into the spotlight.[8] The scene encapsulated part of what made the film so notable: *Crazy Rich Asians* was a profitable celebration of diasporic and transnational Chinese cultures in a conventional romance-comedy genre—without explaining the nuances of its cultural references to an outsider audience.[9]

Changing gender and sexual politics have strengthened rather than weakened mahjong's connections to Asian and Jewish American ethnicity. In the 1980s and 1990s, queer people of color sought to create LGBTQ-identified communities among those who experienced shared vulnerabilities of race, ethnicity, and religion. Within ethnic groups where mahjong already marked a shared culture, individuals could, in turn, use mahjong to identify with the "mainstream" within ethnic communities and also build a positive sense of queer community around their position on the edges. These motivations to gain inclusion but retain distinctiveness overlap with similar feelings that helped propel mahjong's popularity for Jewish American women amid postwar middle-class assimilation. For some Jewish lesbians in the San Francisco Bay Area, mahjong's gender and ethnic resonances lent themselves beautifully to women's community building decades later. In 2000, the Gay Asian Pacific Alliance (GAPA) contributed a float to San Francisco's elaborate Chinese New Year parade complete with "Miss GAPA" playing mahjong in drag. In the 1990s and early 2000s, gay men in New York and California embraced the game as well, including Jewish men. Their politics of gender and sexual transgression meant that mahjong's strongly feminine connotation in the United States would not deter them from playing the game. As in mahjong's earlier history, the San Francisco Bay Area took on a central role. Its historic influx of influences helped make it a center for queer culture as well as a hub of Asian immigration and Asian American populations.[10]

In the early twenty-first century, references to a Jewish American past created an intergenerational bridge. Because mahjong played an iconic role in midcentury Jewish women's culture, it became a focal point. In the 2010s, a traveling exhibit curated by the Museum of Jewish Heritage helped promote the spreading enthusiasm. "Project Mah Jongg" fueled media coverage and ignited local florescence of memories and attention to the game. As the Cold War era's aesthetic profile has risen in popular culture and media representations, the rising generation has retouched mahjong with a touch of glamour and nostalgia. Vacationing camps for young Jewish American adults are, in effect, the Catskills gone millennial. At Trybal Gatherings, mahjong is among a suite of offerings meant to entertain, build community, and connect with ethnic roots.[11] In 2018, the hit streaming series *The Marvelous Mrs. Maisel* depicted a color-saturated vision of the Catskills and its mahjong tables, reinforcing the association for younger viewers distanced from the heyday of the bungalow colonies and beach clubs.[12] As the first generation of National mahjong players aged, the game became associated with older women rather than the young mothers they once were. Although mahjong's revival has occurred primarily among the retiring generation, many young mothers continue to find the same camaraderie their grandmothers did at the mahjong table. As one new mahjong player wrote, "Sure, we were in our thirties, not our eighties, but I liked the idea of getting together with friends for an activity that included neither our children nor our spouses and resembled nothing I had tried with friends before."[13]

Mahjong in the United States continues to reflect the changing face of America, and its endurance is linked to its diverse history across Asia. Particularly after 1965, when the national quota system that excluded Asian immigrants ended with the Immigration and Nationality Act, the growing Asian American population has deepened and diversified America's transpacific ties. The game has continued to evolve and change in China and across Asia, fostering unique Filipino and Japanese mahjong cultures, which in turn shape nationally specific Asian American communities.[14] The Asian American mahjong landscape continues to shift with multidirectional and frequent transpacific travel. Regional Chinese variants of the game have proliferated, with recent immigrants from China sometimes struggling to find a group to play their preferred style. Mahjong has, however, continued to maintain a remarkable spectrum of respectability, from a low-stakes game for families and elderly women, to high-stakes and risky gaming. As Las Vegas casinos increasingly target immigrants and wealthy Chinese tourists, hotels on the Strip have incorporated dim sum and mahjong along with games of chance popular in the Chinese gambling center of Macau. Immigrants' use of the game to build social connections in their communities demonstrates yet again the game's enduring capacity to build ties in the midst of new and uprooted situations.

Well into the twenty-first century, mahjong still connects far-flung Air Force officers' wives, as well as a smaller number of retired female military officers. (It remains a game of officer rank, not the enlisted.) It endures as a way to build relationships amid the transience and hierarchies of base life and also to maintain long-lasting friendships within military circles after re- tirement. The Wright-Patterson Mah Jongg Club leadership releases new standard hands about every six years, while local debates have erupted over whether to incorporate jokers. The conflict reveals the increasing crossover between mahjong cultures and styles of play, in this case among those who know both the Wright-Patterson and National Mah Jongg League rules.[15]

In a change from earlier decades, mahjong enthusiasts have also started intentionally crossing boundaries of ethnicity, gender, and style of game play to unite around a shared love of mahjong. In the annual "Egg Rolls, Egg Creams, and Empanadas" festival, games of mahjong help celebrate the mixed cultural heritage of Manhattan's Lower East Side. In San Francisco, a Chinese American artist and Jewish American chef created "Jews for Dim Sum" snack boxes that combined elements of mahjong with consumable art and wry humor.[16] In 2011, the American Jewish Committee and the Asian Week Foundation co-sponsored an event to bring together Chinese and Jewish players. Meanwhile, the grandson of a National Mah Jongg League player started a new Philadelphia group promoting Japanese riichi mahjong; he was inspired to learn an Asian style of mahjong after watching *Crazy Rich Asians* (though the film featured Chinese, not Japanese mahjong).[17] The group welcomes newcomers, many of whom are not of Japanese descent. Across the country, players' gatherings are increasingly ethnically mixed, and a small but notable population of men has joined the ranks of League players. Women are often eager to have them, perhaps because male players deflect some of the criticisms of mahjong as a frivolous women's game. Indeed, for the first time in its history the National Mah Jongg League is led by men: two sons of longtime president Ruth Unger. The game is also diversifying in other ways that mirror a general increase in informality in American life. Since the 1970s, hostesses are no longer obligated to entertain; groups can play in cafés instead.

Mahjong's adherents have grown among an aging population, though younger players are coming to the game as well.[18] Community centers regularly advertise mahjong meet-ups and classes. In retirement communities, mahjong is once again proving to be a way to forge new relationships. These new networks have encouraged the diversification of mahjong groups, particularly for the League's National game. Often, the epicenters of this growth remain Jewish women, even as others learn it.[19] Many are baby boomers who grew up around the game, but who may have rejected it in youthful rebellion or who simply did not make time for it amid their generation's growing career commitments and more time-intensive approaches to parenting. For them, the game can connect to a sense of family and heritage or simply provide an enjoyable mix of intellectual challenge and social stimulation. These women are teaching new neighbors and friends, and sometimes learning it alongside the next generation of family members. In Dallas, a group of neighbors with Christian backgrounds has picked up the League's game, but the seeds of knowledge were originally planted through lessons from a Jewish mother-in-law.[20] Professional instructors are joining these ad-hoc teachers and mahjong is once again proving to be a career opportunity, particularly for women.[21] One particularly prolific instructor, Linda Feinstein, has taught thousands of players and convenes a popular "Mah Jongg Mondays" gathering in Manhattan, near the Essex House where the National Mah Jongg League first formed. She and other New Yorkers noticed a particular turn toward mahjong in the days after the 9/11 attacks in Manhattan, when people turned to spending time with friends in home-based activities.[22]

Mahjong's adaptability has allowed it to take on new forms amid the digital revolution, though its analog appeal remains irreplaceable. Mahjong has become widely known as a popular computer solitaire game, played with the same game-set structure but entirely different rules. In contrast to the tile game's sensory qualities, role in community building, and complex cultural meanings, this new version is played alone in front of digital screens. Mahjong can also be played against the computer. Drivers of Tesla luxury electric cars will soon be able to enjoy the leisure of self-driving vehicles with mahjong games installed for the Chinese market.[23] Elsie McCormick presaged this development a century earlier when she joked that devotees in Shanghai desired to play the game while being driven in rickshaws, with portable tables strung around player's necks.[24] However, some online venues for interactive, though remote play also exist.[25] Even the National Mah Jongg League, which rarely ventures into the digital realm, has an official membership-based internet game in which players "enter" a virtual space decorated to look like an elegant living room.[26] The League's simulated space echoes the cultural trappings of middle-class America, but the interactions center on speed-based play without the social aspects—and, according to some, with harsher competition. Players can seek out speed in online games or through increasingly popular public mahjong tournaments, while also still hosting social groups in their living rooms. During the coronavirus pandemic and community lockdowns of 2020 and 2021, these digital platforms became vitally important to combat isolation, and many groups who had only played in person began to venture online to meet at a shared time and website.[27] Social media has also helped unite mahjong players and collectors, further fueling its revival. Lively discussion boards about the game and how to collect sets have mushroomed.

Mahjong instructor and collector Johni Levene started a Facebook group named "Mah Jongg, That's It!" after Dorothy Meyerson's book; it boasts nearly 30,000 members.

The sensory appeal of mahjong tiles—their sound, heft, and beauty—endures for players, even as manufacturing for the American market has transformed. By the late twentieth century, the demand for domestically manufactured sets declined as the core market of Jewish women experienced a generational shift away from the game. Those who continued to play often kept the same sets that had held them in good stead. Manufacturing in many industries moved abroad, and in the contemporary global economy China once again supplies most sets for the American market, including the sets sold through the National Mah Jongg League. However, collectors are fueling a rise in value of those old vintage sets, overlapping with the collectors' market for early plastics like Catalin and Bakelite. In 2015, Crisloid, the Rhode Island–based games manufacturer that acquired A&L Manufacturing in 1970, began releasing limited runs of once again hand-crafted mahjong sets, this time for the luxury market. The most recent are characterized by whimsy and showcase entirely new imaginings of craks, bams, dots, and dragons, so that for the first time these sets have lost the visual reminder of their Chinese origins.[28] Crisloid is the sole representative of contemporary American mahjong manufacturing, made within the new high-end collector's market still driven by the appeal of artisanal craftsmanship, as well as the powerful element of nostalgia.

As players and their children age, the meaning of their mahjong sets has grown in psychological importance. Today, many play with the tiles that re-unite them with loved ones who have passed away.[29] Survivors often feel a deep and powerful connection when they hold the heft of the tiles and feel the cool smoothness, or hear the clatter of the tiles that evokes beloved voices in the air. The materiality of mahjong remains deeply important to the game's ongoing appeal.

The current revival of mahjong reveals much about our own historical moment, as well as the enduring patterns and connections to the past. Mahjong's history charts the substantial diversification of American culture, as the nation has become increasingly able to incorporate difference and even, at least rhetorically, to embrace it. By evoking ideas of China, the tiles' aesthetic symbolism offers a spectrum of meaning, whether giving shape to a sense of ancestral homeland, or an exotic otherworldliness, or a cosmopolitan American modernity. Through mahjong, individuals and groups continue to build a sense of belonging in new and possibly anxious situations, to feel a connection to China or what China represents, and to join with those who share heritage or are forming a common identity. It reveals the deeply American experience, sometimes desired and sometimes enforced, of simultaneously belonging and also standing apart.

Acknowledgments

THIS PROJECT HAS only been possible through the generosity of my mentors, colleagues, loved ones, and interviewees. So many have shared so much with me.

I will never cease to be grateful for my incredible good fortune to work with and learn from Estelle Freedman. Her mentorship has provided the rare and invaluable combination of both guidance and empowerment. Words cannot express how much her teaching, scholarship, and friendship continue to enrich my life.

At the other end of the gestation of this project, Susan Ferber midwifed its publication with astonishing skill and support. I am deeply honored to be able to work with an editor who dedicates such time, energy, and incisive feedback to improve a first-time author's work.

In between, many readers shared their time and wisdom by reading portions of this book. I was fortunate to begin my academic training at Whitman College, and I have benefited ever since from the insights of Nina Lerman and Lynn Sharp. In graduate school, Gordon Chang, Estelle Freedman, Allyson Hobbs, and Tom Mullaney set me on a particularly fruitful path with their advice, critiques, and support throughout my dissertation process. My writing group comrades, Natalie Marine-Street, Katherine Marino, and Andy Robichaud, provided astute commentary as well as vital camaraderie. Stephanie Cole, Nancy Cott, and Judy Tzu-Chun Wu generously offered key feedback as I revised the dissertation into a book. With my first position out of graduate school, I landed at the University of Texas at Dallas. One of the greatest gifts to come out of those three years was a multidisciplinary writing group with Ashley Barnes, Erin Greer, Charles Hatfield, Natalie Ring, Eric Schlereth, Shilyh Warren, and Dan Wickberg, who each improved many iterations of this manuscript. I was extremely fortunate to have Lynn Dumenil as a manuscript reader, and she continued to offer keen insight throughout revision. Brenda Frink, Bryna Goodman, and Valerie Matsumoto lent their expertise to individual chapters. Most recently at the University of Oregon, Michelle McKinley and the participants of the Works in Progress group at the Center for the Study of Women in Society contributed helpful feedback during late-stage revisions. Finally, I owe a debt of gratitude to the anonymous readers of *Frontiers: A Journal of Women Studies, American Historical Review,* and Oxford University Press.

For four of the dozen years I've spent writing about mahjong, I worked on a related project reconsidering domesticity in a global perspective, published in the *American Historical Review.* Conversations with and critical advice from my collaborators Antoinette Burton, Julie Hardwick, Victoria Haskins, Elizabeth LaCouture, Abigail McGowan, and Kathryn Kish Sklar greatly improved this book. Linda Kerber, Rebecca Jo Plant, Nayan Shah, Eileen Findlay, and Alex Lichtenstein also shared invaluable commentary.

Over sixty individuals shared their memories and family stories with me. I could not have written this book without their generosity and trust. I wish to especially thank those who shared the invaluable and ephemeral "stuff" of memories and gave me precious mahjong sets, photographs, and keepsakes, including Joyce Chan, Dorothy Toy Fong, Rita Greenstein, Katherine Hartman, Boots Hersh, Hilda Korner, Beth Lean, Ginnie Lo, Hilda Schaffer, and Zelda Schoengold. While I know that not everyone I interviewed will agree with the history I've written, I hope each person who gave me the gift of their time and memories can recognize themselves in this story, and feel that it contributes an understanding and appreciation of their lives. Sadly, some of my interviewees have since passed away; I wish I could have shared this book with them, and I hope my words honor their memories. I would also like to thank the broader mahjong community, from the bustling Mah Jongg Collectors Association and groups on social media to enthusiastic tableside players.

Additional individuals whose contributions are too lengthy to individually enumerate, but who deserve special mention include: Audrey Aldman, Christopher Berg, Jeff Caruso, Von Diaz, Dorlie Fong, Myron Gittell, Mary Greenfield, Betty Duke, Jim Hevia, Destin Jenkins, Brooks Jessup, Al and Nancy Johnston, Amy Jo Jones, Jenna Weissman Joselit, Linda and Charles Kraus, Rachel Kranson, Ellen Johnston Laing, Elizabeth Lasensky, Emory Lee, Johni Levene, Sarah Levine-Gronningsater, Beth Lew-Williams, Sara Levy Linden, Judith Litvich, Ginnie Lo, Sharon Loui, Al Low, Alison

Lustbader, Diana Mark, Lynne Mok, Deborah Dash Moore, Greg Morris, Pamela Nadell, Jaime Oberlander, Phil Orbanes, Stacey Revitz, Marjorie Sablow, Toby Salk, Jonathan D. Sarna, Sharon Edelman and Paul Schreiber, Alida Silverman, Tom Sloper, Lauren Lean, Michael Stanwick, Molly Taylor-Poleskey, Ruth Unger and David Unger, Nathalie Wade, Marin Watts, Rabbi Avi Weiss, Melissa Martens Yaverbaum, Connie Yu, Judy Yung, and Leandra Zarnow. I apologize for any omissions and sincerely appreciate the help of many others not listed here.

Historians are always indebted to the work of archivists, librarians, and curators. I have directly benefited from the expertise and thoughtfulness of numerous individuals, including Chen Xuyan at the Shanghai Library; Hong Cheng at UCLA; Jan Clay at the Oroville Chinese Temple and Museum Complex; Nancy Davis and Jim Roan at the National Museum of American History; Bob Fisher at the Wing Luke Museum; Gabriella Karsch at the Pacific Asia Museum; Ken Klein at USC; Zachary Baker, Anna Levia, and especially Ben Stone at Stanford University Libraries; Joelle Mintz at the Chinese American Museum; Claire Pingel at the National Museum of American Jewish History; Ellen Shea of the Schlesinger Library; Amy Jo Jones of the Wright-Patterson Officers' Spouses' Club; and the staff members of the A/P/A Institute at New York University, San Francisco Public Library, and the National Archives at San Francisco. Arlene Balkansky helped make the Library of Congress infinitely more accessible and welcoming. The unofficial curator of the Parker Brothers Archive, George Burtch, literally unlocked the doors to their treasures next to the factory floor. Finally, Marjorie Meyerson Troum kept the figurative keys to her mother's rich personal papers, and I am grateful to her for sharing them with me.

My work has also benefited from the generosity of other mentors and colleagues. In my home department at the University of Oregon, Leslie Alexander, Bryna Goodman, Allison Madar, Brett Rushforth, and Julie Weise offered particular support. The Arts and Humanities community at the University of Texas at Dallas deepened my scholarship and provided warm fellowship. I am grateful for the individual and collective criticisms and generous support of the Stanford history faculty and graduate student community. Additional thanks go to Stanford faculty members Ari Kelman, Jim Campbell, Matt Sommer, Caroline Winterer, Richard White, and Al Camarillo. Along the way, Zhang Yu, Andrew Elmore, Tom Mullaney, Yvon Wang, and Johannes Voelz provided generous translation assistance. In particular, Luke Habberstad contributed expert translation.

Trips to archives and conferences, in addition to more prosaic sustenance, were made possible with the support of the Brush and Endeavour Faculty Fellowships from the Department of History at the University of Oregon, Michelle R. Clayman Institute for Gender Research Graduate Dissertation Fellowship, the Mellon Foundation Dissertation Fellowship, the Taube Center for Jewish Studies Conference Grant, the Diversity Dissertation Research Opportunity Fellowship, the Schlesinger Library Dissertation Grant at the Radcliffe Institute, and the Bell Family Fellowship at Stanford University.

In the larger community, I wish to thank my co-panelists and the audience members at the conferences of the American Historical Association, the Association for Asian Studies, the Berkshire Conference of Women Historians, the Western Association of Women Historians, the Plastics Heritage Conference with the Portuguese Center for the History of Science and Technology, as well as the audiences for my talks at the Contemporary Jewish Museum in San Francisco and community groups. I appreciate the intellectual community of the US History Workshop and the Gender Workshop at Stanford, as well as the Dallas Area Society of Historians. My undergraduate and graduate students at UO, UTD, and Stanford have consistently invigorated my approach to history.

Friends who are chosen family have immeasurably enriched my life, often adding not only nourishment for the soul and the stomach, but contributing their own intellectual insights and curiosity as well. Heartfelt thanks go to Erin Bray and Eric Marsh, Megan and Malcolm Dunn, Danielle Kraus and Thomas Both, Katherine Marino, Anna Markee and Jen Whipple, Tom Mullaney and Chiara Vernari Mullaney, Kristina Mustacich and Glenn Kessler, Jessie Schreiber and Rory Henneck, Sarah Stein Greenberg, Victoria Sun, Jema Turk, and Simon Weiss. The children who came into the world during this project's development, Alice and Lila Both, Remi and Tula Braymarsh, Simon and Eleanor Dunn, Ana Lucia Heinz, Rose Schreiber Henneck, Morris and Charlie Mustacich Kessler, Milly Krummeck, Orfeo Vernari Mullaney, Althea and Arlo Turkweiss, and Tim Whipple, have each contributed their own joyful senses of wonder.

My extended family, both the Heinz clan and my partner's family, have seen us, this project, and me through many twists and turns, and I am grateful for each of them. My inspiring grandmother, Norma Heinz, not only took me to a mahjong tearoom, but also won her first game there. Susan Weiss deserves special thanks for her enthusiastic interest. I am also thankful for

Mike Beebe's encouragement. In addition, Denise Van Horn has supported this project every step of the way.

I have a lifetime of gratitude for my father, Tom Heinz, and his unequivocal love, and for my sister, Carol Heinz, who has always believed in me. Although I deeply wish I could have benefited from her support and insights, this project is a testimony to my mother, Peggy Heinz, her enduring love, and her passion for history.

There are two people without whom this particular book would not exist. In so many ways, the brilliant mind and constant inspiration of Katie Krummeck sustained this project, as she has enlightened every aspect of my life for over twenty years. From Southwest China to San Francisco, Dallas, and Portland, mahjong infiltrated our lives. She not only tolerated it but welcomed it with astonishing good humor. More than a decade ago, Katie encouraged me to pursue the unconventional research idea that my aunt Jane Heinz first sparked when she visited us in China. Jane had asked a seemingly simple question about why her Jewish friends played this apparently Chinese game, and I soon discovered that the source of this intriguing connection remained unexplained. As she had throughout my life, Jane enthusiastically supported my efforts – from the germ of an idea to the book's cover design. Tragically, we lost Jane to cancer in the final stages of publication. With their shared stubbornness, deep generosity, and mutual admiration, Jane and Katie each wanted me to dedicate the book to the other. In fact, they are both essential to its story. Inasmuch as these pages are mine to give, they are for Katie and for Jane, together.

Many thanks to those who contributed oral histories and correspondence:

Audrey Abel* (pseudonym)	Sylvia Leeds
Diane Baker	David Leong
Ronnie Becher	Frank Lodato
Dorene Beller	Zelda Lubart
Edy Berman-Peterson	Martha Lustbader
Joan Blednick	Joan Mapou
Arlene Brodman	Margaret Masters
Janice Brodsky	Judy Michelson
Joyce (Lee) Chan	Rhoda Persicano
Katherine Chann	Renny Pritikin
Grace Chun	Arlene Revitz

Natalie Cohen

Jamie Corwin

Barbara Dellon

Linda Feinstein

Dorothy Toy Fong

Linda Forth* (pseudonym)

Hilda Grande

Rita Rappoport Greenstein

Stephanie Grossman

Jeff Gurock

Pamela Gurock

Amy Gwilliam

Boots "Boots" Hersh

John Hom

Margo Horn

Kay Hunter

Ann Israel

Judye Kanfer

Kelli Vernon Kirkham

Hilda Korner

Charles Kraus

Linda Kraus

Nancy Kraus

Margaret Kuo

Beth Lean

David Lee

Janae Lee* (pseudonym)

Judi Quan Rizzuto

Marilyn Robinson

Laurence Roth

Eva and Richard Rubel

Marjorie Sablow

Reva Salk

Toby Salk

Elaine Sandberg

Hilda Schaffer

Rochelle "Shelley" Schreiber

Ethel Shapiro

Zelda Shoengold

Carol Shuttleworth

Susan "Sue" Shields

Alida Silverman

Seymour and Edith Silverman

Angelina "Ann" Speranza

Marilyn Starr

Mary Street

Marjorie Meyerson Troum

Ruth Unger

Toby Weiss

Denice Wisniewski

Cee Cee Wu

Al Yu* (pseudonym)

Emily Yue

Notes

PREFACE

1. Michael Stanwick and Hongbing Xu, "From Cards to Tiles: The Origin of Mahjong(g)'s Earliest Suit Names," *The Playing-Card* 41, no. 1 (September 2012), http://themahjongtileset.co.uk/earliest-suit-names/.

2. Tom Sloper, "Identifying a Mah-Jongg Variant: FAQ 2b," *Sloper on Mah-Jongg* (blog), accessed January 5, 2020, http://www.sloperama.com/mjfaq/mjfaq02b. html#Details.

3. For more on how to play, an authoritative source is Tom Sloper, *The Red Dragon & The West Wind: The Winning Guide to Official Chinese & American Mah-Jongg* (New York: HarperCollins, 2007).

INTRODUCTION

1. Han Bangqing, *The Sing-Song Girls of Shanghai*, ed. Eva Hung, trans. Eileen Chang (New York: Columbia University Press, 2005); Hsi-yüan Chen, "Cong madiao dao majiang [Madiao and Mahjong in Popular Culture and Elite Discourse]," trans. Luke Habberstad, *Bulletin of the Institute of History and Philology Academia Sinica*, March 2009, 180.

2. Janet Wulsin, June 28, 1921, Janet Elliott Wulsin Personal Papers, Folder: 2004.7.1.33, Peabody Library, Harvard University.

3. George S. Romanovsky, *Standard Rules and Regulations for the Game of Lung-Chan* (San Francisco: Lung Chan Company, 1923); Georges Romanovsky, *Règles du jeu du Lung Chan*, trans. Paul Verdier (Paris: Lung Chan Company, 1924).

4. Chinese American Museum, "Sun Wing Wo General Store and Herb Shop Exhibit" (Los Angeles, August 21, 2012); "Du Wan and Tom J. Chong Family Photo Album," 1930-1935, Huntington Library.

5. Ted Freudy, "Photograph: Mahjong at Green's Lakeside Hotel, NY," 1955, Lorna Drake, Freudy Photos Archives, LLC.

6. China Trading Co., "Forced Sale!," *Seattle Post-Intelligencer*, November 5, 1922, Mah-Jongg Sales Company (MJSC) Scrapbook 1, Parker Brothers Archive (PB).

7. Borrowing from Philip Deloria, *Playing Indian* (New Haven: Yale University Press, 1998).

8. See, for example, Virginia Yans, "On 'Groupness,'" *Journal of American Ethnic History* 25, no. 4 (Summer 2006): 119–129; Lon Kurashige, *Japanese American Celebration and Conflict: A History of Ethnic Identity and Festival, 1934–1990* (Berkeley: University of California Press, 2002).

9. Sylvia Leeds, interview by author, Phone, August 8, 2014.

10. Donna R. Braden, *Leisure and Entertainment in America* (Dearborn, MI: Henry Ford Museum & Greenfield Village, 1988); Kathy Peiss, *Cheap Amusements: Working Women and Leisure in Turn-of-the-Century New York* (Philadelphia: Temple University Press, 1986); Lizabeth Cohen, *A Consumers' Republic: The Politics of Mass Consumption in Postwar America* (New York: Random House, 2003); Juliet Schor, *The Overworked American: The Unexpected Decline of Leisure* (New York: Basic Books, 1991).

11. David G. Schwartz, *Roll the Bones: The History of Gambling* (New York: Gotham Books, 2006); Jackson Lears, *Something for Nothing: Luck in America* (New York: Viking Penguin, 2003); Ann Fabian, *Card Sharps and Bucket Shops: Gambling in Nineteenth-Century America* (New York: Routledge, 1999).

12. Helen Bullitt Lowry, "Rise and Present Peril of Mah Jong: The Chinese Game Has Escaped from Society's Chaperonage and Is on Its Own," *New York Times*, August 10, 1924.

13. Ronnie Becher, interview by author, Phone, May 15, 2012.

14. Margaret Kuo, interview by author, San Francisco, CA, June 17, 2014.

15. Kristin L. Hoganson, *Consumers' Imperium: The Global Production of American Domesticity, 1865–1920* (Chapel Hill: University of North Carolina Press, 2007); Cohen, *A Consumers' Republic*; Susan Porter Benson, *Counter Cultures: Saleswomen, Managers, and Customers in American Department Stores, 1890–1940* (Urbana: University of Illinois Press, 1986); Emily Remus, *A Shoppers' Paradise: How the Ladies of Chicago Claimed Power and Pleasure in the New Downtown* (Cambridge, MA: Harvard University Press, 2019); Charles McGovern, *Sold American: Consumption and Citizenship, 1890–1945* (Chapel Hill: University of North Carolina Press, 2006).

16. See, for example, Alice Kessler-Harris, *Out to Work: A History of Wage-Earning Women in the United States* (New York: Oxford University Press, 1982); Joanne Meyerowitz, ed., *Not June Cleaver: Women and Gender in Postwar America, 1945–1960* (Philadelphia: Temple University Press, 1994); Nan Enstad, *Ladies of Labor, Girls of Adventure: Working Women, Popular Culture, and Labor Politics at the Turn of the Twentieth Century* (New York: Columbia University Press, 1999);

Cornelia Dayton and Lisa Levenstein, "The Big Tent of US Women's and Gender History: A State of the Field," *Journal of American History* 99, no. 3 (December 2012): 793–817.

CHAPTER 1

1. "Photograph: Granada Theatre," September 1922, MJSC Scrapbook 1, PB; Atlantic Dance Orchestra; "[Snippet about Mah Jongg Blues]," *Moving Picture World*, December 2, 1922, The Moving Picture World Collection, Library of Congress; The Granada Theatre, "Advertisement: George Melford's 'Burning Sands,'" 1922, MJSC Scrapbook 1, PB; "The Granada Theatre Program," September 1922, MJSC Scrapbook 1, PB; "Mah-Jongg Inspiration of Granada Act," *San Francisco Examiner*, September 26, 1922, MJSC Scrapbook 1, PB; "'Mah-Jongg' Blues Stars at the Granada," *San Francisco Daily News*, September 29, 1922, MJSC Scrapbook 1, PB; "Granada Features Big Desert Story, 'Burning Sands,'" *San Francisco Chronicle*, September 25, 1922, MJSC Scrapbook 1, PB.

2. Atlantic Dance Orchestra, *Mah-Jongg Blues*, 1922, http://goo.gl/76PLVu; Columbia Theatre, "Columbiagram: Around the Mah Jongg Table," 1922, MJSC Scrapbook 1, PB.

3. Teresa de Escoriaza, "¡MAH-JONGG!," *La Prensa*, June 2, 1925; "Look Out, Bridge! Mah Jongg Is after Your Title," *Walla Walla Bulletin*, n.d., MJSC Scrapbook 1, PB; "Three Films Being Shown at Central," *Washington Post*, July 6, 1924; "Mah Jongg Shoes," n.d., MJ Scrapbook 2, PB; Sid Reinherz, "Mah Jong Novelty Piano Solo" (Jack Mills Inc., 1923), The Strong National Museum of Play.

4. Babcock may have spoken Mandarin or, perhaps more likely, the local Suzhounese dialect. He also had knowledge of written Chinese. Celia Babcock Smith and Martha Ann Babcock, Joseph Babcock and Mah Jong from Celia Babcock Smith's Oral History, interview by Barbara Babcock Millhouse and Sherold Hollingsworth, January 6, 2007, Christopher Berg Personal Collection.

5. Alma Sierks-Overholt and Norma Babcock, "Mah Jongg Started in Popularity at Catalina," *The Catalina Islander*, April 16, 1924.

6. Joseph Park Babcock, *The Laws of Mah-Jongg: 1925 Code Revised and Standardized by Joseph Park Babcock and an Associated Committee, Containing Also the New Game Du-Lo* (Salem, MA: Parker Brothers, Inc., 1925), 1.

7. "Joseph Park Babcock v. Philip Naftaly," October 10, 1922, Equity Case #848, The National Archives at San Francisco; Anton Lethin, "Letter to Agnes," February 18, 1923, Lisa Lethin Personal Collection; J. P. Babcock, *Babcock's Rules for Mah-Jongg: The Red Book of Rules*, Second (1920; repr., San Francisco: Mah-Jongg Sales Company of America, 1923); Edna Lee Booker, *News Is My Job: A Correspondent in War-Torn China* (New York: Macmillan, 1940), 17.

8. "Majjang Wins Popular Favor of Fair Avalonian Players," *Los Angeles Evening Express*, June 9, 1920, MJSC Scrapbook 1, PB.

9. Sierks-Overholt and Babcock, "Mah Jongg Started in Popularity at Catalina."

10. "Joseph Park Babcock v. Philip Naftaly"; Lethin, "Letter to Agnes," February 18, 1923.

11. R. F. Foster, *Foster on Mah Jong* (New York: Dodd, Mead, 1924), 168; Edith McConn, "Town Mah Jongg Mad; Society Stacks Tiles: Newly Introduced Chinese Game Spreads," *Evening News*, November 27, 1922.

12. Mah-Jongg Sales Company of America, "Mah-Jongg," *Indianapolis Star*, 1922, MJSC Scrapbook 1, PB; Mah-Jongg Sales Company of America, "Mah-Jongg," *Louisville Herald*, 1922, MJSC Scrapbook 1, PB; Mah-Jongg Sales Company of America, "Mah-Jongg," *Times Picayune*, 1922, MJSC Scrapbook 1, PB; Mah-Jongg Sales Company of America, "Mah-Jongg," *The Enquirer*, 1922, MJSC Scrapbook 1, PB; Mah-Jongg Sales Company of America, "Mah-Jongg," *The North American*, 1922, MJSC Scrapbook 1, PB; Mah-Jongg Sales Company of America, "Mah-Jongg," *New York Times*, 1922, MJSC Scrapbook 1, PB; Mah-Jongg Sales Company of America, "Mah-Jongg," *El Paso Times*, 1922, MJSC Scrapbook 1, PB; Mah-Jongg Sales Company of America, "Mah-Jongg," *The Plain Dealer*, 1922, MJSC Scrapbook 1, PB; Mah-Jongg Sales Company of America, "Mah-Jongg," *Boston Post*, 1922, MJSC Scrapbook 1, PB; Mah-Jongg Sales Company of America, "Mah-Jongg," *Pittsburg Gazette Times*, 1922, MJSC Scrapbook 1, PB.

13. "Try Mah Jongg: New Chinese Game Introduced Here," *San Francisco Chronicle*, May 5, 1922; "Atlanta Woman Tells of Visiting War-Torn Korea," *Atlanta Constitution*, May 15, 1922.

14. "Oriental Game Intrigues 'Em: Poker Eclipsed by Chinese Game," *San Francisco Bulletin*, May 5, 1922, MJSC Scrapbook 1, PB.

15. Y. Lewis Mason, "Shipping and Travel News: Planning a Homeward Trip across the Pacific," *Chinese Students' Monthly* 20, no. 2 (December 1924): 75; R. F., "Mah Jongg," *Christian Science Monitor*, November 20, 1922; Elsie McCormick, "China's Ancient Dominoes Now Fascinate Foreigners [Abbreviated Reprint Clipping]," *Unknown*, 1921, MJSC Scrapbook 1, PB.

16. "Oriental Game Intrigues 'Em"; The John Wanamaker Store, "Advertisement: In the Far East Shop," *New York Tribune*, June 14, 1923, MJSC Scrapbook 1, PB. The Admiral Oriental Steamship Line issued free rulebooks—and claimed credit for introducing the game to the United States. *Ma-Chiong* (Seattle: Admiral Oriental Line, 1923); "Mah Jongg Rules Given Away Free by Oriental Line," *Atlanta Constitution*, March 2, 1924.

17. B. H. Dyas Co., "Come to Dyas' for Your Mah-Jongg Set," *Los Angeles Times*, May 7, 1922.

18. Emanie N. Sachs, "China's Fascinating Super Game," *New York Times*, September 3, 1922.

19. Christopher Berg, "Babcock/Fairbanks Photos," August 16, 2014.

20. "World's Biggest Hotel Opens Today," *New York Times*, January 25, 1919.

21. "Fascinating Old Chinese Game Becomes Fad in Cities on the Western Coast," *Pennsylvania Register (Hotel Pennsylvania)*, November 4, 1922, MJSC Scrapbook 1, PB.

22. "Martinelli, Operatic Star, and His Wife Playing Old Chinese Game," *The Sun*, November 10, 1922, MJSC Scrapbook 1, PB.

23. "Mah-Jongg Has Become Fad in Capital Society," *Baltimore American*, December 10, 1922. Lou and Herbert Hoover had lived and traveled together in China at the turn of the century while Herbert worked as a mining engineer, but it is unclear if either of them encountered mahjong while in China. With her California upbringing, residence in China, and her Northeastern political networks, Lou Hoover embodied the nexus of geographic connections that mahjong traveled.

24. "Newport, The Resort of Unfailing Charm," *Vogue*, September 1, 1923; Walter Lionel George, "Humanity at Palm Beach," *Harper's Monthly Magazine*, January 1925; "Miss Marion Angeline Howlett," *Boston Sunday Globe*, March 23, 1924, Marion Angeline Howlett Papers [unprocessed], Schlesinger Library, Radcliffe Institute, Harvard University.

25. Sierks-Overholt and Babcock, "Mah Jongg Started in Popularity at Catalina."

26. "Forms Mah Jong Club," *Chicago Defender*, February 9, 1924, National edition; Theo Burr, "'Long Distance' from Chicago," *The Spur*, June 1, 1923; "Latest Indoor Sport," *Seattle Post-Intelligencer*, August 20, 1922, MJSC Scrapbook 1, PB; "Chinese Parties Are 'All the Rage,'" *Atlanta Constitution*, November 4, 1923.

27. Mah-Jongg Sales Company of America, "Mah-Jongg Catalogue No. 2," 1923.

28. Joseph Park Babcock, Game, United States Patent Office 1554834 (Tsinan, China, Assignor to Mah-Jongg Company of China, of Shanghai, China, a Corporation of Alaska, filed November 4, 1922, and issued September 22, 1925); "Joseph Park Babcock v. Philip Naftaly"; Michael Stanwick, "The Origin and Development of the Mahjong Tile Set, Part 7," *The Mahjong Collector*, 2016.

29. Michael Stanwick, "J. P. Babcock, A. R. Hager, A. N. Lethin and the Mah-Jongg/ Mah-Jong Company of China et Al.," *The Mahjong Tile Set* (blog), accessed February 12, 2020, https://www.themahjongtileset.co.uk.

30. "Muh-Juhng" (Regensteiner Corporation, 1923), PB.

31. Mah Jongg Sales Co. of America, "Advertisement: What Is Mah Jongg?," *Tacoma News-Tribune*, August 22, 1922, MJSC Scrapbook 1, PB; Mah Jongg Sales Co. of America, "Advertisement: What Is Mah Jongg?," *San Francisco Call and Post*, July 22, 1922, MJSC Scrapbook 1, PB.

32. "Mah Jongg Sales Co. Sues for Copyright," *San Francisco Examiner*, October 25, 1922, MJSC Scrapbook 1, PB.

33. "Mah Jongg Suit Filed," *San Francisco Journal*, October 11, 1922, MJSC Scrapbook 1, PB; "Mah Jongg in Patent Tangle," *San Francisco Examiner*, October 11, 1922, MJSC Scrapbook 1, PB.

34. "Chinese Game of Mah Jongg in Legal War," *San Francisco Chronicle*, October 11, 1922, MJSC Scrapbook 1, PB; "Joseph Park Babcock v. Philip Naftaly"; "Joseph

Park Babcock v. H.S. Crocker Company," October 10, 1922, Equity Case #847, The National Archives at San Francisco.

35. Philip Naftaly, *Rules and Directions for the Chinese Game of "Ma Cheuck"* (San Francisco: Philip Naftaly, 1923).

36. "Het Mah-Jongg-Spel," *Nieuwe Rotterdamsche Courant*, December 23, 1924, http://www.mahjongmuseum.nl/1924-2; "Mah-Jongg vor Gericht," *Frankfurter General-Anzeiger*, November 5, 1924, http://www.mahjongmuseum.nl/1924-2; "Der Streit um Mah-Jongg," *Frankfurter Zeitung*, November 8, 1924, http://www.mahjongmuseum.nl/1924-2; Paul Heimann & Co., "Aufklärung über MAH JONGG," November 13, 1924, http://www.mahjongmuseum.nl/1924-2.

37. Babcock, Game.

38. "Fad in Capital Society."

39. "Gossip in Washington," *Los Angeles Times*, March 20, 1923.

40. "Fad in Capital Society."

41. Philip E. Orbanes, *The Game Makers: The Story of Parker Brothers from Tiddledy Winks to Trivial Pursuit* (Boston: Harvard Business School Press, 2004), 70.

42. 1924 Mah-Jongg Purchase Notice, as pictured in Orbanes, *The Game Makers*, 68.

43. Philip E. Orbanes, *The Game Makers*, 34.

44. "The Parker Games 1923–1924" (Parker Brothers, Inc., 1923), Catalogs, PB; "Pung Wo Junior Boxed Set" (Mei Ren Company, Inc., 1923), Project Mah Jongg, The Museum of Jewish Heritage—A Living Memorial to the Holocaust.

45. The Neophyte, "Dragons Clash at Mah-Jongg: Chinese Game Played in Time of Confucius Full of Intriguing Combinations," *Los Angeles Times*, November 5, 1922.

46. A. A. Vantine and Company, "Vantine's" (A. A. Vantine and Company [New York], 1920s), 6, Trade Catalogs, Winterthur Museum Library, http://archive.org/details/vantineso2aava.

47. Ly Yu Sang, *Sparrow: The Chinese Game Called Ma-Ch'iau* (New York: The Lent & Graff Co., for The Long Sang Ti Chinese Curios Co., Inc., 1923).

48. Oleg Grabar, "Roots and Others," in *Noble Dreams, Wicked Pleasures: Orientalism in America, 1870–1930* (Princeton: Princeton University Press and Sterling and Francine Clark Art Institute, 2000), 6.

49. Holly Edwards, "A Million and One Nights: Orientalism in America, 1870–1930," in *Noble Dreams, Wicked Pleasures: Orientalism in America, 1870–1930* (Princeton: Princeton University Press and Sterling and Francine Clark Art Institute, 2000), 11–58; Edward Said, *Orientalism* (New York: Vintage Books, 1978).

50. Einav Rabinovitch-Fox, "[Re]Fashioning the New Woman: Women's Dress, the Oriental Style, and the Construction of American Feminist Imagery in the 1910s," *Journal of Women's History* 27, no. 2 (Summer 2015): 14–36.

51. Kristin L. Hoganson, *Consumers' Imperium: The Global Production of American Domesticity, 1865–1920* (Chapel Hill: University of North Carolina Press, 2007);

Mari Yoshihara, *Embracing the East: White Women and American Orientalism* (New York: Oxford University Press, 2003), Ch. 1.

52. Hoganson, *Consumers' Imperium*, 16.

53. Anne Rittenhouse, "If You Don't Play Mah-Jong, You Should Learn Now," *Atlanta Constitution*, March 18, 1923; "Chinese Parties Are 'All the Rage'"; Ellye Howell Glover, *"Dame Curtsey's" Book of Party Pastimes for the Up-to-Date Hostess*, 6th ed. (Chicago: A. C. McClurg & Co., 1912).

54. Andrew Coe, *Chop Suey: A Cultural History of Chinese Food in the United States* (New York: Oxford University Press, 2009); Madeline Y. Hsu, "From Chop Suey to Mandarin Cuisine: Fine Dining and the Refashioning of Chinese Ethnicity during the Cold War Era," in *Chinese Americans and the Politics of Race and Culture* (Philadelphia: Temple University Press, 2008), 173–94.

55. C. H. Burnett, "Life History of Andrew Kan as Social Document" (Survey of Race Relations, August 22, 1924), Survey of Race Relations: Major Documents, Hoover Archive, Stanford University.

56. China Trading Co., "Forced Sale!," *Seattle Post-Intelligencer*, November 5, 1922, MJSC Scrapbook 1, PB.

57. Steven C. Caton, "The Sheik: Instabilities of Race and Gender in Transatlantic Popular Culture of the Early 1920s," in *Noble Dreams, Wicked Pleasures: Orientalism in America, 1870–1930* (Princeton: Princeton University Press and Sterling and Francine Clark Art Institute, 2000), 99–119.

58. Rupert Arrowsmith, "The Transcultural Roots of Modernism: Imagist Poetry, Japanese Visual Culture, and the Western Museum System," *Modernism/Modernity* 18, no. 1 (January 2011): 27–42; Gordon H. Chang, "Chinese Painting Comes to America: Zhang Shuqi and the Diplomacy of Art," *Journal of Transnational American Studies* 4, no. 1 (2012), www.escholarship.org/uc/item/0207q69j; Anthony W. Lee, *Picturing Chinatown: Art and Orientalism in San Francisco* (Berkeley: University of California Press, 2001).

59. Yoshihara, *Embracing the East*; Edwards, "A Million and One Nights."

60. Notably, in protest of anti-Chinese immigration laws the Qing government refused to send a delegation for a Chinese display; local Chinese Americans and Chinese immigrants volunteered to host a "Chinese Village" in their place. Edwards, "A Million and One Nights," 36–39; Yoshihara, *Embracing the East*, 17–23.

61. Michael Stanwick, "Mahjong(g) before Mahjong(g): Part 2," *The Playing-Card* 32, no. 5 (2004): 208.

62. Sarah Cheang, "Women, Pets, and Imperialism: The British Pekingese Dog and Nostalgia for Old China," *Journal of British Studies* 45 (April 2006).

63. Yoshihara, *Embracing the East*, 7; Gordon H. Chang, *Fateful Ties: A History of America's Preoccupation with China* (Cambridge, MA: Harvard University Press, 2015), Ch. 2; Hoganson, *Consumers' Imperium*.

64. Grace Nicholson, "Advertisement: Have You Ever Visited California's World Famous Treasure House of Oriental Art?," n.d., Grace Nicholson Papers, Box 8,

Huntington Library; Grace Nicholson, "Advertisement: Ma Jong Prizes," n.d., Grace Nicholson Papers, Box 8, Huntington Library; Grace Nicholson, "Advertisement: Regular $50 Ma Jong Sets for $30," n.d., Grace Nicholson Papers, Box 8, Huntington Library; Mary Kellog, "Chia: A Description of a Celestial Garden in Pasadena," *House Beautiful*, March 1927, Grace Nicholson Papers, Box 9, Huntington Library.

65. For relevant discussions of commodified Native American culture including basketry, see Paige Raibmon, *Authentic Indians: Episodes of Encounter from the Late-Nineteenth-Century Northwest Coast* (Durham, NC: Duke University Press, 2005); Boyd Cothran, "Working the Indian Field Days: The Economy of Authenticity and the Question of Agency in Yosemite Valley," *The American Indian Quarterly* 34, no. 2 (Spring 2010): 194–223.

66. David Parlett, *The Oxford History of Board Games* (New York: Oxford University Press, 1999), 225; Thierry Depaulis and Jac Fuch, "First Steps of Bridge in the West: Collinson's 'Biritch,'" *The Playing-Card* 32, no. 2 (October 2003): 67–76.

67. "Look Out, Bridge! Mah Jongg Is after Your Title"; "Chinese Checkers Win Society," *Los Angeles Times*, December 26, 1922; "Latest Indoor Sport"; "Fad in Capital Society." Many more examples abound.

68. "Queer Chinese Game, Invented Centuries Ago, Is Society's Latest Craze. Mah-Jongg, Intricate Pastime, Built around Great Wall of the Orient," *San Francisco Chronicle*, October 15, 1922, sec. F.

69. Robert Patterson, "Horatius at the Bridge," *Judge*, April 5, 1924.

70. See, for example: *Mah-Jongg, Sweet Little Devil* (WB Music Corp., 1923), Gershwin on Broadway; "The Joined Battle of the Games: When Mah Jong, Out of the Chinese East, Meets Old Inhabitant, Auction Bridge," *New York Times*, January 27, 1924.

71. "The Truth about Mah-Jongg: When You Have Trumped Your Partner's Ace and Feel Like Burning Your Bridge Tables behind You—Try Mah-Jongg," *Vogue*, January 15, 1923.

72. China Trading Co., "Advertisement: Mah-Jong 50c," *Vogue*, August 15, 1923; Goldwater's, "Advertisement: Society Puts Its Stamp of Approval on Mah-Jongg," 1922, MJSC Scrapbook 1, PB; MacDougall-Southwick, "Do You Want to Learn to Play Mah Jongg?," n.d., MJSC Scrapbook 1, PB.

73. McConn, "Town Mah Jongg Mad." See also "Chinese Checkers Win Society."

74. "Queer Chinese Game"; "New-Old Game Fascinates," *Seattle Times*, October 19, 1922, MJSC Scrapbook 1, PB.

75. "The Joined Battle of the Games."

76. Harry Murphy, "What Other Games Are There?," n.d., MJ Scrapbook 2, PB.

77. For a few examples, see John Held Jr., "'And the Twain Shall Meet,'" *Auction Bridge and Mah Jong Magazine*, May 1924, Library of Congress; Glenn Cook Morrow, "Never the Twain Shall Meet!," *Judge*, April 5, 1924; Harriette S. Stevens, "Mah Jongg—Its Principles and Interest," *Vogue*, 1923, 82; "Mah Jongg Safer Than Bridge

for Couples, Its Devotees Say," *New York World-Telegram*, April 30, 1941, Dorothy S. Meyerson Scrapbook, Marjorie Troum Personal Collection.

78. For a relevant discussion, see Karen Kuo, *East Is West and West Is East: Gender, Culture, and Interwar Encounters between Asia and America* (Philadelphia: Temple University Press, 2013).

79. Lew Lyle Harr, *Pung Chow: The Game of a Hundred Intelligences, Also Known as Mah-Diao, Mah-Jong, Mah-Cheuk, Mah-Juck and Pe-Ling* (New York: Harper & Brothers, 1922).

80. "Ancient Chinese Game Taking West Parties by Storm," 1922, MJSC Scrapbook 1, PB.

81. "Ancient Chinese Game Taking West Parties by Storm."

82. Albert Hager, Cabinet for Holding Games, United States Patent Office 1477056 (Shanghai, China, Assignor to the Mah-Jongg Company of China, of San Francisco, California, a Copartnership Consisting of Joseph Park Babcock, Anton N. Lethin, and Albert R. Hager, filed May 25, 1922, and issued December 11, 1923); Lucien A. Marsh, Game Board (Mill Valley, CA, filed November 21, 1922, and issued December 9, 1924); Leroy L. Richard and Robert E. Richard, Playing-Game Implement, 1571374 (Coalinga, CA, filed November 11, 1922, and issued February 2, 1926); Ruth J. Maurer, Rack, 1529660 (La Crosse, WI, filed April 20, 1923, and issued March 17, 1925); Scott Products Co., "Advertisement: Scott Rack for Mah Jongg, Pung Chow & Ma Cheuck," *Vogue*, July 15, 1923.

83. R. H. White Co., "Advertisement: The 'Latest' in Handkerchiefs—The 'Mah Jong,'" *Boston Daily Globe*, February 17, 1924; "Advertisement: The Silk Mah Jong Umbrella," *Boston Daily Globe*, May 4, 1924; Saks-Herald Square, "Advertisement: When Society Plays at Dragons and Winds," *New York Times*, August 28, 1924; Jordan Marsh Company, "Advertisement: Mah Jong," *Boston Daily Globe*, October 2, 1924.

84. "[Untitled]," *Olympia Recorder*, October 10, 1922, MJSC Scrapbook 1, PB; "Vogue's Fortnightly Wardrobe," *Vogue*, November 1, 1926; Stewart & Co., "Advertisement: College Club Creations for the College Term," *Vogue*, March 1, 1924; A. A. Vantine and Company, "Vantine's"; Amaizo Oil, "Advertisement: Mah Jong Cakes," *Chicago Daily Tribune*, June 5, 1924; "Chinese Styles in Vogue," *China Review*, September 1923.

85. "Decries Activities of Press Agents: Silk Group of Dry Goods Association Discusses Effect of Mah-Jongg on Styles," *New York Times*, January 15, 1924.

86. "The Business World: Offers a Mah Jongg Stocking," *New York Times*, January 19, 1924.

87. "Mah Jongg Sandals Grip Milady of Discernment," *Los Angeles Examiner*, June 19, 1923, MJSC Scrapbook 1, PB; "Mah Jongg Shoes."

88. "Mah Jong Min Lsing Is Champion Dog," *New York Times*, October 19, 1924; "Prize Steer Brings $4,680," *New York Times*, December 4, 1925; "Pamela of Frere Is Best Pekinese: Mrs. Tarbell's Mah Jongg Judged Best of Opposite Sex at Plaza,"

New York Times, January 20, 1925; "Revenge Is Victor at New Orleans: Mah Jong Fails Talent," *New York Times*, February 23, 1924.

89. "Assorted Stitched Tablecloths," 1920s, Johni Levene Personal Collection; "Ma Jong Party Invitation," 1920s, Johni Levene Personal Collection; Melissa J. Martens, "The Game of a Thousand Wonders," in *Mah Jongg: Crak Bam Dot* (New York: 2wiceBooks, 2010), 9.

90. The first version of the "Mah Jong Doll," likely an earlier prototype, was presented to Marion Howlett by its designer Grace G. Drayton, the originator of the iconic Campbell Soup Kids and a designer for the Averill Company. The Averill Company's factory-produced doll had a molded composition head that was interchangeable with "white" dolls, including blue eyes. In contrast, the Drayton prototype had pronounced slanted eyes painted on a fabric head. Martens, "The Game of a Thousand Wonders," 12. Marion Angeline Howlett, "Palm Beach 1924," 1924, Marion Angeline Howlett Papers [unprocessed], Schlesinger Library, Radcliffe Institute, Harvard University; "Miss Marion Angeline Howlett."

91. Lawrence B. Glickman, "Rethinking Politics: Consumers and the Public Good during the 'Jazz Age,'" *OAH Magazine of History*, Reinterpreting the 1920s, 21, no. 3 (July 2007): 16–20. See also Meg Jacobs, *Pocketbook Politics: Economic Citizenship in Twentieth-Century America* (Princeton: Princeton University Press, 2005); Charles McGovern, *Sold American: Consumption and Citizenship, 1890–1945* (Chapel Hill: University of North Carolina Press, 2006).

92. Martha Olney, *Buy Now, Pay Later: Advertising, Credit, and Consumer Durables in the 1920s* (Chapel Hill: University of North Carolina Press, 1991); Lynn Dumenil, *The Modern Temper: American Culture and Society in the 1920s* (New York: Hill and Wang, 1995), Ch. 2.

93. McGovern, *Sold American*; Janice Williams Rutherford, *Selling Mrs. Consumer: Christine Frederick and the Rise of Household Efficiency* (Athens: University of Georgia Press, 2003).

94. Alice Kessler-Harris, *Out to Work: A History of Wage-Earning Women in the United States* (New York: Oxford University Press, 1982), 226; Kathy Peiss, *Hope in a Jar: The Making of America's Beauty Culture* (Philadelphia: University of Pennsylvania Press, 1998), Chs. 4–5; Estelle Freedman, "The New Woman: Changing Views of Women in the 1920s," *The Journal of American History* 61, no. 2 (September 1974): 372–93; The Modern Girl around the World Research Group, ed., *The Modern Girl around the World: Consumption, Modernity, and Globalization* (Durham, NC: Duke University Press, 2008).

95. The Glazo Company, "Advertisement: Glazo Completes the Picture of Loveliness," *Vogue*, April 1, 1925; Eileen Chang, *Lust, Caution*, trans. Julia Lovell (New York: Penguin Classics, 2007); Martens, "The Game of a Thousand Wonders."

96. Edward Steichen, *Ilka Chase's Hands with Cartier Jewelry*, 1925, Photograph, 1925, Conde Nast Archive/CORBIS.

97. Flora Smith, "When Milady Steps Out," *Los Angeles Times*, February 10, 1924.

98. "Christmas Suggestions," *New York Times*, December 14, 1924, sec. Classified; R. H. White Co., "Advertisement: Chinese Game of a Hundred Intelligences," 1923, Marion Angeline Howlett Papers, Schlesinger Library, Radcliffe Institute, Harvard University; "The Parker Games 1923–1924"; *Sears, Roebuck and Company* (Philadelphia: Sears, Roebuck and Company, 1922), 475; Radio Corporation of America, "Advertisement: For Summer Sport—Radiola RC," *Saturday Evening Post*, June 9, 1923.

99. Susan Porter Benson, *Household Accounts: Working-Class Family Economies in the Interwar United States* (Ithaca, NY: Cornell University Press, 2007).

100. Claude S. Fischer, "Changes in Leisure Activities, 1890–1940," *Journal of Social History* 27, no. 3 (Spring 1994): 453–75.

101. Clare Briggs, "That Guiltiest Feeling," n.d., MJ Scrapbook 2, PB.

102. Constance Grenelle Wilcox, *Mah-Jongg: The Play of One Hundred Intelligences, In a Prologue and One Act* (Boston: C. C. Birchard & Company, 1923).

103. Auto Vacuum Ice Cream Freezer, "Advertisement: Play While the Ice Cream Freezes," *Good Housekeeping*, June 1924, Home Economics Archive: Research, Tradition and History (HEARTH), Cornell University. See also Oh Henry!, "Advertisement: Oh Henry!," *Good Housekeeping*, March 1925, Home Economics Archive: Research, Tradition and History (HEARTH), Cornell University.

104. "Forms Mah Jong Club"; "With the Clubs," *Chicago Defender*, August 9, 1924, National edition.

105. "Buckeye State," *Chicago Defender*, March 15, 1924, National edition; "Missouri," *Chicago Defender*, April 19, 1924, National edition; "Michigan State News," *Chicago Defender*, May 24, 1924, National edition; "Washington," *Chicago Defender*, May 24, 1924, National edition.

106. Eastern Sales Co., "Mah Jong Ring," *Chicago Defender*, May 24, 1924, National edition.

107. For the politics of respectability, see Evelyn Brooks Higginbotham, "African-American Women's History and the Metalanguage of Race," *Signs* 17, no. 2 (Winter 1992): 272.

108. "Forms Mah Jong Club." For race and women's clubs, see also: Glenda Gilmore, *Gender and Jim Crow: Women and the Politics of White Supremacy in North Carolina, 1896–1920* (Chapel Hill: University of North Carolina Press, 1996); Lynn Dumenil, "The New Woman and the Politics of the 1920s," *OAH Magazine of History*, Reinterpreting the 1920s, 21, no. 3 (July 2007): 22–26.

109. "Ancient Chinese Game Taking West Parties by Storm."

110. "Tea Dance with Fashion Show," *San Francisco Call*, July 20, 1922, MJSC Scrapbook 1, PB; "Mah Jongg Tea Dancing by Society Girl," *San Francisco Call and Post*, July 15, 1922, MJSC Scrapbook 1, PB; "Mah-Jongg Tea," *San Francisco Examiner*, April 1, 1923, SFPL.

111. "Omaha Couple Introduce Mah-Jongg to Dinner Guests," *World-Herald*, September 12, 1922, MJSC Scrapbook 1, PB.

112. "Ma-Jung Fete of 1923: Album of Photographs," 1923, Stanford University Special Collections.

113. "'Mah-Jongg Fete' to Aid Big Sisters Is a Bizarre Event," *New York Herald*, December 1923, MJ Scrapbook 2, PB.

114. Myra Nye, "Mah Jongg and Music in Club Circles; Women's Work, Women's Clubs," *Los Angeles Times*, November 12, 1922, MJSC Scrapbook 1, PB; "Woman to Seek Academy; In Aid of Child Study's Work," *New York Times*, March 24, 1923; Myra Nye, "Take Leading Part in Club Activity; Women's Work, Women's Clubs," *Los Angeles Times*, November 19, 1922; "Society Turns to the Orient for New Diversion," *Fresno Republican*, November 12, 1922, sec. Society Clubs Music Books, MJSC Scrapbook 1, PB.

115. "First to Give 'Mah Jongg' Tea in This City," *Seattle Post-Intelligencer*, 1922, MJSC Scrapbook 1, PB.

116. "Business Meeting of Association," *Journal of Home Economics* 15, no. 10 (October 1923): 572.

117. William Leach, *Land of Desire: Merchants, Power, and the Rise of a New American Culture* (New York: Vintage Books, 1994); Emily Remus, *A Shoppers' Paradise: How the Ladies of Chicago Claimed Power and Pleasure in the New Downtown* (Cambridge, MA: Harvard University Press, 2019); Richard Longstreth, *The American Department Store Transformed, 1920–1960* (New Haven: Yale University Press, 2010).

118. R. H. Macy & Co., "Advertisement: 'How Ma-Chiang Saved My Life,'" *New York Times*, February 25, 1924.

119. Frank C. Elliott, *Mah Jongg Section*, October 11, 1923, Photograph, October 11, 1923, Bullock's Department Store Collection of Photographs, Huntington Library; "Shopping with Marie," *San Francisco Bulletin*, October 5, 1922, MJSC Scrapbook 1, PB.

120. Little Jane, "'Mah Jongg' New Word in Tacoma," *Tacoma Ledger*, November 4, 1922, MJSC Scrapbook 1, PB; "Mah Jongg Makes Bow in Tacoma," 1922, MJSC Scrapbook 1, PB.

121. "[Untitled Clipping]," *Berkeley Courier*, September 10, 1922, MJSC Scrapbook 1, PB; B. H. Dyas Co., "Come to Dyas' for Your Mah-Jongg Set"; Mah-Jongg Sales Company of America, "Mah-Jongg Catalogue No. 2"; O'Connor, Moffatt & Co., "Advertisement: Free Lessons Friday and Saturday in Mah-Jong," *Oakland Tribune*, November 1, 1922, MJSC Scrapbook 1, PB.

122. Parker Brothers, Inc., "Advertisement: Mah-Jongg Sets," *National Drug News*, n.d., MJSC Scrapbook 1, PB.

123. "'The Masquerader' Is a Chinese Gambler," *Moving Picture World*, October 14, 1922, MJSC Scrapbook 1, PB.

124. "[Snippet about Mah Jongg Blues]."

125. "[Snippet about Mahjong Hurting Movies]," *Moving Picture World*, January 19, 1924, The Moving Picture World Collection, Library of Congress; "Is Radio a Menace? Mah Jongg Craze, Too," *Moving Picture World*, April 12, 1924, The Moving Picture World Collection, Library of Congress.

126. "'Miami' Well Presented in California Theatre," *Moving Picture World*, August 2, 1924, The Moving Picture World Collection, Library of Congress; "Celebrities Who Enjoy Auction and Mah Jong," *Auction Bridge Magazine*, 1924, Marion Angeline Howlett Papers, Schlesinger Library, Radcliffe Institute, Harvard University.

127. "Many Hooks," *Moving Picture World*, September 13, 1924, The Moving Picture World Collection, Library of Congress.

128. "Mah Jongg Should Be Proud Papa," *Los Angeles Times*, November 15, 1922.

129. Edgar A. Guest, "Just Folks," *Washington Post*, September 18, 1924.

130. Helen Bullitt Lowry, "Rise and Present Peril of Mah Jong: The Chinese Game Has Escaped from Society's Chaperonage and Is on Its Own," *New York Times*, August 10, 1924.

131. McConn, "Town Mah Jongg Mad."

132. "Ancient Chinese Game Taking West Parties by Storm"; Rittenhouse, "If You Don't Play Mah-Jong, You Should Learn Now"; Edna Woolman Chase, "Vogue's-Eye View of the Mode!," *Vogue*, April 15, 1924; "Louise Fazenda Thrilled by 'Mah-Jongg,'" *Los Angeles Times*, August 5, 1923, sec. 7.

133. Amaizo Oil, "Advertisement: Mah Jong Cakes."

134. Catherine Keyser, *Playing Smart: New York Women Writers and Modern Magazine Culture* (New Brunswick, NJ: Rutgers University Press, 2010), 6.

135. Hoganson, *Consumers' Imperium*; Yoshihara, *Embracing the East*; "Louise Fazenda Thrilled by 'Mah-Jongg'"; Vanity Fair, "Advertisement: Mah Jongleurs!," *New York Times*, January 27, 1924.

136. Juana Neal Levy, "Society," *Los Angeles Times*, April 6, 1924.

137. Jell-O, "Advertisement: Your Guests Will Appreciate Your Foresight," *Good Housekeeping*, December 1924, Home Economics Archive: Research, Tradition and History (HEARTH), Cornell University.

138. A. L. Wyman, "Practical Recipes: Mah Jongg Luncheon," *Los Angeles Times*, July 8, 1924.

139. Ladies Home Journal and Genevieve Jackson Boughner, "Catering for the Mah Jongg or Pung Chow Party," in *Women in Journalism: A Guide to the Opportunities and a Manual of the Technique of Women's Work for Newspapers and Magazines* (New York: D. Appleton, 1926), 74.

140. Florence Currier, "Diary, 1920–1924," n.d., Florence May Wyman Currier Personal Papers, Schlesinger Library, Radcliffe Institute, Harvard University.

141. R. H. White Co., "Advertisement: Chinese Game of a Hundred Intelligences"; Jordan Marsh Company, "Advertisement: 1000 Mah Jong Sets," *Boston Daily Globe*, November 27, 1923.

142. Entry October 2, 1923, Currier, "Diary, 1920–1924."

143. Entry December 28, 1923, ibid.

144. Entry June 30, 1924, ibid.

145. Entries June 25–26, 1924, ibid.

146. James Huskey, "Americans in Shanghai: Community Formation and Response to Revolution, 1919–1928" (PhD diss., Chapel Hill, University of North Carolina, 1985), 5; Janet Wulsin, June 28, 1921, Janet Elliott Wulsin Personal Papers, Folder: 2004.7.1.33, Peabody Library, Harvard University; Thyra E. V. Pedersen, "Thyra E. V. Pedersen Personal Papers," 1923–1925, Letter, Folder 19, Schlesinger Library, Radcliffe Institute, Harvard University.

147. Marion Angeline Howlett, "Addenda to Application for US Civil Service," 1942, Marion Angeline Howlett Papers [unprocessed], Schlesinger Library, Radcliffe Institute, Harvard University.

148. Marion Angeline Howlett, "[Notes about Calcutta Statesman Article]," n.d., Marion Angeline Howlett Papers [unprocessed], Schlesinger Library, Radcliffe Institute, Harvard University.

149. Marion Angeline Howlett, "Marion Angeline Howlett: Palm Beach," n.d., Marion Angeline Howlett Papers [unprocessed], Schlesinger Library, Radcliffe Institute, Harvard University.

150. Newspaper accounts further exaggerated Howlett as the only white woman in Nankou, which she attempted to correct in the archival record.

151. Marion Angeline Howlett, "Addenda to Application for US Civil Service"; George, "Humanity at Palm Beach."

152. "Miss Marion Angeline Howlett."

153. "News of Palm Beach, Howlett Montage," *Palm Beach Post*, January 27, 1924, Marion Angeline Howlett Papers [unprocessed], Schlesinger Library, Radcliffe Institute, Harvard University; "Miss Marion Angeline Howlett"; Marion Angeline Howlett, "White Star Notes," 1972, Marion Angeline Howlett Papers [unprocessed], Schlesinger Library, Radcliffe Institute, Harvard University.

154. Marion Angeline Howlett, "Mah Jong—Palm Beach," February 1924, Marion Angeline Howlett Papers [unprocessed], Schlesinger Library, Radcliffe Institute, Harvard University; "Mah Jong in the Surf," *New York Times*, February 10, 1924, Marion Angeline Howlett Papers, Schlesinger Library, Radcliffe Institute, Harvard University.

155. "The Night Bathers' Greatest Thrill of All," *Palm Beach News*, March 24, 1924, Marion Angeline Howlett Papers, Schlesinger Library, Radcliffe Institute, Harvard University; Howlett, "Palm Beach 1924"; "[Clipping of Society News]," *Palm Beach Post*, March 7, 1924, Marion Angeline Howlett Papers, Schlesinger Library, Radcliffe Institute, Harvard University; "From Shanghai to Palm Beach," *Palm Beach Post*, January 29, 1924, Marion Angeline Howlett Papers, Schlesinger Library, Radcliffe Institute, Harvard University; "[Photograph of Mahjong on Palm Beach]," *Cincinnati Sunday Enquirer*, February 1924, Marion Angeline

Howlett Papers, Schlesinger Library, Radcliffe Institute, Harvard University; "News of Palm Beach, Howlett Montage"; "Mah Jongg at Palm Beach: Mrs. Elsie Parsons," *New York Times*, February 3, 1924, Marion Angeline Howlett Papers, Schlesinger Library, Radcliffe Institute, Harvard University; "Catches," *Palm Beach Daily News*, 1924, Marion Angeline Howlett Papers, Schlesinger Library, Radcliffe Institute, Harvard University.

156. "300 Sun Readers Meet Mah Jong and Learn How to Play," *Attleboro Sun*, December 28, 1923, Marion Angeline Howlett Papers, Schlesinger Library, Radcliffe Institute, Harvard University; "Mah Jong Party Due This Evening," *Attleboro Sun*, December 27, 1923, Marion Angeline Howlett Papers, Schlesinger Library, Radcliffe Institute, Harvard University.

157. R. H. White Co., "Advertisement: Chinese Game of a Hundred Intelligences"; Mandel Brothers, "Advertisement: Free Lessons in Mah Jong," *Chicago Daily Tribune*, October 6, 1923; Lansburgh & Brother, "Advertisement: Personal Instruction in Mah-Jong," *Washington Post*, October 14, 1923; Jordan Marsh Company, "Advertisement: We Announce a Number of Genuine Chinese Mah Jong Sets," *Boston Daily Globe*, April 4, 1924.

158. Howlett, "Mah Jong—Palm Beach."

159. "Marion Angeline Howlett Announces Her New Lecture for 1931–1932," 1931, Marion Angeline Howlett Papers, Schlesinger Library, Radcliffe Institute, Harvard University. Howlett remained unmarried and supported herself. After lecturing in the 1930s and unsuccessfully applying to the Civil Service in 1942, she worked as a librarian in a Boys' Club in Boston's South End during the 1940s and 1950s.

160. Claude S. Fischer, "Changes in Leisure Activities"; George A. Lundberg, Mirra Komarovsky, and Mary Alice McInery, *Leisure: A Suburban Study* (New York: Columbia University Press, 1934).

161. Lethin, "Letter to Agnes," February 18, 1923.

162. Namco Products Corporation, "Female Help Wanted, Mah Jong Teachers and Experts," *New York Times*, September 17, 1923, sec. Classified Ads.

163. "Women Teach Fine Points of Mah Jongg," *San Francisco Call*, September 2, 1922, MJSC Scrapbook 1, PB. See also H. W., "Money Made at Home: Teaches Games," *Chicago Daily Tribune*, August 10, 1930.

164. "Hartman's to Stage Game of Mah Jongg," *Merced Star*, November 14, 1922, MJSC Scrapbook 1, PB; "Mah Jongg," *Santa Rosa Press Democrat*, November 16, 1922, MJSC Scrapbook 1, PB; "Society Here to Learn Mah Jongg," *Santa Rosa Republican*, November 13, 1922, MJSC Scrapbook 1, PB.

165. Nye, "Mah Jongg and Music."

166. "The Joined Battle of the Games"; "Classified Ad: Learn to Play Mah Jongg," *San Francisco Examiner*, November 5, 1922, MJSC Scrapbook 1, PB; "Mah Jongg Party for Army Folk," *San Francisco Call*, October 6, 1922, MJSC Scrapbook 1, PB.

CHAPTER 2

1. An "amah" was a Chinese nanny. Elsie McCormick, "China's Ancient Dominoes Now Fascinate Foreigners," *China Press*, September 11, 1921, MJSC Scrapbook 1, PB. For reprints, see: Elsie McCormick, "China's Ancient Dominoes Now Fascinate Foreigners [Abbreviated Reprint Clipping]," *Unknown*, 1921, MJSC Scrapbook 1, PB; "Society Is 'Punging,'" *The Wasp*, July 15, 1922, MJSC Scrapbook 1, PB.

2. The term "expatriate" is embedded in the history of wealthy Westerners temporarily moving to another country to make money before returning home. For more, see Yasmeen Serhan, "'Expat' and the Fraught Language of Migration," *The Atlantic*, October 9, 2018.

3. Michael Stanwick, "Mahjong(g) before Mahjong(g): Part 2," *The Playing-Card* 32, no. 5 (2004): 212–13; Andrew Lo, "China's Passion for Pai: Playing Cards, Dominoes, and Mahjong," in *Asian Games : The Art of Contest*, ed. Irving Finkel and Colin Mackenzie ([New York]: Asia Society, 2004), 216–31; Hsi-yüan Chen, "Cong Madiao Dao Majiang [Madiao and Mahjong in Popular Culture and Elite Discourse]," trans. Luke Habberstad, *Bulletin of the Institute of History and Philology Academia Sinica* (March 2009): 15. See also Maggie Greene, "The Game People Played: Mahjong in Modern Chinese Society and Culture," *Cross-Currents: East Asian History and Culture Review* E-Journal, no. 17 (December 2015): 5. Greene cites Du Yaquan's *Boshi* (1933).

4. Jeffrey Wasserstrom, *Global Shanghai, 1850–2010* (New York: Routledge, 2009).

5. These individuals include William Wilkinson, George Glover, and Stewart Culin. Michael Stanwick, "Mahjong(g) before Mahjong(g): Part 1," *The Playing-Card* 32, no. 4 (2004): 153–62; Stanwick, "Mahjong(g) before Mahjong(g): Part 2."

6. Michael Stanwick and Hongbing Xu, "Flowers and Kings: An Hypothesis of Their Function in Early Ma Que," The Mahjong Tile Set, 2008, https://www. themahjongtileset.co.uk/tile-set-history/flowers-and-kings-an-hypothesis-of-their-function-in-early-ma-que. Chen Yumen, a member of the nineteenth-century literati in Ningbo, is now widely credited with developing the original mahjong combined game. However, scholarship clearly linking Chen as mahjong's sole developer remains inconclusive. The Chinese government built a museum at the turn of the twenty-first century to commemorate Chen and "Mahjong's Birthplace." Conversely, historian Hsi-yüan Chen argues that mahjong developed among commoners and was initially rejected by the literati, but is also without conclusive evidence. Chen, "Madiao and Mahjong." Apocryphal myths of the game's origins abound, including mahjong as a cure for seasick sailors, such as in Harold J. Cooper, "It's 'Mah Chang,' Not 'Mah Jongg'–Sze Says So! And How Nearly the Game's Name Caused the Severance of the US-China Relations," *Brooklyn Daily Eagle*, 1923.

7. The earliest documented use to date of the moniker *májiàng* is in 1909, from a cartoon in a Chengdu journal of a "Majiang Textbook" in a farcical literati mahjong school. Hsi-yüan Chen, "Madiao and Mahjong," 15. The earlier name written as

máquè could be used to refer to either a card or tile game, while *májiàng* referred specifically to the tile game. *Máquè/moziang* also remained in use in writing. Michael Stanwick and Hongbing Xu, "Máquè/Májiàng/Mahjong Terms 1780–1920," *The Mahjong Tile Set* (blog), accessed June 21, 2017, https://www.themahjongtileset.co.uk/mahjong-terms-1780-1920.

8. Quoted in Hsi-yüan Chen, "Madiao and Mahjong," 152.

9. Kariann Yokota, *Unbecoming British: How Revolutionary America Became a Postcolonial Nation* (New York: Oxford University Press, 2011); John E. Willis Jr., "European Consumption and Asian Production in the Seventeenth and Eighteenth Centuries," in *Consumption and the World of Goods* (New York: Routledge, 1993); Lorna Weatherhill, "The Meaning of Consumer Behaviour in Late Seventeenth- and Early Eighteenth-Century England," in *Consumption and the World of Goods* (New York: Routledge, 1993), 206–27; Caroline Frank, *Objectifying China, Imagining America: Chinese Commodities in Early America* (Chicago: University of Chicago Press, 2011); Carole Shammas, "Changes in English and Anglo-American Consumption from 1550 to 1800," in *Consumption and the World of Goods* (New York: Routledge, 1993), 177–205; Christina H. Nelson, *Directly from China: Export Goods for the American Market, 1784–1930* (Salem, MA: Peabody Museum of Salem, 1985).

10. Willis, "European Consumption and Asian Production in the Seventeenth and Eighteenth Centuries," 134.

11. Although in the mid-nineteenth century, American foreign policy established a friendlier, less predatory relationship between the United States and China, by the late nineteenth century the United States' growing economic strength and military aggression in the Caribbean and the Pacific brought it more in line with other imperialist powers. Gordon H. Chang, *Fateful Ties: A History of America's Preoccupation with China* (Cambridge, MA: Harvard University Press, 2015), Ch. 3.

12. This was the 1842 Treaty of Nanking after the First Opium War. The United States' successful declaration of the Open Door Treaty in 1899, which prevented any single power from fully controlling access to China's trade, nominally also sought to protect China's sovereignty. However, in effect it served mainly to balance outside interests against each other, with China relegated to an exploitable position. Bryna Goodman and David S. G. Goodman, "Colonialism and China," in *Twentieth-Century Colonialism and China: Localities, the Everyday, and the World* (New York: Routledge, 2012), 2; Chang, *Fateful Ties*, 49–51, 104.

13. Mu Shiying, "The Shanghai Foxtrot (A Fragment)," trans. Sean Macdonald, *Modernism/Modernity* 11, no. 4 (2004): 803, 807.

14. Jeffrey Wasserstrom, "Locating Old Shanghai: Having Fits about Where It Fits," in *Remaking the Chinese City: Modernity and National Identity, 1900–1950* (Honolulu: University of Hawaii Press, 2000), 193.

15. Christian Henriot, "'Little Japan' in Shanghai: An Insulated Community, 1875–1945," in *New Frontiers: Imperialism's New Communities in East Asia, 1842–1953* (New York: Manchester University Press, 2000), 146–69, 147.

16. Bryna Goodman, *Native Place, City and Nation: Regional Networks and Identities in Shanghai, 1853–1937* (Berkeley: University of California Press, 1995).

17. Bryna Goodman and David S. G. Goodman, "Colonialism and China," 2; Gail Hershatter, *Dangerous Pleasures: Prostitution and Modernity in Twentieth-Century Shanghai* (Berkeley: University of California Press, 1997), 28; James Huskey, "Americans in Shanghai: Community Formation and Response to Revolution, 1919–1928" (PhD diss., Chapel Hill, University of North Carolina, 1985); Nicholas Clifford, *Spoilt Children of Empire: Westerners in Shanghai and the Chinese Revolution of the 1920s* (Hanover, NH: Middlebury College Press, University Press of New England, 1991).

18. Gail Hershatter, *Dangerous Pleasures*, 94; Lo, "China's Passion for Pai"; Michael Stanwick and Hongbing Xu, "From Cards to Tiles: The Origin of Mahjong(g)'s Earliest Suit Names," *The Playing-Card* 41, no. 1 (September 2012), http://themahjongtileset.co.uk/earliest-suit-names. Quoting Han Bangqing, 1892, in Chen, "Madiao and Mahjong," 144.

19. Gail Hershatter, *Dangerous Pleasures*, 94.

20. Han Bangqing, *The Sing-Song Girls of Shanghai*, ed. Eva Hung, trans. Eileen Chang (New York: Columbia University Press, 2005), 203. According to the speaker, mahjong banquets were especially effective at less competitive second-tier courtesan houses.

21. Bangqing, 14, 103–5.

22. Bangqing, 203, 109, 120.

23. Although Qing rule was marked by regulation of morality and propriety, regulation and reality often bore little resemblance to each other. See, for example, Andrea Goldman, *Opera and the City: The Politics of Culture in Beijing, 1770–1900* (Stanford, CA: Stanford University Press, 2012).

24. Bangqing, *The Sing-Song Girls of Shanghai*, 120. Such allowances did not help the Shanghai mahjong player who leapt to his death from an opium establishment in 1882 to escape police who mistook him for a player of *pai jiu*, or Chinese poker. Lo, "China's Passion for Pai," 217.

25. Elizabeth Perry, *Shanghai on Strike: The Politics of Chinese Labor* (Stanford, CA: Stanford University Press, 1993), 35.

26. Greene, "The Game People Played," 4, 12. For more about mahjong in the everyday lives of working people and Shanghai culture, see Hanchao Lu, *Beyond the Neon Lights: Everyday Shanghai in the Early Twentieth Century* (Berkeley: University of California Press, 1999).

27. Edith McConn, "Mah Jongg'd with an Empress; Had to Lose," *San Jose Evening News*, November 10, 1922, MJSC Scrapbook 1, PB.

28. Quoted in Chen, "Madiao and Mahjong," 152.

29. Hyungju Hur, "Staging Modern Statehood: World Exhibitions and the Rhetoric of Publishing in Late Qing China, 1851–1910" (PhD diss., Urbana, University of Illinois at Urbana-Champaign, 2012), 96.

30. Chen, "Madiao and Mahjong," 157; Thomas S. Mullaney, *The Chinese Typewriter: A History* (Cambridge, MA: MIT Press, 2017).

31. Quote from *Jingzhong Ribao* in Chen, "Madiao and Mahjong." In what was either a prescient or influential move, the author also advocated changing the name majiang from 麻雀 (sparrow) to 馬將, meaning "General Ma" or "horses and generals," to emphasize the game's "military and competitive significance." The name majiang would indeed catch on in the following years, though usually in the hybrid form of 麻將 with the nonsensical meaning of "hemp generals."

32. The Chinese Government Bureau of Economic Information, "The Rise of Mahjongg," *Chinese Economic Monthly*, January 1924, 2.

33. Greene, "The Game People Played," 15.

34. Perry, *Shanghai on Strike*, 141.

35. Ibid., 218.

36. For more about this origin myth, see Thierry Depaulis, "Embarrassing Tiles: Mahjong and the Taipings," *The Playing Card* 35, no. 3 (March 2007): 148–53.

37. The author's use of various "kings" also echoes the Taiping nomenclature. Quoted from *Youxi zazhi* in Chen, "Madiao and Mahjong," 165–66.

38. McCormick, "China's Ancient Dominoes Now Fascinate Foreigners."

39. Nan Enstad, "To Know Tobacco: Southern Identity in China in the Jim Crow Era," *Southern Cultures* 13, no. 4 (2007): 12; James Huskey, "Americans in Shanghai," 3.

40. Letter May 20, 1921, "Janet Elliott Wulsin Personal Papers," 1921–1924, Peabody Library, Harvard University.

41. Clifford, *Spoilt Children of Empire*, 42, 53; James Huskey, "Americans in Shanghai."

42. Letter Aug 10, 1923, Thyra E. V. Pedersen, "Thyra E. V. Pedersen Personal Papers," 1923–1925, Schlesinger Library, Radcliffe Institute, Harvard University.

43. James Huskey, "Americans in Shanghai," 6.

44. By the late 1920s, the treaty-port's hierarchy became more class-based, but national origin continued to matter. Jeffrey Wasserstrom, "Cosmopolitan Connections and Transnational Networks," in *At the Crossroads of Empires* (Stanford, CA: Stanford University Press, 2008), 206–24.

45. Chang, *Fateful Ties*, 54.

46. Nara Dillon and Jean C. Oi, "Middlemen, Social Networks, and State-Building in Republican Shanghai," in *At the Crossroads of Empires* (Stanford, CA: Stanford University Press, 2008), 3–21.

47. James Huskey, "Americans in Shanghai"; Jeffrey Wasserstrom, "Cosmopolitan Connections and Transnational Networks"; Robert A. Bickers, "Shanghailanders: The Formation and Identity of the British Settler Community in Shanghai 1843–1937," *Past and Present*, no. 159 (1998): 162–211; Anne-Marie Brady and Douglas Brown, "Introduction: Foreign Bodies," in *Foreigners and Foreign Institutions*

in Republican China (New York: Routledge, 2013), 1–22; "Janet Elliott Wulsin Personal Papers."

48. Joseph and Norma Babcock maintained that he was the first to convince Chinese craftsmen to add Arabic numerals, as he may in fact have been within his own community in Suzhou, but numerous accounts testify to other and earlier tile carvers who added Western numbers. See also "Joseph Park Babcock v. Philip Naftaly," October 10, 1922, Equity Case #848, The National Archives at San Francisco; Alma Sierks-Overholt and Norma Babcock, "Mah Jongg Started in Popularity at Catalina," *The Catalina Islander*, April 16, 1924; R. F. Foster, *Foster on Mah Jong* (New York: Dodd, Mead, 1924), 159–60.

49. Jeffrey Wasserstrom, "Cosmopolitan Connections and Transnational Networks," 214, 216; James Huskey, "Americans in Shanghai," 58.

50. Robert A. Bickers, "Shanghailanders," 183, 187; James Huskey, "Americans in Shanghai," 8.

51. James Huskey, "Americans in Shanghai," 38; Robert A. Bickers, "Shanghailanders," 183; "Janet Elliott Wulsin Personal Papers."

52. Robert A. Bickers and Jeffrey Wasserstrom, "Shanghai's 'Dogs and Chinese Not Admitted' Sign: Legend, History and Contemporary Symbol," *China Quarterly* 142 (June 1995): 444–66; Gail Hershatter, *Dangerous Pleasures*; Jeffrey Wasserstrom, "Cosmopolitan Connections and Transnational Networks"; Foster, *Foster on Mah Jong*, 167; Robert A. Bickers, "Shanghailanders"; Bryna Goodman and David S. G. Goodman, "Colonialism and China," 6.

53. Jeffrey Wasserstrom, "Locating Old Shanghai," 193; Robert A. Bickers, "Shanghailanders," 187; James Huskey, "Americans in Shanghai," 15.

54. James Huskey, "Americans in Shanghai," 15.

55. Lisa Lethin, "My Grandfather Was the Partner of Mr. Babcock," *Mahjong in Holland Museum* (blog), accessed September 28, 2012, http://www.mahjongmuseum.nl.

56. "Joseph Park Babcock v. Philip Naftaly."

57. Foster, *Foster on Mah Jong*, 157.

58. Despite claims by competitors, Babcock's 1920 rulebook was almost certainly the first published in English, and was the most widely circulated in the Western social clubs. At least one Chinese-language rulebook was published in the 1910s and was exported to Chinese consumers in San Francisco, but the game was most likely not primarily learned in China via written rules. The Englishman Harold (Sterling) Carey published a rulebook in Shanghai in 1921 and avoided the changes Babcock introduced. The German company F. Ad. Richter & Cie. claimed that they had applied for a *Gebrauchsmuster* (a utility model similar to a patent) in 1919, though no such record exists. "Joseph Park Babcock v. Philip Naftaly"; Foster, *Foster on Mah Jong*, 170–71; J. P. Babcock, *Babcock's Rules for Mah-Jongg: The Red Book of Rules*, 2nd ed. (1920; repr., San Francisco: Mah-Jongg Sales Company of America, 1923); Edna Lee Booker, *News Is My Job: A Correspondent in War-Torn China* (New York: Macmillan, 1940), 17; Harold Sterling [Harold Carey], *Standard Rules*

and *Instructions for the Chinese Game of Mah Chang (Sparrow)*, 5th ed. (1921; repr., Shanghai: The Shanghai Mercantile Printing Co., Ltd., 1923); *F. Ad. Richter & Cie* (Rudolstadt, Germany: Richters Verlagsanstalt Leipzig, n.d.); Tony Watson, "Richter: German Mahjong Manufacturer," *The Mahjong Collector* (Summer 2015).

59. Jeffrey Wasserstrom, "Cosmopolitan Connections and Transnational Networks," 213.

60. Parker Brothers, Inc., "Advertisement: Mah-Jongg Sets," *National Drug News*, n.d., MJSC Scrapbook 1, PB.

61. Although Baghdadi Jews were among the wealthiest long-term foreign residents, only a handful gained admittance to the Shanghai Club. Chiara Betta, "From Orientals to Imagined Britons: Baghdadi Jews in Shanghai," *Modern Asian Studies* 37, no. 4 (2003): 1005, 1015.

62. The Japanese population would soon skyrocket in the early 1930s. "Growth of the American Community at Shanghai," *China Weekly Review*, February 13, 1926; Huskey, "Americans in Shanghai," 3.

63. Huskey, "Americans in Shanghai," 15–18.

64. "The American Club, Shanghai," *Far Eastern Review*, April 1925, University of California, Los Angeles; "The New American Club Premises," *North China Herald*, November 29, 1924; Ellen Johnston Laing, "The American Club, The Columbia Country Club and the Creation of an American Ambiance in Shanghai, 1920–1943" (Moderne and Modernity: Visual Narratives of Interwar Shanghai, Berkeley Art Museum, March 6, 2010).

65. During the early years of the mahjong fad, however, the American Club was housed in the luxurious Astor House hotel, rather than in a building of its own. While the policies of the American Club were less exclusive than the British, the club self-consciously reflected their overall economic and social positioning.

66. Shanghai was profoundly male-dominated in both its foreign and Chinese populations, but Chinese women provided extensive paid domestic, sexual, and factory labor. By the 1920s, more foreign women arrived singly, in families, or were born as second- and third-generation Shanghailanders. Enterprising American women often worked as teachers, especially in Christian institutions, while wives of settlers and expatriate businessmen created networks within their own social groups, in Shanghai and in expat communities. See Hershatter, *Dangerous Pleasures*; Bickers, "Shanghailanders," 177–78.

67. James Huskey, "Americans in Shanghai," 5.

68. A major player in American attempts to expand the Chinese market, Andersen Meyer imported building materials and served as General Electric's sole agent in China. Letter January 30, 1922, "Janet Elliott Wulsin Personal Papers." Reflecting the game's newness in Beijing expatriate circles, Wulsin wrote about the game under a different spelling until 1922, after J. P. Babcock's rules spread through foreign communities under the standardized (and proprietary) name "Mah Jongg." Even then, expatriates and foreign visitors alternated between a variety of alternative

spellings, including Mah Jung and Mah Jong. Also see: Letters September 20, 1923, April 10, 1924 Pedersen, "Thyra E. V. Pedersen Personal Papers."

69. Grace Thompson Seton, *Chinese Lanterns* (New York: Dodd, Mead, 1924), 272, 277.

70. Huskey, "Americans in Shanghai," 58.

71. Karen J. Leong, *The China Mystique: Pearl S. Buck, Anna May Wong, Mayling Soong, and the Transformation of American Orientalism* (Berkeley: University of California Press, 2005), 4. See also Weili Ye, *Seeking Modernity in China's Name: Chinese Students in the United States, 1900–1927* (Stanford, CA: Stanford University Press, 2001), 176.

72. Mayling Soong frequented Rhoda Cunningham's gatherings and became an important contact for other Americans. Edna Lee Booker, *News Is My Job*, 235.

73. Edna Lee Booker, 17, 115. Neither Booker nor others mentioned difficulty in playing with Chinese players, having learned Babcock's simplified rules. It is unclear if players were switching styles or if the standard Chinese version at the time was close enough to Babcock's version that the difference was easily surmountable.

74. Primary among them were free spirits who worked in mobile office work, while some sold sexual services. Huskey, "Americans in Shanghai," 5, 21.

75. Letter April 10, 1924, Pedersen, "Thyra E. V. Pedersen Personal Papers."

76. Letters September 11, 1923; September 13, 1923; March 27, 1924; January 28, 1924 Pedersen, "Thyra E. V. Pedersen Personal Papers."

77. Letter December 11, 1921, "Janet Elliott Wulsin Personal Papers."

78. Letter November 4, 1923, "Janet Elliott Wulsin Personal Papers."

79. Letter December 27, 1923, "Janet Elliott Wulsin Personal Papers."

CHAPTER 3

1. Chung-Kuei Cheng, "The Financial Phases of China's Foreign Trade," *Chinese Social and Political Science Review*, 1926, 92–119; "China Section," *Pacific Ports*, October 1922, 87.

2. The Chinese Government Bureau of Economic Information, "The Rise of Mahjongg," *Chinese Economic Monthly*, January 1924, 2.

3. The Chinese Government Bureau of Economic Information, "The Rise of Mahjongg." See also "[Untitled]," *The North China Herald*, April 28, 1923.

4. The Chinese Government Bureau of Economic Information, "The Rise of Mahjongg," 3; D. K. Lieu, "Fact-Finding in China: The Chinese Government Bureau of Economic Information," *News Bulletin (Institute of Pacific Relations)*, March 1, 1928, 1–4.

5. "How the New Tax Law Will Help to Lift America's Taxation Load," *Christian Science Monitor*, June 3, 1924. Previously, Congress had decided to tax mahjong sets according to their primary component material, sparing them from the higher tax on dominoes. "Rules on Mah Jong Duty," *New York Times*, June 27, 1923.

6. "Commerce with China: Mah Jongg Sets Sixth in Value of Imports from Shanghai," *New York Times*, March 9, 1924.

7. "Mah-Jong Import Heavy: Sets Valued at $849,833 Reach US from China in 9 Months," *New York Tribune*, December 9, 1923; "Commerce with China."

8. "Mah Jongg Should Be Proud Papa," *Los Angeles Times*, November 15, 1922.

9. The Chinese Government Bureau of Economic Information, "The Rise of Mahjongg," 2.

10. "Stray Stories," *Boston Daily Globe*, May 3, 1925.

11. For more about John B. Powell, see James Huskey, "Americans in Shanghai: Community Formation and Response to Revolution, 1919–1928" (PhD diss., Chapel Hill, University of North Carolina, 1985). For more on the United States' "special relationship" with China, see Gordon H. Chang, *Fateful Ties: A History of America's Preoccupation with China* (Cambridge, MA: Harvard University Press, 2015).

12. J. B. Powell, "Ma Chang Invented in China Spreads All over the World," *China Weekly Review*, June 30, 1923, sec. Special Insert, Microfilm, University of California, Los Angeles.

13. Harold Sterling [Harold Carey], *Standard Rules and Instructions for the Chinese Game of Mah Chang (Sparrow)*, 5th ed. (1921; repr., Shanghai: The Shanghai Mercantile Printing Co., Ltd., 1923); *F. Ad. Richter & Cie* (Rudolstadt, Germany: Richters Verlagsanstalt Leipzig, n.d.).

14. Weymer Mills, "The Genteel Needlework of Other Days Becomes a Modern Party Pastime," *Vogue*, February 1, 1925.

15. "'London Calling': 'Are You There?' Smart America Is, for the Season Is the Gayest in a Decade," *Vogue*, June 15, 1924; "Mah Jong Craze in London: Chinese Game to Be Most Popular Indoor Sport," *China Review*, December 1923.

16. Robertson and Mullens, "Advertisement: 'Mah-Jongg' The Great Chinese Game Grips London," *The Argus*, April 7, 1923.

17. The Western world spent increasing funds on consumer durables in the 1920s. Carole Shammas, "Changes in English and Anglo-American Consumption from 1550 to 1800," in *Consumption and the World of Goods* (New York: Routledge, 1993), 201; Edna Woolman Chase, "Vogue's-Eye View of the Mode!," *Vogue*, April 15, 1924; Princesse Achille Murat, "A Fortnight Spent in Java," *Vogue*, January 1, 1927; "Gala-Days in the Eternal City: A Visiting Frenchwoman in Rome Finds the Cosmopolitan Life of To-Day Scintillate against the Background of Antiquity," *Vogue*, June 15, 1924.

18. "Three American Women of Both Professional and Social Prominence: Members of the European Aristocracy Who Have Achieved Notable Careers," *Vogue*, August 15, 1924.

19. William Bolitho, "Mah Jongg and the Idle Rich," *The Outlook*, December 8, 1923, Library of Congress.

20. The Modern Girl around the World Research Group, "The Modern Girl as Heuristic Device: Collaboration, Connective Comparison, Multidirectional Citation," in *The Modern Girl around the World: Consumption, Modernity, and Globalization* (Durham, NC: Duke University Press, 2008), 1–24.

21. The Modern Girl around the World Research Group, 2.

22. "Mah Jongg," *Time*, July 2, 1923.

23. Powell, "Ma Chang," 3; Chinese Government Bureau of Economic Information, "The Rise of Mahjongg," 3.

24. Chinese Government Bureau of Economic Information, "The Rise of Mahjongg," 2.

25. Ibid., 4.

26. J. B. Powell, "Mah Chang: The Game and Its History, from the China Weekly Review, June 30," *The Living Age*, September 1, 1923, 7; Chinese Government Bureau of Economic Information, "The Rise of Mahjongg," 4; Powell, "Ma Chang," 7.

27. "Mah Jongg Set Frisky; Leaping Larvae Blamed," *San Francisco Examiner*, February 29, 1924, SFPL.

28. Kariann Yokota, *Unbecoming British: How Revolutionary America Became a Postcolonial Nation* (New York: Oxford University Press, 2011). For another example, see Nancy J. Taniguchi, "World War I, the American Interior, and Pacific Markets: A Look at Distant Impacts," in *Studies in Pacific History* (Burlington, VT: Ashgate Publishing Company, 2002), 123–39.

29. Chinese Government Bureau of Economic Information, "The Rise of Mahjongg," 5.

30. R. F. Foster, "The Genesis of Mah Jong," *Auction Bridge and Mah Jong Magazine*, March 1924, 64, Library of Congress; Powell, "Mah Chang," 3–6.

31. AP Night Wire, "Mah Jongg Shin Bones Shipped: Craze for Game Depletes Supply Stocks of Chinese Firms," *Los Angeles Times*, March 1, 1924.

32. Chinese Government Bureau of Economic Information, "The Rise of Mahjongg," 4. In January 1923, bone retailed for "about $400 a ton." A ton of front legs provided "material for 180 sets of mahjongg, while 225 sets can be furnished from a ton of back leg bones."

33. M. E. Falkus, "United States Economic Policy and the 'Dollar Gap' of the 1920's," *Economic History Review* 24, no. 4 (November 1971): 599–623; "Hopeful Trade Outlook Is Seen," *Christian Science Monitor*, February 15, 1924.

34. Chinese Government Bureau of Economic Information, "The Rise of Mahjongg," 5; China Trading Co., "Forced Sale!," *Seattle Post-Intelligencer*, November 5, 1922, MJSC Scrapbook 1, PB.

35. Pung Wo Company, *Photographs: Pung Wo Company Factory*, 1924 copyright 1923, Photograph, 1924 copyright 1923, Games—Mah Jong, Library of Congress, Prints and Photographs; Mah-Jongg Company, *Photographs: Mah-Jongg Manufacturing Company of China*, 1923, Photograph, 1923, MJ Scrapbook 2, PB. The Mah-Jongg Sales Company advertised itself as "by far the largest producer of tiles in the world." Mah-Jongg Sales Company of America, "Mah-Jongg Catalogue No. 2," 1923, 2, www.mahjongmuseum.com/mjsca2.htm, Mah Jong Museum.

36. Pung Wo Company, *Standard Rules for the Chinese Domino Game of Pung Wo Brand of Mah-Jongg* (M. Newmark & Co., 1925).

37. Powell, "Ma Chang"; Powell, "Mah Chang"; Chinese Government Bureau of Economic Information, "The Rise of Mahjongg"; Foster, "The Genesis of Mah Jong"; W. Lock Wei, *The Theory of Mah Jong: Its Principles, Psychology, Tactics, Strategies, and Fine Points, Including the Complete Chinese Rules of Play* (Boston: Small, Maynard & Company, 1925).

38. Although transliterated in the company name as "ren," the character 倫 is "lun" in pinyin.

39. The English placards read variously Pung Wo or Mei Ren in the photographs published by Powell as compared with the set of the same photographs housed at the Library of Congress. The Chinese name transliterated as Mei Ren did not change in the photographs.

40. *All Tools Used in Making Mah Jong and Cabinets*, 1923, Photograph, 1923, Pung Wo Company, Library of Congress, Prints and Photographs.

41. *Engraving Tiles*, 1923, Photograph, 1923, Pung Wo Company, Library of Congress, Prints and Photographs. For more about child labor, see Elizabeth Perry, *Shanghai on Strike*, 60.

42. "Shinbones Are Used for Mah Jong Sets," October 1923, MJSC Scrapbook 1, PB.

43. *A Few of Our Skilled Workers*, 1923, Photograph, 1923, Pung Wo Company, Library of Congress, Prints and Photographs.

44. For more about public spaces, see Robert A. Bickers and Jeffrey Wasserstrom, "Shanghai's 'Dogs and Chinese Not Admitted' Sign."

45. With few beasts of burden (demanding, as they did, both space and food), Shanghai's muscle was mostly human. Alongside rickshaw pullers crowding the streets were "wheel barrow men" for hire. Amy Richardson Holway, 1919/1920, Amy Richardson Holway Papers, Folder: Letters to family, 1917–1929, Schlesinger Library, Radcliffe Institute, Harvard University; Hanchao Lu, *Beyond the Neon Lights: Everyday Shanghai in the Early Twentieth Century* (Berkeley: University of California Press, 1999).

46. *Untitled [Wheelbarrow Worker]*, 1923, MJ Scrapbook 2, PB.

47. Chinese Government Bureau of Economic Information, "The Rise of Mahjongg," 6.

48. *Splitting Shin Bones*, Photograph, 1923, Pung Wo Company, Library of Congress, Prints and Photographs.

49. Powell, "Ma Chang"; Huang Ting-mou, "Ivory and Bamboo," *China Review*, April 1923. Many other Chinese residents in Shanghai also came from the nearby provinces of Jiangsu and Zhejiang. Jeffrey Wasserstrom, "Locating Old Shanghai," 193.

50. Powell, "Ma Chang," 6. When a skilled chef earned less than $10 a month working a foreign household in nearby Hangchow, the reported $50–$100 bonus was significant. Amy Richardson Holway, n.d., presumed 1919 to 1922 .

51. Powell, "Ma Chang," 6.

52. Sin Wen Pao, trans., "China Trade: Mah Jongg Exports Increasing" (Department of Commerce, June 15, 1923), Correspondence of the Military Intelligence Division Relating to General, Political, Economic, and Military Conditions in China, 1918–1941, US National Archives.

53. Chinese Government Bureau of Economic Information, "Wages in China for Various Trades," February 1924. This would put skilled factory workers below the highest-earning category of domestic servants, but above matting weavers and tobacco curers, who averaged 12 and 19 Mexican cents respectively. Most of the Chinese economy ran on Mexican silver dollars; the American gold-standard exchange halved the Mexican total.

54. B. H. Dyas Co., "Advertisement: Come to Dyas' for Your Mah-Jongg Set," *Los Angeles Times*, May 7, 1922. Imported sets with carved tiles flew off the shelves. Although high-end sets could sell for hundreds of dollars, the inexpensive (bamboo only, without bone) Pung Wo. Jr. set made by Mei Ren retailed at Gimbels for $6. Their profits lay in volume. "Pung Wo Junior Boxed Set," Mah Jong Museum, accessed September 18, 2013, www.mahjongmuseum.com/mj261.htm.

55. Michael Stanwick and Hongbing Xu, "Flowers and Kings: An Hypothesis of Their Function in Early Ma Que," The Mahjong Tile Set, 2008, https://www.themahjongtileset.co.uk/tile-set-history/flowers-and-kings-an-hypothesis-of-their-function-in-early-ma-que. Stanwick and Xu cite Liu Yishu's *Maque de jingyan yu jiqiao* (1941).

56. Terese Tse Bartholomew, *Hidden Meanings in Chinese Art* (San Francisco: Asian Art Museum, 2012).

57. For diverse mahjong sets, see the online collection by Michael Stanwick: http://themahjongtileset.co.uk. For more on reformers, see Chapter 2.

58. Ray Heaton, "Ji Gong," *The Mahjong Collector*, Summer 2015. See Heaton's regular contributions in *The Mahjong Collector*, 2015–2016.

59. Additionally, the "honor" tiles included those known in the West as "dragon" tiles, which were white or painted in green or red, and whose faces often contained large, generally standardized characters such as prosperity, dragon, or phoenix.

60. A set exported to the United States by Shanghai's Kwang Liyuen Company advertised the "Far Eastern Trading Company" name on its box cover and flower tiles. Jim May, "Traditional Chinese Boxed Set," *Mahjong Museum*, accessed June 24, 2013, www.mahjongmuseum.com/mjo88.htm. Translation by Luke Habberstad.

61. Mah-Jongg Company, *Photographs: Mah-Jongg Co. Factory*; Babcock, *Babcock's Rules for Mah-Jongg*.

62. Theo Burr, "'Long Distance' from Chicago," *The Spur*, June 1, 1923.

63. Ting-mou, "Ivory and Bamboo"; B. H. Dyas Co., "Advertisement: Come to Dyas' for Your Mah-Jongg Set"; "The Truth about Mah-Jongg: When You Have Trumped Your Partner's Ace and Feel Like Burning Your Bridge Tables behind You—Try Mah-Jongg," *Vogue*, January 15, 1923.

64. "Mah-Jong Ballet by Society Girls," *New York Times*, December 20, 1923.

65. R. W. Beachey, "The East African Ivory Trade in the Nineteenth Century," *Journal of African History* 8, no. 2 (1967): 269–90.

66. "Walrus May Be Wiped Out: Enormous Demand for Ivory for Mah Jong Sets and Cigarette Holders Has Spurred Hunters," *Boston Daily Globe*, April 13, 1924. In yet another spin on global trade and authenticity, the article reported "Japanese and Chinese artisans buy walrus ivory in Seattle, carve 'Eskimo' toys and curios and ship them back to Alaska for sale to tourists." Walrus hunting was propelled by another consumer good associated both with women and the social changes of the 1920s: female smoking.

67. The Chinese Government Bureau of Economic Information, "The Rise of Mahjongg," 3.

68. Mah Jongg Sales Co. of America, "Mah-Jongg [Promotional Text]"; Babcock, *Babcock's Rules for Mah-Jongg: The Red Book of Rules*, 96.

69. "American Who Invented Mah Jongg Discovered," *Baltimore Evening Sun*, n.d., MJ Scrapbook 2, PB.

70. Originally a registered trademark of the Celluloid Manufacturing Company, celluloid later became a generic term.

71. Pao, "China Trade: Mah Jongg Exports Increasing"; "Mah Jong Game Now Manufactured in America," *China Review*, May 1923.

72. "Mah Jong Game Now Manufactured in America."

73. "The Parker Games 1923–1924."

74. Parker Brothers, Inc., "Mah-Jongg Set: Popular Edition," 1923, PB; Parker Brothers, Inc., "Mah-Jongg Set: Hong Kong Set," 1923, PB; Parker Brothers, Inc., "Mah-Jongg Set: Ning-Po Set," 1924, PB. The new sets bore the same stamped designs as the hand-carved tiles from the Mah-Jongg Company's Shanghai factory.

75. Foster, "The Genesis of Mah Jong."

76. "Making Mah Jongg Tiles Is an Important Chinese Industry," *Current Opinion*, March 1, 1924; Mandel Brothers, "Advertisement: Free Lessons in Mah Jong," *Chicago Daily Tribune*, December 4, 1923. Most, but not all, mahjong sets coming out of China in the 1920s were made of bone and bamboo; other materials included wood and plastics. Cheaper sets might be entirely made of bamboo, which reduced both the cost of materials and the quality of the carving, as bamboo proved resistant to finely etched designs.

77. "Tony Watson Galleries," The Mahjong Tile Set, accessed July 17, 2019, https://www.themahjongtileset.co.uk/tony-watson-galleries.

78. "Muh-Juhng" (Regensteiner Corporation, 1923), PB; "The Parker Games 1925" (Parker Brothers, Inc., 1925), Catalogs, PB.

79. Pung Chow Company, "Pung Chow Style 376 Boxed Set," 1923, Mah Jong Museum, www.mahjongmuseum.com/mj111.htm.

80. "Dear Friend" (Tanners Engraved Greetings, 1924), MJ Scrapbook 2, PB. Similar manufacturing patterns occurred in Western Europe as the mahjong fad spread.

81. "Condensed Catalogue of the Parker Games 1924–1925" (Parker Brothers, Inc., 1924), Catalogs, PB; "The Parker Games 1925."

82. Pung Chow Company, "Advertisement: Why the Queen of Norway Sent to America for a Chinese Game," *Vogue*, September 15, 1923.

83. A. C. Becken Co., "Advertisement: If It Isn't Marked Mah-Jongg It Isn't Genuine!," *American Jeweler*, January 1, 1924, American Periodicals; Mah-Jongg Sales Company of America, "Mah-Jongg Catalogue No. 2." Emphasis in original.

84. Judy Yung, Gordon H. Chang, and Him Mark Lai, eds., *Chinese American Voices: From the Gold Rush to the Present* (Berkeley: University of California Press, 2006), 4.

85. Anonymous [G. B. Densmore], *The Chinese in California: Description of Chinese Life in San Francisco. Their Habits, Morals and Manners. Illustrated by [William] Voegtlin* (San Francisco: Pettit & Russ, 1880); Nayan Shah, *Contagious Divides: Epidemics and Race in San Francisco's Chinatown* (Berkeley: University of California Press, 2001).

86. The Pung Chow Company, "Pung Chow: The Most Beautiful Game in the World," n.d 1923, Mah Jong Museum, www.mahjongmuseum.com/pc.htm.

87. T.N.T., "News Twinkles," *Salem News*, 1923, MJ Scrapbook 2, PB.

88. See also: Sam Hellman, *Low Bridge and Punk Pungs* (Boston: Little, Brown, and Company, 1924), 93; Lew Lyle Harr, *Pung Chow in Ten Minutes* (New York: Pung Chow Company, Inc., 1923); G. B. Walker, "Cartoon: The Yellow Peril," *Harper's Monthly Magazine*, December 1923; John Held Jr., "The Ancient Chinese Game According to the More Modern Generation," *Auction Bridge and Mah Jong Magazine*, June 1924, Library of Congress; Collier, "Do You Mah Jong or Pung Chow?," *Boston Herald*, June 1, 1923, MJSC Scrapbook 1, PB; Neal O'Hara, "Lessons and Some Other Danger Signals on That Chinese Game, Mah Jong," *Boston Post*, August 15, 1923, MJSC Scrapbook 1, PB; Chief Seattle, "To Members of the 'Four Hundred,'" *The Seattle Star*, November 13, 1922, MJSC Scrapbook 1, PB.

89. "1923 Mah-Jongg Sales Company of America Catalog," Mah Jong Museum, accessed September 13, 2013, www.mahjongmuseum.com/mjsca1.htm.

90. Parker Brothers, Inc., "The Genuine Always Bears the Printed Title MAH-JONGG and Contains the Copyrighted Babcock Rules," n.d., Warshaw Collection: "Parker" 60/toys Box 3, National Museum of American History, Archives Center. Sierks-Overholt and Babcock, "Mah Jongg Started in Popularity at Catalina."

91. "The Parker Games 1923–1924."

92. Mah-Jongg Company, *Photographs: Mah-Jongg Co. Factory.*

93. The sole exception for the representation of a Chinese craftsman was of Wong Liang Zung, Parker Brothers, Inc., "The Genuine." H. H. Warner, "Cover Design," *Auction Bridge and Mah-Jongg Magazine*, September 1924, Library of Congress; Underwood & Underwood, *[Marietta Minnigerode Andrews]*, Photograph, 1920s, Games—Mah Jong, Library of Congress, Prints and Photographs.

94. Underwood & Underwood, *[Marietta Minnigerode Andrews]*, 1920s, Photograph, 1920s, Games–Mah Jong, Library of Congress, Prints and Photographs.

CHAPTER 4

1. Pung Wo Company, *As Mah Jong "Is Played in China,"* Photograph, 1924 copyright 1923, Games–Mah Jong, Library of Congress, Prints and Photographs; "Pung Wo Junior Boxed Set," Mah Jong Museum, accessed September 18, 2013, www.mahjongmuseum.com/mj261.htm; "Pung Wo Junior Boxed Set" (Mei Ren Company, Inc., 1923), Project Mah Jongg, The Museum of Jewish Heritage—A Living Memorial to the Holocaust.

2. Paige Raibmon, *Authentic Indians: Episodes of Encounter from the Late-Nineteenth-Century Northwest Coast* (Durham, NC: Duke University Press, 2005); Philip Deloria, *Playing Indian* (New Haven: Yale University Press, 1998); T. J. Jackson Lears, *No Place of Grace: Antimodernism and the Transformation of American Culture, 1880–1920* (Chicago: University of Chicago Press, 1994); Martin F. Manalansan IV, "Beyond Authenticity: Rerouting the Filipino Culinary Diaspora," in *Eating Asian America* (New York: New York University Press, 2013), 288–300; Allyson Hobbs, *A Chosen Exile: A History of Passing in American Life* (Cambridge, MA: Harvard University Press, 2014).

3. Deloria, *Playing Indian*. For an example linking "quaint" Native American and Chinese customs, see "Chinese Life Revealed in Vivid Style," *Washington Post*, February 15, 1925.

4. Said, *Orientalism*; Edwards, *Noble Dreams*.

5. Edith McConn, "Town Mah Jongg Mad; Society Stacks Tiles: Newly Introduced Chinese Game Spreads," *Evening News*, November 27, 1922.

6. For relevant discussions, see Gordon H. Chang, *Fateful Ties: A History of America's Preoccupation with China* (Cambridge, MA: Harvard University Press, 2015); Harold R. Isaacs, *Scratches on Our Minds: American Images of China and India* (New York: The John Day Company, 1958).

7. Lynn Dumenil, *The Modern Temper: American Culture and Society in the 1920s* (New York: Hill and Wang, 1995).

8. For relevant discussions, see Raibmon, *Authentic Indians*.

9. A few examples are: Louise Jordan Miln, *The Soul of China: Glimpsed in Tales of Today and Yesterday* (New York: Frederick A. Stokes Company, 1925), 205; Ezra H. Fitch, "Introduction: The Ancient Game of Chinese Scholars and Gentlemen," in *Snyder's Ma-Jung Manual*, by Henry M. Snyder, ed. Robert F. Foster (Boston: Houghton Mifflin Company, 1923), ix–xi; "Now the Game Is Mah Jongg," *San Francisco Sunday Chronicle*, January 7, 1923, sec. Magazine; "Now Comes Mah Jongg Out of the Orient: Fascinating Game Hails from Old China [Edited by Mah Jongg Sales Co.]," *Oregon Sunday Journal*, November 19, 1922, MJSC Scrapbook 1, PB.

10. Out of scores of articles about mahjong and its supposedly ancient origins, the few exceptions generally had links to China-based sources: "Mah Jong a Modern Game Quest in China Indicates," *Washington Post*, March 23, 1924; From the New York Sun, "'Mah Jongg' a Modern Game. Evidence Refutes Assertion It Was Invented by Confucius," *Kansas City Star, Published as the Kansas City Times*, November 21, 1922, 43: 65 edition; New York Sun, "Mah-Jongg, Chinese Game, Too Modern for Confucius," *Boston Daily Globe*, December 24, 1922.

11. Sax Rohmer, *The Return of Dr. Fu-Manchu* (New York: A. L. Burt Company, 1916); Robert G. Lee, *Orientals: Asian Americans in Popular Culture* (Philadelphia: Temple University Press, 1999), Ch. 4; Frank Robinson and Lawrence Davidson, *Pulp Culture: The Art of Fiction Magazines* (Portland, OR: Collectors Press, Inc., 1998).

12. Sax Rohmer, *The Return of Dr. Fu-Manchu*, 2; "Fu-Manchu Ancient Chinese Game," Mah Jong Museum, accessed December 1, 2013, www.mahjongmuseum. com/mj296.htm.

13. A few examples are: E. Ellicott, Esq., "Ancient Game of Confucius Now Confuses Us," *Washington Post*, July 29, 1923; The Neophyte, "Dragons Clash at Mah-Jongg: Chinese Game Played in Time of Confucius Full of Intriguing Combinations," *Los Angeles Times*, November 5, 1922; John Held Jr., "If Confucius Should Return," *Auction Bridge and Mah Jong Magazine*, August 1924, Library of Congress.

14. Philip Naftaly, *How to Play Ma Jong: Played by Confucius 2200 Years Ago the Rage of Today*, 1922.

15. Anne Rittenhouse, "If You Don't Play Mah-Jong, You Should Learn Now," *Atlanta Constitution*, March 18, 1923.

16. Fitch, "The Ancient Game of Chinese Scholars and Gentlemen."

17. "The Truth about Mah-Jongg: When You Have Trumped Your Partner's Ace and Feel Like Burning Your Bridge Tables behind You—Try Mah-Jongg," *Vogue*, January 15, 1923.

18. Rittenhouse, "If You Don't Play Mah-Jong, You Should Learn Now"; Caroline Frank, *Objectifying China, Imagining America: Chinese Commodities in Early America* (Chicago: University of Chicago Press, 2011), 90; Lucy Alsanson Cuddy, *The Green Dragon Emerald: A Mystery Play in Three Acts* (San Francisco: Banner Play Bureau, Inc., 1928).

19. A few examples: *How to Play "Ma-Jong" or "Ma Cheuk" (The Sparrow Game)*, 1920s; Lew Lyle Harr, *Pung Chow: The Game of a Hundred Intelligences, Also Known as Mah-Diao, Mah-Jong, Mah-Cheuk, Mah-Juck and Pe-Ling* (New York: Harper & Brothers, 1922); Rittenhouse, "If You Don't Play Mah-Jong, You Should Learn Now."

20. Philip E. Orbanes, *The Game Makers: The Story of Parker Brothers from Tiddledy Winks to Trivial Pursuit* (Boston: Harvard Business School Press, 2004), 69.

21. "A Distraction," *Washington Post*, October 10, 1923.

22. "Mah Jongg Creates Interest," *San Francisco Examiner*, July 17, 1922, Microfilm, SFPL.

23. Chinese Government Bureau of Economic Information, "The Rise of Mahjongg."

24. Pung Chow Company, "Pung Chow Style 500 Boxed Set," 1923, 500, Mah Jong Museum, www.mahjongmuseum.com/mj172.htm.

25. Pung Chow Company, "Marion Angeline Howlett Business Card," 1923, Marion Angeline Howlett Papers [unprocessed], Schlesinger Library, Radcliffe Institute, Harvard University.

26. "300 Sun Readers Meet Mah Jong and Learn How to Play," *Attleboro Sun*, December 28, 1923, Marion Angeline Howlett Papers, Schlesinger Library, Radcliffe Institute, Harvard University.

27. Thyra E. V. Pedersen, "Mah Jong: The Game de Luxe of China," 1923–1925, Thyra E. V. Pedersen Personal Papers, Folder 19, Schlesinger Library, Radcliffe Institute, Harvard University.

28. Miln, *The Soul of China*, 205. Emphasis in original.

29. "First US Mah Jong Plant Established at Glen Cove; Has Order for 25,000 Sets," *Brooklyn Daily Eagle*, 1923, MJ Scrapbook 2, PB; Harr, *Pung Chow*.

30. "1923 Mah-Jongg Sales Company of America Catalog."

31. Pung Chow Company, "Queen of Norway."

32. Charles Caldwell Dobie, *San Francisco's Chinatown* (New York: D. Appleton–Century Company, 1936), 223; Lee, *Orientals*; *Chinese Immigration: The Social, Moral and Political Effect of Chinese Immigration. Testimony Taken before a Committee of the Senate of the State of California.*, 1876; Moon-Ho Jung, *Coolies and Cane: Race, Labor, and Sugar in the Age of Emancipation* (Baltimore: Johns Hopkins University Press, 2006).

33. "What Is It?," *The Illustrated Wasp*, August 1877, Chinese in California, Bancroft Library.

34. "Events Tonight," *Christian Science Monitor*, May 16, 1923; "Listening-In," *Washington Post*, July 23, 1923.

35. Collier, "Do You Mah Jong or Pung Chow?"

36. "Now Comes Mah Jongg (Edited by Mah Jongg Sales Co.)"; "Cartoon: Chow to Mah-Jongg [Edited Draft]," n.d., MJ Scrapbook 2, PB.

37. Mah-Jongg Sales Company of America, "Mah-Jongg Catalogue No. 2."

38. "Mah Jongg King Arrives in City: Game Originator Frightened, but Not Ashamed; J. P. Babcock Admits Latest Craze Foreign to China; and He Is Blond, Native of Hoosier State," *Los Angeles Times*, October 25, 1923.

39. Joseph Park Babcock, "Advertisement: Mah-Jongg Its Authentic Source," *Vogue*, December 15, 1923.

40. Editor, "Mah Jong and Spiritism," *China Review*, June 1923. See also: "Books and Authors," *New York Times*, July 1, 1923, sec. BR. They were aided in their attacks by Lew Lysle Harr's brother, John Harr, who was angry over being ousted from the Pung Chow Company once it became profitable. "Brother Attacks Harr's Claim

of Games with Li Hung Chang," *New York World, Reproduced in China Review*, September 1923.

41. "Mahjong Set for President and First Lady Harding," 1923, Ohio Historical Society. We will never know what Harding thought of the set, as he died suddenly a few days later in San Francisco's Palace Hotel.

42. Pardee Lowe, "Organizations—Native Sons of the Golden State," n.d., Pardee Lowe Collection, Box 125a, Hoover Archive, Stanford University.

43. Hsi-yüan Chen, "Madiao and Mahjong," 34–35.

44. Lo, "China's Passion for Pai," 222.

45. "Chinese Students Peeved," *Los Angeles Times*, November 2, 1923.

46. For discussions of sincerity in performance, see Butler, "Performative Acts and Gender Constitution," 520; Striff, "Locating Performance Studies," 5. Striff draws from Erving Goffman, *The Presentation of Self in Everyday Life* (New York: Doubleday, 1956). See also William Gow, "A Night in Old Chinatown: American Orientalism, China Relief Fundraising, and the 1938 Moon Festival in Los Angeles," *Pacific Historical Review* 87, no. 3 (August 2018): 439–72.

47. Leong, *The China Mystique*, 88, 91, 188.

48. Olga Racster, *Mah-Jongg: Rules for Playing in the Chinese Manner, The Official Standardised Rules of the Mah-Jongg League Limited* (London: Heath Cranton Ltd., 1924).

49. Wei, *The Theory of Mah Jong*.

50. Tow, *The Outline of Mah Jong*.

51. Ly Yu Sang, *Sparrow: The Chinese Game Called Ma-Ch'iau* (New York: The Lent & Graff Co., for The Long Sang Ti Chinese Curios Co., Inc., 1923). Although he identified himself as "M. A., Member of Kwongtung Economic Research Bureau, Science Society, Etc.," Sang did not mention his position as president of the import business Lang Sang Ti Chinese Curios, Inc. Sang may also have authored the curio's revised 1924 edition of the rulebook under a different title, *Ma-Jong The Ancient Game of China*, 5th ed. (The Lent & Graff Co., for The Long Sang Ti Chinese Curios Co., Inc., 1924). With thanks for information on Ly Yu Sang, also known as Ly Hoi Sang, to Elyse Zorn Karlin and Steve Upton.

52. Sang's book enjoyed wide circulation and suffered from plagiarism as well, as in: *The Dragon Rule Book for Sparrow Ma Ch'iau* (New York: Loring P. Rixford, 1924).

53. "Topics of the Times: Have All of Us Been Misled?," *New York Times*, February 9, 1924.

54. Wei, *The Theory of Mah Jong*.

55. "Mah Jongg," July 2, 1923.

56. "New-Old Game Fascinates," *Seattle Times*, October 19, 1922, MJSC Scrapbook 1, PB; Mah Jongg Sales Co. of America, "America's Newest—China's Oldest Game Adopted by Society," *San Francisco Examiner*, August 16, 1923, SFPL.

57. B. H. Dyas Co., "Advertisement: Come to Dyas' for Your Mah-Jongg Set." See also "'Put and Take' Fails," n.d., MJSC Scrapbook 1, PB.

58. Western Electric Co., Ltd., "Electrical Mah Jong" (Thomas De La Rue & Co., Ltd., 1924), Melissa Martens Personal Collection.

59. " 'Put and Take' Fails."

60. "Now the Game Is Mah Jongg."

61. "1923 Mah-Jongg Sales Company of America Catalog."

62. Missionaries often differed from businessmen in their desired forms of "uplift." Both groups influenced policymakers, but the latter enjoyed increased clout by the 1920s. American government officials and business leaders did not always agree on the best course. American defense of the "Open Door Policy" was in its own best interest, though it was later characterized as a protective move for Chinese sovereignty. Business interests were more invested in Japan and, though they desired equal access to China's markets, were not willing to force the issue with Japan after the Japanese military invaded Manchuria in 1931. James Huskey, "Americans in Shanghai"; Donald W. Treadgold, "The United States and East Asia: A Theme with Variations," *Pacific Historical Review* 49, no. 1 (February 1980): 1–27; William Appleman Williams, "The Legend of Isolationism in the 1920's," *Science & Society* 18, no. 1 (Winter 1954): 1–20; Harold R. Isaacs, *Scratches on Our Minds*, Ch. 2.

63. Vern E. Scott, *The Blue Book of Official Rules for Pe-Ling The Original Chinese Game* (San Francisco: Greeley Corp., 1923).

64. "Literary Gossip," *Los Angeles Times*, December 21, 1924; Miln, *The Soul of China*, 202–33.

65. Held, "The Ancient Chinese Game According to the More Modern Generation"; Hill, "Among Us Moderns."

66. Lears, *No Place of Grace*, Chs. 4 and 7; Kristin L. Hoganson, *Consumers' Imperium: The Global Production of American Domesticity, 1865–1920* (Chapel Hill: University of North Carolina Press, 2007), 248. For a critique of mahjong as part of the degenerate "frenzy" and hectic pace of change in "modern civilization," see Meredith Davis, "Grin and Bear It," *Los Angeles Times*, January 25, 1925. Also Sinclair Lewis, "Main Street's Been Paved!," *The Nation*, September 10, 1924; "When You Hear the Far West Calling," *Vogue*, June 15, 1923.

67. George W. Sutton Jr., "A Bouquet of Motor Cars," *Auction Bridge and Mah Jong Magazine*, May 1924, Library of Congress.

68. *Vogue's Book of Etiquette: Present-Day Customs of Social Intercourse with the Rules for Their Correct Observance* (New York: Conde Nast Publications, 1925), 287.

69. James J. Montague, " 'Fire!' And 'Fore!,' " *Washington Post*, December 16, 1923.

70. "Society Is 'Punging' "; "Native Daughters of the Golden West," *Grizzly Bear Magazine*, August 1924, SFPL.

71. Andrew Coe, *Chop Suey: A Cultural History of Chinese Food in the United States* (New York: Oxford University Press, 2009); Yong Chen, *Chop Suey, USA: The Story of Chinese Food in America* (New York: Columbia University Press, 2014); Madeline Y. Hsu, "From Chop Suey to Mandarin Cuisine: Fine Dining and the Refashioning of Chinese Ethnicity During the Cold War Era," in *Chinese*

Americans and the Politics of Race and Culture (Philadelphia: Temple University Press, 2008), 173–94.

72. "The World Field," *The Chinese Recorder*, May 1924, 339.

73. Fu Liang Chang, "The Christian Teacher—His Job," *The Chinese Recorder* 56 (1925): 40–43.

74. Anna West, "Trip to Peking," August 1922, Amy Richardson Holway Papers, Folder: Letters from Anna West, Schlesinger Library, Radcliffe Institute, Harvard University.

75. Norman Jefferies, "Letter to the Editor: Regarding Pung-Chow or Mah-Jongg," *Christian Science Monitor*, January 5, 1924; "Flappers of Chinatown: East Meets West in Piquant Fashion in San Francisco," *New York Times*, May 27, 1923, ProQuest.

76. Hans Kong Petruchka, "Letter to the Editor: A Defender of Mah Jong," *New York Times*, May 9, 1924; Francis X. Tsu, "Letter to the Editor: Mah Jong in China," *New York Times*, April 27, 1924; Hubert W. Peet, "Letter to the Editor: Regarding 'Mah Jong,'" *Christian Science Monitor*, December 24, 1923; Jefferies, "Letter to the Editor: Regarding Pung-Chow or Mah-Jongg"; Joseph, "Random Thoughts"; W. B. Norton, "Christian Chinese Appeal to America to Abjure Mah Jong," *Chicago Daily Tribune*, January 16, 1924; "The East Wind," *Los Angeles Times*, February 15, 1924.

77. Sang, *Sparrow*, 25.

78. Y. P. Wang, "This Unfortunate Habit, Ma Chiang," *New York Tribune Sunday Magazine*, January 13, 1924.

79. Helen Bullitt Lowry, "Rise and Present Peril of Mah Jong: The Chinese Game Has Escaped From Society's Chaperonage and Is on Its Own," *New York Times*, August 10, 1924.

80. Lears, *Something for Nothing: Luck in America*; Roe Fulkerson, "The Hotel Stenographer," *Boston Daily Globe*, July 16, 1924.

81. David G. Schwartz, *Roll the Bones*, 353.

82. Lynn Dumenil, *The Modern Temper*, 7.

83. Meade Minnigerode, "Mah Jong," *Collier's The National Weekly*, December 1, 1923.

84. "Oriental Game Intrigues 'Em: Poker Eclipsed by Chinese Game," *San Francisco Bulletin*, May 5, 1922, MJSC Scrapbook 1, PB; McConn, "Town Mah Jongg Mad." In another example, the 1923 film *Lawful Larceny* involves big losses at mahjong in a gambling parlor, but the storyline is based on an earlier 1922 stage play. "The Screen: A Gambling Hero's Trouble," *New York Times*, July 24, 1923.

85. Jean Knott, "Penny Ante: How to Bust Up a Poker Party," *Boston Daily Advertiser*, October 19, 1923, MJ Scrapbook 2, PB.

86. T.N.T., "News Twinkles."

87. A few examples include: *Chinese Immigration*; Anonymous [G. B. Densmore], *The Chinese in California: Description of Chinese Life in San Francisco*; "The Truth about Mah-Jongg"; Minnigerode, "Mah Jong."

88. Yung, Chang, and Lai, *Chinese American Voices*, 18.

89. Tsu, "Letter to the Editor: Mah Jong in China." Reformist critics of mahjong in China were also ignored, as Chinese players found it to be a "pleasurable and innocuous diversion." Maggie Greene, "The Game People Played: Mahjong in Modern Chinese Society and Culture," *Cross-Currents: East Asian History and Culture Review* E-Journal, no. 17 (December 2015): 21.

90. "Mah Jong's Depravity," *New York Tribune*, January 17, 1924. The exchange was abbreviated and reprinted in "Mah Jongg's Depravity [reprint]," *Los Angeles Times*, February 5, 1924.

91. "Quit 'Bones' for Mah Jong: Negro Gamblers Surprise Raiders with Chinese Game," *New York Times*, March 17, 1924.

92. "Mah Jong Gambling Banned in Philadelphia Chinatown," *New York Times*, February 6, 1924.

93. "Chinese Mah Jongg Players Robbed by Bandits," *Atlanta Constitution*, January 21, 1924.

94. "Rules Mah Jong Is No Crime, Even When Played by Chinese," *New York Times*, May 1, 1924.

95. "Mah Jongg? Oh No, 'Twas Poker Party: Six Japanese Play US Game in Oriental Atmosphere," *The Tacoma Daily Ledger*, November 10, 1923, MJSC Scrapbook 1, PB.

CHAPTER 5

1. "Big Costume Benefit Plan of Ebell Club," *Los Angeles Examiner*, November 5, 1922, MJSC Scrapbook 1, PB; Nye, "Mah Jongg and Music"; The Neophyte, "Dragons Clash."

2. "Comic Strip: The First Hundred Games of Mah Jong Are the Hardest," *New York Evening Mail*, October 2, 1923, MJ Scrapbook 2, PB. See also Jean Knott, "Penny Ante: Girls Take Up Mah Jong," 1923, MJ Scrapbook 2, PB; Knott, "Penny Ante: How to Bust Up a Poker Party."

3. For relevant discussion, see Bryn Williams, "Chinese Masculinities and Material Culture," *Historical Archaeology* 42, no. 3 (2008): 53–67.

4. William C. Morris, *The Game of Mahjuck* (Los Angeles: William C. Morris, 1922).

5. Elmer Dwiggins, *White Dragons Wild and How to Win at Ma Jong* (Los Angeles: Phillips Printing Company, 1924), 54.

6. Nayan Shah, *Contagious Divides*; David L. Eng, *Racial Castration: Managing Masculinity in Asian America* (Durham, NC: Duke University Press, 2001); Lee, *Orientals*; Gina Marchetti, "American Orientalism," *Pacific Historical Review* 73, no. 2 (May 2004): 299–304; Holly Edwards, "A Million and One Nights: Orientalism in America, 1870–1930," in *Noble Dreams, Wicked Pleasures: Orientalism in America, 1870–1930* (Italy: Princeton University Press and Sterling and Francine Clark Art Institute, 2000), 11–58; Edward Said, *Orientalism* (New York: Vintage Books, 1978).

7. Some men likely dressed in costume at Chinese-themed mahjong parties, though their photographs were not featured as women's were. Juana Neal Levy, "Society," *Los Angeles Times*, November 8, 1929.

8. "Photo Standalone," *New York Times*, February 24, 1924; "Wrestling Training!," *Los Angeles Examiner*, September 14, 1922, sec. 1, MJSC Scrapbook 1, PB.

9. Joseph Park Babcock, *The Laws of Mah-Jongg*.

10. Sachs, "China's Fascinating Super Game"; Lord & Taylor, "Advertisement: Mah Jong"; B. H. Dyas Co., "Ville de Paris"; Hellman, *Low Bridge and Punk Pungs*; "Mah Jong Hands Displayed"; "Pledged Their Troth at Game of Mah Jong."

11. "Mah Jong Hands Displayed."

12. See, for example, J. P. Babcock, *Babcock's Rules for Mah-Jongg: The Red Book of Rules*, 2nd ed. (1920; repr., San Francisco: Mah-Jongg Sales Company of America, 1923); Joseph Park Babcock, *The Laws of Mah-Jongg: 1925 Code Revised and Standardized by Joseph Park Babcock and an Associated Committee, Containing Also the New Game Du-Lo* (Salem, MA: Parker Brothers, 1925); R. F. Foster, *Foster on Mah Jong* (New York: Dodd, Mead, 1924); Philip Naftaly, *How to Play Ma Jong: Played by Confucius 2200 Years Ago the Rage of Today*, 1922; Philip Naftaly, *Rules and Directions for the Chinese Game of "Ma Cheuck"* (San Francisco: Philip Naftaly, 1923); Arthur Julius Israel, *How to Play Mah-Jong: Rules Which Govern the Play in the Principal American, European and Chinese Clubs in Shanghai, Hongkong and Peking, as Well as in the American and British Fleets in the Far East* (New York: Oriental Export Company, 1923); Lew Lyle Harr, *Pung Chow: The Game of a Hundred Intelligences, Also Known as Mah-Diao, Mah-Jong, Mah-Cheuk, Mah-Juck and Pe-Ling* (New York: Harper & Brothers, 1922); George S. Romanovsky, *Standard Rules and Regulations for the Game of Lung-Chan* (Lung Chan Company, 1923); Hugo Manovill, *Standard Rules for "The Ancient Game of the Mandarins" the Original Game of Old China* (New York: Piroxloid Products Corp., 1923); Nanyang Bros., *Rules for Playing Mah Jong* (New York: Nanyang Brothers, 1924); Silas J. Douglass, *Rules of the Game* (Pasadena, CA: Silas J. Douglass, 1923); Dwiggins, *White Dragons Wild*.

13. Work, *Mah-Jongg Up-to-Date*, 77.

14. Irwin, *The Complete Mah Jong Player*, vii, 195.

15. "Mah-Jongg Gives Way to Ma-Chiang," *New York Herald*, November 18, 1923, MJ Scrapbook 2, PB; Mary Greenfield, "'The Game of One Hundred Intelligences': Mahjong, Materials, and the Marketing of the Asian Exotic in the 1920s," *Pacific Historical Review* 79, no. 3 (August 2010): 342.

16. "Mah Jongg Experts Can't Agree on Playing Rules, Decide to Form League," *Brooklyn Daily Eagle*, October 11, 1923, MJ Scrapbook 2, PB; International Ma Chiang Players' Association, *Laws of Ma Chiang*.

17. International Ma Chiang Players' Association, *Laws of Ma Chiang*.

18. "Mah-Jongg Gives Way to Ma-Chiang"; L. S. Hsu, "Leland Stanford," *The Chinese Students' Monthly*, 1921.

19. "Mah-Jongg Gives Way to Ma-Chiang"; "Mah Jong Fans Decide to Call Game Ma Chiang," *Brooklyn Daily Eagle*, November 17, 1923, MJ Scrapbook 2, PB.

20. R. H. Macy & Co., "Advertisement: Sets, Racks and Tables for Ma Chiang," *New York Times*, March 12, 1924; R. H. Macy & Co., "Advertisement: Direct from China 650 Sets of Ma Chiang," *New York Times*, December 16, 1923; R. H. Macy & Co., "Advertisement: 'How Ma-Chiang Saved My Life'"; Parker Brothers, "The Genuine Always Bears the Printed Title MAH-JONGG and Contains the Copyrighted Babcock Rules," n.d., Warshaw Collection: "Parker" 60/toys Box 3, National Museum of American History, Archives Center; Greenfield, "Mahjong, Materials, and the Marketing of the Asian Exotic," 339.

21. Work, *Mah-Jongg Up-to-Date*; "Mah-Jongg Gives Way to Ma-Chiang"; "Mah Jongg Experts Can't Agree"; "Mah Jong Fans Decide to Call Game Ma Chiang."

22. Joseph Park Babcock, *The Laws of Mah-Jongg*.

23. "Mah-Jong Ballet by Society Girls"; "Youthful Dancer," *San Francisco Chronicle*, October 29, 1922, MJSC Scrapbook 1, PB; "Mah Jongg Tea Dancing by Society Girl."

24. Constance Grenelle Wilcox, *Mah-Jongg: The Play of One Hundred Intelligences, in a Prologue and One Act* (Boston: C. C. Birchard & Company, 1923).

25. "Mah Jongg Party for Army Folk"; Ladies Home Journal and Genevieve Jackson Boughner, "Catering for the Mah Jongg or Pung Chow Party," in *Women in Journalism: A Guide to the Opportunities and a Manual of the Technique of Women's Work for Newspapers and Magazines* (New York: D. Appleton, 1926).

26. "Ancient Game of China"; "Latest Indoor Sport"; "Look Out, Bridge! Mah Jongg Is after Your Title."

27. Krystyn R. Moon, *Yellowface: Creating the Chinese in American Popular Music and Performance, 1850s–1920s* (New Brunswick, NJ: Rutgers University Press, 2005); Eric Lott, *Love and Theft: Blackface Minstrelsy and the American Working Class* (New York: Oxford University Press, 1993); Robert Toll, *Blacking Up: The Minstrel Show in Nineteenth-Century America* (New York: Oxford University Press, 1974); Rhae Lynn Barnes, "The Birth of Blackface Minstrelsy and the Rise of Stephen Foster," *US History Scene* (blog), accessed June 17, 2020, https://ushistoryscene.com/article/birth-of-blackface; David Roediger, *The Wages of Whiteness: Race and the Making of the American Working Class* (New York: Verso, New Left Books, 1991); Deloria, *Playing Indian*; Thomas C. Holt, "Marking: Race, Race-Making, and the Writing of History," *American Historical Review* 100, no. 1 (February 1995): 1–20; Gina Marchetti, *Romance and the "Yellow Peril": Race, Sex, and Discursive Strategies in Hollywood Fiction* (Berkeley: University of California Press, 1993); John Kuo Wei Tchen, *New York before Chinatown: Orientalism and the Shaping of American Culture, 1776–1882* (Baltimore: Johns Hopkins University Press, 1999).

28. Holly Edwards, "A Million and One Nights: Orientalism in America, 1870–1930," in *Noble Dreams, Wicked Pleasures: Orientalism in America,*

1870–1930 (Princeton: Princeton University Press and Sterling and Francine Clark Art Institute, 2000), 34, 48.

29. Einav Rabinovitch-Fox, "[Re]Fashioning the New Woman: Women's Dress, the Oriental Style, and the Construction of American Feminist Imagery in the 1910s," *Journal of Women's History* 27, no. 2 (Summer 2015): 14–36; Amy Sueyoshi, *Discriminating Sex: White Leisure and the Making of the American "Oriental"* (Urbana: University of Illinois Press, 2018), Ch. 3; William R. Leach, "Transformations in a Culture of Consumption: Women and Department Stores, 1890–1925," *Journal of American History* 71, no. 2 (September 1984): 341.

30. Ellye Howell Glover, *"Dame Curtsey's" Book of Party Pastimes for the Up-to-Date Hostess*, 6th ed. (Chicago: A. C. McClurg & Co., 1912), 197; Edwards, "A Million and One Nights," 34, 40, 49.

31. Mari Yoshihara, *Embracing the East: White Women and American Orientalism* (New York: Oxford University Press, 2003); Kristin L. Hoganson, *Consumers' Imperium: The Global Production of American Domesticity, 1865–1920* (Chapel Hill: University of North Carolina Press, 2007); Sueyoshi, *Discriminating Sex*.

32. "Forms Mah Jong Club"; "With the Clubs."

33. For relevant context, see Hasia Diner, *The Jews of the United States, 1654 to 2000* (Berkeley: University of California Press, 2004), 111; Deborah Dash Moore, *At Home in America: Second Generation New York Jews* (New York: Columbia University Press, 1981); Riv-Ellen Prell, *Fighting to Become Americans: Jews, Gender, and the Anxiety of Assimilation* (Boston: Beacon Press, 1999).

34. "Ma-Jung Fete Album."

35. In 1923, a Los Angeles Reform synagogue sisterhood held an "unusual social meeting," where incense and Chinese costumes made for a "decidedly Oriental" ambiance. "News and Notes of Sisterhoods," *Jewish Chronicle*, April 6, 1923.

36. Alys Eve Weinbaum, "Racial Masquerade: Consumption and Contestation of American Modernity," in *The Modern Girl around the World: Consumption, Modernity, and Globalization*, ed. The Modern Girl around the World Research Group (Durham, NC: Duke University Press, 2008), 120–46; Mari Yoshihara, *Embracing the East*; Moon, *Yellowface*; A. A. Vantine and Company, "Vantine's."

37. The Modern Girl around the World Research Group, "The Modern Girl as Heuristic Device," 2.

38. D'Emilio and Estelle Freedman, *Intimate Matters: A History of Sexuality in America*, 240.

39. "[Untitled Clipping: Ebell Club]," *Los Angeles Evening Herald*, November 15, 1923, MJSC Scrapbook 1, PB.

40. Erté (Romain de Tirtoff), *Costume Design for "Mah-Jongg,"* Gouache and metallic paint, 1924, Drawings, Metropolitan Museum of Art. The costumes that were acutally used were somewhat less fantastical and revealing than Erté's original vision. (See photos of costumes in "Mah-Jongg on the Stage," *Auction Bridge and*

Mah Jong Magazine, Sept. 1924.) Wilcox, *Mah-Jongg: The Play*; "Mah-Jong Ballet by Society Girls."

41. "Now The Game Is Mah Jongg."

42. Florence Irwin, *The Complete Mah Jong Player* (New York: Brentano's, 1924). Mahjong slang was a transnational phenomenon, as slang flowed from the Shanghai social clubs via expats and tourists. McCormick, "China's Ancient Dominoes Now Fascinate Foreigners." American mahjong players still refer to the blank white dragon tile as "Soap."

43. Held, "The Ancient Chinese Game According to the More Modern Generation." The cartoons were published in a specialty magazine, but Held was an artist with national reach. His magazine covers helped define the flapper image.

44. Sachs, "China's Fascinating Super Game."

45. Held, "If Confucius Should Return."

46. Peggy Paige, "Advertisement: There's an Easter Dress for You"; Eastern Sales Co., "Mah Jong Ring"; "Silk Group Discusses"; Helen Koues, "Fashions," *Good Housekeeping*, July 1924, Home Economics Archive: Research, Tradition and History (HEARTH), Cornell University; "Mah Jong Wields Influence," *China Review*, September 1923; "Vogue's Fortnightly Wardrobe."

47. "Flappers of Chinatown."

48. *Mah-Jongg*, Sweet Little Devil (WB Music Corp., 1923), Gershwin on Broadway; Moon, *Yellowface*. Moon examines how the characterization of Chinese music as "noise" influenced larger perceptions of assimilability and social evolution. An exception to this pattern was Sid Reinherz's straightforward ragtime tune "Mah Jong." Sid Reinherz, "Mah Jong Novelty Piano Solo" (Jack Mills, 1923), The Strong National Museum of Play.

49. *Mah-Jongg*, 1923. Although Bret Harte's poem, officially titled "Plain Language from Truthful James," was intended as a satirical jab at anti-Chinese sentiments attributed to working-class Irishmen, Harte's poem quickly circulated in anti-Chinese circles and entered popular culture. For decades after, the "heathen Chinee" was a cultural reference point in media and was used to taunt Chinese Americans on the streets. Harte later called it "trash." Gary Scharnhorst, "'Ways That Are Dark': Appropriations of Bret Harte's 'Plain Language from Truthful James.'" *Nineteenth-Century Literature* 51, no. 3 (December 1996): 377–99.

50. Lee, *Orientals*; Gina Marchetti, *Romance and the "Yellow Peril"*; Judy Yung, *Unbound Feet: A Social History of Chinese Women in San Francisco* (Berkeley: University of California Press, 1995); Fitch, "The Ancient Game of Chinese Scholars and Gentlemen"; Held, "'. . . and the Twain Shall Meet.'"

51. "Some Girl—Some Game!," *Los Angeles Examiner*, October 14, 1922, MJSC Scrapbook 1, PB.

52. "News of Los Angeles Cafes and Newest Attractions," *Los Angeles Examiner*, November 1, 1922, MJSC Scrapbook 1, PB.

53. Hamburger's, "Advertisement: A Popular Gift 'Mah Jongg'—the Game of a Thousand Wonders," *Los Angeles Times*, December 22, 1922; "Warrants in Cafe Raid," *Los Angeles Times*, October 28, 1921; "Dry Agent Here Only to Testify," *Los Angeles Times*, January 19, 1922; "County to Modernize Dance Law," *Los Angeles Times*, April 28, 1924.

54. The café was respectable enough to host a corporate dinner party: "Sales Record Cause of Celebration," *Los Angeles Times*, February 4, 1923.

55. "LA Society Takes Up Mah Jongg, Chinese Game," *Los Angeles Evening Herald*, July 26, 1922, MJSC Scrapbook 1, PB.

56. "Students Teach Mah Jong," *New York Times*, March 18, 1923. "Colleges Report on Summer Jobs," *New York Times*, August 3, 1924.

57. Erika Lee, "Defying Exclusion: Chinese Immigrants and Their Strategies during the Exclusion Era," in *Chinese American Transnationalism*, ed. Sucheng Chan (Philadelphia: Temple University Press, 2006), 1.

58. Jorae, *The Children of Chinatown*, 47.

59. For relevant discussions, see Shirley Jennifer Lim, *A Feeling of Belonging: Asian American Women's Public Culture, 1930–1960* (New York: New York University Press, 2006); Lisa Lowe, *Immigrant Acts: On Asian American Cultural Politics* (Durham, NC: Duke University Press, 1996).

60. Wu, *Doctor Mom Chung of the Fair-Haired Bastards*, 97–102; Leong, *The China Mystique*, 57; Haiming Liu, "Chinese Herbalists in the United States," in *Chinese American Transnationalism*, ed. Sucheng Chan (Philadelphia: Temple University Press, 2006), 148; Moon, *Yellowface*, Ch. 6.

61. "Institute of Pacific Relations: Preliminary Paper Prepared for Second General Session July 15–29, 1927" (Institute of Pacific Relations, 1927), 15, Pardee Lowe Collection, Box 97, Hoover Archive, Stanford University.

62. Jorae, *The Children of Chinatown*, 211; "Institute of Pacific Relations, 1927." See also Pardee Lowe's sociological notes and interviews in Boxes 96, 97, 99 in Pardee Lowe Collection, Hoover Archive, Stanford University.

63. "Wrestling Training!" For additional depictions of attractive and flirtatious Chinese female instructors, see Held Jr., " '. . . and the Twain Shall Meet' "; Jefferies, "Mysteries of Mah Jong Description."

64. "Mah Jongg, Orient Game, Replacing Bridge in SF," *San Francisco Call*, June 23, 1922, MJSC Scrapbook 1, PB.

65. Elliott, *Mah Jongg Section*.

66. Lim, *A Feeling of Belonging*, 50.

67. Moon, *Yellowface*; Leong, *The China Mystique*; Lim, *A Feeling of Belonging*; Lowe, *Immigrant Acts*; Shehong Chen, *Being Chinese, Becoming Chinese American* (Urbana: University of Illinois Press, 2002); Anthony W. Lee, "Another View of Chinatown: Yun Gee and the Chinese Revolutionary Artists' Club," in *Reclaiming San Francisco: History, Politics, Culture; A City Lights Anthology* (San Francisco: City Lights Books, 1998), 163–82.

68. Some voices in popular media explicitly undercut Chinese Americans' mahjong authority by questioning whether contemporary working-class Chinese people would know anything about an ancient royal game. See Montague, "'Fire!' and 'Fore!.'"

69. Wu, *Doctor Mom Chung of the Fair-Haired Bastards*, 101.

70. Lawton Mackall, "Tiles on Parade," *Auction Bridge and Mah Jong Magazine*, May 1924, Library of Congress; Knott, "Penny Ante: Girls Take Up Mah Jong." Some Chinese American instructors advertised home-based instruction, though they were generally outnumbered by others, often white women, advertising similar services. "Classified Ad: S. C. Hung, Mah-Jong Instructor," *Vogue*, October 1, 1923.

71. Similar themes were featured in the form of Japanese influence (and a set full of Chinese objects), in the hit film *The Cheat*. Cecil B. DeMille, *The Cheat* (Paramount Pictures, 1915).

72. Held Jr., "'. . . and the Twain Shall Meet.'"

73. Jefferies, "Mysteries of Mah Jong Description."

74. Norman Jefferies, "Mysteries of Mah Jong: Film Copyright Descriptive Material," 1924, Copyright Descriptive Material, microfilm, Library of Congress, Motion Pictures. Actor Amelia Ruth Parker used "Princess Nai Tai Tai" as her stage name.

75. Lee, *Orientals*.

76. Nayan Shah, *Contagious Divides*.

77. Sax Rohmer, *The Return of Dr. Fu-Manchu*.

78. Nayan Shah, *Contagious Divides*; Mary Ting Yi Lui, *The Chinatown Trunk Mystery: Murder, Miscegenation, and Other Dangerous Encounters in Turn-of-the-Century New York City* (Princeton: Princeton University Press, 2005).

79. I. W. Taber, *White Women in Opium Den, Chinatown, S.F.*, Photograph, May 31, 1892, Album of views of California and the West, Canada, and China, Bancroft Library; Nayan Shah, *Contagious Divides*.

80. Lui, *The Chinatown Trunk Mystery*.

81. Emma Jinhua Teng, *Eurasian: Mixed Identities in the United States, China, and Hong Kong, 1842–1943* (Berkeley: University of California Press, 2013).

82. Clement Wood, *The Truth about New York's Chinatown*, Little Blue Book 1057 (Girard, KS: Haldeman-Julius Company, 1926); Chad Heap, *Slumming: Sexual and Racial Encounters in American Nightlife, 1885–1940* (Chicago: University of Chicago Press, 2008).

83. In *Orientals*, Robert Lee identifies six alienating Asian stereotypes: the pollutant, the coolie, the deviant, the yellow peril, the model minority, and the gook. I see the faux-assimilated trickster figure as an additional stereotype, predominant in the 1910s–1930s. Lee, *Orientals*, 8.

84. G. B. Walker, "Cartoon: The Yellow Peril," *Harper's Monthly Magazine*, November 1923.

85. "Queer Chinese Game, Invented Centuries Ago, Is Society's Latest Craze. Mah-Jongg, Intricate Pastime, Built around Great Wall of the Orient," *San Francisco*

Chronicle, October 15, 1922, sec. F. See also Lawton Mackall, "Tiles on Parade," *Auction Bridge and Mah Jong Magazine*, May 1924, Library of Congress; Ring Lardner, "Memories of Mah Jongg Raked Over by Lardner," *Boston Daily Globe*, April 26, 1925.

86. Cuddy, *The Green Dragon Emerald*; Sam Hellman, "Punk Pungs," *Saturday Evening Post*, November 3, 1923, MJ Scrapbook 2, PB.

87. Lui, *The Chinatown Trunk Mystery*.

88. Hellman, "Punk Pungs"; Hellman, *Low Bridge and Punk Pungs*.

89. Hellman, *Low Bridge and Punk Pungs*, 85.

90. Ibid., 88.

91. Ibid., 89.

92. Ibid., 99, 112.

93. As in *Birth of a Nation* and other mainstream post-emancipation white suprem-acist media portrayals, the dangerous and uppity upwardly mobile non-white threat is juxtaposed against the figure of the simple servant who did not threaten the racial hierarchy. See Jack Temple Kirby, "D. W. Griffith's Racial Portraiture," *Phylon* 39, no. 2 (Qtr 1978): 118–127.

94. Cuddy, *The Green Dragon Emerald*, 41–42. Common stereotypical Chinese di-alect included switching "L" and "R," frequently inserting "L," and adding "ee" suffixes. Also see Lee, *Orientals*, re: childlike sexuality.

95. Cuddy, *The Green Dragon Emerald*; "Senior Class of Mariposa High to Give Play," May 14, 1931.

96. Cuddy, *The Green Dragon Emerald*, 84–85, 88, 89.

97. Ibid., 23.

98. Demonstrated in colonial-era "Japanning" lacquered furniture designs, Orientalist consumerism, and popular media such as D. W. Griffith's *Broken Blossoms*. See Frank, *Objectifying China, Imagining America*; Holly Edwards, "A Million and One Nights"; Mae M. Ngai, "American Orientalism: Review of New York before Chinatown," *Reviews in American History* 28, no. 3 (September 2000): 408–415; Gina Marchetti, "American Orientalism"; Mari Yoshihara, *Embracing the East*; Jack Temple Kirby, "D. W. Griffith's Racial Portraiture," 119–20; Lee, *Orientals* Ch. 4.

99. "American Who Invented Mah Jongg Discovered"; "Mrs. Edwin S. Webster," *Town Topics*, February 15, 1923; Stevens, "How the Mah Jongg Fiend Scores His Victories."

100. For additional examples, see: Auto Vacuum Ice Cream Freezer, "Advertisement: Ice Cream Freezer"; R. H. Macy & Co., "Advertisement: 'How Ma-Chiang Saved My Life'"; "Now the Game Is Mah Jongg."

101. Josephine M. Burnham, "Three Hard-Worked Suffixes," *American Speech*, February 1927, 244–246. A linguist in 1927 identified the creation of a new term: "mah-jong-itis." Borrowed from the medical suffix meaning "inflammation of," popular use of "-itis" came to mean, "excessive tendency to." The author in-cluded "mah-jong-itis" with Charlestonitis, flapperitis, crosswordpuzzleitis, and

[Ku Klux] klanitis, revealing 1920s cultural preoccupations ranging from hobbies to white supremacy.

102. "Woman Must Return to the Corset," *San Francisco Examiner*, March 27, 1923, Microfilm, SFPL; Adams, "A Maker of Heirlooms."

103. *Since Ma Is Playing Mah Jong* (New York: M. Witmark & Sons, 1924), Sam DeVincent Collection, National Museum of American History, Archives Center.

104. See also Hellman, "Punk Pungs"; Judy Tsou, "Gendering Race: Stereotypes of Chinese Americans in Popular Sheet Music," *Repercussions* 6, no. 2 (Fall 1997): 37.

105. The Modern Girl around the World Research Group, "The Modern Girl as Heuristic Device." Chad Heap, *Slumming*.

106. Eddie Cantor was a very popular comedic Jewish entertainer who successfully transitioned from vaudeville to film. He often performed in blackface, including in partnership with the African American vaudevillian Bert Williams. His humor included ethnic humor based on Jewish stereotypes, but he was simultaneously an early pioneer in embracing his Jewish heritage in front of mixed audiences.

107. Miriam Van Waters, *Youth in Conflict* (New York: Republic Publishing Co., 1925), 274.

108. "Mah Jongg and the Husbands' Protective League," *Vancouver Sun*, November 11, 1923. McConn, "Town Mah Jongg Mad."

109. "Divorce Wrecks 148,554 Homes in One Year! Yearning for 'Self Expression' Brings Menace to Institutions of Civilization," *San Francisco Chronicle*, November 15, 1923, Microfilm, SFPL; Hall, "The Screen"; Guest, "Just Folks"; "Comic Strip: The First Hundred Games of Mah Jong Are the Hardest."

110. Montague, "More Truth Than Poetry: Mah Jong."

111. "Mah Jongg and the Husbands' Protective League."

112. John McCallan, "Why the Chinese Left Humboldt," July 1923.

113. Sidney Smith, "The Gumps," n.d., MJ Scrapbook 2, PB.

114. "The Mahjongg Neck," *Hawaii Herald*, September 21, 1922, MJSC Scrapbook 1, PB; "Chink Game Raises Rubber," *Casper Herald*, September 3, 1922, MJSC Scrapbook 1, PB.

115. "Woman Scared by Mah Jongg: Thought Game a Germ and Asked Physician to Vaccinate Her," *Los Angeles Times*, February 19, 1924.

116. Breuner's, "Advertisement: Mah-Jongg the Game That Is Taking the Country by Storm," *Sacramento Bee*, October 5, 1922, MJSC Scrapbook 1, PB.

117. "'Mah Jongg Eyes' Held New American Malady," *San Francisco Examiner*, December 26, 1923, SFPL.

118. "Mah Jongg Eye Remedy Suggested," *Los Angeles Times*, January 6, 1924.

119. "The Mah Jongg Eye," *Los Angeles Times*, January 2, 1924.

120. Oscar H. Fernbach, "4 Eyes Needed in Mah Jongg," *San Francisco Examiner*, December 27, 1923, SFPL.

121. "Leaping Larvae." The bouncy tiles were likened to another foreign import, "Mexican jumping beans." The 1922 animated short film by Max Fleischer, *Jumping Beans*, featured Mexican jumping beans, but without racialized representation.

122. Frank Thone, "Poison Ivy Conquered by Chemicals," *Science News-Letter*, July 2, 1927, 10; "Letters, Notes, and Answers: Mah Jongg," *British Medical Journal*, March 15, 1924, 506. Cultural concerns remained preeminent, however: the *British Medical Journal* began its cautionary notice by reassuring readers that bridge would not likely be replaced by an encroaching mahjong "craze."

123. Caroline Little, "Correspondence: Dermatitis Produced by Chinese Lacquer," *British Medical Journal*, June 21, 1924, 1112.

124. "Pen Points," *Los Angeles Times*, December 4, 1924; "Too Much Wind," *Los Angeles Times*, February 21, 1926; "Topics of the Times: Another Fad Has Passed," *New York Times*, June 17, 1926.

125. "Bankruptcy Proceedings," *New York Times*, April 10, 1925. "Topics of the Times: Will He Get Any Bids?," *New York Times*, June 13, 1925.

126. After graduating from Yale in 1927, Joseph Babcock joined a New York law firm; perhaps his legal experiences with mahjong informed his future career as chief counsel of the General Electric Company. Norma apparently kept many of the sets in the divorce settlement. Celia Babcock Smith and Martha Ann Babcock, Joseph Babcock and Mah Jong from Celia Babcock Smith's Oral History, interview by Barbara Babcock Millhouse and Sherold Hollingsworth, January 6, 2007, Christopher Berg Personal Collection.

127. Philip E. Orbanes, *The Game Makers*, 71, 75.

128. "Mah Jongg," *Chinese Digest* 4, no. 2 (February 1938): 19.

129. "Mah Jongg Boom Dies, but China Plays On," *Washington Post*, June 3, 1928.

130. "Pen Points."

131. For an alternative comparison, see Philip Orbanes, "The Canasta Story," *The Games Journal*, August 2000, www.thegamesjournal.com/articles/Canasta.shtml.

132. Nancy R., "Charades Win Way Back to Favor as Rival of Mah Jongg," *Chicago Daily Tribune*, March 18, 1925; "The Passing of Mah Jong and Cross-Words," *The China Press*, February 19, 1926; Currier, "Diary, 1920–1924."

133. Lowry, "Rise and Present Peril."

134. The Poe Sisters, "Washington Scene," *Washington Post*, July 19, 1936; "Annual Dinner Party of Nau Wah Mah Jongg Club," *The Chicago Defender*, June 18, 1932; "Nau Wah Mah Jongg," *The Chicago Defender*, March 30, 1935, National edition.

135. Fong Tai Co., "Advertisement: Fong Tai Co.," trans. Andrew Elmore, *Young China*, January 23, 1934, Pardee Lowe Collection, Box 125b, Folder: Imported Skills and Technology, Hoover Archive.

136. George R. Clark, *[The Gay Twenties I]*.

CHAPTER 6

1. Victor G. Nee and Brett de Bary Nee, *Longtime Californ'*, 158.

2. Karen J. Leong, *The China Mystique: Pearl S. Buck, Anna May Wong, Mayling Soong, and the Transformation of American Orientalism* (Berkeley: University of California Press, 2005); Gordon H. Chang, *Fateful Ties: A History of America's Preoccupation with China* (Cambridge, MA: Harvard University Press, 2015), Ch. 4.

3. By the 1920s, many residents of Chinese heritage were long-term residents or citizens by birth. Although the term "Chinese American" was not yet in wide circulation, it is an appropriate term to encompass the wide range of claims to residence and citizenship in this relatively stable population. The mostly male "sojourner" migrant population was no longer the predominant type, in part as a result of Chinese immigration exclusion. The proportion of women had grown from less than one seventh of the US Chinese population in 1900 to one fourth in 1930. By 1940, 51 percent of the Chinese American population was born in the United States. See Wendy Rouse Jorae, *The Children of Chinatown: Growing Up Chinese American in San Francisco, 1850–1920* (Chapel Hill: University of North Carolina Press, 2009), 216.

4. Immigrants who entered the United States in the 1910s recalled, "At that time there was no mah-jong." Mr. Quan, interview; Mr. Low, interview by Him Mark Lai, Laura Lai, and Judy Yung, December 27, 1975, Angel Island Oral History Project, Ethnic Studies Library, University of California Berkeley. See also Lu Xun, "Our Story of Ah Q," 113; Greene, "The Game People Played."

5. Pardee Lowe, *Father and Glorious Descendant*, 219.

6. Mah-Jongg Sales Co., "Advertisement: Da Bang Ma Jiang Fa Xing [Boosting Ma Jiang Sales]," trans. Thomas Mullaney, *Chung Sai Yat Po*, October 5, 1922, MJSC Scrapbook 1, PB.

7. In the early 1910s, writer Hu Shi recorded in his college diary playing "Chinese pai" with other Chinese students studying at Cornell University. Many other entries mention generic "playing pai." It is uncertain whether this "Chinese pai" was mahjong, although the phrasing indicates he may have been playing mahjong along with other card and/or tile games. Diary entry: April 29, 1911. Hu Shi, *Hu Shi Riji Quanbian [A Complete Collection of Hu Shi's Diaries]*, trans. Yvon Wang (Hefei, China: Anhui Education Press, 2001), 90.

8. Mr. Quan, interview; Mr. Low, interview; Laverne Mau Dicker, *The Chinese in San Francisco: A Pictorial History* (New York: Dover Publications, 1979), 78; George Kao, *Cathay by the Bay: San Francisco Chinatown in 1950* (Hong Kong: Chinese University Press, 1988), 63.

9. The Chinese Government Bureau of Economic Information, "The Rise of Mahjongg," 2.

10. Lowe, *Father and Glorious Descendant*, 219. Lowe's book, informed by his extensive sociological research on the California Chinese American communities of his roots, was the first full-length book by a Chinese American published in the United States and was commercially successful. Pardee Lowe, "Second-Generation

Dilemmas (1930s)," in *Chinese American Voices: From the Gold Rush to the Present*, ed. Judy Yung, Gordon H. Chang, and Him Mark Lai (Berkeley: University of California Press, 2006), 164–66. Despite Lowe's father's initial resistance to mahjong as gambling, the "whole family learned" to play and his stepmother "became a superb player."

11. Maggie Greene, "The Game People Played: Mahjong in Modern Chinese Society and Culture," *Cross-Currents: East Asian History and Culture Review* E-Journal, no. 17 (December 2015): 1–25. "Afternoon Translation: A Strange Story of Shanghai," in *Files on Noulens Associates: Anniversary of the Coup d'Etat at Sian Falling on December 12* (Shanghai, 1936), 74; Wong Koh Hwa, "Shanghai Municipal Police Report of Police Investigations," in *Files on Noulens Associates: Shanghai Police Investigation Reports Regarding Japanese Military Arrests and Searches*, trans. Yao Dinain, 1938, 25–26.

12. "Gambling at Public Places," in *Files on Noulens Associates: People's Educational Institute—Anti-Foreign and Anti-Japanese*, 1936. "Comments on Current Events," March 14, 1936, Correspondence of the Military Intelligence Division Relating to General, Political, Economic, and Military Conditions in China, 1918–1941, US National Archives.

13. Adam McKeown, *Chinese Migrant Networks and Cultural Change: Peru, Chicago, Hawaii, 1900–1936* (Chicago: University of Chicago Press, 2001), 31.

14. Sucheng Chan, "Against All Odds: Chinese Female Migration and Family Formation on American Soil during the Early Twentieth Century," in *Chinese American Transnationalism*, ed. Sucheng Chan (Philadelphia: Temple University Press, 2006), 34–135; Andrea Rees Davies, *Saving San Francisco: Relief and Recovery after the 1906 Disaster* (Philadelphia: Temple University Press, 2011), 45; Lowe, *Father and Glorious Descendant*, 27–29.

15. For more on transnational migrant networks among Chinese Americans in Chicago, Hawaii, and Peru, see McKeown, *Chinese Migrant Networks and Cultural Change*.

16. Victor G. Nee and Brett de Bary Nee, *Longtime Californ': A Documentary Study of an American Chinatown* (New York: Pantheon Books, 1972), 61.

17. Leong Gor Yun, *Chinatown Inside Out*, 176.

18. Gordon L'Allemand, "Old Chinatown."

19. Larson, *Sweet Bamboo*, 144.

20. "[Note to Newspaper]."

21. Lowe, *Immigrant Acts*, 121.

22. Chinese American Museum, "Sun Wing Wo General Store and Herb Shop Exhibit" (Los Angeles, August 21, 2012); Charles Caldwell Dobie, *San Francisco's Chinatown* (New York: D. Appleton–Century Company, 1936); Pardee Lowe, "Recreation—Stores as Social Centers, 1930–1933," 1930s, Pardee Lowe Collection, Box 128a, Hoover Archive, Stanford University; Katherine Chann, interview by author, Phone, February 13, 2017.

23. Yu, *Chinatown San Jose, USA,* 67–68; Madeline Y. Hsu, "Trading with Gold Mountain: Jinshanzhuang and Networks of Kinship and Native Place," in *Chinese American Transnationalism,* ed. Sucheng Chan (Philadelphia: Temple University Press, 2006), 22–33.

24. Leong Gor Yun, *Chinatown Inside Out,* 21.

25. Lowe, *Father and Glorious Descendant,* 98–99. See also Dobie, *San Francisco's Chinatown.*

26. Rose Hum Lee, "Social Institutions of a Rocky Mountain Chinatown," *Social Forces* 27, no. 1 (October 1948): 10. See also Mae M. Ngai, *The Lucky Ones: One Family and the Extraordinary Invention of Chinese America* (New York: Houghton Mifflin Harcourt, 2010), 202.

27. Ibid., 160.

28. Gordon L'Allemand, "Old Chinatown," *Los Angeles Times,* October 4, 1930.

29. "Jesse Brown Cook Scrapbooks," Vol. 6, 63–64a.

30. " 'Twas Poker Party."

31. Liu, "Chinese Herbalists in the United States," 155; Lowe, *Father and Glorious Descendant,* 51.

32. William Wong, "Arthur Tom," in *Chinese America: History & Perspectives— The Journal of the Chinese Historical Society of America* (San Francisco: Chinese Historical Society of America with UCLA Asian American Studies Center, 2011), 49.

33. Years earlier, Chinese Americans joined with Chinese consumers for a transpacific boycott of American goods in protest of the anti-Chinese US immigration policy. See Yong Chen, "Understanding Chinese American Transnationalism during the Early Twentieth Century: An Economic Perspective," in *Chinese American Transnationalism,* ed. Sucheng Chan (Philadelphia: Temple University Press, 2006), 161.

34. Yung, Chang, and Lai, *Chinese American Voices,* 5; Yung, *Unbound Feet,* 25.

35. Wing Luke Museum of the Asian Pacific American Experience, "Gee How Oak Tin Association Hall" (Seattle, n.d.), accessed February 14, 2012; John Hom, interview by author, Wing Luke Museum, Seattle, February 14, 2012.

36. Xavier Paules, "An Illustration of China's 'Paradoxical Soft Power': The Dissemination of the Gambling Game Fantan by the Cantonese Diaspora, 1850-1950," *Translocal Chinese: East Asian Perspectives* 11 (2017): 187–207; Fred W. Mueller Jr., "Gaming and Gaming Pieces," in *An American Chinatown: Archaeology,* ed. Wong Ho Leun, vol. 2 (San Diego: The Great Basin Foundation, 1987), 385–95; Julia G. Costello, Kevin Hallaran, and Keith Warren, *The Luck of Third Street: Historical Archaeology Data Recovery Report for the Caltrans District 8 San Bernadino Headquarters Demolition Project* (San Bernadino: California Department of Transportation District 8, 2004).

37. Joyce (Lee) Chan, interview by author, San Francisco, CA, July 19, 2012.

38. Judy Yung, *Unbound Feet: A Social History of Chinese Women in San Francisco* (Berkeley: University of California Press, 1995), 80; Chan, interview; Pardee Lowe, "[Handwritten Notes]," n.d., Pardee Lowe Collection, Box 128a Folder: Recreation—Play, Hoover Archive, Stanford University; Chinese Women's Association, Inc., "Souvenir Program Chinese Women's Association, Inc.," June 29, 1936; Connie Young Yu, *Chinatown San Jose, USA* (San Jose, CA: History San Jose, 1991), 79; Asian American Studies Center, University of California, Los Angeles, and Chinese Historical Society of Southern California, *Linking Our Lives: Chinese American Women of Los Angeles* (Los Angeles: Chinese Historical Society of Southern California, Inc., 1984), 59; Chann, interview.

39. Louise Leung Larson, *Sweet Bamboo: A Memoir of a Chinese American Family* (Berkeley: University of California Press, 1989), 144.

40. Pardee Lowe, "Recreation—Women's—Ma Jong—1934," n.d., Pardee Lowe Collection, Box 128a Folder: Recreation—Play (2), Hoover Archive, Stanford University; Pardee Lowe, "Ma Jong Game," February 1935, Pardee Lowe Collection, Box 128a Folder: Recreation—Play, Hoover Archive, Stanford University. See also Lowe, *Father and Glorious Descendant*, 301.

41. Pardee Lowe, "Recreation—Women's—Ma Jong—1934."

42. Pardee Lowe, "Biography of a Second-Generation Chinese Woman," 1930s, Pardee Lowe Collection, Box 128a Folder: Women's Status, Hoover Archive, Stanford University.

43. Lowe, "Second-Generation Dilemmas," 173.

44. Amy Tan, *The Joy Luck Club* (New York: Ballantine Books, 1989).

45. Al Yu [pseud.], Millbrae, CA, August 3, 2012. For other examples of conversation and the game's rhythm, see Agatha Christie, *The Murder of Roger Ackroyd* (London: W. Collins Sons & Co. Ltd., 1926), 16; Alice Gerstenberg, *Four Plays for Four Women* (New York: Brentano's, Inc., 1924); Eileen Chang, *Lust, Caution*.

46. Lowe, *Father and Glorious Descendant*, 220.

47. Roberta Park, "Sport and Recreation among Chinese American Communities of the Pacific Coast from Time of Arrival to the 'Quiet Decade' of the 1950s," *Journal of Sport History* 27, no. 3 (Fall 2000): 445–70; Jorae, *The Children of Chinatown*; Ruth Fong Chinn, "Square and Circle Club of San Francisco: A Chinese Women's Culture" (Senior thesis, University of California, Santa Cruz, 1987), Stanford University Special Collections (Alice Fong Yu Papers).

48. Rose Hum Lee, "Social Institutions of a Rocky Mountain Chinatown," 10.

49. Victor G. Nee and Brett de Bary Nee, *Longtime Californ'*, 150.

50. Jorae, *The Children of Chinatown*, 47.

51. Yung, Chang, and Lai, *Chinese American Voices*, 105–6; Jorae, *The Children of Chinatown*, 208–9.

52. Pardee Lowe, "Americanization—Increased Mingling of the Sexes," 1930s, Pardee Lowe Collection, Box 125a, Hoover Archive, Stanford University.

53. "Interview with Flora Belle Jan, Daughter of Proprietor of the 'Yet Far Low,' Chop Suey Restaurant, Tulare St., and China Alley, Fresno" (Survey of Race Relations, 1924–1927), Survey of Race Relations: Major Documents, Hoover Archive, Stanford University; Judy Yung, "'It Is Hard to Be Born a Woman but Hopeless to Be Born a Chinese': The Life and Times of Flora Belle Jan," *Frontiers: A Journal of Women Studies* 18, no. 3 (1997): 66–91.

54. Miss Ya-Tsing Yen, "College Wives and College Citizens," *The Chinese Students' Monthly* 19, no. 4 (February 1924): 21–22; Burnett, "Life History of Andrew Kan"; Shehong Chen, "Republicanism, Confucianism, Christianity, and Capitalism in American Chinese Ideology," in *Chinese American Transnationalism* (Philadelphia: Temple University Press, 2006), 183–84.

55. Yung, *Unbound Feet*, 147–48.

56. Pardee Lowe, "Assimilation: Pathetic Features: Over-Assimilation, 1934," Pardee Lowe Collection, Box 125a, Hoover Archive, Stanford University.

57. Larson, *Sweet Bamboo*, 143. Chinese Students' Alliance, "Chinese Students' Alliance Twenty-Sixth Annual Conference, Stanford University, August 16–19, 1928," Pardee Lowe Collection, Box 196, Hoover Archive, Stanford University.

58. Louise Leung, "Night Call—In Chinatown," *Los Angeles Times*, July 26, 1936.

59. Larson, *Sweet Bamboo*, 143.

60. Lowe, *Father and Glorious Descendant*, 68.

61. William Hoy, "Newspaper Clipping: Through a Chinatown Window," December 27, 1940, Alice Fong Yu Papers, Stanford University Special Collections.

62. Pardee Lowe, "New Year's Day Celebration (American); Native-Born Men & Women," 1930s, Pardee Lowe Collection, Box 125a, Hoover Archive, Stanford University.

63. Pardee Lowe, "Celebration of American New Year's Eve—Older Native-Born's Activities," 1930s, Pardee Lowe Collection, Box 125a, Hoover Archive, Stanford University.

64. Pardee Lowe, "Celebration of American New Year's Eve—Chinatown Street Scene," 1930s, Pardee Lowe Collection, Box 125a, Hoover Archive, Stanford University.

65. Virginia Yans, "On 'Groupness,'" *Journal of American Ethnic History* 25, no. 4 (Summer 2006): 119–29; K. Scott Wong, "Chinatown: Conflicting Images, Contested Terrain," *MELUS* 20, no. 1 (Spring 1995): 3–15.

66. Sources show a deafening silence from Christian sources in contrast to the chatter about mahjong in contemporaneous non-Christian circles. Notable absences include the records of the Square and Circle and Ging Hawk Clubs of young Chinese American women, Chinese Christian college groups, and Pardee Lowe's discussion of his own life and habits (as opposed to those of his non-Christian mahjong-playing stepmother).

67. Chen, "Republicanism, Confucianism, Christianity, and Capitalism in American Chinese Ideology," 187.

68. As one example, a multi-denominational Taoist, Buddhist, and Confucian temple complex in Northern California housed mahjong sets in the 1920s and 1930s. "Mahjong Set," n.d., City of Oroville Chinese Temple and Museum Complex.

69. James Mo, "Critical Judgments," *The Chinese Students' Monthly*, April 1929, 273.

70. Weili Ye, *Seeking Modernity in China's Name: Chinese Students in the United States, 1900–1927* (Stanford, CA: Stanford University Press, 2001), 7; Joan Judge, "Talent, Virtue, and the Nation: Chinese Nationalisms and Female Subjectivities in the Early Twentieth Century," *American Historical Review* 106, no. 3 (June 2001): 765–803.

71. Chen, "Understanding Chinese American Transnationalism," 160.

72. Yong Chen, *Chinese San Francisco, 1850–1943: A Trans-Pacific Community* (Stanford, CA: Stanford University Press, 2000), 237; McKeown, *Chinese Migrant Networks and Cultural Change*, 86–94.

73. Chen, "Understanding Chinese American Transnationalism," 156.

74. Ting-mou, "Ivory and Bamboo," 158.

75. Hsi-yüan Chen, "Madiao and Mahjong," 19.

76. Chen, "Republicanism, Confucianism, Christianity, and Capitalism in American Chinese Ideology," 177.

77. Other cultural forms like Peking Opera underwent similar transformations from associations with disreputable sexuality to "national treasure" status in the early twentieth century. Hsi-yüan Chen, "Madiao and Mahjong," 1; Andrea Goldman, *Opera and the City: The Politics of Culture in Beijing, 1770–1900.*

78. Hsi-yüan Chen, "Madiao and Mahjong," 30.

79. Hsi-yüan Chen, "Madiao and Mahjong," 32–33.

80. Hallett Abend, "Chinese in Mukden Have Orgy of Vice," *New York Times*, January 3, 1932.

81. Lin Yutang, "Some Hard Words about Confucius," *Harper's Monthly Magazine*, December 1934, 717. For an example of mahjong as a symptom of feudalism, see "Shanghai Municipal Police Report: Shanghai Vocational Chinese Women's Lien Nyi Society," in *8754* (Shanghai, 1939), 33–44.

82. For a particularly striking depiction of empowered Communist women physically fighting male mahjong gamblers, see "No Sacrifice . . . No Victory: Agnes Smedley, China Correspondent, Writes of China's War-Wise Women, Who Have Made Their Choice," *Vogue*, April 15, 1942. For more on differences between radical and conservative nationalist portrayals of women's roles, see Prasenjit Duara, "Of Authenticity and Woman: Personal Narratives of Middle-Class Women in Modern China," in *Becoming Chinese: Passages to Modernity and Beyond*, ed. Wen-hsin Yeh (Berkeley: University of California Press, 2000), 342–64.

83. Duara, 347. See also Ye, *Seeking Modernity in China's Name*, 151.

84. Roberta Chang, "Some of the Problems of Women," *The Chinese Recorder* 68 (1937): 682–85.

85. Ibid., 685.

86. Judge, "Talent, Virtue, and the Nation," 802.

87. Ibid., 803.

88. Chang, "Some of the Problems of Women," 682.

89. Asian American Studies Center, University of California, Los Angeles, and Chinese Historical Society of Southern California, *Linking Our Lives: Chinese American Women of Los Angeles* (Los Angeles: Chinese Historical Society of Southern California, Inc., 1984), 103.

90. "Shanghai Municipal Police Report: Illegal Functioning by Chapei Police," in *Further Report Re: Illegal Functioning by Chapei Police* (Shanghai, 1933), 1–4.

91. Jim May, "#230 Traditional Chinese Boxed Set," Mah Jong Museum, accessed August 23, 2013, www.mahjongmuseum.com/mj230.htm. See also Ann Israel and Gregg Swain, *Mah Jongg: The Art of the Game* (Rutland, VT: Tuttle Publishing, 2014), 118.

92. Gregg Swain, "Scenes of War on Mahjong Tiles," *Mahjong Treasures*, January 26, 2015, www.mahjongtreasures.com.

93. Ye, *Seeking Modernity in China's Name*.

94. Lowe, *Father and Glorious Descendant*, 190; "Interview with Flora Belle Jan."

95. Gloria Heyung Chun, "Shifting Ethnic Identity and Consciousness: US-Born Chinese American Youth in the 1930s and 1950s," in *Asian American Youth: Culture, Identity, and Ethnicity* (New York: Routledge, 2004), 120.

96. "Institute of Pacific Relations, 1927," 15.

97. Francis Y. Chang et al., "From the Preparation Committee for the Formation of the S.F. Bay Region Chinese Students' Association, Chinese Y.M.C.A., San Francisco," January 20, 1936, Pardee Lowe Collection, Box 128a Folder: Chinese Patriotism, Hoover Archive, Stanford University.

98. Chun, "Shifting Ethnic Identity and Consciousness," 117.

99. Larson, *Sweet Bamboo*, 143.

100. Chang et al., "From the Preparation Committee."

101. San Francisco Museum and Historical Society, "Swinging Chinatown: The Golden Age of Chinese Nightclubs," February 2010.

102. Arthur Dong, *Forbidden City, USA: Chinese American Nightclubs, 1936–1970* (Los Angeles: DeepFocus Productions, Inc., 2014), 153.

103. Quoted in Yung, *Unbound Feet*, 202.

104. Yung, 204. Most of the clubs in San Francisco were located on Grant Avenue, the busiest thoroughfare in Chinatown.

105. P'ing Yu, "The Jade Box," *Chinese Digest*, February 1938; "Clothing for War Refugees in China," *Chinese Digest*, November 1937; Lawrence Glickman, "'Make Lisle the Style': The Politics of Fashion in the Japanese Silk Boycott, 1937–1940," *Journal of Social History* 38, no. 3 (Spring 2005): 579.

106. William Gow, "A Night in Old Chinatown: American Orientalism, China Relief Fundraising, and the 1938 Moon Festival in Los Angeles," *Pacific Historical Review* 87, no. 3 (August 2018): 439–72.

107. George Chauncey, *Gay New York : Gender, Urban Culture, and the Making of the Gay Male World, 1890–1940* (New York: Basic Books, 1995); Chad Heap, *Slumming: Sexual and Racial Encounters in American Nightlife, 1885–1940* (Chicago: University of Chicago Press, 2008).

108. Clement Wood, *The Truth about New York's Chinatown*, Little Blue Book 1057 (Girard, KS: Haldeman-Julius Company, 1926), 10.

109. China Trading Co., "Forced Sale!"; "Nanyang Brothers, Expanding Import-Export Business."

110. "Fad in Capital Society."

111. Mah-Jongg Sales Co., "Advertisement: 大幫麻雀發行 Boosting Ma Jiang Sales," trans. Thomas Mullaney, 中西日報 *Chung Sai Yat Po*, October 5, 1922, MJSC Scrapbook 1, PB.

112. William G. Merchant, "Letter to the Editor," *Chinese Digest*, April 10, 1936, Alice Fong Yu Papers, Stanford University Special Collections.

113. Ngai, *The Lucky Ones*, 8; Nayan Shah, *Contagious Divides*, 153.

114. Philip P. Choy, *San Francisco Chinatown: A Guide to Its History and Architecture* (San Francisco: City Lights Books, 2012), 43; Judy Yung and Chinese Historical Society of America, *San Francisco's Chinatown*, Images of America (Chicago: Arcadia Publishing, 2006), 44–45.

115. "Advertisement: Grandview Gardens," *Los Angeles Times*, June 18, 1941. Despite its tourist-oriented designs, many Chinese American Angelenos preferred the "New Chinatown," with Chinese American leadership, over the rival "China City," which was developed by Christine Sterling and closely patterned after movie sets for *The Good Earth* film. Fire helped determine the victor, as China City burned in 1938 and again in 1949. Sojin Kim, "Curiously Familiar: Art and Curio Stores in Los Angeles' Chinatown," *Western Folklore* 58, no. 2 (1999): 131–47.

116. Jorae, *The Children of Chinatown*, 6; Chen, *Chinese San Francisco*, 172; Lee, "Another View of Chinatown," 171.

117. Chinese Digest, "Advertisement: A Message to Chinatown Merchants," *Chinese Digest*, November 15, 1935, Alice Fong Yu Papers, Stanford University Special Collections.

118. *China's Gifts to the West*, 16 mm, 1936.

119. Connecticut Inter-racial Commission, *Aids in the Teaching of Intercultural Understanding* (1945; repr., Hartford, CT: Connecticut Inter-racial Commission, 1946).

120. Leong, *The China Mystique*.

121. Madeline Y. Hsu and Ellen D. Wu, "'Smoke and Mirrors': Conditional Inclusion, Model Minorities, and the Pre-1965 Dismantling of Asian Exclusion," *Journal of American Ethnic History* 34, no. 4 (Summer 2015): 43–65.

122. Madeline Y. Hsu, "From Chop Suey to Mandarin Cuisine: Fine Dining and the Refashioning of Chinese Ethnicity during the Cold War Era," in *Chinese Americans and the Politics of Race and Culture* (Philadelphia: Temple University Press, 2008), 173–94.

CHAPTER 7

1. "Internment" means the legal confinement of enemy aliens, but has been conflated with the unconstitutional mass expulsion and incarceration of mostly American citizens of Japanese ancestry. Historians have objected to "internment" as a euphemism linked to the official propagandistic nomenclature of "evacuation" (as opposed to expulsion) and "relocation centers" (as opposed to concentration camps). Roger Daniels, "Words Do Matter: A Note on Inappropriate Terminology and the Incarceration of the Japanese Americans," in *Nikkei in the Pacific Northwest: Japanese Americans & Japanese Canadians in the Twentieth Century*, ed. Louis Fiset and Gail M. Nomura (Seattle: Center for the Study of the Pacific Northwest in association with the University of Washington Press, 2005), 190–214.

2. Adam McKeown, "Ritualization of Regulation: The Enforcement of Chinese Exclusion in the United States and China," *American Historical Review* 108, no. 2 (April 2003): 401–2.

3. Lee and Yung, *Angel Island*, 69.

4. Mae M. Ngai, *Impossible Subjects: Illegal Aliens and the Making of Modern America*, 7.

5. Lee, "Defying Exclusion," 1.

6. Lee and Yung, *Angel Island*, 70–89.

7. McKeown, "Ritualization of Regulation," 378.

8. Ibid., 113.

9. Ibid., 394.

10. Sam Chang, "Sam to Tennyson on 15 February 1923," in *The Transnational History of a Chinese Family: Immigrant Letters, Family Business, and Reverse Migration*, by Haiming Liu (New Brunswick, NJ: Rutgers University Press, 2005), 83.

11. Erika Lee and Judy Yung, *Angel Island: Immigrant Gateway to America* (New York: Oxford University Press, 2010), 85–90.

12. Mr. Quan, interview.

13. Mr. Dea et al., interview by Him Mark Lai and Judy Yung, 1976, Angel Island Oral History Project, Ethnic Studies Library, University of California Berkeley.

14. Mr. Quan, interview; Mr. Low, interview; Mr. Tom, interview by Him Mark Lai and Judy Yung, April 17, 1977, Angel Island Oral History Project, Ethnic Studies Library, University of California Berkeley. Xavier Paulès, "An Illustration of China's 'Paradoxical Soft Power': The Dissemination of the Gambling Game Fantan by the Cantonese Diaspora, 1850–1950," *Translocal Chinese: East Asian Perspectives* 11 (2017): 187–207.

15. Mr. Yip, interview by Genny Lim and Judy Yung, August 29, 1976, Angel Island Oral History Project, Ethnic Studies Library, University of California Berkeley. One interviewee remembered the guards forbade gambling in 1913 (though he did not mention mahjong, which likely not yet present). This may relate to individual variation or to an earlier history. Mr. Wong [1913], interview by Him Mark Lai and Philip Fong, July 16, 1977, Angel Island Oral History Project, Ethnic Studies Library, University of California Berkeley.

16. Mr. Lee, interview by Him Mark Lai, Judy Yung, and Genny Lim, February 12, 1977, Angel Island Oral History Project, Ethnic Studies Library, University of California Berkeley. See also Henry Tom, Thomas Wu, and Fred Schulze, interview by Him Mark Lai and Judy Yung, 1977, Angel Island Oral History Project, Ethnic Studies Library, University of California Berkeley.

17. Mr. Tong, interview by Him Mark Lai, Judy Yung, and Genny Lim, August 15, 1976, Angel Island Oral History Project, Ethnic Studies Library, University of California Berkeley; Lee and Yung, *Angel Island*, 99.

18. McKeown, "Chinese Diasporas," 317.

19. Mr. Tong, interview.

20. Mr. Mock, interview by Judy Yung, April 9, 1984, Angel Island Oral History Project, Ethnic Studies Library, University of California Berkeley.

21. Mr. Tong, interview.

22. Mr. Mock, interview.

23. Mr. Poon, interview by Judy Yung and Him Mark Lai, August 17, 1977, Angel Island Oral History Project, Ethnic Studies Library, University of California Berkeley; Mr. Dea, interview by Him Mark Lai and Judy Yung, March 24, 1976, Angel Island Oral History Project, Ethnic Studies Library, University of California Berkeley; Douglas Wong, Martin Owyoung, and Dennis Owyoung, interview by Judy Yung, July 12, 1990, Angel Island Oral History Project, Ethnic Studies Library, University of California Berkeley.

24. Judy Yung, "'A Bowlful of Tears': Lee Puey You's Immigration Experience at Angel Island," in *Asian/Pacific Islander American Women: A Historical Anthology* (New York: New York University Press, 2003), 126.

25. Jennifer Gee, "Housewives, Men's Villages, and Sexual Respectability: Gender and the Interrogation of Asian Women at the Angel Island Immigration Station," in *Asian/Pacific Islander American Women: A Historical Anthology* (New York: New York University Press, 2003), 90–105.

26. Mr. Tong, interview; Mr. Mock, interview; Mr. Wong [1933], n.d., Angel Island Oral History Project, Ethnic Studies Library, University of California Berkeley.

27. Lee and Yung, *Angel Island*, 56–58, 79, 100.

28. Because the Immigration Act barred all "aliens ineligible to citizenship," foreign-born wives of citizens and merchants were ineligible. The US Supreme Court allowed merchants' wives in 1925. Chinese wives of citizens were not allowed until 1930, and only those who were married before the law was in place. Lee and Yung, *Angel Island*, 76.

29. Suspicion against women as prostitutes likely declined in the twentieth century, but admission was still weighted explicitly around questions of "respectability." Immigration Inspector #3, interview by Felicia Lowe, n.d., Angel Island Oral History Project, Ethnic Studies Library, University of California Berkeley; Jennifer Gee, "Housewives, Men's Villages, and Sexual Respectability: Gender and the Interrogation of Asian Women at the Angel Island Immigration Station," in *Asian/*

Pacific Islander American Women: A Historical Anthology (New York: New York University Press, 2003), 90–105; Adam McKeown, *Chinese Migrant Networks and Cultural Change: Peru, Chicago, Hawaii, 1900–1936* (Chicago: University of Chicago Press, 2001), 31.

30. Lee and Yung, *Angel Island*, 80.

31. Mrs. Jew, n.d., Angel Island Oral History Project, Ethnic Studies Library, University of California Berkeley.

32. Mr. Tong, interview.

33. These functions enhanced the wealth, prestige, and access to power held by these networks of associations, which in turn encouraged their own investments in the immigration system as predicated on exclusion. McKeown, "Ritualization of Regulation," 397.

34. Mr. Low, interview; Mr. Tom, interview; Mr. Chew, interview by Him Mark Lai and Laura Lai, December 13, 1976, Angel Island Oral History Project, Ethnic Studies Library, University of California Berkeley.

35. Chingwah Lee, "Remember When?," *Chinese Digest*, January 1937, Alice Fong Yu Papers, Stanford University Special Collections.

36. Kathleen Norris, "Newspaper Clipping: An Abused Amusement Is a Hard Master," January 5, 1936, Alice Fong Yu Papers, Stanford University Special Collections.

37. Mrs. Chong, interview by Felicia Lowe, October 12, 1981, Angel Island Oral History Project, Ethnic Studies Library, University of California Berkeley.

38. Mrs. Leong, interview by Judy Yung, Genny Lim, and Him Mark Lai, August 15, 1980, Angel Island Oral History Project, Ethnic Studies Library, University of California Berkeley.

39. Lee and Yung, *Angel Island*, 81; Gee, "Gender and the Interrogation of Asian Women."

40. Immigration Interpretor #1 and #2, interview by Him Mark Lai et al., May 8, 1976, Angel Island Oral History Project, Ethnic Studies Library, University of California Berkeley.

41. Gee, "Gender and the Interrogation of Asian Women," 98.

42. Kitty Calavita, "The Paradoxes of Race, Class, Identity, and 'Passing': Enforcing the Chinese Exclusion Acts, 1882–1910," *Law & Social Inquiry* 25, no. 1 (Winter 2000): 1–40; McKeown, "Ritualization of Regulation," 398.

43. Jorae, *The Children of Chinatown*, 37.

44. Maggie Greene, "The Game People Played: Mahjong in Modern Chinese Society and Culture," *Cross-Currents: East Asian History and Culture Review* E-Journal, no. 17 (December 2015): 10–16.

45. Pardee Lowe, *Father and Glorious Descendant*.

46. Mrs. Lim, interview by Him Mark Lai, Genny Lim, and Judy Yung, September 12, 1976, Angel Island Oral History Project, Ethnic Studies Library, University of California Berkeley; Mrs. Woo, interview by Him Mark Lai and Judy Yung, June

19, 1977, Angel Island Oral History Project, Ethnic Studies Library, University of California Berkeley; Yung, "'A Bowlful of Tears,'" 126.

47. Lee and Yung, *Angel Island*, 300–1.

48. Erika Lee, *The Making of Asian America: A History* (New York: Simon and Schuster, 2015), 256–257.

49. Madeline Y. Hsu and Ellen D. Wu, "'Smoke and Mirrors': Conditional Inclusion, Model Minorities, and the Pre-1965 Dismantling of Asian Exclusion," *Journal of American Ethnic History* 34, no. 4 (Summer 2015): 43–65.

50. War Relocation Authority, "Relocating Japanese-American Evacuees," 1942, 3, Stanford University. See Wendy L. Ng, *Japanese American Internment during World War II: A History and Reference Guide* (Westport, CT: Greenwood Press, 2002); Roger Daniels, *Prisoners without Trial: Japanese Americans in World War II* (New York: Hill and Wang, 1993); Valerie Matsumoto, *Farming the Home Place: A Japanese American Community in California, 1919-1982* (Ithaca, NY: Cornell University Press, 1993); Gary Y. Okihiro, *Whispered Silences: Japanese Americans and World War II* (Seattle: University of Washington Press, 1996); Greg Robinson, *A Tragedy of Democracy in North America* (New York: Columbia University Press, 2009).

51. The determination and confiscation of "contraband" was highly capricious and invasive. See Gary Y. Okihiro, *Encyclopedia of Japanese American Internment* (Santa Barbara, CA: ABC-CLIO, Inc., 2013), 170; Valerie Matsumoto, "Japanese American Women during World War II," *Frontiers: A Journal of Women Studies* 8, no. 1 (1984): 7.

52. War Relocation Authority, "The Relocation Program: A Guidebook for the Residents of Relocation Centers," May 1943, 12, Stanford University.

53. Elliott Chaze, *The Stainless Steel Kimono* (New York: Simon and Schuster, 1947), 170.

54. For more on Nishimoto, see Ng, *Japanese American Internment During World War II*, 142–43.

55. Richard S. Nishimoto, "Gambling at Poston," May 24, 1943, 11–13, The Japanese American Evacuation and Resettlement, Bancroft Library.

56. Mr. Langdon, "Elements of Weakness in the Japanese People and in the Japanese Position," in *Central File: Decimal File 894.00, Internal Affairs of States, Japan, Political Affairs*, 1942.

57. Nishimoto, "Gambling at Poston," 71.

58. Konrad Linke, "Dominance, Resistance, and Cooperation in the Tanforan Assembly Center," *Amerikastudien/American Studies* 54, no. 4 (2009): 628.

59. "Six-Day Exhibit Displays Worlds of 130, Attracts All," *Rohwer Outpost*, January 20, 1943, Japanese-American Relocation Camp Newspapers: Perspectives on Day-to-Day Life, Library of Congress.

60. Yukiko Furuto, Issei Experience in Orange County, California: Yukiko Furata, interview by Yasko Gamo and Arthur A. Hansen, June 17, 1982, Oral Histories, Japanese American Relocation Digital Archive.

61. Doris Hayashi, "Family Study," 1942, 4, The Japanese American Evacuation and Resettlement, Bancroft Library.

62. Doris Hayashi, "Family Study," 1942, 3, 18, The Japanese American Evacuation and Resettlement, Bancroft Library. These beliefs were likely informed by both Japanese and American discourse that legitimated imperialism and ethnic nationalism. Japanese Americans may have looked down on Chinese culture but did not feel the same motivation to reject it as Chinese Americans who boycotted Japanese goods in response to invasion.

63. Ibid., 12, 37.

64. War Relocation Authority, "The Relocation Program," 1; "The Social World: Recreation Halls Get Funds for Purchase of Equipment," *Heart Mountain Sentinel*, November 20, 1943, Japanese-American Relocation Camp Newspapers: Perspectives on Day-to-Day Life, Library of Congress.

65. "Rohwer," *Densho Encyclopedia*, accessed May 7, 2015, http://encyclopedia.densho.org; "Poston (Colorado River)," *Densho Encyclopedia*, accessed May 7, 2015, http://encyclopedia.densho.org.

66. War Relocation Authority, "The Relocation Program," 7.

67. "Amano Wins Top Tourney Prize," *Granada Pioneer*, December 31, 1943, Japanese-American Relocation Camp Newspapers: Perspectives on Day-to-Day Life, Library of Congress; "Evacu-Ways," *Minidoka Irrigator*, July 10, 1943, Japanese-American Relocation Camp Newspapers: Perspectives on Day-to-Day Life, Library of Congress; "Mah-Jong Experts to Clash Sunday," *Granada Pioneer*, December 24, 1943, Japanese-American Relocation Camp Newspapers: Perspectives on Day-to-Day Life, Library of Congress; "Mah Jongg," *Tanforan Totalizer*, August 1, 1942, Japanese-American Relocation Camp Newspapers: Perspectives on Day-to-Day Life, Library of Congress; "Tournament for Mah Jong Players," *Rohwer Outpost*, February 10, 1943, Japanese-American Relocation Camp Newspapers: Perspectives on Day-to-Day Life, Library of Congress.

68. "Untitled: English Translation of Japanese Text," *Daily Tulean Dispatch*, July 23, 1943, sec. Japanese Section, Japanese-American Relocation Camp Newspapers: Perspectives on Day-to-Day Life, Library of Congress; Hayashi, "Family Study," 70.

69. Shotaro Hikida, "C.A.S. Coordinator Weekly Reports and Related Material," 1943, The Japanese American Evacuation and Resettlement, Bancroft Library.

70. Matsumoto, "Japanese American Women during World War II," 9.

71. "20–30 Social Slated," *Denson Tribune*, October 15, 1943, Japanese-American Relocation Camp Newspapers: Perspectives on Day-to-Day Life, Library of Congress.

72. "YBA to Hold Fellowship," *Heart Mountain Sentinel*, November 20, 1943, Japanese-American Relocation Camp Newspapers: Perspectives on Day-to-Day Life, Library

of Congress; "Canal Y Working Girls Party Saturday," *Gila News-Courier*, July 8, 1943, Japanese-American Relocation Camp Newspapers: Perspectives on Day-to-Day Life, Library of Congress.

73. Henry Kusaba, James Lindley, and Joe McClelland, "Amache," 1944, 17, The Japanese American Evacuation and Resettlement, Bancroft Library.

74. "Amano Wins Top Tourney Prize."

75. Matsumoto, "Japanese American Women during World War II," 9.

76. Tami, "Dis and Data," *Topaz Times*, June 12, 1943, Japanese-American Relocation Camp Newspapers: Perspectives on Day-to-Day Life, Library of Congress.

77. Nishimoto, "Gambling at Poston," 70.

78. Hayashi, "Family Study," 70.

79. Ibid., 52.

80. Ibid., 70, 78, 112.

81. Nishimoto, "Gambling at Poston," 77.

82. Ibid., 3.

83. War Relocation Authority, "The Relocation Program," 12.

84. Hayashi, "Family Study," 12, 18.

85. Rosalie Hankey, "Report on Tule Lake, Draft" (Japanese American Evacuation and Resettlement Study, 1943), 8, The Japanese American Evacuation and Resettlement, Bancroft Library.

86. The sponsoring groups were the Philadelphia Federal Council of Churches, the Citizens' Cooperating Committee on Resettlement, and the Women's International League for Peace and Freedom. *While Refreshments Are Served at a Social in the Philadelphia, Pennsylvania, Hostel, Mrs. Arnold Nakajima, of Princeton, N.J., and Miss June Amamoto, a Philadelphian from Manzanar, Continue with Their Game of Mah Jong*, Photograph, July 8, 1944, War Relocation Authority Photographs of Japanese-American Evacuation and Resettlement, Bancroft Library; *A Mah Jong Game Engages the Attention of This Group at a Social at the Philadelphia, Pennsylvania, Hostel*, Photograph, July 8, 1944, War Relocation Authority Photographs of Japanese-American Evacuation and Resettlement, Bancroft Library.

87. *At the Relocation Hostel in Philadelphia, Pennsylvania, the Local Nisei Steering Committee Is Holding Its Weekly Social for Players of Bridge and Mah Jong and for Other Resettlers Who Come to See Friends and Catch Up with Their Reading of Project Newspapers*, Photograph, August 1944, War Relocation Authority Photographs of Japanese-American Evacuation and Resettlement, Bancroft Library. For more about resettlement, see Greg Robinson, *After Camp: Portraits in Midcentury Japanese American Life and Politics* (Berkeley: University of California Press, 2012); Valerie Matsumoto, *City Girls: The Nisei Social World in Los Angeles, 1920–1950* (New York: Oxford University Press, 2014), Ch. 5.

88. Walter Muramoto, *Untitled: Photograph at Rohwer*, Photograph, October 1, 1944, Japanese American National Museum.

CHAPTER 8

1. "Old Game," *The New Yorker*, October 2, 1937, Dorothy S. Meyerson Scrapbook, Marjorie Troum Personal Collection; "To Set Mah Jongg Rules: 200 Women Expected at Meeting Friday to Standardize Game," *New York Times*, September 12, 1937.

2. "Old Game."

3. Evelyn Keene, "The Inscrutable Addiction to Mah-Jongg," *Boston Globe*, January 1, 1974.

4. "Growth of the National League," *National Mah Jongg League News*, Spring 1940; Viola Cecil, *Maajh: The American Version of an Ancient Chinese Game* (New York: Hallco, 1938), 3.

5. "Mah-Jong Popularity Revived as Queens Group Takes Up Play," *Brooklyn Daily Eagle*, June 27, 1937, Dorothy S. Meyerson Scrapbook, Marjorie Troum Personal Collection.

6. Ben Wickham, "Mah Jong Stages a Streamlined Comeback to Woo Parlor Favor," *Cleveland News*, February 8, 1938, Marjorie Troum Personal Collection; "League Simplifies and 'Streamlines' Mah-Jongg Game," *Chicago Daily Tribune*, November 27, 1938.

7. Marjorie Meyerson Troum, interview by author, Los Angeles, August 21, 2012.

8. Herma Jacobs, interview by Tom Sloper, Phone, June 25, 2002, Tom Sloper Personal Collection; Marjorie Meyerson Troum, interview by author, Los Angeles, August 21, 2012; "Growth of the National League."

9. "Gift Show Opening Draws Many Buyers," *New York Times*, February 25, 1936. The trade show was held at none other than the Hotel Pennsylvania, site of the Mah-Jongg Sales Company's initial whisper campaign in New York in 1922.

10. Dorothy S. Meyerson, *"That's It:" A New Way to Play Mah Jong*, 4th ed. (Forest Hills, Long Island: Dorothy Meyerson, 1938), vi.

11. Ibid., v–vii.

12. Meyerson, *That's It*; Cecil, *Maajh*. Meyerson had a complicated and often fractious relationship with some of the other founders of the League, who objected to her apparent competition. She maintained her unique importance in shaping the game before the League's founding and kept up her own business ventures of *That's It!* book sales and sales of mahjong sets. Dorothy Meyerson to J. B. Lazurus, n.d., Dorothy S. Meyerson Scrapbook, Marjorie Troum Personal Collection; Marjorie Meyerson Troum, interview.

13. Macy's, "Advertisement: Mah Jong* Sale," *New York Herald Tribune*, February 20, 1938, Dorothy S. Meyerson Scrapbook, Marjorie Troum Personal Collection.

14. Natalie Marine-Street, "Agents Wanted: Sales, Gender, and the Making of Consumer Markets in America, 1830–1930" (PhD diss., Stanford University, 2016).

15. "Advertising News and Notes," *New York Times*, October 20, 1937; "Writes Book on New Mah Jong System," *Sunday Times*, June 13, 1937, Dorothy S. Meyerson Scrapbook, Marjorie Troum Personal Collection; Ben Wickham, "Mah Jong Stages a Streamlined Comeback to Woo Parlor Favor," *Cleveland News*, February 8, 1938, Marjorie Troum Personal Collection; Bamberger's, "Advertisement: Everyone's Playing Mah Jong Again!," *Star-Eagle*, February 14, 1938, Dorothy S. Meyerson Scrapbook, Marjorie Troum Personal Collection; Walgreen's, "Advertisement: The Chinese Tile Game Returns to Popularity," *Chicago Daily Tribune*, December 18, 1939.

16. Wickham, "Mah Jong Stages a Streamlined Comeback to Woo Parlor Favor."

17. "Former Park Woman to Speak over WOR 8:30 A.M. Tomorrow," *Daily Home News*, September 15, 1937, Dorothy S. Meyerson Scrapbook, Marjorie Troum Personal Collection; "Mrs. Meyerson Gives Broadcast on 'That's It'," *Kew Forest Post*, September 1937, Dorothy S. Meyerson Scrapbook, Marjorie Troum Personal Collection.

18. "Mah Jongg Authority to Give Television Broadcast Sundays," *Forest Hills–Kew Gardens Post*, early 1940s, Dorothy S. Meyerson Scrapbook, Marjorie Troum Personal Collection.

19. Dorothy Meyerson, "That's It: Practice While Learning," n.d. [possibly 1943], Dorothy S. Meyerson Scrapbook, Marjorie Troum Personal Collection.

20. "Old Game."

21. Dorothy Meyerson, "Mah Jong Taught and Explained by the World's Greatest Authority on Mah Jong [ad copy]," 1938, Dorothy S. Meyerson Scrapbook, Marjorie Troum Personal Collection. For a description of Meyerson as "aggressive," see the note from one of her advertising targets, "Mah Jong Rule Book Exhibits," *The Modern Stationer*, April 1938, Dorothy S. Meyerson Scrapbook, Marjorie Troum Personal Collection.

22. "Mah-Jong Popularity Revived as Queens Group Takes Up Play."

23. Marjorie Meyerson Troum, interview.

24. "Mah Jong, a Hobby and Serious Business Enterprise," n.d., Dorothy S. Meyerson Scrapbook, Marjorie Troum Personal Collection.

25. Hasia Diner, *The Jews of the United States, 1654 to 2000* (Berkeley: University of California Press, 2004), 229–31.

26. Robert Putnam, "Bowling Alone: America's Declining Social Capital," *Journal of Democracy* 6, no. 1 (January 1995): 69, fn. 6.

27. Dorothy S. Meyerson, *"That's It" Mah Jongg Instruction Book*, 13th ed. (New York: Dorothy Meyerson, by Permission of the National Mah Jongg League, Inc., 1953); Tom Sloper, "Column 509," *Sloper on Mah-Jongg* (blog), February 26, 2012, www.sloperama.com/mahjongg/column509a.html; Ruth Unger, interview by author, Phone, June 1, 2012; Marilyn Starr, interview by author, Manhattan, NY, May 31, 2012; Herma Scheffer, "President's Message [1960]," *National Mah Jongg League News*, January 1960, National Mah Jongg League Private Collection.

28. In Thomas Lane's 1938 book *Modern Mah Jong*, he describes similar ways of playing that would become commonplace in National mahjong: a passing process akin to the League's Charleston that he calls "rutching," a five-player mode with the fifth person serving as a bettor, which he calls "Race Horse"; and a "cat" that was perhaps a precursor to the shared pot of money unofficially called a "kitty." Lane's book probably reflected the evolution of table rules and differing styles of play that Meyerson, Cecil, and the League were also working to consolidate. However, it is also possible that he was directly influenced by Meyerson's efforts of the previous few years, or vice versa. Thomas Lane, *Modern Mah Jong* (Chicago: Rand McNally & Company, 1938).

29. Viola Cecil, *Maajh: The American Version of an Ancient Chinese Game* (New York: Hallco, 1939), 7.

30. Originally, in a continuation from 1920s rules, points doubled for the player in the "East Wind" position in rotation. Today, points increase or decrease for certain hands depending on if the hand is completed through a blind draw or through acquiring a discarded tile.

31. "Return of the Dragon," *Newsweek*, November 13, 1961.

32. Herma Jacobs, interview by Tom Sloper, Phone, June 25, 2002, Tom Sloper Personal Collection.

33. "National Explains Lists Versus Memberships."

34. "Editor's Mail Bag," *National Mah Jongg League News*, Winter 1940, Dorothy S. Meyerson Scrapbook, Marjorie Troum Personal Collection.

35. Viola Cecil, "To Change or Not to Change!," *National Mah Jongg League News*, Spring 1942, Dorothy S. Meyerson Scrapbook, Marjorie Troum Personal Collection.

36. National Mah Jongg League, "Charities We Proudly Proclaim," *National Mah Jongg League News*, Spring 1940, Dorothy S. Meyerson Scrapbook, Marjorie Troum Personal Collection.

37. International Ma Chiang Players' Association, *Laws of Ma Chiang*; Racster, *Mah-Jongg: Rules for Playing in the Chinese Manner*; "Those Who Know Game Form Mah-Jong Club," n.d., MJSC Scrapbook 1, PB; Joseph Park Babcock, *The Laws of Mah-Jongg*; "The Auction Bridge Magazine Mah Jong Ballot," *Auction Bridge Magazine*, April 1924, Library of Congress; Bray, "Americanizing Mah Jong."

38. Adele Tripp, "Editorial," *National Mah Jongg League News*, Winter 1940. For an example of a competitor, see Mattye Kreindler, "1940 Adopted Hands & Rules For Players of 'Mah Jong'" (Mattye Kreindler, 1939).

39. "Ten Flowers—No, No, No!," *National Mah Jongg League News*, Winter 1940, Dorothy S. Meyerson Scrapbook, Marjorie Troum Personal Collection.

40. "National Explains Lists Versus Memberships," *National Mah Jongg League News*, Winter 1940, Dorothy S. Meyerson Scrapbook, Marjorie Troum Personal Collection; Marjorie Meyerson Troum, interview. The government, however, eventually decreed that they were not tax exempt as either a charitable corporation or

a recreational club because they were not "organized and operated exclusively" for either purpose. See Judge Henry Goddard, "National Mah Jongg League, Inc., v. United States" (District Court, Southern District New York, December 18, 1947), www.leagle.com.

41. Hasia Diner, *The Jews of the United States*, Ch. 5.

42. She began by teaching other women her version of the game, and as her lessons proved successful, sold a mimeographed and stapled set of her rules as a fundraiser for the Forest Hills Synagogue Sisterhood.

43. Wyman, "Mah Jongg Luncheon"; "Dorothy Meyerson to Advise on Mah Jong Play Friday," December 1937, Dorothy S. Meyerson Scrapbook, Marjorie Troum Personal Collection.

44. Viola Cecil, "To the Members of the National Mah Jongg League, Inc.," *New York Times*, November 26, 1939, sec. Classified Advertisements; "News and Views of the Branches," *National Mah Jongg League News*, Winter 1940, Dorothy S. Meyerson Scrapbook, Marjorie Troum Personal Collection.

45. "1943 Donations Top All Records," *National Mah Jongg League News*, Winter 1943, Dorothy S. Meyerson Scrapbook, Marjorie Troum Personal Collection; Jacobs, interview.

46. George A. Lundberg, Mirra Komarovsky, and Mary Alice McInery, *Leisure: A Suburban Study*, v, 4; L. P. Jacks, "Leisure: A New and Perplexing Problem," *New York Times Magazine*, July 5, 1931; Jesse Frederick Steiner, *Americans at Play: Recent Trends in Recreation and Leisure Time Activities*, Recent Social Trends in the United States (New York: McGraw-Hill Book Company, 1933).

47. Susan Currell, *The March of Spare Time: The Problem and Promise of Leisure in the Great Depression* (Philadelphia: University of Pennsylvania Press, 2010), 10. For a revealing example of this discourse, see Mary Borden, "The Man Protests Against Organized Gaiety," *Vogue*, February 1, 1931.

48. Dulles, *America Learns to Play*, viii.

49. "News and Views of the Branches," *National Mah Jongg League News*, Spring 1940, Dorothy S. Meyerson Scrapbook, Marjorie Troum Personal Collection.

50. Virginia W. Musselman, *Home Play in Wartime* (National Recreation Association, 1942).

51. "Mah Jongg Safer Than Bridge for Couples, Its Devotees Say"; Edgar W. Knight, "The 'Roll' of Education," *School and Society* 54 (September 13, 1941): 190–91. An accompanying radio broadcast featured an elite philanthropist from the Rockefeller family, and a representative from "Bundles for Britain."

52. "News and Views of the Branches," *National Mah Jongg League News*, Spring 1942, Dorothy S. Meyerson Scrapbook, Marjorie Troum Personal Collection.

53. "News and Views of the Branches," *National Mah Jongg League News*, Winter 1943, Dorothy S. Meyerson Scrapbook, Marjorie Troum Personal Collection.

54. "A Three-Cent Stamp Makes Us Feel Like a Million," *National Mah Jongg League News*, Winter 1943, Dorothy S. Meyerson Scrapbook, Marjorie Troum Personal Collection.

55. "Editorial: Be Smart—Act Dumb," *National Mah Jongg League News*, Spring 1942, Dorothy S. Meyerson Scrapbook, Marjorie Troum Personal Collection.

56. "Reprint of League Broadcast in April," *National Mah Jongg League News*, Winter 1943, Dorothy S. Meyerson Scrapbook, Marjorie Troum Personal Collection.

57. *Untitled [Mobile Canteen]*, Photograph, November 18, 1942, Dorothy S. Meyerson Scrapbook, Marjorie Troum Personal Collection; "150 'Bundles for Buddies,'" *New York Times*, June 12, 1942.

58. "1943 Donations Top All Records."

59. For more maternal examples, see "Recreation Room Furnished for Boys at Camp Shanks, NY," *National Mah Jongg League News*, Winter 1943, Dorothy S. Meyerson Scrapbook, Marjorie Troum Personal Collection; "Coast Guard Soldiers Enjoying Day-Room," *National Mah Jongg League News*, Winter 1943, Dorothy S. Meyerson Scrapbook, Marjorie Troum Personal Collection.

60. Marjorie Meyerson Troum, interview.

61. National Mah Jongg League, "Charities We Proudly Proclaim."

62. "Official Standard Hands and Rules" (National Mah Jongg League Inc., 1943), Author Personal Collection.

63. "1943 Donations Top All Records," 7.

64. Rose Daitch, "Members Earn Gifts for Charity by Sending 25 or More Applications," *National Mah Jongg League News*, January 1960, National Mah Jongg League Private Collection.

65. Daitch, "Members Earn Gifts for Charity by Sending 25 or More Applications"; "League's Contributions to Charity in 1959 Surpass Donations of Any Previous Year"; "League's Contributions Continue to Grow"; "Hadassah Plays Mah Jong."

66. National Mah Jongg League, "Official Standard Hands and Rules," 1950, Toby Salk Personal Collection.

67. Antler, *The Journey Home*, 134, 255; Wolf, "Selling Hadassah in the Postwar Era."

68. "Reprint of League Broadcast in April."

69. Louise Andrews Kent, *The Terrace* (Boston and New York: Houghton Mifflin Company, 1934), 148.

70. Montague, "More Truth Than Poetry: Mah Jong"; "[Untitled Humor Snippet]." For representation of mahjong as recreation at a Depression-era "community house" for the poor, see Lenora Mattingly Weber, "Where Shall I Wander?," *Good Housekeeping*, January 1933, Home Economics Archive: Research, Tradition and History (HEARTH), Cornell University.

71. "Events Today," *New York Times*, October 10, 1941; "Finding Aid," in *Lee Ya-Ching Papers 1938–1970* (National Air and Space Museum: Smithsonian Institution,

Accession 2008–2009); Harold R. Isaacs, *Scratches on Our Minds: American Images of China and India* (New York: The John Day Company, 1958), 120.

72. Madeline Y. Hsu, "From Chop Suey to Mandarin Cuisine: Fine Dining and the Refashioning of Chinese Ethnicity during the Cold War Era," in *Chinese Americans and the Politics of Race and Culture* (Philadelphia: Temple University Press, 2008), 173–94.

73. "Board of Directors Redoubles Efforts in National Crisis"; "League Celebrates 25th Anniversary," *National Mah Jongg League News*, January 1962, Project Mah Jongg, Museum of Jewish Heritage—A Living Memorial to the Holocaust; "Postcard: Ruby Foo's Den," n.d., Project Mah Jongg, Museum of Jewish Heritage—A Living Memorial to the Holocaust.

74. "Chain Mah Jongg Party to Be Given for China," *National Mah Jongg League News*, Spring 1942, Dorothy S. Meyerson Scrapbook, Marjorie Troum Personal Collection.

75. Leong, *The China Mystique*.

76. Herb Caen, "It's News to Me: Chinatown Is Where," *San Francisco Chronicle*, January 30, 1942, Pardee Lowe Collection, Box 190, Folder: Chinatown History, Hoover Library.

77. "Rice Is Tops to Visitors at This Center," *Chicago Daily Tribune*, November 7, 1943.

78. Chinese Women's Association, Inc., "Souvenir Program Chinese Women's Association, Inc.," 53; Louise Bailey Lowe to Click Idea Contest Editor, "SAN FRANCISCO CHINATOWN CHANGES AND BECOMES 100% AMERICAN," May 29, 1938, Pardee Lowe Collection, Box 382, Folder: California, Hoover Archive, Stanford University; "A Chinatown Beautiful for 1939," *Chinese Digest*, February 1938.

79. "Party on Chinese Junk: Supper Event Tonight Aboard Amoy to Aid United Relief," *New York Times*, June 5, 1941.

80. "Anna May Wong Backs Benefit," *Los Angeles Times*, May 26, 1940.

81. Karen J. Leong and Judy Tzu-Chun Wu, "Filling the Rice Bowls of China: Staging Humanitarian Relief during the Sino-Japanese War," in *Chinese Americans and the Politics of Race and Culture* (Philadelphia: Temple University Press, 2008), 132–52.

82. Miss Pickwick, "Girl about Town," February 1938, Dorothy S. Meyerson Scrapbook, Marjorie Troum Personal Collection.

83. The exact timing of the bank's booklet origins has been lost in the historical record, but it is possible that the "free booklet" mentioned in the bank's advertisement in 1936 was of mahjong. Oklahoma City Federal Savings and Loan Assn., "Loans," *Daily Oklahoman*, May 2, 1936.

84. Helen Ford Sanger, "The Chinese Began It . . . ," *Daily Oklahoman*, October 17, 1965, sec. Women's News; Oklahoma City Federal Savings and Loan, "Rules and Scoring Mah Jongg, 8th Edition," n.d., Author Personal Collection; Continental Federal Savings and Loan, "Mah Jongg Rules and Scoring, 26th Edition," 1983; Phoenix

Federal Savings and Loan, Muskogee OK, "Mah Jongg Rules and Scoring," n.d., Katie Albert Personal Collection; Doris J. Blazy, "Email," March 5, 2015.

85. Sanger, "The Chinese Began It . . . ," 1; Oklahoma City Federal Savings and Loan, "Rules and Scoring Mah Jongg, 8th Edition."

86. Joan Schillo, "Oriental Game Revived: Mah Jongg Players To Hold Tournament," *Journal Herald*, February 20, 1964, Scrapbook, Wright-Patterson Mah Jongg Group. In 1964, Morris explained that the original group's knowledge was gained in the fad years, but that the group was formed in 1941. Nonetheless, the Wright-Patterson rule book has long declared that group's game dates from the 1920s, when Wright-Patterson was still McCook field, and that is the story that has remained most widely known. McCook Army Airfield near Dayton, Ohio, was closed in 1927 and its operations transferred to the nearby Wilbur Wright Field. The Air Force became its own branch of the military in 1947. In 1948, Wright and Patterson Fields combined to form the Wright-Patterson Air Force Base.

87. Schillo.

88. Linda Forth [pseud.], interview by author, Phone, July 23, 2012.

89. Dorothy Odland, "Mah Jongg," September 1970, Scrapbook, Wright-Patterson Mah Jongg Group; "Untitled Photograph: W-P Lesson," n.d. 1960s, Scrapbook, Wright-Patterson Mah Jongg Group.

90. Denice Wisniewski, Phone, August 6, 2014.

91. Nanette Kutner, "If You Were Mrs. Eisenhower," *Good Housekeeping*, January 1944, Home Economics Archive: Research, Tradition and History (HEARTH), Cornell University.

92. Robert Wallace, "They Like Mamie, Too," *Life*, October 13, 1952, 156.

93. Wisniewski, interview. Eventually, as the numbers of female officers slowly grew, Wright-Pat mahjong groups involved women who served as officers and even base commanders.

94. The club transferred to the OWC between 1971 and 1986. Mrs. [Evelyn] William G. Comstock, "Letter from Officers' Wives' Club," April 5, 1971, Scrapbook, Wright-Patterson Mah Jongg Group; Forth [pseud.], interview; Amy Jo Jones, "MJ Inquiry," May 14, 2012.

95. Eve Swarts, "Mah Jongg," *WTTW*, September 1967, Scrapbook, Wright-Patterson Mah Jongg Group.

96. Wisniewski, interview.

97. "Clicking of Tiles Is Sure Sign of Mah Jongg Season Opening," October 1964, Scrapbook, Wright-Patterson Mah Jongg Group.

98. "Clicking of Tiles Is Sure Sign of Mah Jongg Season Opening"; Forth [pseud.], interview.

99. The graphics for advertising the game in base newspapers continued to depict an Orientalist mashup of a kimono-clad cartoon canine with a mandarin mustache in 1970. Odland, "Mah Jongg."

100. Wisniewski, interview; Laurence Roth, interview by author, Manhattan, NY, May 23, 2012; Grace Chun and Amy Gwilliam, interview by author, Chinese-American Museum of Chicago, August 18, 2011.

101. Shirley Mohr, "Foreword," in *Mah Jongg: Wright-Patterson Rules* (Wright-Patterson Air Force Base, Ohio: Mah Jongg Group, 1976). See also Odland, "Mah Jongg."

102. Wisniewski, interview.

103. Forth [pseud.], interview; Marjorie Meyerson Troum, interview; Al Rosenthal's, Inc., "Advertisement: That's It," 1938, Dorothy S. Meyerson Scrapbook, Marjorie Troum Personal Collection.

104. Plastic was the dominant material for mahjong manufacturing, but at least one small manufacturer in New York City made cheaper mahjong sets with wooden tiles. "Mah Jongg Set" (Jaymar Specialty Co., 1955), Tony Watson Personal Collection.

105. Jeffrey Meikle, *American Plastic: A Cultural History* (New Brunswick, NJ: Rutgers University Press, 1995), 92; Sol Swerdloff and Calman Winegarden, "Job Prospects in the Plastics Products Industry," *Monthly Labor Review* 65, no. 3 (September 1947): 294.

106. Diner, *The Jews of the United States*, 229–31.

107. Francis Lodato, *Eboli to Brooklyn, One Way* (Self-Published, 2017), 79–84; Joan Blednick, interview by author, Phone, June 7, 2018.

108. Swerdloff and Winegarden, "Job Prospects in the Plastics Products Industry," 293.

109. Seymour Silverman and Edith Silverman, interview by author, Hartsdale, NY, May 29, 2012.

110. Meikle, *American Plastic*, 14, 17, 22.

111. A. P. Peck, "A Plastic Is Born," *Scientific American*, January 1938, 18.

112. Quoted in Meikle, *American Plastic*, 75.

113. Meikle, 76.

114. Francis Lodato, interview by author, Telephone, March 9, 2018.

115. Mandel Brothers, "Advertisement: Chinese Tile Sets," *Chicago Daily Tribune*, September 10, 1947; TYL Manufacturing Co., "Advertisement: Mah-Jongg Sets $18.95," *National Jewish Monthly*, 1949. The 1930s were a transition period, when advertisements featured both the older wooden boxes and the new style of cases with racks, or customers could choose to purchase racks separately. Macy's, "Advertisement: Mah Jong* Sale," *New York Herald Tribune*, February 20, 1938, Dorothy S. Meyerson Scrapbook, Marjorie Troum Personal Collection; Bloomingdale's, "Advertisement: 500 Imported Games," *New York Times*, September 18, 1938.

116. Lodato, interview; Silverman and Silverman, interview, May 29, 2012.

117. The chips resembled a hybrid of American and Chinese coins: about the size and thickness of a dime, with a hole in the center to slide onto small metal rods at the end of the tile racks. Not unlike poker chips, different colors represented different points and/or coin denominations.

118. Meikle, *American Plastic*, 92.

119. Lodato, interview.

120. Blednick, interview.

121. Ruth Milkman, "Redefining 'Women's Work': The Sexual Division of Labor in the Auto Industry During World War II," *Feminist Studies* 8 (1982): 336–72.

122. Seymour Silverman and Edith Silverman, interview by author, Phone, June 12, 2018.

123. Lizabeth Cohen, *Making a New Deal: Industrial Workers in Chicago, 1919–1939* (New York: Cambridge University Press, 1990), 209; Blednick, interview.

124. Swerdloff and Winegarden, "Job Prospects in the Plastics Products Industry," 301.

125. Macy's, "Advertisement: You Pronounce It Ma-Jongg," *New York Times*, May 3, 1954; "Advertisement: Fortunoff's 3 Day Sale," *New York Times*, April 20, 1958.

126. "Some 'No's' for Mah Jongg Players," *National Mah Jongg League News*, January 1960, National Mah Jongg League Private Collection.

127. Meikle, *American Plastic*, 170–75. Indeed, a new kind of plastic fabric, rayon, was the basis of a popular dress fabric, "Mah-Jong." Russeks, "Advertisement: 'Jelly Bean,'" *New York Times*, March 7, 1954; Bloomingdale's, "Advertisement: The Look of Shangtung," *New York Times*, March 9, 1955.

128. "Advertisement: Gimbels Storewide Jubilee," *New York Times*, January 11, 1955.

129. By the early 1930s, manufacturers had developed a process to make white Catalin, which could then mimic the historic white bone of mahjong tiles. Today, many of these tiles are a butterscotch yellow, but that is a result of discoloration over time—not the original color. Lodato, interview.

130. Today there is a cottage industry of joker tiles to make pre-1968 vintage sets usable for contemporary 8-Joker play by applying stickers to transform other tiles into jokers. Many of the stickers still evoke Chinese or even Japanese images. Others offer political commentary, such as Donald Trump appearing as Joker after the 2016 presidential election.

131. Dan MacMasters, "America's Own . . . The Coffee Table," *Los Angeles Times*, April 23, 1950; Kerwin Hoover, "Home-Town Flavor," *Los Angeles Times*, February 14, 1954.

CHAPTER 9

1. Rita Rappoport Greenstein, interview, May 21, 2012. Rita worked outside the home as a teacher but still felt a need to actively build local relationships, particularly due to the enormous loss of an extended family and community network that she experienced upon relocation.

2. Rita Rappoport Greenstein, interview, February 3, 2010.

3. Hasia Diner, *The Jews of the United States, 1654 to 2000* (Berkeley: University of California Press, 2004), 240, 111; Joyce Antler, *The Journey Home: Jewish Women and the American Century* (New York: Free Press, 1997), 137.

4. For more on the idea of ethnicity as "nexus," see anthropologist James Clifford's work as discussed by Antler, *The Journey Home*, xiv.

5. Charles Kraus, interview by author, Lake Forest Park, Wash., February 14, 2012; Alida Silverman, interview by author, San Francisco, Calif., September 14, 2014. Similar characterizations were expressed by Beth Lean, telephone interview by author, June 25, 2014; Judye Kanfer, telephone interview by author, February 29, 2012; Susan Shields, telephone interview by author, May 1, 2013; Alan H. Rosenberg, director, producer, and writer, *Mah Jongg Mavens and Memories* (Alan H. Rosenberg, 1997), VHS.

6. Nana Judith "Judy" Michelson, interview by author, Phone, April 12, 2013; Rosenberg, *Mah Jongg Mavens and Memories*; Jenna Weissman Joselit, *The Wonders of America: Reinventing Jewish Culture 1880–1950* (New York: Hill and Wang, 1994), 156.

7. Ethel Shapiro et al., interview by author, Brooklyn, New York, May 22, 2012.

8. Alida Silverman, interview by author, San Francisco, CA, October 11, 2014; Susan Shields, interview by author, Phone, May 1, 2013. As Judy Michelson remembered from the Baltimore suburbs: "The women that I met were pretty much all Jewish. I don't think that I planned it that way, that's just who happened to be doing what I was learning to do at that time." Nana Judith "Judy" Michelson, interview by author, Phone, April 12, 2013.

9. Stephanie Grossman, interview; Silverman, interview, October 11, 2014. Echoed by many others.

10. Margo Horn, "Email," May 12, 2014; Rosenberg, *Mah Jongg Mavens and Memories*; Shields, interview.

11. As anthropologists have argued, culture is best understood "not simply as a product, but also as production." William Roseberry, *Anthropologies and Histories: Essays in Culture, History, and Political Economy* (New Brunswick, NJ: Rutgers University Press, 1994), 28.

12. The field of ethnic history has been shaped by the "uprooted" and "transplanted" debate of its early works by Oscar Handlin and John Bodnar. Since the 1990s, George Sánchez and others initiated an ongoing push against what Lon Kurashige calls the "false dichotomy between assimilation and ethnic retention." See, for example, Oscar Handlin, *The Uprooted: The Epic Story of the Great Migrations That Made the American People* (Boston: Little, Brown, 1951); John Bodnar, *The Transplanted: A History of Immigrants in Urban America* (Bloomington: Indiana University Press, 1985); George J. Sánchez, *Becoming Mexican American: Ethnicity, Culture and Identity in Chicano Los Angeles, 1900–1945* (New York: Oxford University Press, 1993); Adam McKeown, *Chinese Migrant Networks and Cultural Change: Peru, Chicago, Hawaii, 1900–1936* (Chicago: University of Chicago Press, 2001); Virginia Yans, "On 'Groupness,'" *Journal of American Ethnic History* 25, no. 4 (Summer 2006): 119–29; Lon Kurashige, *Japanese American Celebration and Conflict: A History of Ethnic Identity and Festival, 1934–1990* (Berkeley: University

of California Press, 2002); Matthew Frye Jacobson, "More 'Trans-,' Less 'National,'" *Journal of American Ethnic History* 25, no. 4 (Summer 2006): 74–84; Hasia Diner, "American Immigration and Ethnic History: Moving the Field Forward, Staying the Course," *Journal of American Ethnic History* 25, no. 4 (Summer 2006): 130–141.

13. Sklare and Greenblum, *Jewish Identity on the Suburban Frontier*, 283, 289; Benjamin B. Ringer, *The Edge of Friendliness: A Study of Jewish-Gentile Relations* (New York: Basic Books, 1967).

14. Larson, *Sweet Bamboo*, 144; Pardee Lowe, "New Year's Day Celebration (American); Native-Born Men & Women."

15. Sklare and Greenblum, *Jewish Identity on the Suburban Frontier*, 289.

16. Alida Silverman, interview by author, San Francisco, CA, September 14, 2014. Marshall Sklare and Mark Vosk, *The Riverton Study: How Jews Look at Themselves and Their Neighbors* (New York: The American Jewish Committee, 1957), 26; Jack Wertheimer, "The Conservative Synagogue," in *The American Synagogue: A Sanctuary Transformed* (New York: Cambridge University Press, 1987), 111–49; Andrew R. Heinze, *Adapting to Abundance: Jewish Immigrants, Mass Consumption, and the Search for American Identity* (New York: Columbia University Press, 1990); Deborah Dash Moore, *At Home in America: Second Generation New York Jews* (New York: Columbia University Press, 1981). For more about the debate over the merits of what can be called "symbolic ethnicity" and tensions over Judaism as religion versus Jewishness as ethnicity, see Herbert J. Gans, "Symbolic Ethnicity: The Future of Ethnic Groups and Cultures in America," *Ethnic and Racial Studies* 2, no. 1 (January 1979): 1–20; Deborah Dash Moore, "At Home in America?: Revisiting the Second Generation," *Journal of American Ethnic History* 25, no. 2/3 (Winter–Spring 2006): 156–68. For an alternative perspective, Stephen J. Whitfield, *In Search of American Jewish Culture* (Hanover, NH: Brandeis University Press, 1999).

17. Marshall Sklare and Joseph Greenblum, *Jewish Identity on the Suburban Frontier: A Study of Group Survival in the Open Society* (New York: Basic Books, 1967), 16. See also Hanna Miller, "Identity Takeout: How American Jews Made Chinese Food Their Ethnic Cuisine," *Journal of Popular Culture* 39, no. 3 (2006): 430–465; Jennifer 8. Lee, "Why Chow Mein Is the Chosen Food of the Chosen People," in *Mah Jongg: Crak Bam Dot* (New York: 2wiceBooks, 2010), 62–67; Martha Lustbader, Arlene Revitz, and Stacey Revitz, interview by author, San Francisco, February 20, 2015. Scholars have speculated about why Chinese American food became a Jewish American staple, citing shared immigrant neighborhoods and the absence of dairy in Chinese food. (While not necessarily kosher, avoiding the mixing of meat and dairy prevented an obvious breach of dietary rules.)

18. M. Avrum Ehrlich, ed., *The Jewish-Chinese Nexus: A Meeting of Civilizations* (New York: Routledge, 2008); Vera Schwarcz, *Bridge across Broken Time: Chinese and Jewish Cultural Memory* (New Haven: Yale University Press, 1998); Rudolf Glanz, "Jews and Chinese in America," *Jewish Social Studies* 16, no. 3 (July 1954): 219–34.

19. Charles Kraus, interview by author, Lake Forest Park, WA, February 14, 2012; Seymour Silverman and Edith Silverman, interview by author, Hartsdale, NY, May 29, 2012; Zelda Lubart, interview.

20. Jonathan Freedman, *Klezmer America: Jewishness, Ethnicity, Modernity* (New York: Columbia University Press, 2008), 29–34, Ch. 6; Leonard Rogoff, "Is the Jew White?: The Racial Place of the Southern Jew," *American Jewish History* 85, no. 3 (September 1997): 195, 207; Zhou Xun, "The 'Kaifeng Jew' Hoax: Constructing the 'Chinese Jew,'" in *Orientalism and the Jews*, ed. Ivan Davidson Kalmar and Derek J. Penslar (Waltham, MA: Brandeis University Press, 2005), 76.

21. For a relevant analysis of Jewish actors and blackface, see Michael Rogin, *Blackface, White Noise: Jewish Immigrants in the Hollywood Melting Pot* (Berkeley: University of California Press, 1998). For a critical review of Rogin's influential work, see Hasia Diner, "Trading Faces," *Common Quest: The Magazine of Black-Jewish Relations*, 1997.

22. Viola Cecil, *Maajh*; "Photograph: Women Playing Mahjong in Catskills," n.d., Project Mah Jongg, Collection of Harvey Abrams, Museum of Jewish Heritage— A Living Memorial to the Holocaust.

23. Madeline Y. Hsu and Ellen D. Wu, "'Smoke and Mirrors': Conditional Inclusion, Model Minorities, and the Pre-1965 Dismantling of Asian Exclusion," *Journal of American Ethnic History* 34, no. 4 (Summer 2015): 43–65; Christina Klein, *Cold War Orientalism: Asia in the Middlebrow Imagination, 1945–1961* (Berkeley: University of California Press, 2003); Madeline Y. Hsu, "From Chop Suey to Mandarin Cuisine: Fine Dining and the Refashioning of Chinese Ethnicity during the Cold War Era," in *Chinese Americans and the Politics of Race and Culture* (Philadelphia: Temple University Press, 2008), 173–94; Ellen D. Wu, *The Color of Success: Asian Americans and the Origins of the Model Minority* (Princeton: Princeton University Press, 2014).

24. Dorothy S. Meyerson, *"That's It" Mah Jongg Instruction Book*, 13th ed. (New York: Dorothy Meyerson, by Permission of the National Mah Jongg League, Inc., 1953), Preface.

25. Donna R. Braden, *Leisure and Entertainment in America* (Dearborn, MI, 1988).

26. Claude S. Fischer, "Changes in Leisure Activities, 1890–1940," *Journal of Social History* 27, no. 3 (1994): 453–75.

27. Albert H. Morehead, "Bridge: Still Going Strong at 30," *New York Times*, December 30, 1956; Morehead, "Games: Who Plays What and Why," *New York Times*, October 13, 1957.

28. Albert H. Morehead, "Rummy from Argentina," *New York Times*, August 28, 1949.

29. Braden, *Leisure and Entertainment in America*, 68, 103.

30. Gwendolyn Wright, *Building the Dream: A Social History of Housing in America* (New York: Pantheon, 1981), 255; James A. Jacobs, "Social and Spatial Change in the Postwar Family Room," *Perspectives in Vernacular Architecture* 13, no. 1

(2006): 70–85, here 81; Laura J. Miller, "Family Togetherness and the Suburban Ideal," *Sociological Forum* 10, no. 3 (1995): 393–418, here 394.

31. Hilda Schaffer, interview, May 29, 2012.

32. Alan H. Rosenberg, *Mah Jongg Mavens and Memories*, VHS, 1997.

33. Jenna Weissman Joselit, *The Wonders of America: Reinventing Jewish Culture 1880–1950* (New York: Hill and Wang, 1994), 5. See also Riv-Ellen Prell, *Fighting to Become Americans: Jews, Gender, and the Anxiety of Assimilation* (Boston: Beacon Press, 1999).

34. Rita Rappoport Greenstein, interview by author, Phone, February 3, 2010.

35. Moore, *To the Golden Cities*, 1; Hasia Diner, *The Jews of the United States*, 2004, 241.

36. Moore, *At Home in America*.

37. Mary Dudziak, *Cold War Civil Rights: Race and the Image of American Democracy*, 2nd ed. (Princeton: Princeton University Press, 2011).

38. Eric L. Goldstein, *The Price of Whiteness: Jews, Race, and American Identity* (Princeton: Princeton University Press, 2006), 190.

39. Sklare and Vosk, *The Riverton Study*; Diner, *The Jews of the United States*, 2004, 161; Riv-Ellen Prell, "Triumph, Accommodation, and Resistance: American Jewish Life from the End of World War II to the Six-Day War," in *The Columbia History of Jews and Judaism in America* (New York: Columbia University Press, 2008), 137.

40. Prell, "Triumph, Accommodation, and Resistance," 126.

41. Sklare and Greenblum, *Jewish Identity on the Suburban Frontier*.

42. Prell, "American Jewish Life from the End of World War II to the Six-Day War," 119.

43. Lizabeth Cohen, *A Consumers' Republic: The Politics of Mass Consumption in Postwar America* (New York: Random House, 2003), 216, 222. Residential housing covenants used since the 1920s to keep "undesirables" (including Jews) out of neighborhoods were declared unconstitutional by the Supreme Court in 1948. However, new zoning strategies against multi-family and lower-cost housing emerged to create class boundaries. By the 1960s and 1970s, the majority of white Americans, regardless of class, were moving from urban to suburban areas.

44. Ibid., 23. Amid ongoing dispersal, Jewish migration patterns remained clear and distinctive. By the early 1960s, Los Angeles had usurped Chicago as the nation's second most populous city and one of the world's largest Jewish cities. The size of LA's Jewish population ranked third in the world, after New York City and Tel Aviv. Los Angeles in particular mushroomed in overall population, and Jews made up more than 10 percent of new residents. Comparatively, 3 percent of the national population was Jewish. *American Jewish Year Book 1969* (American Jewish Committee, Jewish Publication Society, 1969); United States Census Bureau, "1960 Census," accessed July 30, 2014, https://www.census.gov.

45. Moore, *At Home in America*; Jenna Weissman Joselit, "The Special Sphere of the Middle-Class American Jewish Woman: The Synagogue Sisterhood, 1890–1940," in *The American Synagogue: A Sanctuary Transformed*, ed. Jack Wertheimer (New York: Cambridge University Press, 1987), 206–30. Antler, *The Journey Home*;

Joellyn Wallen Zollman, "Every Wise Woman Shoppeth for Her House: The Sisterhood Gift Shop and the American Jewish Home in the Mid-Twentieth Century," in *Jews at Home: The Domestication of Identity*, ed. Simon J. Bronner (Portland, OR: The Littman Library of Jewish Civilization, 2010), 75–106; Joselit, "The Special Sphere of the Middle-Class American Jewish Woman."

46. Kevin Schultz, *Tri-Faith America: How Catholics and Jews Held Postwar America to Its Protestant Promise* (New York: Oxford University Press, 2011); Diner, *The Jews of the United States*, 252.

47. Joselit, *The Wonders of America*. Jewish Americans of German descent also played mahjong, though perhaps at lower rates than the majority of Jewish Americans who were of Eastern European heritage. See statements regarding class and denomination distinctions, which roughly map onto divergent patterns between the more established and assimilated descendants of earlier German immigrants, and those of the more recent Eastern European immigrants, who as a group had been poorer and more discriminated against than their German counterparts.

48. Linda Kraus, interview by author, Lake Forest Park, WA, February 15, 2012. Emphasis in speech.

49. Dorene Beller, interview by author, Manhattan, NY, May 23, 2012.

50. Goldstein, *The Price of Whiteness*, 5; Hsu and Wu, "Smoke and Mirrors."

51. Matthew Frye Jacobson, *Whiteness of a Different Color: European Immigrants and the Alchemy of Race* (Cambridge, MA: Harvard University Press, 1998), 176.

52. Ringer, *The Edge of Friendliness*; Sklare and Greenblum, *Jewish Identity on the Suburban Frontier*. For roots in the 1920s, see Alexander, *Jazz Age Jews*.

53. Antler, *The Journey Home*, 233.

54. Goldstein, *The Price of Whiteness*; Lila Corwin Berman, "American Jews and the Ambivalence of Middle-Classness," *American Jewish History* 93, no. 4 (December 2007): 409–34; Karen Brodkin, *How Jews Became White Folks and What That Says about Race in America* (New Brunswick, NJ: Rutgers University Press, 1998).

55. Diner, *The Jews of the United States*, 2004, 277–81; Prell, "American Jewish Life from the End of World War II to the Six-Day War," 120.

56. Prell, "American Jewish Life from the End of World War II to the Six-Day War," 120; Cohen, *A Consumers' Republic*; Deborah Dash Moore, *To the Golden Cities: Pursuing the American Jewish Dream in Miami and LA* (New York: Free Press, 1994); Kenneth T. Jackson, *Crabgrass Frontier: The Suburbanization of the United States* (New York: Oxford University Press, 1985).

57. Moore, *To the Golden Cities*, 26, 48.

58. Prell, "American Jewish Life from the End of World War II to the Six-Day War," 119. For more about definitions of "suburbia" in the New York context and 1920s migration, see Moore, *At Home in America*; Daniel Horowitz, "Jewish Women Remaking American Feminism/Women Remaking American Judaism: Reflections on the Life of Betty Friedan," in *A Jewish Feminine Mystique? Jewish Women in Postwar America* (New Brunswick, NJ: Rutgers University Press, 2010), 235–56.

59. "League's Contributions to Charity in 1959 Surpass Donations of Any Previous Year," *National Mah Jongg League News*, January 1960, National Mah Jongg League Private Collection; "League's Contributions Continue to Grow," *National Mah Jongg League News*, January 1965, National Mah Jongg League Private Collection.

60. May Co., "Advertisement: New 1960 Mah Jongg Rules Just Released," *Los Angeles Times*, May 3, 1959.

61. Cohen, *A Consumers' Republic*, Ch. 6.

62. Moore, *To the Golden Cities*, 50.

63. Phil Brown, "A Movable Community in the Catskills," in *The Other Promised Land: Vacationing, Identity, and the Jewish American Dream*, ed. Avi Y. Decter and Melissa Martens (Baltimore: The Jewish Museum of Maryland, 2005), 62–75.

64. Brown, *Catskills Culture* Chs. 2–3.

65. Other transliterations include cochalein, kocheleyn, and kuchalein. Ibid., 45.

66. Silverman, interview, October 11, 2014; Rochelle "Shelley" Schreiber, interview by author, Phone, August 25, 2011.

67. David Boroff, "The Catskills," 62. See also M. S., "A Bungalow in the Hills," *New York Times*, June 10, 1956.

68. Brown, *Catskills Culture*, 43; David Boroff, "The Catskills," 56.

69. M. S., "A Bungalow in the Hills."

70. The Concord Hotel, "Advertisement: Hotels, Like People, Are Judged by the Company They Keep," *New York Times*, May 8, 1955; "Grossinger News Notes," *New York Times*, February 6, 1966.

71. Brown, *Catskills Culture*, 43.

72. David Boroff, "The Catskills," 61.

73. Ibid., 62. For more on Boroff's commentary about Jewish women's corrupting cultural influence, see Prell, *Fighting to Become Americans*, 152.

74. Dellon, interview.

75. Charles Kraus, interview.

76. David Kaufman, *Shul with a Pool: The "Synagogue-Center" in American Jewish History* (Hanover, NH: Brandeis University Press, 1999).

77. Barbara Dellon, interview by author, June 25, 2014.

78. Shtetl is a Yiddish word for Jewish towns in Eastern and Central Europe, before pogroms and the Holocaust. Quoted in Brown, "A Movable Community in the Catskills," 72.

79. Brown, *Catskills Culture*, 90; Dellon, interview; Charles Kraus, interview.

80. Silverman, interview, October 11, 2014.

81. Eva Rubel and Richard Rubel, interview by author, Riverdale, Bronx, NY, May 30, 2012; Brown, *Catskills Culture*, 44.

82. David Boroff, "The Catskills," 63.

83. Decter, "Foreword," 6.

84. Margo Horn, "Email"; Dellon, interview; "Photograph: Mah Jong," 1957, Frieda Spieler Family Papers, The William Breman Jewish Heritage Museum; Judye

Kanfer, interview by author, Phone, February 29, 2012; Hilda Schaffer, interview, May 29, 2012; Joan Mapou, "Email," October 23, 2014.

85. "New Way of Life: The Beach Clubs," *New York Times*, August 19, 1959. Miller, "Family Togetherness and the Suburban Ideal"; Elaine Tyler May, *Homeward Bound: American Families in the Cold War Era* (New York: Basic Books, 1988).

86. "New Way of Life: The Beach Clubs."

87. Dellon, interview.

88. Ruth Unger, interview by author, Phone, June 1, 2012.

89. Herma Scheffer, "President's Message [1960]," *National Mah Jongg League News*, January 1960, National Mah Jongg League Private Collection.

90. For postwar pluralism, see Daryl Michael Scott, "Postwar Pluralism, *Brown v. Board of Education*, and the Origins of Multicultural Education," *Journal of American History* 91, no. 1 (June 2004): 69–82.

91. Judye Kanfer, interview by author, Phone, February 29, 2012; Nancy Kraus, interview by author, Brooklyn, NY, May 22, 2012; Beth Lean, interview by author, Phone, June 17, 2014; "Mah Jongg, That's It! Facebook Group Discussion," January 13, 2020.

CHAPTER 10

1. The concept of "doubled vision" developed by Kathy Peiss in her analysis of young working women's culture in the early twentieth century is useful here, too. She argues that their "embrace of style, fashion, romance, and mixed-sex fun could be a source of autonomy and pleasure as well as a cause for their continuing oppression." Kathy Peiss, *Cheap Amusements: Working Women and Leisure in Turn-of-the-Century New York* (Philadelphia: Temple University Press, 1986), 6.

2. Elaine Tyler May, *Homeward Bound: American Families in the Cold War Era* (New York: Basic Books, 1988). For examples that complicate generalizations about Cold War culture, see Joanne Meyerowitz, ed., *Not June Cleaver: Women and Gender in Postwar America, 1945–1960* (Philadelphia: Temple University Press, 1994).

3. For a comprehensive review of early foundational work examining home as analytic, see Linda Kerber, "Separate Spheres, Female Worlds, Woman's Place: The Rhetoric of Women's History," *Journal of American History* 75, no. 1 (June 1988): 9–39. For analysis of domestic labor, see especially Jeanne Boydston, *Home and Work: Housework, Wages, and the Ideology of Labor in the Early Republic* (New York: Oxford University Press, 1990); and Thavolia Glymph, *Out of the House of Bondage: The Transformation of the Plantation Household* (New York: Cambridge University Press, 2008). For more on the historiography of American domesticity, see Kathryn Kish Sklar, "Reconsidering Domesticity through the Lens of Empire and Settler Society in North America," *American Historical Review* 124, no. 4 (October 2019): 1249–66.

4. Kerber, "Separate Spheres, Female Worlds, Woman's Place."

5. May, *Homeward Bound*, 138–41; Margaret Marsh, "Suburban Men and Masculine Domesticity, 1870–1915," *American Quarterly* 40, no. 2 (1988): 165–86.

6. However, nearly 40 percent of Jewish women older than forty-four were back in the workplace, as many reentered the workforce once their children were older. Riv-Ellen Prell, "Triumph, Accommodation, and Resistance: American Jewish Life from the End of World War II to the Six-Day War," in Marc Lee Raphael, ed., *The Columbia History of Jews and Judaism in America* (New York: Columbia University Press, 2008), 114–41, here 127. For national data on women's employment, see Susan M. Hartmann, "Women's Employment and the Domestic Ideal in the Early Cold War Years," in Meyerowitz, *Not June Cleaver*, 84–100.

7. Hasia Diner, Shira Kohn, and Rachel Kranson, "Introduction," in Diner, Kohn, and Kranson, *A Jewish Feminine Mystique? Jewish Women in Postwar America* (New Brunswick, NJ: Rutgers University Press, 2010), 1–12, here 3–4.

8. Diner, Kohn, and Kranson, *A Jewish Feminine Mystique?*

9. Steven M. Gelber, *Hobbies: Leisure and the Culture of Work in America* (New York: Columbia University Press, 1999); Cowan, *More Work for Mother*; Janice Brodsky, telephone interview by author, March 28, 2012.

10. Natalie Cohen, Phone, May 15, 2013.

11. Danny Davis, *My Son the President: Mah Jong Tea*, 12in LP (Strand, 1962), Dartmouth Jewish Sound Archive; Allan Sherman, *My Son the Folk Singer: Shticks and Stones*, 12in LP (Warner Brothers Records, 1962), Dartmouth Jewish Sound Archive; Joyce Antler, *You Never Call! You Never Write!: A History of the Jewish Mother* (New York: Oxford University Press, 2007); Dan Greenburg, *How to Be a Jewish Mother: A Very Lovely Training Manual* (Los Angeles: Price/Stern/Sloan Publishers, Inc., 1964).

12. Beth Lean, interview by author, Phone, June 17, 2014. For an example of a children's game set, see "Advertisement: Fortunoff's 3 Day Sale," *New York Times*, April 20, 1958.

13. Beth Lean, interview by author, Phone, June 25, 2014; Allen Meyers, *The Jewish Community of West Philadelphia*, Images of America (Charleston SC: Arcadia Publishing, 2001), 8.

14. Sylvia Leeds, interview.

15. Arleen Winston Goldman, "Mah Jongg League Brought Ancient Game of China to Modern Jewish Community," *Jewish News*, April 6, 2000.

16. For literary depictions of conversation and the game's rhythm, see Christie, *The Murder of Roger Ackroyd*, Ch. 16; Gerstenberg, *Four Plays for Four Women*; Eileen Chang, *Lust, Caution*; Amy Tan, *The Joy Luck Club*.

17. *Audio Piece by Timothy Nohe for "Project Mah Jongg" Exhibition*, n.d., Museum of Jewish Heritage—A Living Memorial to the Holocaust.

18. Rita Rappoport Greenstein, interview, May 21, 2012; Sylvia Leeds, interview.

19. Heller and Pearlman, *Mah-Jongg: The Tiles That Bind*.

20. Donna R. Braden, *Leisure and Entertainment in America* (Dearborn, MI: Henry Ford Museum & Greenfield Village, 1988), 105; James A. Jacobs, "Social and Spatial Change in the Postwar Family Room," *Perspectives in Vernacular Architecture* 13, no. 1 (2006): 70–85.

21. Laura J. Miller, "Family Togetherness and the Suburban Ideal," *Sociological Forum* 10, no. 3 (September 1995): 393–418; Elaine Tyler May, *Homeward Bound: American Families in the Cold War Era* (New York: Basic Books, 1988).

22. Beth Lean, interview by author, Phone, June 25, 2014; Hilda Schaffer, interview by author, Hartsdale, NY, May 29, 2012; "Photograph [1940s]," 1940s n.d., Louis Silver Family Papers, The William Breman Jewish Heritage Museum.

23. Geraldine S. Foster, "'Click, Click, Click': The Sound of Mah Jongg," *Rhode Island Jewish Historical Notes* 15, no. 1 (2008): 107–8.

24. Alan H. Rosenberg, *Mah Jongg Mavens and Memories*, VHS, 1997; Toby Weiss, interview by author, Riverdale, Bronx, NY, May 30, 2012; David Unger, interview by author, Manhattan, NY, May 31, 2012.

25. Dorene Beller, interview by author, Manhattan, NY, May 23, 2012. Emphasis in speech. Echoed by Marjorie Meyerson Troum, interview by author, Los Angeles, August 21, 2012. For memories of housebound immigrant grandmothers, see Hilda Schaffer, interview by author, Phone, November 11, 2010. Echoed by virtually every interviewee and description of mahjong groups.

26. Lynn Spigel, *Make Room for TV: Television and the Family Ideal in Postwar America* (Chicago: University of Chicago Press, 1992), Ch. 3.

27. Lisa McGirr, *Suburban Warriors: The Origins of the New American Right* (Princeton: Princeton University Press, 2001); Bennett M. Berger, *Working-Class Suburb: A Study of Auto Workers in Suburbia* (Berkeley: University of California Press 1960); Reva Salk, interview by author, Floral Park, Long Island, NY, May 22, 2012.

28. Nancy Kraus interview, May 22, 2012; Dorene Beller interview, May 23, 2012; Zelda Lubart, interview by author, Manhattan, NY, May 23, 2012; Ethel Shapiro et al., interview by author, Brooklyn, NY, May 22, 2012; Hilda Schaffer, interview by author, Hartsdale, NY, May 29, 2012; Rita Rappoport Greenstein, telephone interview by author, February 3, 2010; Barbara Dellon interview, June 25, 2014; Natalie Cohen, telephone interview by author, May 15, 2013. Foster, "'Click, Click, Click': The Sound of Mah Jongg," 111.

29. Eva Rubel and Richard Rubel, interview; Cohen, interview.

30. Dorene Beller, "Email," January 16, 2020; Jill Shuman, "Mahjong Community Facebook Group Discussion," January 13, 2020.

31. Charles Kraus, "Email," January 16, 2020; "Mah Jongg, That's It! Facebook Group Discussion," January 13, 2020; "Mahjong Memories Facebook Group Discussion," January 13, 2020; "Mahjong Community Facebook Group Discussion," January 13, 2020.

32. Marjorie Meyerson Troum interview, August 21, 2012.

33. Norris Leap, "Baby Sits with Papa When Mom Goes Out," *Los Angeles Times*, August 7, 1959, A1.

34. Fortunoff's, "Advertisement: I Gave My Mommy $1.62 for Mother's Day!," *New York Times*, May 4, 1958; Seymour Silverman and Edith Silverman, interview; Hilda Schaffer, interview, May 29, 2012.

35. Marilyn Starr, interview.

36. Dorothy Stern and Sarah Blustain, "Tiles and Tribulations," *Lilith* 35, no. 2 (Summer 2010): 21–23.

37. Silverman, interview, October 11, 2014.

38. Audio Piece by Timothy Nohe for "Project Mah Jongg" Exhibition.

39. Sylvia Leeds, interview.

40. Reva Salk, interview.

41. National Mah Jongg League, "National Mah Jongg League News," January 1965, National Mah Jongg League Private Collection.

42. Marjorie Sablow, interview by author, Hartsdale, NY, May 29, 2012.

43. Sylvia Leeds, interview by author, Phone, August 8, 2014. Echoed by Boots Hersh, "Email," September 25, 2015.

44. *[Tablecloth]*, n.d., Toby Salk Personal Collection; *[Apron]*, n.d., Toby Salk Personal Collection; *[Apron]*, n.d., Project Mah Jongg, Museum of Jewish Heritage—A Living Memorial to the Holocaust.

45. *[Dorothy S. Meyerson Teaching Mah Jongg on Television, 1951]*, Photograph, 1951, Project Mah Jongg, Museum of Jewish Heritage—A Living Memorial to the Holocaust.

46. Toby Weiss, interview; Pamela Gurock, interview by author, Riverdale, Bronx, NY, May 30, 2012; "Mah Jongg, That's It! Facebook Group Discussion"; Zelda Schoengold to author, November 2014.

47. Renny Pritikin, "Email 1," June 25, 2014; Marjorie Meyerson Troum, interview; Rosenberg, *Mah Jongg Mavens and Memories*; Fern Bernstein, "Catskills Mah Jongg Memories," Mah Jongg Mondays, May 4, 2020.

48. Beller, "Email," January 16, 2020.

49. Linda Kraus, interview by author, Lake Forest Park, WA, February 15, 2012; Barbara Dellon, interview by author, Telephone, June 25, 2014.

50. Hilda Schaffer, interview, May 29, 2012.

51. Nancy Kraus, interview by author, Brooklyn, NY, May 22, 2012; Dorene Beller, interview; Zelda Lubart, interview by author, Manhattan, NY, May 23, 2012; Ethel Shapiro et al., interview by author, Brooklyn, New York, May 22, 2012; Hilda Schaffer, interview, May 29, 2012; Rita Rappoport Greenstein, interview by author, Phone, February 3, 2010; Dellon, interview; Cohen, interview.

52. Ethel Shapiro et al., interview.

53. Dorothy S. Meyerson, *"That's It:" A New Way to Play Mah Jong*, 1937. A minority of groups played for no money at all, though most enjoyed the added motivation provided by having some skin in the game.

54. Dellon, interview; Ethel Shapiro et al., interview; Eva Rubel and Richard Rubel, interview by author, Riverdale, Bronx, NY, May 30, 2012; Foster, "'Click, Click, Click': The Sound of Mah Jongg," 112.

55. Marion Banks, "Coin Purse," 1950, National Museum of American Jewish History; "The Ever-Popular Mah Jongg Purse," *National Mah Jongg League News*, January 1965, National Mah Jongg League Private Collection; "Letter to the Editor: Jane Civins-Mills."

56. Arthur Tanney, "Vendors, Peddlers and Knishmen in the Summer," *In the Mountains Newsletter of the Catskills Institute*, March 1999, Catskills Institute Files, American Jewish Historical Society, New York.

57. Dorothy S. Meyerson, *"That's It:" A New Way to Play Mah Jong*, 1937, 18. Foster, "'Click, Click, Click': The Sound of Mah Jongg," 109.

58. Rolaine Hochstein, "Mah-Jongg Returns"; Ethel Shapiro et al., interview; Rita Rappoport Greenstein, interview, May 21, 2012.

59. Lustbader, Revitz, and Revitz, interview.

60. Ethel Shapiro et al., interview.

61. Rosenberg, *Mah Jongg Mavens and Memories*.

62. Sklare and Greenblum, *Jewish Identity on the Suburban Frontier*, 258.

63. Silverman, interview, October 11, 2014.

64. Prell, "American Jewish Life from the End of World War II to the Six-Day War"; Horowitz, "Jewish Women Remaking American Feminism/Women Remaking American Judaism"; Moore, *B'nai B'rith and the Challenge of Ethnic Leadership*.

65. Lustbader, Revitz, and Revitz, interview.

66. Alexander Grinstein, "Profile of a 'Doll'—A Female Character Type," *Psychoanalytic Review* 50, no. 2 (Summer 1963): 161–74; Davis, *My Son the President: Mah Jong Tea*; Sherman, *Shticks and Stones*.

67. Antler, *You Never Call! You Never Write!*; Riv-Ellen Prell, *Fighting to Become Americans: Jews, Gender, and the Anxiety of Assimilation* (Boston: Beacon Press, 1999).

68. Rebecca Jo Plant, *Mom: The Transformation of Motherhood in Modern America* (Chicago: University of Chicago Press, 2010).

69. Philip Roth, *Portnoy's Complaint* (New York: Random House, 1969), 98.

70. Roth, 43.

71. Indeed, another young man dies by suicide and leaves as his last note a phone message for his mother from her mahjong group. Roth, 120.

72. "The Mah-Jongg Craze," *Newsweek*, February 24, 1969, 15; Kingsley Amis, "Waxing Wroth," book review, *Harper's Magazine*, April 1, 1969, 104–7.

73. Antler, *You Never Call! You Never Write!*, 8–9; Joyce Antler, "'We Were Ready to Turn the World Upside Down': Radical Feminism and Jewish Women," in Diner, Kohn, and Kranson, *A Jewish Feminine Mystique?*, 210–34.

74. Stephanie Grossman, telephone interview by author, April 23, 2013.

75. Gwen Gibson Schwartz and Barbara Wyden, *The Jewish Wife* (New York: Paperback Library, 1969), 211; Friedan, *The Second Stage*, 80. Echoing Friedan, see Robert Sward, "Kaddish," *The Massachusetts Review*, Summer 1964.

76. Rolaine Hochstein, "Mah-Jongg Returns—One Bam, Two Crack, How about a Little Snack?," *Ms. Magazine*, January 1977, 14–18; Civins-Mills, letter to the editor.

77. Dorothy Stern, "Tiles and Tribulations," *Lilith* 35, no. 2 (Summer 2010): 20–23.

78. Hasia Diner, *The Jews of the United States, 1654 to 2000* (Berkeley: University of California Press, 2004), 304; Juliet Schor, *The Overworked American: The Unexpected Decline of Leisure* (New York: Basic Books, 1991).

79. Claire Cain Miller, "The Relentlessness of Modern Parenting," *New York Times*, December 25, 2018; Sharon Hays, *The Cultural Contradictions of Motherhood* (New Haven: Yale University Press, 1998); Philip Cohen, *Enduring Bonds: Inequality, Marriage, Parenting, and Everything Else That Makes Families Great and Terrible* (Oakland: University of California Press, 2018).

EPILOGUE

1. Quotation is from Rochelle "Shelley" Schreiber et al., Group observation, San Francisco, CA, October 3, 2011; Rochelle "Shelley" Schreiber, interview by author, Phone, August 25, 2011.

2. Lucette Lagnado, "Dust Off Your Old Game Table: Mah-Jongg Is Making a Comeback," *Wall Street Journal*, October 18, 2010; Kara Baskin, "The New Age of Mahjong," *Boston Globe*, May 18, 2016; Lisa Keys, "Gen-X and Web Spurring a Revival of Mah-Jongg, the Game of Bubbes," *Forward*, October 19, 2001.

3. "Julia Roberts Calms Down by Playing Mahjong," *The Late Show with Stephen Colbert*, December 5, 2018.

4. Chinese American Women's Club, "A Humble Beginning," 2012, temporary exhibit, Pioneering the Valley: The Chinese American Legacy in Santa Clara Valley, Martin Luther King Jr. Library, San Jose; Emily Yue, "Email," February 27, 2012.

5. Amy Tan, *The Joy Luck Club*; Wayne Wang, *The Joy Luck Club* (Buena Vista Pictures, 1993); Alan Patureau, "'The Joy Luck Club' Renews Interest in Age-Old Mah-Jongg," *Chicago Daily Tribune*, November 18, 1993. A few other references to the game scattered through other popular media at the time, including Chinatown mahjong players in the film *Eat a Bowl of Tea* (1989) and a scene in the 1989 film *Driving Miss Daisy* wherein the game helps mark Daisy Werthan as Jewish. These films may have helped prime the cultural ground for the *Joy Luck Club*'s more significant effect. Bruce Beresford, *Driving Miss Daisy* (Warner Bros. Pictures, 1989); Wayne Wang, *Eat a Bowl of Tea* (Columbia Pictures, 1989).

6. Beverly Beyette, "Hands (and Strategies) across the Mah-Jongg Table," *Los Angeles Times*, March 18, 1996, sec. Life & Style.

7. Sonaiya Kelley, "'Crazy Rich Asians' Dominates the Box Office, Makes History for Representation," *Los Angeles Times*, August 19, 2018, sec. Movies. Another recent Hollywood portrayal that brought mahjong to the screen but engendered

less popular conversation about the game was Ang Lee's 2007 adaptation of Eileen Chang's *Lust, Caution,* in Mandarin. Ang Lee, *Lust, Caution* (Focus Features, 2007).

8. Jon Chu, *Crazy Rich Asians* (Warner Bros. Pictures, 2018); Kevin Kwan, *Crazy Rich Asians* (New York: Anchor Books, 2013). Chu added the mahjong scene to the film; it was not in the book.

9. Jeff Yang, "The Symbolism of Crazy Rich Asians' Pivotal Mahjong Scene, Explained," *Vox,* August 31, 2018.

10. "Games Night at London Arms," *The Other Side,* July 1980, Series 9: Gay and Lesbian Community, Support, and Spirit, Gay, Lesbian, Bisexual and Transgender Historical Society; Ethan Mordden, "Beach Blanket Mah-Jongg," in *Everybody Loves You: Further Adventures in Gay Manhattan* (New York: St. Martin's Press, 1988), 155–73; "3 Crack, 2 Bam, Fan of Bridge Mix?," *Jewish Gaily Forward,* April 2001; Caryn Aviv, "Thank You and Goodbye," *Jewish Gaily Forward,* September 2003; Chiou-ling Yeh, *Making an American Festival: Chinese New Year in San Francisco's Chinatown* (Berkeley: University of California Press, 2008), 194, 197; Nan Alamilla Boyd, *Wide Open Town: A History of Queer San Francisco to 1965* (Berkeley: University of California Press, 2003). Amy Sueyoshi, *Discriminating Sex: White Leisure and the Making of the American "Oriental"* (Urbana: University of Illinois Press, 2018).

11. Rachel Levin, "Jewish Summer Camp with Campfires, Crafts and No Lights Out," *New York Times,* September 18, 2019.

12. Emily Burack, "The Best Jewish References in 'The Marvelous Mrs. Maisel' Season 2," *Kveller,* December 12, 2018, https://www.kveller.com.

13. Nina Badzin, "Why I Love My Mah-Jongg Group," *TC Jewfolk,* May 5, 2015, http://tcjewfolk.com. See also Selah Maya Zighelboim, "Playing Mahjong with the Granddaughters," *Jewish Exponent,* November 24, 2019, https://www.jewishexponent.com; Lagnado, "Dust Off Your Old Game Table."

14. Angelo Bautista, "Picking Up the Pieces of Mahjong," *To the Best of Our Knowledge* (Wisconsin Public Radio and PRX, November 30, 2019); Erika Lee, *The Making of Asian America: A History* (New York: Simon and Schuster, 2015).

15. Denice Wisniewski, Phone, August 6, 2014; Forth [pseud.], interview; Grace Chun and Amy Gwilliam, interview by author, Chinese-American Museum of Chicago, August 18, 2011.

16. "2019 Egg Rolls, Egg Creams & Empanadas Festival," Museum at Eldridge Street, accessed March 16, 2020, https://www.eldridgestreet.org/festival; Imin Yeh and Leah Rosenberg, "Jews for Dim Sum," Imin Yeh, accessed June 17, 2020, http://iminyeh.info/jews-for-dim-sum.

17. Bethany Ao, "Philly's Mahjong Club Brings a Time-Honored Game to Bottle Shops, Board-Game Cafes," *Philadelphia Inquirer,* August 7, 2019. For a similar reaction to the film, see Laurie Levy, "Learning to Play Mahjong," *Still Advocating* (blog), October 11, 2018, www.chicagonow.com/still-advocating/2018/10/learning-to-play-mahjong.

18. Amy Jacobs, "Mah Jongg Unites People of All Ages, Places in the Bay Area," *Jewish News Weekly of Northern California*, November 17, 2000.

19. Penny Schwartz, "It's Not Their Mother's Game: A New Generation of Women Embrace Mah Jongg," *Jewish Advocate*, October 16, 2003; Gloria Shukert Jones, "Getting to Know You Takes Precedence at Mah Jongg," *The Jewish Press*, April 3, 2009.

20. Kelli Vernon Kirkham, interview by author, Dallas, TX, June 10, 2016.

21. Toby Salk, interview by author, Berkeley, CA, April 20, 2012; Linda Feinstein, interview by author, Manhattan, NY, May 21, 2012.

22. Xinyan Yu, "How Mahjong Shaped America," *Inkstone, South China Morning Post*, September 13, 2019; Keys, "Gen-X and Web Spurring a Revival of Mah-Jongg, the Game of Bubbes."

23. Abacus, "Tesla Owners in China Can Soon Play Mahjong and Poker in Cars," *South China Morning Post*, December 20, 2019, sec. Tech.

24. Elsie McCormick, "China's Ancient Dominoes Now Fascinate Foreigners," *China Press*, September 11, 1921, MJSC Scrapbook 1, PB.

25. Marcia Biederman, "An Ancient Game with Fresh Appeal," *New York Times*, August 21, 2003.

26. *Official National Mah Jongg League Internet Game*, n.d., https://www.nmjl.org/game/home.html.

27. Fern Bernstein, "Game Interrupted: How the Coronavirus Is Affecting Mah Jongg," Mah Jongg Mondays, March 16, 2020.

28. "Crisloid," accessed July 30, 2018, https://crisloid.com/product-category/mahjong. For the historically inspired, see "Crisloid and Red Coin," accessed July 30, 2018, https://crisloid.com/product/the-dragon-mah-jong-set-by-red-coin-and-crisloid.

29. Natalie Cohen, Phone, May 15, 2013; Rochelle "Shelley" Schreiber, interview; Toby Salk, interview by author, Phone, February 6, 2020; Reva Salk, interview by author, Floral Park, Long Island, NY, May 22, 2012; Schwartz, "It's Not Their Mother's Game."

Selected Bibliography

ARCHIVAL AND MANUSCRIPT COLLECTIONS

American Jewish Historical Society, New York, New York
   Catskills Institute Records
   Kurt K. Field Film Collection
Brooklyn Museum, Brooklyn, New York
   Stewart Culin Papers
Chicago History Museum
   World's Columbian Exposition Collection
   Olga H. Huncke Scrapbook
Christopher Berg Personal Collection, Columbia, South Carolina
   Joseph and Norma Babcock Collection
Columbia University, New York, New York
   Butler Library, Rare Books & Manuscripts Library
      Leo Lerman Papers
Harvard University, Cambridge, Massachusetts
   Peabody Library
      Janet Elliott Wulsin Papers
   Radcliffe Institute for Advanced Study, Schlesinger Library
   Amy Richardson Holway Papers
      Florence May Wyman Currier Papers
      Julia Coolidge Deane Papers
      Marion Angeline Howlett Papers
      Mary M. Wilbur Papers
      Thyra Pedersen Papers
Hasbro Factory, East Longmeadow, Massachusetts (now a Cartamundi factory)
   Parker Brothers Archive (PB)
      Mah Jongg Sales Company of America Collection (MJSC)
Huntington Library, San Marino, California
   Chong Family Album

Grace Nicholson Papers
Hong Family Papers
Johni Levene Personal Collection, Berkeley, California
    Mahjong sets and ephemera
Library of Congress
    American Folklife Center
        StoryCorps Archive
        Veterans History Project
    Motion Pictures Division
        Copyright Descriptive Material
    Music Division
        Richard Rodgers Collection
        Vol Tilzer/Gumm Collection
        George and Ira Gershwin Collection
    Prints and Photographs Division
        George Clark, Swann Collection
        Herbert Frank National Photo Company Collection
        New York World-Telegram & Sun Collection
        Pung Wo Company Collection
        Underwood & Underwood Collection
Marjorie Meyerson Troum Personal Collection, Pacific Palisades, California
    Dorothy Meyerson Scrapbook
Metroplitan Museum of Art, New York, New York
    Erté Collection
Museum of Jewish Heritage—A Living Memorial to the Holocaust, New York, New York
    Project Mah Jongg Exhibit
National Archives at San Francisco, San Bruno, California
    Equity Case #847
    Equity Case #848
National Mah Jongg League (NMJL), New York, New York
    NMJL Private Collection
National Museum of American History Archives Center, Washington, DC
    Warshaw Collection of Business Americana
New York Public Library, New York, New York
    Library for the Performing Arts, Billy Rose Theatre Division
    Otto Harbach Papers
San Francisco Public Library (SFPL), San Francisco, California
    San Francisco History Archives
        Square and Circle Club Collection
Scripps College, Claremont, California
    Denison Library
    Bess Hovey Games Collection

Stanford University, Stanford, California
   Green Library, Special Collections
      Alice Fong Yu Papers
      Chinese Immigration Pamphlets
      Emory M. Lee Collection
   Hoover Archive
      Pardee Lowe Collection
      Survey of Race Relations
Toby Salk Personal Collection, Berkeley, California
   Mahjong sets and ephemera
Tom Sloper Personal Collection, Los Angeles, California
   Interview with Herma Jacobs
   Mahjong sets
University of California, Berkeley, California
   Bancroft Library
      Chinese in California Collection
      Jesse Brown Cook Scrapbooks
      San Francisco News-Call Bulletin Newspaper Photograph Archive
      War Relocation Authority Collection
   Ethnic Studies Library
      Angel Island Oral History Project
      Chinese-American Business Miscellany
      Chinese American Citizens Alliance Organizational Materials
      Him Mark Lai Papers
      Kem Lee Collection
University of California, Los Angeles, California
   Southern California Chinese American Oral History Project
William Breman Jewish Heritage Museum, Atlanta, Georgia
   Louis Silver Family Papers
   Frieda Spieler Family Papers
Wright-Patterson Mah Jongg Group, Wright-Patterson Air Force Base, Ohio
   Wright-Patterson Mah Jongg Group Scrapbook

ARCHIVES ACCESSIBLE ONLINE

Catskills Institute
   Mountain Memoirs and Historical Essays
Japanese American National Museum
      Walter Muramoto Photographs
Mah Jong Museum
   Mah Jong History and Collection
San Francisco Maritime National Historical Park
   American President Lines Records

University of California, Berkeley
Japanese American Relocation Digital Archives
The Japanese American Evacuation and Resettlement
Winterthur Library
A. A. Vantine and Company Collection

FURTHER READING, SELECTED

Antler, Joyce. *The Journey Home: Jewish Women and the American Century*. New York: Free Press, 1997.

Antler, Joyce. *You Never Call! You Never Write!: A History of the Jewish Mother*. New York: Oxford University Press, 2007.

Braden, Donna R. *Leisure and Entertainment in America*. Dearborn, MI: Henry Ford Museum & Greenfield Village, 1988.

Chang, Gordon H. *Fateful Ties: A History of America's Preoccupation with China*. Cambridge, MA: Harvard University Press, 2015.

Chen, Shehong. *Being Chinese, Becoming Chinese American*. Urbana: University of Illinois Press, 2002.

Chen, Yong. *Chinese San Francisco, 1850–1943: A Trans-Pacific Community*. Stanford, CA: Stanford University Press, 2000.

Coe, Andrew. *Chop Suey: A Cultural History of Chinese Food in the United States*. New York: Oxford University Press, 2009.

Cohen, Lizabeth. *A Consumers' Republic: The Politics of Mass Consumption in Postwar America*. New York: Random House, 2003.

Daniels, Roger. *Prisoners without Trial: Japanese Americans in World War II*. New York: Hill and Wang, 1993.

Decter, Avi, and Melissa Martens, eds. *The Other Promised Land: Vacationing, Identity, and the Jewish American Dream*. Baltimore: The Jewish Museum of Maryland, Inc., 2005.

Deloria, Philip. *Playing Indian*. New Haven: Yale University Press, 1998.

Densho Encyclopedia. Accessed May 7, 2015. http://encyclopedia.densho.org.

Diner, Hasia. *The Jews of the United States, 1654 to 2000*. Berkeley: University of California Press, 2004.

Diner, Hasia, Shira Kohn, and Rachel Kranson, eds. *A Jewish Feminine Mystique? Jewish Women in Postwar America*. New Brunswick, NJ: Rutgers University Press, 2010.

Dumenil, Lynn. *The Modern Temper: American Culture and Society in the 1920s*. New York: Hill and Wang, 1995.

Edwards, Holly. "A Million and One Nights: Orientalism in America, 1870–1930." In *Noble Dreams, Wicked Pleasures: Orientalism in America, 1870–1930*, 11–58. Italy: Princeton University Press and Sterling and Francine Clark Art Institute, 2000.

Frank, Caroline. *Objectifying China, Imagining America: Chinese Commodities in Early America*. Chicago: University of Chicago Press, 2011.

Gelber, Steven. *Hobbies: Leisure and the Culture of Work in America.* New York: Columbia University Press, 1999.

Goldstein, Eric L. *The Price of Whiteness: Jews, Race, and American Identity.* Princeton: Princeton University Press, 2006.

Goodman, Bryna and David S. G. Goodman, eds. *Twentieth-Century Colonialism and China: Localities, the Everyday, and the World.* New York: Routledge, 2012.

Grover, Kathryn, ed. *Hard at Play: Leisure in America, 1840–1940.* Amherst: University of Massachusetts Press, 1992.

Gulliver, Katrina. "Finding the Pacific World." *Journal of World History* 22, no. 1 (March 2011): 83–100.

Heinze, Andrew R. *Adapting to Abundance: Jewish Immigrants, Mass Consumption, and the Search for American Identity.* New York: Columbia University Press, 1990.

Hershatter, Gail. *Dangerous Pleasures: Prostitution and Modernity in Twentieth-Century Shanghai.* Berkeley: University of California Press, 1997.

Hing, Bill Ong. *Making and Remaking Asian America through Immigration Policy, 1850–1990.* Stanford, CA: Stanford University Press, 1993.

Hoganson, Kristin. *Consumers' Imperium: The Global Production of American Domesticity.* Chapel Hill: University of North Carolina Press, 2007.

Hsu, Madeline Y. "From Chop Suey to Mandarin Cuisine: Fine Dining and the Refashioning of Chinese Ethnicity during the Cold War Era." In *Chinese Americans and the Politics of Race and Culture,* 173–94. Philadelphia: Temple University Press, 2008.

Huskey, James. "Americans in Shanghai: Community Formation and Response to Revolution, 1919–1928." PhD diss., University of North Carolina, 1985.

Jackson, Kenneth T. *Crabgrass Frontier: The Suburbanization of the United States.* New York: Oxford University Press, 1985.

Jacobs, Meg. *Pocketbook Politics: Economic Citizenship in Twentieth-Century America.* Princeton: Princeton University Press, 2005.

Jacobson, Matthew Frye. *Whiteness of a Different Color: European Immigrants and the Alchemy of Race.* Cambridge, MA: Harvard University Press, 1998.

Jorae, Wendy Rouse. *The Children of Chinatown: Growing Up Chinese American in San Francisco, 1850–1920.* Chapel Hill: University of North Carolina Press, 2009.

Joselit, Jenna Weissman. *The Wonders of America: Reinventing Jewish Culture 1880–1950.* New York: Hill and Wang, 1994.

Kanfer, Stefan. *A Summer World: The Attempt to Build a Jewish Eden in the Catskills, from the Days of the Ghetto to the Rise and Decline of the Borscht Belt.* New York: Farrar, Straus & Giroux, 1989.

Klein, Christina. *Cold War Orientalism: Asia in the Middlebrow Imagination, 1945–1961.* Berkeley: University of California Press, 2003.

Larson, Louise Leung. *Sweet Bamboo: A Memoir of a Chinese American Family.* Berkeley: University of California Press, 1989.

Leach, William. *Land of Desire: Merchants, Power, and the Rise of a New American Culture*. New York: Vintage Books, 1994.

Lears, T. J. Jackson. *No Place of Grace: Antimodernism and the Transformation of American Culture, 1880–1920*. Chicago: University of Chicago Press, 1994.

Lears, T. J. Jackson. *Something for Nothing: Luck in America*. New York: Viking Penguin, 2003.

Lee, Anthony W. *Picturing Chinatown: Art and Orientalism in San Francisco*. Berkeley: University of California Press, 2001.

Lee, Erika, and Judy Yung. *Angel Island: Immigrant Gateway to America*. New York: Oxford University Press, 2010.

Leong, Karen J. *The China Mystique: Pearl S. Buck, Anna May Wong, Mayling Soong, and the Transformation of American Orientalism*. Berkeley: University of California Press, 2005.

Levine, Lawrence W. *The Unpredictable Past*. New York: Oxford University Press, 1993.

Lim, Shirley Jennifer. *A Feeling of Belonging: Asian American Women's Public Culture, 1930–1960*. New York: New York University Press, 2006.

Liu, Haiming. *From Canton Restaurant to Panda Express: A History of Chinese Food in the United States*. New Brunswick, NJ: Rutgers University Press, 2015.

Lo, Andrew. "China's Passion for Pai: Playing Cards, Dominoes, and Mahjong." In *Asian Games: The Art of Contest*, edited by Irving Finkel and Colin Mackenzie, 216–31. [New York]: Asia Society, 2004.

Lowe, Lisa. *Immigrant Acts: On Asian American Cultural Politics*. Durham, NC: Duke University Press, 1996.

Lui, Mary Ting Yi. *The Chinatown Trunk Mystery: Murder, Miscegenation, and Other Dangerous Encounters in Turn-of-the-Century New York City*. Princeton: Princeton University Press, 2005.

Marchand, Roland. *Advertising the American Dream: Making Way for Modernity, 1920–1940*. Berkeley: University of California Press, 1986.

Marchetti, Gina. "American Orientalism." *Pacific Historical Review* 73, no. 2 (May 2004): 299–304.

Marchetti, Gina. *Romance and the "Yellow Peril": Race, Sex, and Discursive Strategies in Hollywood Fiction*. Berkeley: University of California Press, 1993.

Martens, Melissa J. "The Game of a Thousand Wonders." In *Mah Jongg: Crak Bam Dot*, 8–21. New York: 2wiceBooks, 2010.

Matsumoto, Valerie. *City Girls: The Nisei Social World in Los Angeles, 1920–1950*. New York: Oxford University Press, 2014.

May, Elaine Tyler. *Homeward Bound: American Families in the Cold War Era*. New York: Basic Books, Inc., 1988.

McKeown, Adam. "Ritualization of Regulation: The Enforcement of Chinese Exclusion in the United States and China." *American Historical Review* 108, no. 2 (April 2003): 377–403.

Meikle, Jeffrey. *American Plastic: A Cultural History*. New Brunswick, NJ: Rutgers University Press, 1995.

Meyerowitz, Joanne, ed. *Not June Cleaver: Women and Gender in Postwar America, 1945–1960*. Philadelphia: Temple University Press, 1994.

Miller, Hanna. "Identity Takeout: How American Jews Made Chinese Food Their Ethnic Cuisine." *Journal of Popular Culture* 39, no. 3 (2006): 430–65.

Moon, Krystyn R. *Yellowface: Creating the Chinese in American Popular Music and Performance, 1850s–1920s*. New Brunswick, NJ Rutgers University Press, 2005.

Moore, Deborah Dash. *At Home in America: Second Generation New York Jews*. New York: Columbia University Press, 1981.

Moore, Deborah Dash. *To the Golden Cities: Pursuing the American Jewish Dream in Miami and LA*. New York: Free Press, 1994.

Nee, Victor G., and Brett de Bary Nee. *Longtime Californ': A Documentary Study of an American Chinatown*. New York: Pantheon Books, 1972.

Ngai, Mae M. *Impossible Subjects: Illegal Aliens and the Making of Modern America*. Princeton: Princeton University Press, 2004.

Okihiro, Gary Y. *Whispered Silences: Japanese Americans and World War II*. Seattle: University of Washington Press, 1996.

Orbanes, Philip. *The Game Makers: The Story of Parker Brothers from Tiddledy Winks to Trivial Pursuit*. Boston: Harvard Business School Press, 2004.

Perry, Elizabeth. *Shanghai on Strike: The Politics of Chinese Labor*. Stanford, CA: Stanford University Press, 1993.

Plant, Rebecca Jo. *Mom: The Transformation of Motherhood in Modern America*. Chicago: University of Chicago Press, 2010.

Prell, Riv-Ellen. *Fighting to Become Americans: Jews, Gender, and the Anxiety of Assimilation*. Boston: Beacon Press, 1999.

Richman, Irwin. *Borscht Belt Bungalows: Memories of Catskill Summers*. Philadelphia: Temple University Press, 1998.

Ringer, Benjamin B. *The Edge of Friendliness: A Study of Jewish-Gentile Relations*. New York: Basic Books, 1967.

Robinson, Greg. *After Camp: Portraits in Midcentury Japanese American Life and Politics*. Berkeley: University of California Press, 2012.

Roediger, David. *The Wages of Whiteness: Race and the Making of the American Working Class*. New York: Verso, New Left Books, 1991.

Rutherford, Janice Williams. *Selling Mrs. Consumer: Christine Frederick and the Rise of Household Efficiency*. Athens: University of Georgia Press, 2003.

Said, Edward. *Orientalism*. New York: Vintage Books, 1978.

Schwarcz, Vera. *Bridge across Broken Time: Chinese and Jewish Cultural Memory*. New Haven: Yale University Press, 1998.

Schwartz, David G. *Roll the Bones: The History of Gambling.* New York: Gotham Books, 2006.

Shah, Nayan. *Contagious Divides: Epidemics and Race in San Francisco's Chinatown.* Berkeley: University of California Press, 2001.

Sklare, Marshall, and Joseph Greenblum. *Jewish Identity on the Suburban Frontier: A Study of Group Survival in the Open Society.* New York: Basic Books, 1967.

Sklare, Marshall, and Mark Vosk. *The Riverton Study: How Jews Look at Themselves and Their Neighbors.* New York: The American Jewish Committee, 1957.

Sloper, Tom. *The Red Dragon & The West Wind: The Winning Guide to Official Chinese & American Mah-Jongg.* New York: HarperCollins Publishers, 2007.

Stanwick, Michael. "Mahjong(g) before Mahjong(g): Part 1." *The Playing-Card* 32, no. 4 (2004): 153–62.

Stanwick, Michael. "Mahjong(g) before Mahjong(g): Part 2." *The Playing-Card* 32, no. 5 (2004): 206–15.

Tchen, John Kuo Wei. *New York before Chinatown: Orientalism and the Shaping of American Culture, 1776–1882.* Baltimore: Johns Hopkins University Press, 1999.

The Modern Girl around the World Research Group, ed. *The Modern Girl around the World: Consumption, Modernity, and Globalization.* Durham, NC: Duke University Press, 2008.

Wasserstrom, Jeffrey. *Global Shanghai, 1850–2010.* New York: Routledge, 2009.

Yeh, Chiou-ling. *Making an American Festival: Chinese New Year in San Francisco's Chinatown.* Berkeley: University of California Press, 2008.

Yokota, Kariann. *Unbecoming British: How Revolutionary America Became a Postcolonial Nation.* New York: Oxford University Press, 2011.

Yoshihara, Mari. *Embracing the East: White Women and American Orientalism.* New York: Oxford University Press, 2003.

Yu, Connie Young. *Chinatown San Jose, USA.* San Jose, CA: History San Jose, 1991.

Yung, Judy. *Unbound Feet: A Social History of Chinese Women in San Francisco.* Berkeley: University of California Press, 1995.

Yung, Judy, Gordon H. Chang, and Him Mark Lai, eds. *Chinese American Voices: From the Gold Rush to the Present.* Berkeley: University of California Press, 2006.

Index

For the benefit of digital users, indexed terms that span two pages (e.g., 52–53) may, on occasion, appear on only one of those pages.
Note: page numbers followed by n refer to notes, with note number.

A&L Manufacturing Company, 179–80,
181, 182, 183–84, 204f, 227
advertising, 15, 29
and department stores, 31–32,
33–34, 36
and Dorothy Meyerson, 165
and mahjong rules, 50
by Mah-Jongg Sales Company of
America, 14, 141
and marketing of mahjong, 67–68, 70,
71, 81, 184f, 185–86, 212, 225–26
and Marion Angeline Howlett,
38, 39–40
and National Mah Jongg League, 171
and Orientalism, 20–21, 23,
26–27, 31–32
and women, 27–28, 35–36
African Americans, 18, 29–30, 93–94,
100–1, 102, 121, 156
See also blackface
American Catalin Corporation, 181
American Council of the Institute of
Pacific Relations, 142
Amsterdam, 19
Andersen Meyer, 51

Angel Island Immigration Station, 9, 11–
13, 144, 146, 154
and Angel Island Liberty Association,
149, 150–51, 152
design of, 146–48
and detention and interrogation of
Chinese migrants, 145
fire (1940), 154
and gambling, 149, 150–51, 152,
153, 161
and Japanese Americans, 156
and Japanese migrants, 147–48
and mahjong, 145–46, 148–50, 150f,
151, 153, 161
museum exhibit, 150f
and procedures, 148–49
and psychological challenges for
detainees, 152
and women, 151, 152–54
antimodernism, 88–89
anti-Semitism, 7, 171, 193–94,
195–97
Antler, Joyce, 195–97
Arnold, Julean, 51
Art Deco, 21, 102–3, 162

Asian Americans, 8, 9, 107, 223, 224
  See also Chinese Americans Japanese
    Americans
Atlanta, 11–12, 16, 18, 93–94,
    201–2, 209–10
Atlantic Dance Orchestra, 14–15
Averill Company, 27

Babcock, Joseph, 7–8, 49–50, 84–85
  and Anton Lethin, 50
  and California, 16
  claim to inventing mahjong, 85
  departure from mahjong
    industry, 120
  and George Parker, 20
  and ivory, 69–70
  and Mah-Jongg Manufacturing
    Company of China, 61, 70
  and Mah-Jongg Sales Company of
    America, 15–16, 17f, 19, 80f, 83–84
  and mahjong tiles, 49, 72–73
  and marketing of mahjong, 17, 40, 84,
    88, 104–5, 165
  and patent for mahjong, 18–20
  and Pung Chow, 83–84
  and "Red Book of Rules," 17f, 18, 36–
    37, 50, 51–53, 84, 87–88, 98
  and Shanghai, 15–16, 49–50, 51–53,
    61, 87–88
  and Standardization Committee of
    the American Official Laws of Mah-
    Jongg, 99, 120–21
Barnett, George, 19–20
Barnett, Lelia Montague, 19–20
Bauer, Sylva, 175–76, 178f, 178
Beijing, 1–2, 23, 44, 99–100, 114–15
  as imperial capital, 42
  and invasion by Japan, 134–35
  and Janet Wulsin, 53
  and Marion Angeline Howlett, 37, 39f
  and spread of mahjong, 43, 46, 48, 49
  and YMCA, 90–91

Berkeley, 144–45, 156, 160f
blackface, 100–1, 113
Bolitho, William, 59
Booker, Edna Lee, 51–53
Boston, 38, 57–58, 69, 83–84
  and department stores, 38–39
  and Frank Currier, 36
  and Jewish women, 202
  and Mah-Jongg Sales Company of
    America, 16
  and spread of mahjong, 18
bridge, 29, 34, 93–94, 99–100, 113, 120–
    21, 133–34, 165
  and Air Force wives, 175
  as barrier to mahjong, 58–59
  comparisons to mahjong, 9–10, 23,
    34–35, 92, 209
  as competitor to mahjong, 5, 24, 25f,
    41, 49–50, 106
  contrasts to mahjong, 24–26
  and Florence Irwin, 99, 103
  and foreigners in China, 14–41,
    49–50, 53
  fundraisers, 30
  and Helen Bullitt Lowry, 34–35
  and Jewish Americans, 185,
    192–93, 203–4
  and leisure, 192
  and the National Mah Jongg
    League, 168–69
  and status of, 23, 41
  and women, 36, 53, 117, 205–6, 210–11,
    213, 217–18
  and youth, 132, 192
Britain, 25–26, 43–44, 87, 88, 137,
    207–9
  and Boxer Rebellion, 23
  and bridge, 24
  diplomats of, 99–100
  empire, 58–59, 98
  and Hong Kong, 44
  and Orientalism, 21

Buck, Pearl S., 142–43
Buddhism, 45–46, 112*f*, 156–57,
  159–60
Bullock's, 32, 33*f*

Caen, Herb, 173–74
California, 36, 111–13, 117, 119, 132,
  156, 175–76
  and agriculture, 123–24, 146
  and anti-Chinese sentiment,
    71–72, 123–24
  and anti-Japanese sentiment, 21,
    123–24, 146
  Chinatowns, 11
  and Chinese American Women's
    Club, 222
  and Chinese Americans, 85
  and current mahjong revival, 223
  and Foster City Chinese Club, 222
  and incarceration of Japanese
    Americans, 159, 160*f*
  and Jewish Americans, 195–97
  and Joseph Babcock, 16
  landholders in, 123–24
  and mahjong instructors, 35, 39–40
  and mahjong parties, 30
  and mahjong tournaments, 156–57
  and Marion Angeline Howlett, 37
  newspapers, 36, 39–40
  theaters, 34
  See also Berkeley; Los Angeles; Los
    Angeles Times; Oakland; San
    Francisco
canasta, 167–68, 192–93, 205–6
Canton, 43, 90–91, 124
  and opera, 126, 144, 149–50, 150*f*
Cantor, Eddie, 116–17, 120
Cecil, Viola, 162, 164, 165, 171,
  172*f*, 173
  and book *Maajh,* 191–92
  See also National Mah Jongg League
Chan, Eleanor, 85

Chan, Joyce, 222, 230, 233
Chan, Lily, 136–37
  See also New Life Movement
Chang, Cecilia, 89–90
Chang, Roberta, 136–37
Chen, Yong, 134–35
Chengdu, 42, 43
Chiang Kai-shek, 123–24, 125,
  134–35, 136
  See also Madame Chiang Kai-shek;
    New Life Movement
Chicago, 18–19, 71, 173–74, 180
  Chinatown, 125–27
  and Jewish Americans, 194
  and mahjong clubs, 29, 121
  and mahjong market, 180
  slaughterhouses, 60–61
  and spread of mahjong, 18
  World's Fair, 22–23
China, 10, 99–100, 106, 116–17, 227–28
  and American expatriates, 12, 16, 40,
    41–42, 48, 51, 53, 82
  and American search for authenticity,
    77, 82, 84
  and American views of, 6, 77, 85, 89,
    123–24, 173, 221–22
  and Boxer Rebellion, 23
  and Chinese Americans, 12, 85, 124,
    137–38, 142
  and communism, 134–35, 191–92
  and courtesan culture, 153
  and Dorothy Meyerson, 165
  and Elsie McCormick, 41
  and First Opium War, 42
  and gambling, 90–93, 135–36,
    192–93, 224
  and immigration, 21, 128–29,
    147, 151–52
  and imperialism, 43–44, 88
  and ivory, 69
  and Janet Wulsin, 48, 53
  and Japan, 135–36, 141, 142–43, 145

China (*cont.*)
  and J. B. Powell, 61–62, 66–67
  and Jewish women, 190
  and Joseph Babcock, 84, 85, 88, 165
  and L. L. Harr, 82–83, 84–85
  and mahjong as "ancient game," 18, 75,
    77, 79, 85–86, 88, 121, 135
  and mahjong export boom, 59,
    60–61, 124
  and mahjong's journey to US,
    2–3, 17, 24
  and mahjong manufacturing, 19–20,
    62, 63–65, 71, 163, 180–81, 185, 227
  and mahjong as national game, 122,
    123–24, 134–38
  and mahjong sets, 3*f*, 33*f*, 67–68, 70,
    141, 159–60, 222
  and mahjong today, 131, 224, 227–28
  and Mah-Jongg Manufacturing
    Company of China, 18–19, 56*f*, 61,
    65*f*, 68*f*, 70, 87–88
  and Marion Angeline Howlett, 37, 39–
    40, 39*f*, 82, 165
  and May Fourth Movement, 134
  and Ming Empire, 42
  missionaries in, 48–49, 53, 90–91, 93,
    119–20, 133–34
  and modernity, 79–81, 86, 87–88, 89,
    91, 110, 135
  Nationalist government of, 123–24, 125
  and nationalists, 134–35, 136
  and Orientalism, 21, 23, 26, 32,
    79, 95–97
  and Pung Chow, 82–84
  and Qing era, 42, 44–48, 78, 135
  and regional variants of mahjong, 224
  and relations with US, 56–57, 58, 74,
    145, 154, 174
  and Republican Revolution, 78, 134–35
  and rise and spread of mahjong,
    4–5, 6, 17, 41–42, 46, 59, 81,
    124–25, 149–50

  and Shanghai, 42, 43–44, 48,
    49–50, 51, 75
  and social clubs, 87–88
  and Taiping rebellion, 47–48
  and Thyra Pedersen, 53, 82
  and trade with US, 43–44,
    50–51, 57–58
  and US military presence, 23, 177–78
  and women, 39–40, 136
  and World War II, 154, 171,
    173, 177–78
  and Yangzi Delta, 42–43, 60, 61–62
  See also Beijing; Canton; Hangzhou;
    Ningbo; Shanghai
China Trade Bureau, 84–85
Chinatowns, 10, 12–13, 83–84, 126–27,
    138, 139–43, 190
  in American imagination, 92, 113
  in California, 11, 122
  and Chinese American ethnicity,
    122, 133
  and Chinese New Year, 133
  curio shops in, 107
  and family association halls,
    128–29, 130*f*
  and gambling, 92–94, 124, 127, 129
  and immigration to US, 147
  Los Angeles, 127, 141–42
  and mahjong styles, 124
  and marketing of mahjong, 56
  and men, 110
  New York, 128*f*, 140–41, 180
  representations of, 125–26, 141–42
  San Francisco, 108*f*, 113–14, 122, 125–
    26, 152, 173–74, 221–22
  and sexuality, 105, 139–40
  and "slumming," 89–90, 111, 140–41
  as source of economic
    opportunities, 125–26
  and white tourists/consumers,
    124, 141–42
  and white women, 111

and women and mahjong, 129, 132
and World War II, 171, 173–74
China Trading Company, 21
Chinese American Women's Club, 222
Chinese Americans, 4, 6–7, 11–12, 78–
79, 106, 110, 121, 122–23
and authenticity, 78, 84, 86–87, 108–9
and debates about mahjong, 91–92
and Chinatowns, 122, 124, 125–26
and Chinese nationalism, 134
and Christian communities, 133–34
detention of, 145
and discrimination, 5–6, 123–24, 142
and ethnicity, 122, 126, 133
and exclusion, 123–24
and food, 89–90
and general stores, 127
and generational conflict, 131–32
and image of China, 84–85
as instructors of mahjong, 106
and Japan, 139–40
laborers, 89, 110
in Los Angeles, 2
and mahjong instructors, 4, 109
and mahjong retailers, 141
and marketing of mahjong,
122–23, 142
and meanings of mahjong, 2–3,
6, 142–43
and Orientalism, 85–86, 174
and Pardee Lowe, 7–8
and rise of mahjong, 124–25
students, 132–33, 137–38
and survival of mahjong, 186
and "trickster stereotype," 111–13
as US soldiers, 173–74
and violence, 116
and women, 11, 85, 139–40
and World War II, 154–55, 173–74
See also China; Chinatowns
Chinese food, 89–90, 110, 115
Chinese New Year, 2, 53, 131, 133, 223

Cold War, 7, 191–92, 195–97,
204–5, 223–24
Colorado, 156–57
Columbia University, 87, 91–92, 106
communism, 38–39, 59, 134–35, 187, 191–
92, 193–94, 195–97
Confucius, 5, 79, 80*f*, 81–82, 91–92, 103,
177, 191–92
consumerism, 12, 15, 27–29, 69–74
and Chinatown, 138, 141–42
and leisure, 28, 197
and Orientalism, 20–21, 23, 27, 40, 95–
97, 109–10, 177
transnational, 10
and women, 115, 164
"coolie," 6, 71–72, 89, 94, 113–14, 191–92
and Chinese Americans, 86
and mahjong, 82–85, 124
origins of term, 83.
See also nativism/xenophobia
Corrigan, Joseph, 94
Crazy Rich Asians, 222–23, 225
Crisloid, 227
Culin, Stewart, 23
cultural seduction, 109–10, 111,
115–17, 118–19
Cunningham, Edwin, 51–53
Cunningham, Rhoda, 51–53
Currier, Florence, 36–37

Decter, Avi, 201
department stores, 28–29, 36, 75, 105–6,
118–19, 164, 213–15
and Joseph Babcock, 20
and Ma Chiang Players'
Association, 99–100
and mahjong instructors, 39–40, 109
and mahjong sets, 141
and marketing of mahjong, 16, 31–32,
33*f*, 33–34
and Marion Angeline Howlett, 38–39
and Parker Brothers, 32

department stores (*cont.*)
  Ville de Paris (Los Angeles), 106
  and women, 35–36
  See also advertising; Bullock's; Macy's
DeSylva, B. G., 104–5
domesticity, 13, 97, 205–6, 207–12,
    213, 219
  and Catskills, 197–98
  and Jewish American women, 7, 194,
    201–2, 203–4, 207, 216–17
  in postwar US, 203, 205, 209–10, 218
dominoes, 28–29, 42–43, 144
  and Americanization of
    manufacturing, 180, 181
  and Angel Island Immigration Center,
    149, 150*f*
  and Chinatown, 127, 133
  and Chinese Americans, 142
  and gambling, 126, 149
  and mahjong's origins in the US, 23
  and postwar consumer society, 197
Dulles, Foster Rhea, 169–70
Dwiggins, Elmer, 97–98

Ebell Club, 95, 96*f*, 100
Eisenhower, Dwight, 176
Eisenhower, Mamie, 176
Elks Lodge, 92
Empire Games, 180–81, 182, 184
Eng, Frank, 122
ethnicity, 6–7, 8, 125–34, 189, 223
  Chinese American, 122, 126, 133, 145, 225
  as gendered, 193
  Jewish American, 12–13, 187, 188–89,
    195, 223
  and triangulation, 190

Fahnestock, Carolyn Snowden
    Andrews, 19–20
Fahnestock, Gibson, 19–20
Fairbanks, Douglas, 17, 17*f*
feminism, 217–18

flappers, 27–28, 100, 103–5, 110, 114, 132
  See also Jazz Age
Florida, 18, 38–39, 39*f*, 195–97
Foster, Robert, 50, 99–100, 103
France, 43–44, 59
Frederick, Christine, 27–28
Friedan, Betty, 203, 205, 207, 217–18
Fu Manchu, 78–79, 89–90, 110, 114–15,
    142–43, 185

gambling, 72, 92–93, 113–14, 131, 137, 153,
    192–93, 215
  and Angel Island Immigration Center,
    149, 150–51, 152, 153–54
  in American culture, 92
  and American views of China,
    92–93, 133–34
  and Chinese Americans, 126, 127, 133
  and Chinese restrictions against, 44–
    46, 53, 125
  and Chinese immigrants, 9, 124–25
  and emergence of mahjong, 4–5, 42–
    43, 44–46, 47–49, 91, 128–29
  and enforced leisure, 9, 146
  and Janet Wulsin, 48
  and Japanese Americans, 9, 155, 157–59
  and leisure, 126
  and Macau, 224
  and meanings of mahjong, 9, 78,
    82–83, 91–92, 93–94, 123, 124, 133,
    135–36, 161
  and missionaries, 9, 48–49, 90–91,
    93, 152–53
  as moral threat, 9, 90–91, 134
  and women, 151, 152, 157
Germany, 19, 181
Gershwin, George, 104–5
Gilded Age, 10
Glick, Carl, 173
Great Depression, 2, 122, 141–42, 155,
    162–63, 182–83
  and Jewish Americans, 198

and discrimination against Chinese
    Americans, 137–38, 142
and leisure, 169–70
The Green Dragon Emerald,
    111–13, 114–15
Greenstein, Rita, 187, 188*f*, 188, 193–
    94, 197, 230, 234

Hager, Albert, 16, 18–19, 50, 51–53, 87–88
Hammond, William A., 16
Hangzhou, 42, 53, 82
Harding, Warren G., 4–5, 85
Harmon Foundation, 142
Harr, Lew Lyle (L. L.), 71–72, 84–85,
    86–87, 88, 91
    and Orientalism, 26
    and origins myth of mahjong,
        81–83, 91
    and Pung Chow Company, 81–84,
        91, 120
Harte, Bret, 104–5
Hasbro, 11
Hawaii, 37, 38, 107
Hawes, Harry, 19–20
Hayashi, Doris, 156, 158–59
Held Jr., John, 103, 104*f*, 110
Ho, Sang M., 99–100
Hollywood, 4–5, 17, 27–28,
    100–1, 222–23
Hong Kong, 42, 44, 57, 87, 179
Hoover, Herbert, 18
Hoover, Lou Henry, 18
Howlett, Marion Angeline, 37–40, 39*f*,
    82, 165
H. S. Crocker Company, 19

immigration, 9, 21, 24, 93, 115–16, 147,
    161, 223
    and 1924 Immigration Act, 147, 148,
        151–52, 153
    and 1943 Chinese Exclusion Repeal
        Act, 154

and Angel Island Immigration Station,
    9, 11–12, 144, 146–47, 148–49,
    150*f*, 153
    and Chinese exclusion, 145, 147
    and gender, 151–52, 153, 161
    and Immigration and Nationality
        Act, 224
    in interwar years, 123–24, 131–32
    and Japanese Americans, 146
    and Jews, 193–94
    and "paper sons," 148, 151–52
    reform, 124
    restrictions, 5, 9, 89, 106–7, 151, 241n.59
imperialism, 43–44, 88, 98, 138, 146
Indiana, 15–16
International Ma Chiang Players'
    Association, 99–100
Irwin, Florence, 99, 103
Israel, 171–72, 194, 216
ivory, 4, 31*f*, 34–35, 55, 69–71, 72–73, 179,
    180–81, 184*f*

Japan, 19–20, 23, 43–44, 60–61, 82,
    142, 145
    and anti-Japanese sentiment, 21, 123–
        24, 139–40, 146, 154–55, 157–58
    and invasions of China, 123–24, 134–
        36, 137, 141, 145, 179
    and ivory, 69
    and mahjong, 120, 155–56, 159–61,
        177–78, 179, 224
    and Orientalism, 21, 102
    and US Army, 177–78
    and World War II, 138, 142–43,
        154–55, 173–74
Japanese Americans, 160*f*, 173–74
    in American racial framework, 146
    and Angel Island Immigration
        Station, 147–48
    and Christianity, 158–59
    wartime incarceration of, 4, 6–8, 9, 11,
        12–13, 144–46, 156, 159–61

Japanese Americans (*cont.*)
  hostility to, 139, 146, 157–58, 159
  and mahjong, 155–57, 186, 225
  and "The Three Mah Jongs," 139
  and World War II, 154–55
  See also Poston incarceration
    camp Rohwer incarceration
    camp Tanforan racetrack and
    assembly center
Jazz Age, 4, 5–6, 11, 103, 120
  See also flappers
Jewish Americans, 6–8, 11–12, 156
  and anti-Semitism, 195–97
  Big Sisters organization, 30, 102
  and the Catskills, 2, 197–98, 201
  and Dorothy Meyerson,
    163–64, 165–66
  and ethnic formation, 12–13,
    188–89, 194–95
  and immigration, 147, 188–89, 193–94
  interviews with, 11–12
  and National Mah Jongg League,
    162–63, 165–66, 169
  and New York City, 183, 198
  refugees, 169, 191
  suburbanization of, 194, 195–97,
    199–200
  and upward mobility, 11–12, 102, 179,
    193–94, 195, 202
  and Viola Cecil, 162
  and whiteness, 195–97
Jewish American women, 2–3, 179–80,
  186, 190, 207–9, 218–19, 221, 227
  and American Orientalism,
    190, 191–92
  and anti-Semitism, 171
  and the Catskills, 199, 201–2
  and charity, 171, 207–9, 216
  and current mahjong revival, 222,
    223–24, 225–26
  and ethnicity, 12–13, 187–89, 193,
    194–95, 223

  and feminism, 217–18, 219
  and leisure, 186, 187, 192, 201–2,
    203–4, 207
  and mahjong and community, 188,
    189, 202
  and mahjong as exclusively a women's
    game, 192–93
  as middle-class, 8–9, 195, 203–4, 223
  as mothers, 10, 203, 216–18
  and National Mah Jongg League, 191,
    206, 222
  and "National" mahjong, 189
  and postwar domesticity, 11, 205–6,
    207–9, 210–11
  and suburbanization, 12–13, 212
  and upward mobility, 207–9, 216–17
  and World War II, 171, 187
Joy Luck Club, 222–23
Judge (magazine), 24, 25*f*
Judge, Joan, 136–37

Kan, Andrew, 21, 59, 61, 87, 141
Kan, Johnny, 89–90
Kansas, 11, 29, 212
Kipling, Rudyard, 26, 110
Kohl, Elisabeth Godey, 99–100
Khrushchev, Nikita, 204–5
Ku Klux Klan, 5

Larson, Louise Leung, 126–27, 133, 138
Las Vegas, 224
Lee, Chingwah, 142
Lee, Joyce, 129, 197
Lee, Rose Hum, 131
leisure, 2–4, 9–10, 27–35, 126, 135–36, 183,
  187, 192
  and Americans in China, 41–42, 50
  and the Catskills, 197–98, 199
  decline of, 218–19
  in China, 47
  and Chinese Americans, 131
  and class privilege, 8, 35–36

and domesticity, 97, 203–4, 205–6, 207, 209–10, 216–17, 218

enforced, 9, 145, 146, 149–50, 155, 156, 157, 160–61

and ethnic formation, 8–9, 12–13

as fraught in American life, 8

and Jewish women, 186, 187, 192, 193, 201–2, 203–4

and mahjong's "ancient" origins, 97

and mass consumerism, 28

and meanings of mahjong, 47, 78

and middle classes, 35–36, 93–94, 192

and National Mah Jongg League, 166, 169–70

and plastics, 183, 197

as a problem, 169–70

and "smart women" in the 1920s, 35–37

and suburbs, 197

and wealth, 18, 38

and women, 10, 11, 13, 97, 115–16, 117, 136–37, 152–53, 219

and women in postwar America, 206–7, 209–10

and youth, 38

Leong, Karen, 142–43

Lethin, Anton, 16, 50

Leung, Lam Ping, 87

Lodato, Alfonso, 179–80, 182–83
    See also A&L Manufacturing Company

Lodato, Anthony "Lucky," 182–83
    See also A&L Manufacturing Company

Long Island, 162, 187, 188*f*, 193–94, 197, 201–2, 212

Los Angeles, 87, 96*f*, 105–6, 107, 126–27
    Chinatown, 127, 141–42
    and Chinese Americans, 2
    and department stores, 32, 33*f*, 106
    and Ebell Club, 95, 96*f*
    and Japanese Americans, 155
    and Jewish Americans, 194, 202, 222

and Joseph Babcock, 69–70

and Louise Leung Larson, 126–27

and mahjong market, 180

and mahjong parties, 95

and Marion Angeline Howlett, 37

and New Life Movement, 136–37

and Orientalism and mahjong, 5–6, 23, 32, 33*f*, 107

and "The Three Mah Jongs," 139

Los Angeles Times, 20, 95, 211
    and Chinatown, 127
    on dangers of mahjong, 119
    and mahjong advertisements, 16
    on mahjong's appeal to women, 28
    on mahjong craze, 57–58
    and mahjong during Prohibition, 34
    recipe column, 36

Low, Charlie, 139–40

Lowe, Pardee, 7–8, 124–25, 129–31, 132, 133

Lowry, Helen Bullitt, 34–35

Macy's, 31–32, 99–100, 164, 185–86, 197

Madame Chiang Kai-shek, 51–53, 136

mahjong instructors, 11, 14, 40, 82, 99–100, 105–6, 107, 174
    and African Americans, 29–30
    Chinese American, 4, 95–97, 106–7, 108–9, 124
    as dangerous, 109–10, 111, 113–14
    and department stores, 32, 39–40
    and Jewish women, 212, 225–26
    and Marion Angeline Howlett, 37–40, 39*f*
    male, 108–9, 111
    and white women, 11, 35, 39–40, 109

"Mah Jongg Kid" doll, 27

mahjong manufacturing, 11, 18–19, 66–68, 70, 72–73, 76*f*
    and bamboo and bone, 60, 70, 75
    in China, 19–20, 61–62, 73, 179
    and exporters, 60

mahjong manufacturing (*cont.*)
  in Europe, 19, 70–71
  and interviews, 11–12
  and ivory, 71
  and L. L. Harr, 71–72, 82–83
  and modernity, 57
  and Orientalism, 75
  and plastic, 71, 179–80, 183
  in transnational factories, 61
  in the United States, 71, 74, 162, 163,
    179, 181–82, 183, 184, 227
  See also A&L Manufacturing Company
    Crisloid Empire Games Mah-Jongg
    Manufacturing Company of China
    Mei Ren Company Parker Brothers
    Pung Chow
Mah-Jongg Manufacturing Company
  of China, 56*f*, 61, 62, 65*f*, 67–68,
  68*f*, 70
Mah-Jongg Sales Company of America,
  11, 14, 18–20, 33*f*, 63–65, 76*f*, 80*f*
  and Chinese Americans, 141
  and Joseph Babcock and creation of,
    15–16, 17*f*, 19–20, 80*f*, 83–84
  mass marketing by, 32, 39–40, 71
  and purchase by Parker Brothers,
    20, 72–73
  and Vice President J. M. Tees, 17–18
mahjong sets, 2, 22*f*, 31*f*, 68*f*, 72–73, 85,
  119, 126–27
  adaptability of, 226–27
  and Angel Island Immigration
    Center, 149
  and Americanization of, 183–84
  bone-and-bamboo, 28–29,
    37–38, 60, 70
  and Chicago World's Fair, 23
  and Chinatown, 128*f*
  cost of, 16, 34, 75, 92
  at department stores, 31–32, 33*f*, 33–34,
    75, 185–86
  and Dorothy Meyerson, 164–65, 213

and Florence Currier, 36
in *The Green Dragon Emerald,* 114–15
and ivory, 69–70
and Jewish American women, 201–2,
  204*f*, 207, 213–15
and Mah-Jongg Sales Company, 14,
  17*f*, 18–19, 84
and Marion Angeline Howlett, 37–38,
  39*f*, 39–40
and National Mah Jongg League, 162,
  166–67, 171
and origins of mahjong, 42–43
and Pung Chow, 81–83
in Shanghai, 135–36
See also mahjong manufacturing
mahjong tournaments, 16, 156–57, 169,
  170, 198–99, 226–27
Martinelli, Giovanni, 18
The Marvelous Mrs. Maisel, 223–24
Massachusetts, 11, 18, 26–27, 38
  and Florence Currier, 36
  and Marion Angeline Howlett,
    37, 39–40
  and Parker Brothers, 20
May, Elaine Tyler, 204–5
McCormick, Elsie, 41, 48, 226–27
McKeown, Adam, 146–47
Meh, W. C., 99–100
Mei, Lanfang, 85
Mei Ren Company, 61–62, 63–65, 66*f*,
  75, 182
  workers, 55, 62, 63, 64*f*, 66–67, 181
Mexico, 152
Meyerson, Dorothy, 7–8, 163–66, 169,
  172*f*, 175, 211–12
  and *"That's It!:" A New Way to Play
    Mah Jong,* 164, 226–27
  and television appearances,
    164–65, 213
  and Wright-Patterson mahjong
    players, 178
Meyerson, Perry, 165–66

Miln, Louise Jordan, 82, 88

missionaries, 49–50, 93, 111–13, 119–20
  and anti-missionary sentiment, 134
  and Chinese nationalists, 134
  and critiques of mahjong, 9, 48–49, 91,
    94, 133–34, 152–53
  in Shanghai, 48–49, 53
  and Thyra Pedersen, 53

modernism, 21, 121

Montague, James, 118

Morris, Helene, 175–76, 178

Muramoto, Walter, 159–60

Naftaly, Philip, 19, 80*f*

Nanyang Brothers, 141

Nashville, 34

National Mah Jongg League (NMJL),
    172–73, 174–75, 176, 178–79, 185,
    212–13, 224–25
  and the Catskills, 198–99
  and current mahjong revival, 225–27
  and Dorothy Meyerson, 163–65,
    211–12, 213
  formation of, 7, 9–10, 162–63,
    168–69, 179–80
  and gendered mahjong culture, 7
  and Jewish women, 165–66, 186, 189,
    191, 206, 222
  and mahjong manufacturers, 184
  membership of, 163, 164–65, 168, 186
  and "national" version of mahjong,
    162, 163, 166–67, 168–69, 225–26
  philanthropy of, 7, 9–10, 168, 169–70,
    171–72, 206, 222
  and rule cards, 168–69, 202, 214*f*, 215,
    221, 222
  and rule committee, 167–68
  and Ruth Unger, 202, 225
  and Viola Cecil, 162, 164, 165,
    171, 191–92
  and World War II, 7, 170–72, 172*f*,
    173–74, 191–92

Native Daughters of the Golden
    West, 89

Native Sons of the Golden State, 85

nativism/xenophobia, 5–6, 193–94
  See also Ku Klux Klan Native
    Daughters of the Golden West
    United States and exclusion and
    inclusion

New Life Movement, 136–37

Newark, 18, 29

New Orleans, 16, 174–75

newspapers, 91–92, 96*f*, 115–16, 139–40,
    149–50, 159
  and ads for mahjong
    instructors, 39–40
  and anti-Chinese sentiment, 72, 73
  from Japanese American incarceration,
    11, 156–57
  on mahjong, 4–5, 14–15, 29, 31*f*, 36,
    100, 120
  and women, 36
  See also Los Angeles Times New York
    Times Washington Post

New York City, 11, 17, 141, 164–65, 174,
    180, 183, 221–22
  and bridge, 24
  Chinatown, 125–26, 128*f*, 140–41
  and Chinese Americans, 191
  and Chinese Consulate, 86
  and current mahjong revival, 225–26
  department stores, 20, 99–100
  and domesticity, 211, 213, 214*f*
  and Empire Games, 180
  and Jewish Americans, 183, 189, 191,
    193–94, 197–98, 201, 203
  and Jewish women, 162, 187, 212, 216
  and J. M. Tees, 16, 17–18
  and mahjong instructors, 39–40,
    99–100, 213
  and mahjong manufacturing, 163, 179–
    80, 182, 204*f*
  migration patterns, 197

New York City (*cont.*)
  and National Mah Jongg League, 171,
    173, 179, 202
  and Orientalist consumerism, 20
  and plastics, 181
  and society elites, 5–6, 30, 31*f*, 102–3
  and suburbanization, 165–66,
    209–10, 212
  and white society, 5–6, 30, 31*f*
New York *Times,* 25–27, 103, 104–5, 132,
    192, 201–2
  and debates on mahjong, 91
  and "democratization" of
    mahjong, 34–35
  and games columnist Albert
    Morehead, 192
  and Marion Angeline Howlett, 37
  and popularity of mahjong, 17, 106
Nicholson, Grace, 23
Ningbo, 23, 42–43, 55
Nishimoto, Richard, 155–56, 157–58
Nixon, Richard, 204–5

Oakland, 34, 127
Oklahoma, 174–76, 178, 186, 212
opium, 43–45, 47–48, 111, 112*f*, 114–15,
    140–41, 179
  and First Opium War, 42
Orientalism, 73, 87–88, 94, 97,
    100–1, 191–92
  American, 20–21, 23, 85–86, 190
  and "authenticity" of mahjong, 75, 79, 86
  and Chinese Americans, 138, 174
  and Chinese "backwardness," 78
  and Chinese costuming, 100–2
  and consumerism, 20–21, 23, 26–27, 32,
    33*f*, 40, 95–97, 109–10, 177
  and European colonization, 75–77
  and gender, 98
  and Jewish women, 190
  in late nineteenth century, 191–92
  and mahjong culture, 191–92

  and mahjong sets, 67
  and sexuality, 102–3
  visual culture of, 22–23
  and women, 36, 95–97, 102–3

Palm Beach. *See* Florida
Parker Brothers, 32, 65*f*, 70–71,
    72–73, 120
  Archive, 56*f*, 68*f*, 96*f*, 98*f*,
    101*f*, 108*f*
  and trademarks, 20, 70, 99–100
Parker, George, 20, 79–81, 120
Pedersen, Thyra, 53, 82
Peking. *See* Beijing
Philadelphia, 10, 11–12, 209–10, 225
  Chinatown, 93–94
  and Japanese American
    "resettlement," 159–60
  and Jewish Americans, 202,
    207–9, 208*f*
Philippines, 38, 177–78
Piroxloid Products
    Corporation, 33*f*, 70
plastic, 2–3, 67, 137, 178, 197, 203, 214*f*
  Bakelite, 181, 227
  Catalin, 180–82, 184*f*, 185–86, 227
  and development of industry, 7–8,
    179–80, 183
  and Empire Games, 180
  factories, 62, 71–72, 182–83
  and "French ivory," 70
  and Jewish Americans and
    mahjong, 202
  and leisure, 197
  and L. L. Harr, 82–83
  and Parker Brothers, 70, 71
  phenolic, 181
  pyralin, 81
  and shift from natural materials, 4,
    70–71, 179, 180–81, 183–84, 185–86
  thermosetting, 180–81
  and World War II, 163, 181

poker, 10, 92, 94, 132, 155–56, 158, 180, 192–93

Portland, Oregon, 21, 100, 233

Poston incarceration camp (Arizona), 156, 157–59

Powell, John B. (J. B.), 58, 61–62, 63, 66–67

Previtali, Adele, 18

Prohibition, 34, 92, 93, 105–6, 139

Protestants, 30, 102, 191, 194, 216–17
  and gambling, 9
  and missionaries, 90–91, 152–53
  and New Life Movement, 136
  and women, 152–53

Pung Chow Company, 18–19, 81–84, 91, 120

Punk Pungs, 111–13

Pye, Watts O., 90–91

pyralin, 71, 81

radio, 27–29, 34, 83–84, 87, 115, 164–65, 171

Rhode Island, 18, 38, 99, 227

Rittenhouse, Anne, 79

Roberts, Julia, 221–22

Rohmer, Sax, 78–79

Rohwer incarceration camp (Arkansas), 155–57, 159–60

Roosevelt, Franklin, 154

Roth, Philip, 203, 205, 207, 217–18

Russia, 38–39, 43–44, 50–51, 165–66, 171, 207–9
  See also Soviet Union

San Francisco, 60, 107, 108f, 113–14, 119, 132, 141, 221
  and Angel Island Immigration Station, 144, 149–50, 154
  and anti-Chinese sentiment, 83, 85, 126
  Chinatown, 122, 125–26, 129, 133, 139–40, 141–42, 152, 173–74, 221–22
  and Chinese food, 89–90, 225

  earthquake of 1906, 148
  and the Gay Asian Pacific Alliance (GAPA), 223
  and Granada Theatre movie palace, 14–15, 33–34, 95
  and International Exposition (1939), 141–42
  and Jewish Americans, 223, 225
  and Mah-Jongg Sales Company of America, 16, 19, 141
  and mahjong sets, 16, 19–20
  and mahjong's history and spread, 17–18, 39–40, 223
  and Orientalism, 30
  San Francisco Bay Region Chinese Students' Association, 138
  and women, 11, 30, 117–18, 223
  and World War II, 173–74

Sang, Ly Yu, 86–87, 91

Schlesinger Library, 11, 39f, 231, 232

Seattle, 14–15, 18, 30, 33–34, 100, 101f, 130f
  and importer Andrew Kan, 21, 59

sexuality, 4, 53–54, 95–97, 98, 102–6, 115, 139–40

Shanghai, 1–2, 63–65, 79–81, 85, 226–27
  and American Club, 51, 52f
  American expatriates in, 4–5, 41, 48–54, 52f, 83
  British expatriates in, 44, 48–51
  cosmopolitanism of, 12, 43–44, 48, 50, 51–53, 78
  and courtesans, 1, 44–45, 45f
  and Elsie McCormick, 41, 226–27
  and export industry, 57
  history and status of, 43–45
  and International Correspondence School, 16
  and International Settlement, 44, 48–50, 137

Shanghai (*cont.*)
  and invasion by Japan, 134–35, 179
  and Japanese residents, 50–51, 83
  and J. B. Powell, 62
  Jewish refugees, 191
  and J. M. Tees, 17–18
  and Joseph Babcock, 15–16, 17
  and mahjong craftsmen, 60, 61,
    62, 137
  and mahjong industry, 4–5, 11, 18–19,
    56–57, 70, 179
  and Mah-Jongg Sales Company of
    China, 14
  and Marion Angeline Howlett, 37–38,
    39*f*, 82
  and Mei Ren Company, 55, 61–62,
    66–67, 75, 182
  and modernization debates, 46–47
  Municipal Council of, 44,
    48–49, 62
  and origins of mahjong, 41,
    42–43, 47–48
  as treaty port city, 42, 43–44, 83
  press, 118–19
  and Republican Revolution,
    45–46, 47–48
  and Roberta Chang, 136
  and self-determination, 137
  and social clubs, 10, 51
  and trade, 44
  and women, 11
  and workers, 47
  See also Mah-Jongg Manufacturing
    Company of China Mei Ren
    Company
Silverman, Edith, 182, 183
Silverman, Seymour, 180, 182,
  183, 184
Soong, Mayling. *See* Madame Chiang
  Kai-shek
Soviet Union, 38–39, 193–94, 204–5
sports, 25–26, 28, 131, 132, 133–34

Standardization Committee of the
  American Official Laws of
  Mah-Jongg, 99–100
Stanford University, 31*f*, 99–100,
  231–32
Steichen, Edward, 28
St. Louis, 19–20, 141–42
suburbs, 8–9, 12, 188*f*, 192, 198, 204*f*
  and criticism, 217–18
  and domesticity, 209–10, 211
  and Jewish Americans, 165–66,
    188, 190, 193–94, 197,
    199–200, 201
  and Jewish American women, 4, 7, 187,
    207–9, 210, 212–13, 216
  and leisure, 197
  and segregation, 195–97, 204–5
  and working women, 213–15
Sun Yatsen. *See* China and Republican
  Revolution

Taiping Rebellion, 47–48, 78
Taiwan, 177–78
Tan, Amy, 129–30, 222
Tanforan racetrack assembly center,
  144–45, 156–58
tea, 1–2, 30, 96*f*, 105–6, 108*f*, 134
  and Japanese tea socials, 20–21
  and Orientalist consumerism, 21
Tees, J. M., 16, 17–18
television, 164–65, 175
Texas, 14–15, 16, 60–61, 212, 225–26
Tianjin, 43
tourism, 37–38, 57–58, 88–89, 224
  and Chinatown, 111, 124, 127,
    141–42
trade, 23, 42, 43–44, 57–58,
    60–61, 84–85
  mahjong, 87
  silk, 139–40
Troxler, Alice, 105–6
Tow, Julius Su, 86

Toy, Dorothy, 139, 140*f*
Toy, Helen, 139, 140*f*
Troum, Marjorie Meyerson, 172*f*,
   211–12, 231, 234

Unger, Ruth, 202, 209, 225, 231, 234
United China Relief, 173
United States, 2, 125, 128–29, 140*f*, 160–
   61, 205, 224
   and Air Force officers' wives,
      175, 177–78
   and Angel Island Immigration Station,
      146–47, 148–49, 153–54
   and bridge, 24, 25–26, 58–59, 92
   and China, 23, 43–44, 50–51, 56–58,
      74, 77, 142–43, 145, 174
   and Chinatowns, 122, 142
   and Chinese Americans, 6, 85, 106–7,
      113–14, 124, 131–32, 137–38, 154–55
   Congress, 4–5
   and "the coolie," 83
   and debut of mahjong at World's
      Fair, 23
   and exclusion and inclusion, 6, 86,
      147, 148–49
   and history of mahjong, 9–10
   and immigration, 21, 146, 147, 148–49,
      153–54, 193–94, 224
   and incarceration of Japanese
      Americans, 160–61
   and Japan, 145, 173–74
   and Jews, 193–94
   and Joseph Babcock, 15–16, 18
   and mahjong's journey from China,
      2–3, 4–5, 24, 41, 57–58, 124–25
   and mahjong manufacturing, 18–19,
      62, 65*f*, 67, 70–71, 74, 179, 185
   and mahjong's popularity, 14–15, 67–
      68, 73, 90–91, 122–23, 162–63
   and Marion Angeline Howlett, 37–38
   and modernity, 3–4, 77–78, 89
   as multiracial democracy, 142–43

   and National Mah Jongg League,
      168–69, 173
   Native Americans, 75–77
   and rise and popularity of mahjong,
      124–25, 162–63
   and trade, 50–51, 60–61, 179
   and women, 10, 11, 53–54, 97–98, 99,
      136, 223
   and World War II, 146, 154–55
United States Air Force, 8–9, 162–63,
   175, 176–77, 178*f*, 186
   and postings abroad, 177–78
   and race, 177
   officers' wives, 4, 7, 175, 186, 224–25
   and Wright-Patterson Mah Jongg,
      175–76, 177–78, 178*f*, 186, 224–25
United States Women's Army Corps
   (WAC), 171
University of Southern
   California, 85, 138

Vancouver, 117
Van Waters, Miriam, 117
Vanderbilts, 5–6, 36, 94, 102
Vanderbilt, Muriel, 31*f*
Vanderbilt, Virginia Fair, 30
Vogue, 28, 58–59, 79, 89

Wang, Y. P., 91–92, 93
War Relocation Authority (WRA), 154–
   55, 156, 158–59, 160*f*
   See also Japanese Americans,
      incarceration of
Washington DC, 18, 19–20, 29, 58,
   121, 141
Washington Post, 34, 35, 79–81
Washington (state), 29, 32, 94, 100. *See
   also* Seattle
Wayburn, Ned, 30
Wei, W. Lock, 87
whiteness, 102, 107, 116–17, 191–92
   and Jewish Americans, 188–89, 195–97

white supremacy, 29–30
See also nativism/xenophobia
Wilkinson, William H., 23
Wing, Paul, 139, 140*f*
Wong, Anna May, 85–86, 174
Wong, William, 106, 108–9
Work, Milton C., 99–100
World War I, 41, 78, 173, 192
World War II, 12–13, 181, 191–92, 207–9
    and American ethnicities, 3–4
    and China, 146
    and Chinese Americans, 154–55
    and Japanese American incarceration,
        9, 11, 145–46
    and Jewish Americans, 188–89,
        197–98, 207–9
    and Jewish refugees, 191
    and Jewish women, 11, 187
    and mahjong manufacturing, 163
    and mahjong's origins, 191–92

    and the National Mah Jongg
        League, 7, 170
    and Officers' Wives' Club, 7
    and Pearl Harbor attack, 139, 146, 154–
        55, 157–58, 170, 173–74
    and plastics, 181
World's Fair, 22–23
Wright-Patterson Air Force Base, 7, 175,
    177, 178*f*
    and "Wright-Pat Mah Jongg," 7, 175–
        76, 177–78, 178*f*, 186, 224–25
Wulsin, Janet, 48, 49–50, 51, 53

Xu, Ke, 46
Xu, Zhiyan, 46

Ya-Ching, Lee, 173
"yellowface," 100–1, 142–43
YMCA, 90–91, 122, 131, 133–34, 158–59
YWCA, 131, 134